Towards
the
Light

To
my parents,
Pauline,
and Jan,
with love and gratitude

Author and Pauline, Yellowhead Pass, 1989

P.A. Condon

Towards
the
Light

"So the common dandelion,
growing through the paving cracks,
turns its gaze towards the light
and bares its being to the sun."

Every effort has been made to contact copyright holders of material reproduced in this book. If any have been inadvertently overlooked, the author will be pleased to rectify the omission at the earliest opportunity.

Towards the Light was first published in 2007 under the title *Circuits & Bumps.*

Printed in the United States of America.

ISBN: 978-1-4669-4585-2 (sc)
ISBN: 978-1-4669-4584-5 (e)

Trafford rev. 05/31/2014

 www.trafford.com

North America & international
toll-free: 1 888 232 4444 (USA & Canada)
fax: 812 355 4082

Contents

	ACKNOWLEDGEMENTS	vi
I.	A LONDON CHILDHOOD 1926 – 1940	1
II.	THE HILLS OF YOUTH 1940 – 1944	141
III.	ROYAL AIR FORCE 1944 – 1947	207
IV.	PHOENIX RISING 1947 – 1956	289
V.	ASHES 1956 – 2006	373
	APPENDIXES	433

Acknowledgements

I would like to thank first those dead writers who have enriched my life and whose works I have cheerfully plundered or adapted. [See "Sources" in the Appendixes.] I wish also to express my thanks to the Heritage Centre, Greenwich, for providing me with details from the Domesday Book; to the Dawson Museum and Historical Society for a map of the Klondike goldfields and details of the dredges; to Yukon Archives for permission to use the photograph of Hans Oiom from the Tidd Collection; and to the University of Exeter for their gracious permission to quote selections from Marion Glasscoe, ed., *Julian of Norwich: A Revelation of Love*, University of Exeter, 1976.

I owe a very special debt to John and Wendy Hale for their many kindnesses and for sharing their green haven with me; and to Pauline Hawkins, my sister, for her contributions to this memoir. Begun at her urging, it was finished only because of her unfailing support.

PAC

PART ONE

A London Childhood

1926 – 1940

Chapter 1 The Thompsons   3
Chapter 2 The Condons   17
Chapter 3 Early Days   34
Chapter 4 Sex ...   44
Chapter 5 ... and Violence   55
Chapter 6 "Come, Lassies and Lads"   72
Chapter 7 Return to Plumstead I   88
Chapter 8 Evacuee   116

CHAPTER ONE

The Thompsons

1

The Family

Although my birth certificate has me as a "Philip", I was christened "Philip Alfred". The discrepancy, my mother told me, was due to beer. My father had celebrated my christening with a few pints beforehand and had been well fortified at the registrar's office as well. My mother liked passing on titbits of family history like this, often about my father, as I saw little of him as a boy. Except to say "Now you do what your mother tells you," he never talked to me about her, though. Had he followed his own advice and listened to her himself, we may well have been happier. However, beery befuddlement did not explain the choice of names. A part explanation arose during the course of a farewell party in 1975. After a stay in England of four years, I was returning to Canada next day, and the occasion was marked with a little beer and wine and much laughter. As the conversation was taped and I shall be quoting from it at length, I here offer a list of the cast:

3

Mum:	Seventy-five and the star of the gathering
Doll:	A Condon cousin of mine, seventy-one and co-star
Pauline:	My sister, forty-six
Lin:	Her married daughter, twenty-one
Self:	Forty-nine
George:	Mum's common-law second husband
Ralph:	a friend and, following George's death, Mum's lover

Scene: *The living-room of Mum's old house on Plumstead Common. It is a pleasantly warm evening.*

Phil:	What was Grandfather Condon's name? *[Assuming I was named after him.]*
Mum:	"Christopher".
Pauline:	No, that's Dad's name.
Mum:	No. Oh yes, "William", "William Anthony". *[Watney's Barley Wine is a little strong for her.]*
Phil:	Well, how come I'm named "Philip Alfred"? Doesn't seem to be anyone's name.
Doll:	That was your mum, getting all posh.
Mum:	I never.
Doll:	Didn't you?
Mum:	No. I never had the selection of his name. No, 'cause when he was christened, his father was half cut, and he was very friendly with a naval officer who used to come into the pub. And when his father said he was going to have his son christened, the officer said,"Can I be godfather to him?" And when we all went to the church to have him christened, he stood godfather to him, this naval feller. And I didn't know him from A to Z. Never seen the bloke before.
Doll:	Was he a "Philip", then?
Mum:	I don't know."Albert" I think his name was. *[A short silence, as minds grapple with this glorious non sequitur]*
Phil:	*[Laughing]* What's this got to do with…
Mum:	No, "Alfred" his name was. *[Laughs asthmatically]*

4

I still don't know why I'm a "Philip." Perhaps Dad, having served in the Royal Horse Artillery, had loved horses. As for my godfather, Naval Officer Alf, none of us ever saw him again.

When I was born, my parents were living in Plumstead. Registered in the Domesday Book as an estate held by the Abbot of St. Augustine's from the Conqueror's half brother Odo, Bishop of Bayeux[1], it lies on the south bank of the Thames and marks the southeastern extremity of Greater London. It was then bordered to the east by the open farmland of Kent and to the north by marshes that stretched downriver from Woolwich. Although part of the western reach of this marshland was occupied by the Arsenal, most remained open, with high dikes that were ideal for walking. In Dickens' day, the hulks moored off the south bank provided convicts for labour in the docks or the Arsenal, although Pip's convict probably came from a hulk on the Medway, further downriver.

Immediately south of Plumstead, the land slopes steeply up to Plumstead Common and thence up to the local landmark, Shooters Hill, so-called as in medieval days it was a favourite place for practice with the longbow. This vantage point commands a fine view of the Thames. There was much to see when I was a boy, for London was still one of the world's great ports, bustling with activity, and the Thames a major waterway with river craft and ships of all kinds passing up and down on the tides. Now, the farmland adjoining Plumstead is buried beneath the suburban monotony of Welling, and river traffic has dwindled to a trickle. Thanks to the ban on coal fires, however, one can see farther.

Mum and Dad began their married life living next door to my maternal grandparents, Jack and Florence Thompson, who rented a Victorian two up two down terrace house on The Slade, at the east end of Plumstead Common. Grandpa, an erect, slender man of medium height, worked in the Arsenal as a minor office manager. As a young man he must have been something of a dandy. I have a photograph of him and Nanna as a young

---

[1]   For this detail I am indebted to Heritage Centre, Greenwich.

married couple. Nanna is dressed late Victorian style in a white bustled dress, many petticoats and an enormous frilly hat. The dress, worn at her wedding, has leg-of-mutton sleeves, stuffed with tissue paper to make them stand up, and is eighteen inches around the waist. She has two daughters with her, one three and the other (my mother) a baby. They also are formally dressed, with abundant petticoats, frills and bows. Grandpa is wearing a black frock coat, starched collar with cravat, and a top hat. He sports a cane, too. With piercing eyes he looks, I always thought, like Dr. Crippen – or, rather, as I thought the good doctor should look. Stern, anyway. He was head of the family and something of a tyrant. Everything had to be just so for him. Dinner, for example, had to be on time and hot, and then he would complain if it was too hot. He was not an affable man.

Nanna, born in 1875, was a warm, loving woman with a sweet smile that she passed on to my mother. She was quiet and rather shy, perhaps intimidated by her husband. Her maiden name was Knight, but the only one of her family I ever met was Great-Aunt Rose, who was deaf and difficult to talk with. I met none of Grandpa's relatives. His mother had been in service with a Scottish family, supposedly titled with a stag's head as a family crest – but all Celts have nobles or kings in their ancestry. It seems that Grandpa, born in 1873, was the product of a close employer-employee relationship. After his mother married, no doubt hastily, she later produced a half-brother, George, who was killed in France in 1914.

Though Grandpa's house was a modest one, it had a fine location. Not only did it front on the common, overlooking a small ravine known locally as "the 'Oller", but it was also at the end of a bus route. The emptied buses would turn there and park for a while in front of *The Woodman*, the local pub. Most convenient. Until the late 'Fifties little traffic passed by, and so it was a quiet place, too – except on Sunday mornings, when the Boys' Brigade marched by with bugle and drum. Facing north, the house had a miniscule garden in front that consisted mostly of dust, small pebbles and a few discouraged plants behind a privet hedge. At the rear, though, stretched a much longer garden with room for a shed, a small greenhouse and enough space to grow flowers and vegetables. As Grandpa was a keen gardener – he also had an allotment on Shooters Hill – there was always plenty of both, for he enriched the poor soil with manure, then delivered free almost to the door by obliging horses.

The rooms in the house were small, each with its own tiny fireplace; and there were only two built-in cupboards, one beneath and one above the stairs. By the time you put a chest of drawers, dressing table, beds and a wardrobe in a bedroom, little space remained. The living-room was even more crowded: table, four bentwood chairs, two small easy chairs by the fire, a small settee, bookcase, knick-knacks everywhere, and a coal scuttle and fender to trip over. One learned not to make sudden movements.

The house was lit by gas. Not as convenient as electricity, perhaps, it nonetheless had a comforting hiss and the mantle gave off a fine light. The primitive kitchen contained a gas stove, a sink and cold-water tap, and a copper where water could be heated over a small fire. There were also small, standing cupboards for pots and pans, crockery and food. So little space remained that there was barely room for the tub on bath night. Bathrooms for such houses were unnecessary, as the occupants would not be able to afford them, would not want to take a bath anyway, and would no doubt use the tub to store coal – or so I have been told by superior persons. The lavatory, or water closet, was in the backyard. The front room, or parlour, was used for entertaining rare guests or for a family singsong around the piano. Nanna played well enough to earn a little money giving lessons. It was by sitting in on these that her own children learnt to play. They seldom practised if Grandpa was in, though, as he would lock the piano if his patience ran out – and he was not noted for patience.

As a young man Grandpa took up photography, making his first camera out of a cigar box, with a pinhole as lens. Later he bought a camera and took photographs on glass plates, developing them in a small shed in the backyard. Nearly all the family photographs that antedate the Great War are his. One of the best is of Nanna and their youngest boy, Little Len. Nanna is holding the child high in her arms and gazing at him lovingly, while the child is laughing down at her. How Grandpa captured those magical expressions with such primitive equipment, I don't know. By the time I arrived, however, he had abandoned the hobby.

His bookcase contained over a hundred books, probably bought as a set or through a book club, as they were all in the same cheap edition. They were by good authors, too – Scott, Thackeray, Twain, Dickens. He must have read at least some of them, I suppose, but they were not well-thumbed and I never saw him read anything but the newspaper. When we were living with him just prior to the War, I borrowed one from time to time – but not often, for the paper was yellowing and the print too small for comfortable reading.

He spoke and smiled seldom. Mealtimes were devoted to the business of eating, not chatter. Sitting sideways to the table, chewing slowly and staring down the garden, he would now and then exclaim "Look at those birds at my plants" or "There's that damned cat again." Afterwards, he would roll a cigarette from Wills' Golden Virginia and smoke it through a holder in the manner of Roosevelt. He did unbend at times, though. When I was six, he taught me how to tell the time and play chess, deriving amusement from my efforts but taking pains to explain what I was doing wrong. Sometimes I was allowed to help him on his allotment on Shooters' Hill, which I found more fun than chess. Willing though he was to talk to me if I showed interest, he generally ignored my sister. Girls were creatures merely to be tolerated – provided they had the grace to keep quiet.

One day, he became positively lively when he recalled two holiday trips. On a day tour by motor coach ("charabangs" we called them), he felt the need to relieve his bladder. Too embarrassed to ask the driver to stop, he piddled in his shoe and emptied it furtively out of the window. Perhaps he did enjoy the occasional pint after all. The second was a bicycle ride to Brighton and back. His demeanour as he described this marathon suggested that it was the adventure of his life, apart from the Zeppelin raids. I doubt if he thought of marriage as an adventure. But fate was to provide him with another – the London blitz. While bombs were demolishing whole streets, he lived alone in the house and continued working in the Arsenal.

I am inclined to think that Nanna had no hobbies. She hadn't the time, not with a demanding husband and five children to care for. Early morning in the kitchen must have been organized chaos. While Nanna prepared breakfast, the children were washing in the sink, with the older ones helping the younger – after Grandpa had finished, of course. The Friday bath, although less frenzied, took up much of the evening. While the little fire smoked away under the copper and every pot was filled and heated on the gas stove, the galvanized bath was brought in from the yard and wiped clean. Children bathed first, then Mum, and finally Dad, by which time the water was less than clean. I asked Mum once, when we were living there, how she managed to keep so fresh with only one bath a week. "Ah," she said, "I'm always up first, and I wash myself from top to toe while you lot are stinking in bed." I rather think Nanna did the same.

Nanna's busiest day was Monday, laundry day. Soiled linen was boiled in the copper and scrubbed on a washing board. After rinsing, the wash was wrung through the mangle, a cast-iron monster with wooden rollers. Drying was a problem in winter with all the coal fires lit, for the wind was invariably damp and better for carrying soot than anything else. Finally, the ironing had to be done with irons heated on the stove. As this work took up most of the day, dinner was usually bubble-and-squeak (a fried-up mix of leftover potatoes and greens), pickles and cold cuts from the Sunday joint.

Keeping the house clean was a struggle. Sometimes the coalman would call just after the cleaning had been done. Then newspapers had to be spread on the floors, clothes removed from pegs in the hallway and furniture pushed aside in the living-room, for the coal was kept in the cupboard under the stairs. Hooded with sacks and shouldering bags, the coalmen would trudge through like a procession of grimy monks and shoot the coal into the cupboard. Spillage and the billowing coal dust necessitated another clean-up. If you kept the coal in the yard, you gained nothing. Then the coalmen had to squeeze through the kitchen as well. The battle against dirt was unending.

Aside from sewing machine and mangle, Nanna had no labour-saving devices – and Mum had no more, either, until the

'Fifties. The eldest girls could help on holidays and after school, of course; but upon turning fourteen, to earn their keep they found work as soon as possible. Having no refrigerator, on top of her other tasks, including occasional nursing, Nanna usually had to visit the fishmonger or the butcher, for they didn't call at the door like the milkman, the baker and sometimes a greengrocer. Dinner was around noon, for the school was close and Grandpa cycled home from the Arsenal; and tea was in the evening, when he had finished work. Knowing when to expect him, Nanna would watch through the curtains until she saw him coming up Lakedale Road. Then she would dish up his meal so he could hang up his cap, rub his hands together and sit down to eat immediately. And if it was a cold day, she would first warm his chair cushion by the fire! To economize, she made most of the girls' clothes herself; and to supplement the family income, in addition to giving piano lessons she sewed tennis balls for a penny apiece and during the Boer War stitched covers onto pith helmets for the soldiers of the Queen.

Not all mothers worked so hard, of course. But most did, as a matter of pride. Social pressure was strong then. Clean curtains at the windows, doorsteps whitened, path and pavement swept, laundry on Monday, best clothes on Sunday – all were expected. People who failed to conform were looked down upon. As for those who lived in squalor, who didn't take a bath from one year to the next and seldom washed either, who were foulmouthed, who cheated and stole, who roistered in a pub while their children ate chips outside – they were quite simply "the gutter":

Pauline: You don't mean cami-knickers, do you?

Doll: No, dear, they were just two legs on a tape, so the front and the back were all free; and they used to stand one foot on the path and one foot on the road…

Mum: That's right. They used to do it in the gutter. *[Laughter]*

Doll: It's true, it's true, I tell you. It used to plop – just like horses! *[Screams of laughter]*

Pauline: *[Ironically]* I thought we were class.

Doll: Oh, I'm not talking about our family. The old girls used to do it. Not our family. Yes, all the old girls, when I was a kid.

> *Phil:*　I suppose that's what those signs meant: "Do not commit a nuisance".
>
> *Doll:*　Yes, that's right.
>
> *Pauline:* 'Struth!

In my childhood, some of the "old girls" wore a kind of uniform: a drab dress over grubby petticoats; a piece of sackcloth tied round the waist as an apron; perhaps, if it was cold, a shabby cardigan, out at the elbows; ankle-high carpet slippers; and a man's cap, fastened with a hat pin. Often they went armed with a large jug, for fetching beer from the local. Thanks to public toilets, they no longer fouled the streets.

Naturally, it was recognized that people down on their luck could become destitute, especially in hard times, for social safety nets were tenuous. That was different. Most people made every effort to keep a roof over their heads; for, despite jokes about it, they had a horror of the workhouse. But if there was a roof over your head and some money, no matter how little, well, soap was cheap and so were needle and thread. As for food, one could make do with day-old bread,"cooking eggs" (old eggs), potatoes, fruit and tired greens bought cheap late on Saturday, and scrag ends of meat for stews. From 1936-1938 my mother had to practice many of these economies.

Life was not all work, of course. Togged up in their finery, on Sundays the family might promenade on the common, watch people at bowls or tennis and then go on to the bandstand to listen to a military band; or they might picnic in Bostall Woods. And then there were the holidays. They were not generous. In those days most people worked long hours, six days a week, and had to be satisfied with Bank Holidays and one week off a year. On a Bank Holiday, if one was ambitious, one could take a cheap train excursion to the seaside – a pleasant change but hard on poor old mum. As for Grandpa's week off, the family usually went to their favourite resort, Bognor Regis. If they returned home with a fine sunburn, the holiday was accounted a success.

☙❧

The youngest child, Little Len, died when he was five – a terrible shock for Nanna. With a mass of curly blond hair, he'd resembled the boy in the Pear's soap picture, and Grandpa had photographed him in similar dress and pose. After the boy died, they kept a framed enlargement of it in the parlour.

The other children left school at the age of fourteen, as most did then, those not lucky enough to go to public school or a grammar school, that is. They did not have much of an education, but at least they could read, write and figure well enough. The eldest girl, Lil, who possessed a fine contralto voice, was invited to try out for a well-known band; but she developed intense stage fright and dropped the idea of a public career. Instead, she married Bert Green, a printer in the City, and had two boys, John and Peter. John, four years older than I, was a keen naturalist and kept his own zoo – a garden shed full of birds, lizards, snakes, beetles and other creatures. With these, and the tales he made up, he kept both Peter and me enthralled. Later, he became interested in butterflies and moths and over the years built a fine collection, all properly mounted in glass-covered trays.

At first they lived next door but one to my grandparents, but later they moved to a new semi on Westmount Road. Lil joined a tennis club and seemed set on moving up socially. Unhappily, at the beginning of the War she died suddenly; and when a new woman moved into the house a few weeks later, the family fell apart.

George, Nanna's surviving son, married his first cousin, Lil, called "Little Lil" to differentiate her from my mother's sister, and moved into a new semi on Garland Road, opposite the Optical Building. I liked Uncle George. A quiet, kind man, who looked rather like George Orwell, he was a self-employed decorator and a careful craftsman. As a young man he had been a fine pianist and banjo player, but all that stopped after he married. When he wasn't busy on a contract, Little Lil kept him working at home, slaving away in an attempt to turn heavy clay into a garden and decorating and redecorating the house.

The product of an unhappy childhood, Little Lil was perhaps as a result a little cold, although not unkind. She was house-proud and kept everything immaculate. Whenever I came visiting, she greeted me with a characteristic combination of smile and worried frown, "Hello, ducks, take your shoes off." Then she watched me like a hawk, as she did her sons, in case I scratched the woodwork, knocked over a vase, or left grubby fingerprints somewhere. Usually, the parlour was out of bounds. However, it contained a good upright piano and, despite the ban, her eldest son had somehow learnt to play it well. Resembling his mother, John (Little John, of course) was a pallid, slender boy, diffident and unsmiling. His childhood could not have been a happy one. For some reason, Little Lil did not favour him and often booted him out of the house to spend more time in the streets than was good for him.[2] She was warmer to Paul, who at six resembled a cherubic chorister from a della Robbia bas-relief, and perhaps more so to Barry, a child she bore in middle age in a vain attempt to have a girl.

Violet, Nanna's youngest girl, was nicknamed "Doll." A warm-hearted woman, she married "Billy" Billing, a regular in the RAF, and followed him into married quarters, first to Egypt and then to Calshot, where they remained until the outbreak of war. They had one boy, Peter. Like Little Lil, Doll made a late attempt to produce a girl, and at war's end presented her husband with twins, Pam and Pat. Billy's response, to run off with a young WAAF, left her understandably upset. Eventually, she married again, this time to a widower, and he proved a good husband. By the time she died in her eighties, Doll had grandchildren in both Britain and America.

❧

2

My Mother

My mother, born May 12, 1900, and christened May Katherine, was the second of Nanna's children. So it was upon her and Lil that the burden fell for helping around the house. Though this responsibility cut into childhood's supposedly carefree days, she

---

[2]   John married soon after the War, but not well. He would come home from work to find his wife in her dressing-gown, reading movie magazines – with the breakfast dishes still in the sink and no dinner. When eventually he complained, she ran home to her mother and refused to see him again. Rejection by his mother and then by his wife proved altogether too much. In despair he returned home and hanged himself in his father's garden shed.

accepted it willingly and as a result received good training for her own hardworking life as a wife and mother. On leaving school, she and Lil set up a small milliner's shop in Blackheath. Unfortunately, although they were deft seamstresses and produced good copies of West End hats, trade proved slow and they had to give it up. She next worked as a clerk, first with Siemens and then in Grandpa's office; but during the Great War she moved to a factory in the Arsenal, where she made shell cases. She remembered the guns on the Common firing during the Zeppelin raids and retained a vivid image of a Zeppelin coned in the searchlights.

As a mother, she was faultless. She was always "there" and I was never in any doubt that she loved me. Even when we were living in poverty, the house was clean, we were well dressed, and the meals, though simple, were delicious. She was faithful in large matters and in the thousand-and-one small things good mothers do yet think their children take for granted and don't notice. But they *are* noticed – and remembered with love afterwards. At the same time she never overprotected me. She gave advice, usually sound, but then allowed me to make my own decisions. Though I must often have given her cause for worry, she allowed me a remarkably free rein. On the other hand, she never let me get away with anything, either. If I did something wrong, she knew it and soon set me straight. At times, I thought her psychic. Outgoing and fun-loving, she had a genuine compassion for both people and animals and a sunny personality that drew all to her – men, women and children alike. Except when Grandpa or Dad was around, our home was filled with warmth and laughter.

As a woman, though, she was not perfect. A touch of vanity made her susceptible to flattery, especially from men. That may have been one of the causes of the rows my parents had. Well, women know that men can be lying swine, but they will listen! Someone once told her that she had a wonderful profile. As a result, she adopted a characteristic pose in public – one designed to show her profile to advantage. In later years, Pauline and I sometimes teased her when we caught her at it. "Oh, shut up," she would snap, nettled – but then would have the grace to blush. Another flatterer told her that she looked like Gladys Cooper, and she repeated the lie *ad nauseum* for the rest of her life. A photo of her, taken when she was eighteen, shows she didn't resemble Gladys Cooper in the least. Jean Harlow, Gladys Cooper and so on, may have been glamorous, even beautiful. My mother was lovely.

She was not well educated, certainly no intellectual, her focus being on people and things rather than on ideas. Though she could read well enough, I never caught her at it, although Pauline tells me that she once found her reading a novel by Ruby M. Ayres. Her handwriting was mature – a flowing, unadorned style reflecting the unpretentious honesty of her nature.

In most things Mum was level-headed, far from a fool. When my parents became licencees in their own pub, it was she who was really the manager, who attracted the customers and the loyalty of the staff. Dad tended to accept too many drinks, never enough to become drunk but enough to get argumentative with the customers. He never could suffer a fool in silence. Mum enjoyed a drink too, usually a glass or two of Guinness, but always in moderation. Well, almost always. Though she knew that too much confused her and made her vague as to facts and vocabulary, she sometimes relaxed her rule on special occasions – such as my farewell party, when she declared a liking for "Handel's Lager"! At one family Christmas dinner, a little flushed, she stood up to give a toast, "Here's health, wealth, and prostitution to us all." Not a malapropism, though she was capable of those, but perhaps a Freudian slip, this went down so well that she often repeated the performance. Well, we all have our stock jokes.

When she met Dad I don't know – probably some years after the Great War. Anyhow, she was twenty-five and he, twenty-nine when they married. It was not a whirlwind romance. In fact, I doubt whether it was much of a romance at all:

> *Mum:* I remember one day Chris was going to take me to meet one of his aunts. I was waiting for him, when along the road came this apparition. It was Chris, looking like an old Jewish pawnbroker decked out in his best. He was wearing a large Harris tweed overcoat with padded shoulders – you know, like a Teddy boy. And on his head he had a bowler hat. It was set straight, and was resting on his ears. And

he was wearing spats, but they were on the wrong feet. He
looked horrible!

Pauline: Tell Doll about the time he took you to a fancy-dress
dance.

Mum: Oh yes. I was all ready and waiting for him. He was late,
as usual, and after a while I went to the door and looked
along the road. There was not a soul in sight, except an old
Turkish carpet-seller. He was wearing a red fez, a baggy
chalk-stripe suit and a shirt without a collar. Over his
shoulder he was carrying a rolled-up bit of carpet. When
he suddenly turned into our path, I almost wet myself.
Then I realized it was Chris. Well, I was ashamed to be
seen with him, he was so scruffy. He had boot polish
on his face, too.

That hardly sounds like a woman in love. I suspect the Jewish
pawnbroker outfit to have been a joke. Dad was never a dandy,
but he usually dressed well enough. They first met at a dance.
Spotting this ravishing brunette, Dad sent his friend Tich to ask
for a dance. Then, as they left the floor, he casually wandered over
and introduced himself. An odd gambit! During the courtship
Tich continued to act as a go-between, sometimes collecting her
for Dad and then taking her home afterwards. Good old Tich.
Good old romantic Dad! However, Mum gave me another clue to
the lack of romance in the courtship. She said that Grandpa had
given her a push, telling her it was high time she was married
and out of the house. When we were living with him after the
second War, he gave my sister a somewhat rougher hint. She,
too, entered a marriage with less than a whole heart.

CHAPTER TWO

The Condons

1
The Family

I know little of my paternal grandfather, for he died before I was born – while Dad was serving his guns on the Western Front. He was of Anglo-Irish stock and no doubt a Protestant, although the Condons, like the Thompsons, were not churchgoers. About the only time they saw the inside of a church was at weddings, christenings and funerals, and not always at weddings. Why he died fairly young, I don't know. Perhaps he faded away gracefully to escape a surfeit of females, for he and Gran produced nine children, five at least of whom were girls.

Pauline: What was Grandfather Condon like? We never did know.

Doll: He was red-headed...

Mum: He had a bright ginger moustache...

Doll: Yes. And he had your noses. [*Looking at my sister and me, our noses being the generous Roman variety, known in the family as the "Condon conk"*] He was a nice-looking man.

Phil: More booze, anyone?

Mum: Thanks, darling. He was a king wasn't he, King Alfred?

Doll: No, dear, that was his ancestor. Grandfather Condon had trouble with his vowels, so we could never quite make out whether his ancestor shot himself or shit himself. *[Lin nearly chokes on her wine.]* No, he died falling off his horse. That's the way the story goes, anyway. Grandfather Condon used to wear a frock coat and dog's-tooth trousers. He was well-spoken, and a knowledgeable man – no fool. And he liked the ladies.

Phil: That sounds like a Condon, anyway.

Pauline: What did Grandfather Condon do?

Doll: He was something in the Arsenal, in an office, until they got that pub.

Born into the Sutch family, Dad's mother, Gran, was in her eighties and bedridden the first time I recall seeing her. She seemed large to me then, but really she was short and plump. She and her husband had been managers of *The Cornish Arms*, near General Gordon Square in Woolwich. It was a small backstreet pub of the kind with sawdust on the floor and a rough trade. Probably Gran was the moving spirit in the business, for after her husband's death she continued managing it until her retirement many years later. All told, she was licensee there for forty-eight years and saved enough to buy houses, one for herself and at least one other for rental income. Favouring black dresses and boots, she was respectable but no saint:

Doll: I remember going with Gran to visit her sister, Great-Aunt Hetty. You know what Gran was like – 54 around the arse and 54 around the chest – and she wore black boots. She could only do them up part way, because of her fat little legs. And I had a great big hat on and a pink dress. And she said to me, "Be careful how you eat when you get to your Aunt Hetty's. Eat with your mouth shut." Great-Aunt Hetty had a daughter. What was her name? She married a Honeybun. I forget. She was a bit younger than me. I was ten. And I can remember Gran was playful. Now, Gran was *never* playful...

Mum: No...

Phil: *[Laughing]* I can't imagine Gran being playful. But how did

Doll:	*[Ignores him]* And Great-Aunt Hetty had a toy shop. She took Gran and me around it. Showed me all the lovely dolls. Of course, I wanted the lot, didn't I? Got a clip around the ear-hole instead. And I think Grandma Condon had a lover at one time…
Pauline and Phil: [Together, astounded]	What!!!!?
Doll:	Yes, she had a baby…
Pauline:	Cor, 'struth, was it before or…
Mum:	*[Tactfully]* Was it a bastard child?
Doll:	No. I don't know if it was Grandfather's or not. But I know she had a lover. And the child died; and when the child was buried, Grandfather made her swear on the child's grave never to see this bloke again. And she never did.
Pauline:	Oh, then they were married?
Mum:	Oh, so she was married a second time, then?
Pauline:	No, she was doing that when she was – when they were married.
Mum:	Ooooh, I never knew. *[Laughs]* What a dirty old woman!
Doll:	Well, someone comes up and kisses your hand and says, "I love you. Come around the corner." What are you going to do – say "No"? You're not, are you? No. You're going to say, "Yes, please."

Despite her lack of height, Gran had spirit and brooked no nonsense from anyone – not from her children, her customers, nor from insolent knaves in office. I suspect she tolerated none from her husband, either. In short, while Mum's family was a patriarchy, Dad's was very much a matriarchy. Following my parents' wedding, neither family had anything to do with the other. We were the only connecting link, and Dad was not welcomed with any enthusiasm by Mum's side. The Thompsons looked down on the Condons and thought them rather common, certainly their social inferiors. I doubt whether the Condons gave much thought to the Thompsons at all, but they treated Mum well.

Gran's eldest girl was Kate. I recall seeing her only once, although she probably saw me often enough when I was very young. She married, into which family I don't know, and had a number of children. It seems she was generously proportioned. "When she went out shopping for her bras," commented Doll one day, "and the assistant asked for the size of the cups, she should have said 'buckets'!"

I saw a little more of Esther, Doll's mother. She had an odd way of talking that made her sound like a female Fagin. "Yes, my dear," for instance, came out as "Yerz, my dear" in a nasal drawl. She married a Mackenzie, "Uncle Mac", a fine, even-tempered man with an accent as rich as Drambui. I liked him very much. When Mum was going through a desperate period in early 1936, he proved a true Samaritan. Esther, it seems, was not the best of mothers:

Doll: I could never understand what he saw in my mother. He was a gentleman and she was a terrible person. He never swore, never lost his temper. But of course she ruined him, didn't she. It's funny, they were married for fifty years, longer than anyone else in the family, yet they were the unhappiest of the lot. I think disliking one another so much helped to keep them together. But she was a bitch.

Pauline: She used to borrow your clothes, didn't she?

Doll: Yes. She would borrow underwear from my sister and me – without asking, mind you – and then put it back in the drawer without washing it. My sister, who was a bit older than me, was always falling in love. She kept a diary. One day she showed me a page where she had written "Oh, I did love him! I feel ever so unhappy." Underneath, my mother had scribbled, "Poor bitch!" Well, a diary is private, isn't it? Not to my mother.

Pauline: Tell us the story about the steak. Lin hasn't heard it.

Doll: Well, one day, when I was little, I came home from school for my dinner and my mother gave me a shilling for a pound of rump steak. "And make sure there's no fat on it or I'll make you take it back." So off I go to the butcher's. "Yes, ducky?" he said, when he finally noticed my nose resting on the counter. "My mother wants a pound of rump steak, and she doesn't want any fat on it," I whispered. So he cut some off and then threw in a big piece of fat to make the weight up. "Please, my mother doesn't want any fat," I said. "She won't have it." "That's all right, ducky," he said and wrapped it up.

Well, on the way home I unwrapped it and threw the piece of fat in the gutter, among all the oats and bits of straw from the horses. When I got home, my mother hefted it and said, "That don't feel like a pound." Then she started poking at it with her fingers. "Don't feel like a pound at all." Poke, poke, poke. "Take it round to Mrs. Dennis's and get her to weigh it." So off I go to Mrs. Dennis's. We used to buy fish paste and tea from her, a pennyworth at a time, and then pay her on Saturday. The fish paste was scooped from a big enamel tin and it had yellow fat on it. It was horrible. Mrs. Dennis slapped the steak on the scales. "What's it supposed to weigh?" I told her. "It's not a pound, dear. No, it's an ounce short."

So back home I go, in fear and trembling. "Well, did she weigh it?" "Mrs. Dennis says it's an ounce short," I said. "Then you take it back to the butcher's and tell him I want my shilling back." Well, there wasn't a pound, was there? So I had to look in the gutter for the piece of fat I'd thrown away. I eventually found it, all covered with bits of straw, and I lifted up my skirt and wiped it off on my knickers – they weren't washed very often so it didn't matter.

When I got to the butcher's, I said, "Please, my mother doesn't want this steak, because there's too much fat on it. And she wants her shilling back." "Too much fat?" said the butcher, unwrapping the meat and looking at it. "'Ere, what's all these 'oles? It's full of 'oles." "I don't know," I said in a small voice. "But you must know," he said, holding it up. My mother had poked at it until it looked like a bit of old red lace. "No, I don't know, but I know my mother wants her shilling back."

Well, it was a struggle, but he finally gave me the shilling and I took it home. By this time it was nearly two o'clock and I was late for school, wasn't I? And they kept me in. I never did get any dinner that day.

Print cannot do the story justice. With its musical expressiveness, Doll's voice rivalled that of Kathleen Harris or, with a different accent, that of Edith Evans. The world lost a fine comedienne when it failed to discover Doll. She would have made a fortune on the stage or screen. Doll and my mother first met at the funeral of Hetty, another of Gran's daughters. Nearly the same age, they got along famously, and the laughter they shared probably added years to their lives.

Maud, third of Gran's daughters, lived in Southend. I remember seeing her only twice. While I was on leave after the war, Dad and I visited her over a weekend and spent Saturday evening playing four-handed crib for pennies. She trounced us thoroughly, mocking us as she raked in her winnings. Next morning, after breakfast and a perusal of the Sunday papers, we were told, "Go on. You men bugger off." I didn't need to ask where. She knew Dad and knew when the pubs opened. (I should pause here to point out that the Condons were by no means foul-mouthed. They did not consider the meaning of the terms "sod" and "bugger" at all. In our family they were terms of endearment.) When we returned, awash in mild and bitter, we were greeted with plates of food heaped up like pyramids. I asked if I could help with the washing-up. "No, darling, just you relax." So I returned to the Sunday papers, while Dad went upstairs to snore his head off. On the way back to London, I discovered half a crown had been slipped into my pocket, more than enough to make up for my losses at crib. My aunt knew that British servicemen at that time were not paid generously.

Maud married into the Reeman family, but her husband died long before I met her. She had three children that I know of, two boys and a girl. One boy became a major in the Army during the War. A second joined the Royal Navy as a regular in the 'Thirties and became a Navy boxing champion. I'm not sure at what weight. Later, he was badly wounded when his ship was torpedoed under him. In 1946 my father and I went up to London to see him. We found him lying on a couch, still in a great deal of pain from his wounded back. He was a fine-looking man in his thirties. The daughter, Muriel, was living with her mother when I visited. She was a pleasant woman, with a touch of the Condon about her, but she was not like her mother.

Years later, when I was working in Canada, Maud sent me bundles of newspapers and magazines. She thought I might be homesick. Like her secretly slipping the half crown into my pocket, it was a simple act of loving kindness. Of that visit, so long ago now, my only vivid memory is of Maud herself. Warm and intelligent, of all the daughters she most resembled Gran. I was to meet her only once more, in the 'Sixties.

Hetty, fourth of the daughters, did not resemble the others. Perhaps she took after her father. Though short like her sisters, she was little more than skin and bone. If you pushed the chip off her shoulder, the first thing it hit would have been the floor. I felt little of the warmth of Maud in her; yet warmth there was, though it might be hidden behind a dour appearance and protected by a tongue like a razor. Pauline claims that, when she was young, the only thing Hetty ever said to her was "If you were my child, I'd smack your arse." She never said that to me. But then there were so many women in Gran's family that a tight rein had to be kept on them. Boys and men? Well, the women knew they were really the weaker sex and had to be indulged.

Pauline: Aunt Hetty was married, wasn't she?

Doll: Yes, dear, but it only lasted two or three years. Then she lived with Wally. They weren't married, but they went through a form of marriage after seven years.

Pauline: I remember going to her funeral. Your husband Charlie, you and me were sitting around in Hetty's little room having a drink, while Hetty lay in her coffin outside on the hearse. Charlie used to swear terribly, didn't he? But he was very witty. Then the vicar came and we thought we'd better go outside and get on with it. Apart from the hearse, there was only this one car. The vicar sat in front with the driver and we three sat in the back. Well, all the way to the cemetery Charlie kept cracking jokes and we were laughing fit to burst. Even the vicar was doubled up. And I thought afterwards, what must it have looked like from outside? There was the hearse with the coffin, and following it was a car full of mourners laughing themselves silly!

Phil: It was an Irish wake on wheels, dear.

Doll: Yes, we all had a good laugh to send her on her merry way.

When Dad returned from his second war, he found himself unwelcome at home and went to live with Hetty. After I was demobbed, I used to visit them every week. Hetty was certainly not a happy woman. Although given to making sardonic comments, she never complained, though. She really didn't have much to be happy about. The house, on Elmdene Road in Plumstead Common, was part of a terrace built on the side of a hill. There were three floors, and the two rooms on each were cramped because of the passageways and staircases. The top floor was occupied by Hetty's son, Bill Martin. An elderly lady lodged in one of the rooms on the second. When she was carried off to hospital, terminally ill, her room was found to be like a maze. She had saved all her newspapers and magazines for years and piled them up in stacks. Among these she had nested like a mouse.

Hetty and Dad had the rest of the house, consisting of three rooms and a kitchen. One entered their part by descending into a small area. The gloomy front room was Dad's bedroom. Overlooking a small yard at the back was the living-room, if one may call it that, for it was about fifteen feet by nine. With only the minimum of furniture, there was still barely room to move; and the fire had to be kept small or it would have blistered the varnish on the furniture. It could seat three people, no more. The kitchen was not a separate room but the rear half of the passageway, widened at the expense of the living-room. There was no bathroom, of course, and the one lavatory in the yard served the whole house. Hetty kept her part of the house clean, but it must have been a discouraging task.

Apart from the rents paid by her three lodgers, Hetty's only source of income was her work. Until she became too old, she was a charlady, and a very independent one. She neither expected nor wanted help from anyone – no "bloody charity," as she put it. When I knew her, she wore blue-tinted glasses, as her eyes were weak. Perhaps that is an understatement: she was blind in one eye and had less than fifty percent vision in the other. Hetty was not an easy person to love, and Dad did not find her easy to live with. Her eyes may have been weak, but he feared her tongue. I was fond of her and respected her greatly.

The last of the daughters, unless Gran's dead baby had been a girl, was Mary, the gentlest and quietest of the sisters. She never married. She once had a boy friend who wanted to marry her, but Gran apparently refused her consent and he was afterwards killed on the Western Front. Thus it was her lot to stay with Gran and care for her when she became old. I saw quite a bit of Mary, for I used to visit her and Gran nearly every Sunday just before the War. She would greet me with a warm kiss and then immediately heat milk to make me a cup of Camp coffee. She had a slight cast in one eye and wore glasses, for like Hetty she had weak eyes. After Gran's death early in the War, Mary continued to live in the house on her own, her eyesight gradually deteriorating until, by the 'Fifties, she had become completely blind. With poor eyesight, Mary and Hetty must have found the Blitz especially terrifying, for both lived less than a mile from the Arsenal, a prime target.

I last saw Mary in the late 'Seventies, when Mum and I visited her in St. Nicholas's Hospital, Plumstead. She was in a coma and looked remarkably like Gran. She died several days later, the last of her generation of Condons. Two years previously, we had called on her at the old house on Hector Street. Well over eighty but in good health, she was serene and cheerful; and before long she and Mum were weeping with laughter as they talked over old times. Mary was being cared for by her lodger, a seaman in his seventies. He seemed a pleasant man. I like to think she had found a lover after all. Mary enters my thoughts now more than ever – and it is not because of the bottle of Camp coffee I keep in her memory. In some strange way her warm, uncomplaining gentleness speaks louder to me today than many a living voice.

Of Gran's eldest sons, Tom and Ant (Anthony), I know little. When they married, they moved away from Woolwich, presumably to live near their wives' parents. Although I saw both of them just after the War, I can recall only Ant's face now, as we have a photograph of him. He looked an older, more battered version of my father. In the 'Thirties he was an enthusiastic Communist, of the kind that would turn out for street rallies and if necessary mix it up with Oswald Mosley's Blackshirts. So far as I know, he was the only Condon to be involved in politics. I should imagine that the Condons, like most of the British public, voted Labour in 1945. Apart from that act of perhaps cynical insurance, their attitude to politics and politicians probably resembled my father's attitude to religion and priests.

ॐ

2
My Father

Dad was born September 22, 1895. He was a late child, his siblings then being in their teens or even married, and so he was very much the baby of the family. As often happens in such cases, Gran softened and doted on him. Hetty put it to me more bluntly. "Your father," she said sourly, "was Gran's darling. She thought the sun shone out of his arse."

Mum: Chris was the last one born, wasn't he. He was the baby.

Doll: Yes, he was born the same year as Maudy, my sister, my eldest sister, I should say. Of course, they ruined him, she absolutely ruined him.

Mum: Didn't she fuss-arse over him! When he was off to a dance, she'd fuss over his tie, stick his diamond pin in for him…

Doll: I wish she had stuck it up his arse!

Pauline: [Amid general laughter] You're not talking well of our dad!

Phil: Poor old Dad!

Doll: He was horrible.

Pauline: Why?

Doll: Because he used to tell tales. Get us all good hidings. Of course, my mother was such a loving person, Chris would only have to say "That Dolly, so and so, and so and so", she would say "Come here," shake the liver and lights out of you – you know, knock you all about – and send you up to

bed. *[With a touch of bitterness]* You'd be black and blue, she
was so gentle and tender. So I used to hate Chris. He knew
I hated him, too. When he looked at me I used to go *[Pulls
a face]*.

The last time I saw Mum, four months before her death at the age
of eighty-two, I asked, "When you die, darling, and you meet Dad
again, what will you say to him?"

Quietly and without hesitation she replied, "I'll punch the
bugger in the nose!" Poor old Dad!

He may have been spoilt as a child, but life soon redressed the
balance. Between childhood and his death at the age of seventy,
he served in the Army throughout the Great War, experienced
bankruptcy and prison in the 'Thirties, and rejoined the Army
for the second World War. Then, after demobilization in 1945,
he experienced the bitterness of finding that he was not wanted
at home, that his wife had taken up with another man. The last
decades of his life were not happy ones.

Like Mum, he was not well-educated. However, he was far
from ignorant. Though he did not have her business sense, he
was more knowledgeable, with the kind of knowledge that comes
from experience rather than books. Yet he must have done quite
a bit of reading at one time, for he had a sense of history. When
we wandered the streets of London after the War, he usually
had something knowledgeable and sensible to say about historic
buildings and monuments. It was he who first told me about
General Gordon and the Mahdi uprising. He often talked about
the Army, as it had been in the past, but he never spoke about his
own military experience. I asked him once what it had been like
during the Great War. He looked at me, then said quietly, "Well,
I'll tell you. We thought it was never going to end." That was all.
He was wise enough to know that trying to communicate the
reality of war was a waste of time.

He had abundant commonsense, and I cannot recall hearing
him say anything foolish or ill-considered. In many ways, he
and I were alike, only he was more down-to-earth. While I have
tended to be a romantic, he had more of the Anglo-Saxon in him,
more of the pragmatist. He was never cynical, never envious or

small-minded. On the contrary, I found him generous, tolerant in his judgment of others and willing to see things from their point of view. With fools and knaves, however, he had little patience. In 1940, soon after returning from Dunkirk, he was in a pub having a drink with Mum. Primed with a little Guinness, she touched a sailor's collar. "That's for luck," she cried.

The sailor swung around, "Leave me alone, you silly cow."

At this Dad thrust his face forward, "If it weren't for the fact that the Navy was so efficient, I'd knock your bloody head off!" Having finished their drinks, my parents then left.

"Hey!" A man in civilian clothes had followed them out. "Wotcha mean by calling my mate 'fishent'?" he snarled belligerently.

Dad punched his nose, hard, bouncing his head off the brick wall. And then, as the fool stood staring at him cross-eyed, he leant forward and said quietly, "Now I'll tell you what the word 'efficient' means."

As an old miner once said to me, if you want to teach a donkey, you first have to whack it over the head with a two-by-four to get its attention. Sound pedagogic advice.

The following year, Dad again had his patience tested. He was one of the guard commanders on a troopship, part of a convoy outward bound around the Cape for the Middle East. One day the Duty Officer sent for him. "Sergeant…er…Condon, I've noticed that when you are on duty you rarely bring anyone up on a charge. Now, I don't know why this is, but you really must do better, you know. We must keep the men up to the mark, keep them keen."

Of course, the man was a fool. And he was the kind of fool Dad detested above all others – one with pips on his shoulders. Accordingly, on his next guard duty he wandered around the ship charging men on the slightest pretext – boots unpolished, hair too long, unshaven and – that most useful charge – dumb insolence. When something like a platoon presented itself at the defaulters' parade, the Duty Officer received his lesson – not as painful as a punch in the nose, perhaps, but equally salutary.

Dad was not foul-mouthed, and I never heard him tell an off-colour joke. Nor, despite my mother's suspicions at one time, was he a womanizer. Like most soldiers of his generation, he was marked by the Great War and the experience of comradeship under fire. Preferring the company of men, after the War he sought that of old comrades-in-arms. Like the survivors of the Holocaust, he belonged to a select company, one from which others, even welcomed guests, are forever excluded.

The family album has two photographs of him as a young man. In the first, taken when he was eighteen, he bears a remarkable resemblance to me when I was his age. In fact, from the nose up he might be my identical twin, only he is rather fuller in the lips and firmer around the jaw. He is facing the camera, looking directly into the lens, and there is something attractive in the steady gaze of his wide-set grey eyes. We differed in physique, though. He was around five feet eight, rather more than average for his time, with a muscular build, whereas I top six feet and am slender. The second photograph is a full-length shot of him in uniform, probably taken in France, as his uniform looks well lived-in. His face, too, is worn – and haunted. It is no longer the face of a youth.

Shortly after the first photo was taken, he enlisted in the Royal Horse Artillery, a regiment with a splendid best uniform. In August, 1914, he landed in France with the British Expeditionary Force – that "contemptibly little army" as the Kaiser called it – in time for the Battle of Mons and the subsequent retreat. When the German onrush was halted and thrown back at the Battle of the Marne, he was still two weeks short of his nineteenth birthday and must have been one of the younger "Old Contemptibles". And there on the Western Front, except for brief periods of leave, he remained until the end of the war. Though fortunate not to have been in the "poor bloody infantry", for his survival then would have been most unlikely, he was close enough to the Front for a man at his side to be killed by a sniper, and the gun batteries were subject to intense counter-battery fire. As if this were not enough, in 1919 he was part of a British expeditionary force landed in Russia to fight the Reds. It is against this background that his later behaviour is to be viewed.

I doubt whether Mum really loved him at the time they married. He was not romantic, not given to whispering the sweet nothings that women sometimes like to hear, even if they don't always believe them. In fact, his pet name for Mum was "Face", or "Face-ache"! Before long, Mum had good reason to detest and fear him. One reason, no doubt, was his spoiled childhood. He was accustomed to having his own way, to placing his own pleasure first. When they were in business, too often he left Mum to run the pub while he went off somewhere. "Running around the West End with some tart, I suppose," she remarked to me years later. Perhaps, but I think it more likely he was sinking beer with his chums.

Such thoughtlessness and a preference for the company of men, combined with his drinking, proved disastrous to the marriage. I never saw him drunk, slurring his speech or staggering, but he certainly enjoyed his beer. As a boy in Plumstead, I loathed Sundays. Each followed the same pattern. The day would begin pleasantly enough with the best breakfast of the week, and then we would read the papers and listen to the wireless. At one time, I recall, there was a regular half hour of Hawaiian music. Soon Dad would begin to fidget and glance at the clock. Then, as opening time approached, he would grunt and go off to the pub. That day, of course, dinner was delayed until the pubs closed and he had had his skinful. It was usually a quiet affair, as drink made him surly, even menacing, and no one wished to provoke him. After the washing up, the ritual would continue. "Your mother and I are going upstairs for a nap. Now you children be quiet." And off they would go. What a boring way to spend the afternoon! Decades were to pass before I realized they were not going for a nap. Mum was fastidiously clean – in the house, in her handling of food, and in her person. Having to submit to sex – it could hardly be called "lovemaking" – with a husband who stank of beer, and in the same ritual pattern, week after week for years, must have been torment. But submit she did, lying on her back and thinking not of England but her children. As for Hawaiian music, I detest it still.

He was not a brutal man, certainly no bully. Normally, he was reasonable and pleasant enough. Nor was he a violent man, although he was capable of violence. Yet he could certainly be intimidating, and both Mum and Pauline were fearful of him. He could intimidate men, too – he hadn't been a sergeant in the Army for nothing. Although I never saw him lose control, I'm sorry to say that drinking sometimes made him turn ugly. After his death, Pauline told me something I hadn't known before – in rows with my mother, he sometimes hit her:

> I remember him hitting Mum full force with the flat of his hand, first on one side of the face and then on the other. It made me feel sick. I was always afraid of him. And on another occasion he hit her right across a double bed so that she fell off and hit her head against the wall. Then he picked me up, threw me on the bed and shouted, "Here, take your fucking daughter." I felt like a jelly.

Hearing about something years after the event is not the same as witnessing the reality. Had I seen him hitting Mum like that, I know my attitude towards him would have been different. I would have found it difficult to forgive him.

It would be wrong to suppose that fear permeated the family atmosphere, or that Dad was a systematic abuser of the kind we hear of so often now, with the abuser becoming more and more violent. His outbursts were rare explosions brought on by a combination of drink and frustration, although I never really knew the reason for the family rows. I was never fearful of him, but I wasn't foolish enough to cross him when he had been drinking. However, I did defy him once, when I was seven and we were living in Islington. One Sunday, as he sat down to dinner, exuding beer through every pore, he was more than normally surly. Resentful, I looked at him. Why did he drink stuff that changed grown-ups so unpleasantly? "All right," he said unexpectedly, pointing his knife at me. "Now, before we start, I want you to say grace."

Grace? We never said grace. I looked at his flushed face. He didn't look very grateful for what he was about to receive. I didn't know the word, but I smelt it – bullshit. Resentment suddenly flared into outrage. "No, I won't," I burst out.

He glowered at me, surprised and angry. Then his chair scraped back as he rose to his feet. "Why, you little bugger, I'll kick your arse!"

"Chris, don't," pleaded Mum, alarmed.

He couldn't. Sensing that this time he actually meant it, I had

31

outsped Mercury and was already flying up the first flight of stairs on winged feet. Two floors up, listening carefully for sounds of pursuit, I could hear angry voices below. A little later, Mum called me down and we finished dinner in unpleasant silence. Dad didn't look at me.

He never cuffed Pauline or me, though no doubt we sometimes deserved it. Except in the "grace" episode, I interpreted his threats to "kick my arse" as rough, comradely jesting. Once he did administer formal corporal punishment, though. "You two be home before ten. I won't tell you again." We were not home by ten, and we were sent to our rooms to await punishment. In my case, I was to wait with my trousers down. There he let us stew for ten minutes. Pauline was first, and I could hear her pleading, "Don't hurt me, Daddy, don't hurt me," followed by the sound of smacking. Then it was my turn. I had not taken my trousers down. A beating was one thing but humiliation was another. He would have to tear them from me. But he made no comment. Slowly unbuckling his heavy leather belt, he gave me six deliberate and careful strokes. For half an hour I hated him – but then I had to admit he had given me fair warning.

Years later, after he had died, I again had occasion to hate him – for a few minutes. While seated on the sofa next to Mum at a small family gathering, I suddenly raised my hand to scratch my head. At that, Mum flinched. "Why did you do that?" I asked her, astonished. She replied in a small voice, "I thought you were going to hit me"!

Nevertheless, despite his faults – and they weren't many – he was a soldier and a man. I loved him and knew he loved me; and during our times together after the War, I came to like him too. Perhaps his experience of bankruptcy and prison had mellowed him. Or perhaps it was time and his second war. At the age of forty-five, while based in Northern Ireland after his return from Dunkirk, he was confirmed almost by accident. Out of boredom he had attended a class to learn German, only to find it was a confirmation class. And in his last letter to me, written just before a stroke destroyed his ability to read and write, he said, "One thing I have discovered – that God is love." There was nothing mean or small about my father.

Perhaps he didn't deserve my mother. But which of us does deserve love?

In 1965, while I was on a visit to England during the summer, Dad asked if I would drive Mary and Hetty to Southend to see Maud. "It's only for the day," he said quietly. "It's years since they last saw each other, and once you go back there may never be another chance."

It was a joyful reunion. As the four sat together in Maud's living-room, sharing memories, joking about death and laughing, I sat quietly apart. The day was theirs, and for the time being I had ceased to exist for them. Looking on, I felt it a privilege to be part of the family. My father, old soldier yet the youngest there, no longer able to read or write; Mary blind and Hetty nearly so; and Maud, a stroke having impaired her ability to speak, every so often spluttering and swearing as she struggled to find the words – all old, all infirm, and yet such bright spirits! At this point there was a burst of hilarity; and then, almost as if she had been reading my thoughts, Hetty laughed, "Yes, and if you put the four of us together, you'd have one good one."

I am grateful I could do that small service for them. Before the year's end, and within weeks of one another, all save Mary were gone.

33

CHAPTER THREE

Early Days

1

Early Traumas

I was born at 151 Griffin Road, in one of the terrace houses that climb in rows from Plumstead to Plumstead Common. The birth certificate has Dad as a Licensed Victualler's Manager, although he really worked as a barman for his mother. His own father was listed, less grandly, as a Beerhouse Keeper. I emerged at the usual ungodly hour in the morning of February 13, 1926, year of the General Strike. The delivery was a difficult one, for I weighed over eleven pounds. (*I lost nearly all my life's blood giving birth to you!*) Clearly I'd been in no hurry to appear. Whether I was a slow starter, a procrastinator, or an early striker, I don't know. But my birth seems to have set the pattern for my life. I have since been late for nearly everything!

Nevertheless, I began with a splash. On Friday, July 16, 1926, amid a tinny fanfare of publicity, I leapt into the world's spotlight for the first and, I hope, last time. That day's edition of *The Daily Express* shows me posing with two other pudgy infants under the headline "Three of Britain's Wonderful Babies". When Mum first told me about this honour, I was most impressed. Fancy being chosen out of all those babies, I thought, supposing I had won a gruelling competition. The truth dawned later, when I inspected the newspaper cutting that she saved throughout her life. Apparently there had been, not a competition, but an appeal for baby photographs in an effort to distract the populace from economic misery.

In any case, it was not long before I became heartily sick of the whole affair. I think seeing my picture in the paper unhinged Mum's mind on the subject of my infancy, for she trumpeted the tidings to almost everyone she showed me to. The last time she blew a triumphant blast was during the summer break in 1978, when I was showing her around my school. I had left her in the empty staff room while I fetched some papers and returned to find she had the janitor backed into a corner and was talking at him excitedly. When she saw me enter, she cried, "There he is. There's my son. He was one of Britain's Wonderful Babies!" In response to the appeal in the bemused janitor's eyes, I fixed what I hoped was a reassuring smile on my face, made our excuses and we left. Given another few minutes, she might have started on toilet training and weaning. I mention this recurrent trauma only to explain why I turn from praise. When some kindly soul gives me a pat on the back, I shrink. This I do, not purely, but from apprehension. To me, praise is often prelude to torment.

Leaving aside the topic of toilet training, I should recount two other anecdotes about my early childhood that may shed some light on my character.

"I used to hate taking you to see Gran," Mum said, as we sat shucking peas one day.

"Why is that, dear?"

"Well, when Gran and your aunts saw you, they'd say, 'Ah, here's Chris's boy. Look at the little darling!' Then they'd whip off half your clothes. 'Ah, look at his little tootsies! Kootchie, kootchie. Look at his little belly button! Look at his little winkle!' Kiss, kiss, kiss. Then they would dip a dummy into a tin of condensed milk and shove it into your mouth. In a few minutes you would become a sticky mess. And I used to take so much trouble to make you look nice!"

None of this remains in my conscious memory, thank goodness, but who knows what lurks in the subconscious? Does this explain why I tend to edge nervously away on those rare occasions when a woman shows me more than casual interest? All I know is that I once nearly drove off the road when a female passenger suddenly whipped out a sticky pastry and thrust it at me as an offering. And then there was the terrifying experience on the cruise ship *Oronsay*. I had found a quiet corner to do some sunbathing, but as I began drifting peacefully into oblivion, something warm and wet splattered on my back. Cursing all sea gulls, I began to rise – only to find myself pinned to the deck by a blue-rinsed female armed with suntan lotion. When she began to massage me, I cast her and all dignity aside and fled. At the time, there was another reason why I was deeply suspicious of females. I was being pursued by a self-confessed predatory female who happened to be a friend's wife. But more of that later – perhaps.

The last anecdote concerns my weaning. It seems that I clung to my mother's breast for so long that it was almost indecent. "I had a hell of a time weaning him," Mum told one of her friends, while I sat cringing. "He simply wouldn't leave me alone, long after the normal time. I tried everything – even smearing my nipples with mustard, but he merely pulled a face and carried on sucking. He would even climb out of his cot and crawl into my bed. Finally, in sheer desperation, I gave him a sip of Guinness. 'There, you little sod, try that.' That did it! He smacked his lips, gave a gurgling smile and never gave me any more trouble." Was that an early sign of intelligence and good taste? Or heredity?

❦

2
First Memories

But for blurred impressions, my first memories are of Marylebone. Somewhere between Regent's Park and Marylebone Road, and not far from the Baker Street Underground, sat a pub called *The King Alfred*. (Sherlock Holmes may once have been a patron, perhaps.) By 1929, Dad was the licensee there. The trade was good to begin with, as many customers were business people, drawn there by the cooked lunches; but before long it was flourishing, for Mum was an excellent cook in the traditional English style and soon proved to be the main asset to the business.

She further improved the assets of the family by giving birth in March to my sister, Pauline. The timing proved unfortunate, though, for she was no longer able to devote the care to us that I had enjoyed for three years. As a result, Pauline and I were looked after by a nanny, a situation that was to last in my sister's case for about three years. This had little effect on me that I am aware of, as I already felt emotionally secure, but it proved devastating for Pauline. She grew up feeling that she was not wanted, a feeling that was to be reinforced by ill fortune and that was to last. When we were discussing our childhood some time ago – she was then in her late fifties – she said, "Yes, I know *now* that it wasn't true, that I have nothing to blame Mum for, that I was wanted then and am wanted now; but, you know, I still *feel* unwanted!"

There are many reasons, not just bad parenting, for a less than ideal childhood, and most us grow up under some handicap or other. However, as we mature, nearly all of us become capable of choosing what we think and what we try to do. What counts is the way we live despite handicaps. In Pauline's case, her experience made her resolve that her own child should never feel unwanted; and so she lavished care and love on her own daughter – and without spoiling her, either. As for compassion, Pauline is kinder than I.

Of *The King Alfred* period, I remember playing in Regent's Park or hanging out the window watching passers-by and sometimes envying small boys trundling by on scooters made of boxwood and ball bearings. There were periodic visits to the zoo, of course, and those I enjoyed immensely. At night I would sometimes cry because my legs ached. "Growing pains, darling," Mum said. So I just had to put up with it. When Pauline was about two, I would take her for short walks. Mum made it clear that I was responsible for her. "Now don't go too far, and don't take any sweets from strange men. And hang on to her tight. You know what she is." I did know what she was. She was a darter. She was perfectly happy toddling by my side, her hand in mine, but if she saw something that interested her, all other thoughts would dart off – and so would she. Apprehensive, not wanting to see her mashed by a car, I held her hand firmly and kept my other hand ready to grab her dress. One day, a couple of years later, Mum added, "If you get lost, always ask a policeman." Get lost? What an interesting idea! And so I made the next walk an expedition for the pleasure of asking a policeman the way home. A well-dressed small boy leading a toddler through busy city streets might not be a common sight today, but we seem to have more "strange men" about now.

To this period belongs the first Christmas I can remember, Christmas, 1931. We had a family gathering – all, save Dad, from Mum's side. I was excited as my cousins John and Peter were there and could stay over the holiday. When Christmas morning came, I received what I thought was a sack of toys. Actually, it was a small pillowcase; and it wasn't all toys, for it contained what were to be the usual Christmas "fillers" – fruit, sweets, nuts and, "for luck", a lump of coal wrapped in paper. In fact I can recall only one toy, a medieval miller dressed in traditional white smock and blue hood. When you wound up the clockwork, he climbed a pole with a sack of flour on his head. Perhaps it was a shadow of the future, for I was to be doughmaker in a bakery for a while. Also in the "sack" were the first two books I recall reading. One was about two English children in India who had to hide in a ruined temple to avoid a fearsome band of thugs. The other was R.M. Ballantyne's *The Young Lion Hunters*. Although I recall nothing of it, except that I helped make Christmas decorations for our classroom, I had started school and could read with ease.

☙❧

3

Recognition

Next year, my parents were on the move again. *The King Alfred*, old and rat-infested though it was, had provided a good living, but my parents wanted a free house and decided to leave. Mum later told me that the move resulted in a substantial loss of money.

In a deal over the stock, Dad had evidently accepted smiles and fair words instead of demanding a written agreement. "Done in the eye by a fellow Mason," she complained. Though dashed by this experience, they eventually found another pub, whether a free house or not, I don't know, and built it into a thriving business. Again the moving spirit was my mother. At one time she was serving nearly two hundred cooked lunches a day to local business people and staff from a nearby cigarette factory. This attracted so much custom and goodwill to the pub that, in addition to hiring a cook to help in the kitchen, my parents had to hire several barmen as well. In fact business became so good that they became ambitious again and set themselves up for another knockdown. But that was yet to come.

While still between pubs, we moved into a spacious one-room flat above a garage. It was a worrying time for my parents. Their livelihood was gone and with it a great deal of money, and they had not yet found another pub. One result is that they had a thundering row. I retain a vivid picture of it. Mum is bathing my thumb, which has been infected, and Dad is standing on the other side of the table with a glass of beer in one hand and a beer bottle in the other. "You bloody bitch," he shouts, raising the bottle, "I've a damned good mind to throw this at you!" At this, I burst into tears, "Oh, my thumb hurts, Mummy." "Now look what you've done, Chris," she cries. "You've upset the boy." She was right. I was afraid he had meant what he said. It was the only serious row between them that I remember, the only time I saw my father threaten violence – other than offering to kick my arse, that is.

While out walking with my parents at this time, I had a curious experience. It was a grey winter afternoon and the lamplighter was on his round early, reaching up with his pole to bring a little cheer to the street. As I padded along, holding Dad's hand, I heard a rumbling behind me and turned to see the cause. A man was following us, pushing an empty barrow along the gutter. He was dark, like a Gypsy, and wore an open jacket, waistcoat, and the usual cap. He must have been in his early forties. As I gazed at him, something happened that I cannot pretend to understand. Suddenly, as if scales had fallen from my eyes, I seemed to be seeing my father and I felt a surge of compassion for him. Yet he looked nothing like Dad! I was holding him by the hand.

"Mummy," I said, tugging her coat, "look at that poor man. Can we give him some money?"

She turned to look. "He's not a poor man, darling. He's a costermonger, a barrow boy."

Confused, I put the matter from my mind.

More than a quarter of a century later, as I sat in the staff room enjoying a smoke during a spare period, the school librarian popped in for a coffee. "You know, Dolly," I remarked, "I had the most peculiar experience yesterday."

"What was that?" she asked.

"Well, I'd had supper at my usual café and was on my way back to the car. A few young children were playing in the lane and I glanced at them casually. Then one looked up at me, a girl of about eight, I should say – and suddenly my heart turned a somersault! It was as if I had unexpectedly seen a well-loved person after an absence of years. I didn't slacken my stride and had only the vaguest impression of her features, and yet there had been some kind of recognition. As I passed them – I'm not sure about this – I seemed to hear her say, 'What a nice man!' Do you think she might have experienced something similar? Isn't that odd?"

"Yes, it is odd," she said, looking at me oddly.

Bloody fool, I thought as she went out with her coffee. *Now she probably thinks you're a paedophile or something.*

☙❧

4

A Shadow of Things to Come

Just as I was getting used to our new home, I found myself shipped off to Nanna's on Plumstead Common. I think my parents had found their new pub and wanted me out of the way while settling in. Of the time I spent there little remains clear now. My palate reminds me that this was when I fell in love with Nanna's apple tarts, made with cooking apples, decorated with strips of pastry and dusted with icing sugar. And my ear reminds me that this period is the first I associate with a piece of music, in this case a dolorous popular song. I enjoyed the evenings spent with Nanna and Grandpa. As we sat before a coal fire listening to the wireless, the sound of the wind about the eaves made the room seem only cosier. Years later I found that it wasn't the wind at all, but drafts. Whistling eerily through cracks around the window frame, they fed the fire and carried most of the heat up the chimney.

By day I attended Timbercroft Lane School, but I can recall only the first class. A teacher was at the board, rabbiting on about something and being watched by rows of silent boys, seated in pairs. I wasn't interested. Turning to the boy by my side, I whispered, "Who's the toughest boy in class?"

"You are," he replied instantly. Evidently he was a survivor.

"No, apart from me," I said modestly.

"Whatsit, over there."

I scowled at "Whatsit," but had no intention of doing anything.

One day, having decided to visit Gran on Hector Street, I ran down Lakedale Road, took an appreciative sniff of the Beasley brewery and turned into Conway Road. The brewery wall was on my left and on my right there soon appeared another. It was guarding a school I hadn't seen before, a tall Victorian building with the lower windows protected by wire netting. A sign proclaimed "Conway Road School". With its defensive wall of soot-blackened brick topped with broken glass and its black iron-bar gates, it resembled a prison. And that, in my innocence, is what I thought it to be – a prison to keep children in. Oppressed by the thought, I said aloud, "Well, one thing I'm sure of – I'll never have to go to that school." Do the gods take account of such words from a child and consider it hubris? Or did they merely decide to sport with me? I know only that four years later, with those words ringing mockingly in my ears, I found myself being dragged unwillingly to that very school – and at exactly that period in my childhood when I was most vulnerable.

As Christmas approached, I sometimes walked down to Woolwich to rub my nose against shop windows and wander around the street market in the square, the first London street market I can recall seeing. I found them particularly fascinating on winter evenings, for they are vibrant with life. Men, women and children mill around the brighty-lit stalls to compare prices or admire the gleaming pyramids of oranges and apples, the rows of silvery herring and haddock and the deep trays of slimy eels, all alive-o; or stop to finger garments, or peer at stacks of plates and rows of tea pots and cake stands; or cluster around to watch some magician demonstrate the latest gadget for slicing vegetables or beating eggs. In summer, people stand eating winkles, cockles and mussels from little dishes; and in winter, crack hot chestnuts, tossing them from hand to hand to avoid burning their fingers. Meanwhile the air is filled with the hum of voices, the shuffling of feet, the jangling of a barrel-organ outside a pub – all punctuated by the cries of the vendors:

"Rrrripe bananers!"

"Come on, darlin', treat yourself to some o' these luvly Coxes. Yer 'usband'll luv yer for it."

"Look at this luvly set o' dishes. They're seconds, near perfect, just like the ones ordered for Lord and Lady Muck!"

"Fresh fish! Nice 'addock! Come along, nah, look at all these luvly eels!"

"Chestnuts! 'Ot roasted chestnuts!"

A lifetime later, while teaching in a Woolwich school, I was struck by the volume of noise issuing from one small student. "Boy," I said caustically, "you've got a voice that could sell fruit in the market."

"That's what I do, sir," he boomed hoarsely.

Mum was less romantic about markets: "Cheating sods. They put all the best stuff in front and serve you from behind." But then she had to watch her pennies. The vendors sell dreams as much as wares.

Shortly before Christmas I rejoined my parents and sister in our new pub, a small and old one, really – *The Lady Owen Arms* in Islington. And the next morning, as that busy old servant, the sun, was rising to bestow his cheer upon the fog and cloud, I burst from my slumbers, threw open my chamber window and looked out upon the world beneath. Goswell Road was on my right hand as far as the eye could reach, Goswell Road extended on my left, and the opposite side of Goswell Road stared back at me from across the way – but of Mr. Pickwick there was no sign! A new period of my life had begun.

CHAPTER FOUR

Sex...

1
My Sister Makes Herself Heard

I was nearly seven. I suppose I must have seen my sister naked before; but as we shared a room in our new home, I was about to see her naked more often than I would have wished, even had I been interested. Her sense of insecurity was now reinforced by circumstance. She already felt unwanted, from the days of nannies at *The King Alfred*. This feeling had been temporarily assuaged while we were between pubs; but now Mum was busy again and, to make matters worse, we had no nanny. Moreover, Pauline had grown to fear her father, a fear that probably started from a habit he once had of throwing her into the air and then catching her while shouting with delight. While he was only too effective in showing disapproval, he was less so in demonstrating affection; and Pauline was not to know that treating her like a basketball was his way of showing that he loved her. The fear, of course, was not diminished by the family rows.

One day Dad decided to enact a little drama to entertain friends. "What do you mean by sleeping with my wife?" he roared, throwing a glass into a bucket. "I'll teach you a lesson you won't forget." Crash, another glass. "I'll kill you, you swine." Crash. Crash. It was amusing, no doubt, but Pauline was in the next room and thought he was killing someone. She was terrified. With painful regularity, she now began to wet the bed. Night after night, Mum would put us to bed and then go down to the bar. Night after night, Pauline would stir from her sleep and begin to cry. If this brought no attention, and usually it didn't, she would cast off the bedclothes and begin to scream, loudly, persistently, all the while rubbing her ankles together until they were raw. This would go on for about five minutes – more like five hours to me – and sometimes it brought Mum up. However, if it was not yet closing time, well, Mum was in a noisy bar two floors down. Then Pauline would go into the third stage of her attention-getting repertoire. Standing up and casting her nightdress aside, she would use the bed as a trampoline and bounce with incredible energy, using the momentum to crank up the screaming until it drilled through my skull. This she would keep up until lung-power triumphed over distance and Mum arrived at the run.

After several weeks of this purgatory, a succession of nannies arrived. The first was Biddy, whom we had had before at *The King Alfred*. This time she lasted only a few weeks. She was caught pilfering cigarettes and throwing them down to her boy friend in the street. The next was an elderly black woman. Common enough in America, black nannies were unusual in Britain and Mum hesitated to take her on. In response to the woman's pleas, however, she decided to give her a try. Unfortunately, the old dear was plagued by colds and in the evenings would stoke the fire until it roared, hoist her skirts to her knees and then sit almost on top of it, roasting herself and drying her snotty handkerchiefs. She didn't last long, either, for one day she accidentally burned Pauline's leg with the hot poker and was instantly replaced. As for me, Pauline may have needed a nanny, but I needed something else – a separate room. To my profound relief I got one and, except for a brief period, did not have to share a room with her again.

I think this period of over-exposure to her problems had its effect on me. I detest emotional scenes, having witnessed too many as a child. I find them ugly and avoid a quarrel – especially with a woman, for I have the dreadful fear that she might suddenly rip off her clothes and start jumping up and down and screaming.

2
Strange Doings

Islington was then a borough with little park space. If there were parks, I found only one. It consisted of a small square of trees, shrubs, flower beds and manicured grass. Paved paths ran through it, high iron railings guarded it and "Keep off the grass" signs adorned it. It provided a little habitat for birds and a few seats for adults, but it was no place for children. Goswell Road was a busy thoroughfare, and City Road, which joined it at the Angel, was even busier; and so we snotty-nosed kids played in alleys, side streets and odd corners – but not too far away, for strangers aroused the territorial sensibilities of local kids.

In the early weeks at *The Lady Owen Arms*, I sometimes played with neighbouring children in a cul-de-sac next door. It was "L"-shaped, with the pub on one side and a high brick wall on the other. If we played in the short arm of the "L", we could not be seen from the street and were safe from traffic. It was here that I discovered sex could be a social activity – as distinct from the solitary and boring wank. Several of us were playing there one day, including a couple of older girls, and the conversation turned to babies, not my favourite topic. However, one of the girls told us what made babies. "Yes, the man gets his thingy and puts it on the woman's thingy," she said omnisciently.

Fancy that! I digested this interesting news for a moment. Then "Could we do it?" I asked. I think I meant "could" and not "shall".

"I suppose so." She spoke hesitantly, but looked expectant.

Undoing my fly, I fished for my thingy, eventually found it, and then, holding it firmly, advanced on her from the side as she lifted her dress accommodatingly. By dint of much painful pulling,

I reached what I thought were her bloomers. Close enough. "Are they touching?" My voice was betraying the strain.

She frowned in concentration and said uncertainly, "I think so."

"Good," I gasped. "Now you'll have a baby." It was over twenty years before I tried again.

It was about this time that I had my first encounter with a "strange man." While we were playing jacks, much more fun than all that silly baby stuff, into the cul-de-sac walked a man of about thirty. He was wearing a raincoat – all right, a shabby raincoat. He approached us and stood there awhile, watching us play. When we stopped to look up, he suddenly opened his coat wide with a flourish and stood there like Batman. "There," he said, his voice betraying ill-concealed triumph, "what do you think of that?" "That" was an enormous penis, rampant. In complete silence we looked at it respectfully. At last, satisfied with the impression he had made, he folded his wings and scuttled off, hugging his pride and joy closely. "What a funny man!" exclaimed one of the girls, as we looked at one another in puzzlement. Crikey, yes. A jolly good thing he hadn't offered us any sweets! Then we resumed our game.

A little later I clattered in and sat down for tea. "What have you been doing, darling?" Mum asked, smiling.

With my mouth full of bread and butter, I answered, "Nothing, Mum. Just playing jacks, that's all. It was fun." Then I remembered. "Mum," I said, chattily, "I saw a really funny man just now."

"A funny man, dear? Whatever do you mean?"

"Well, he came up and he had a long pink balloon between his legs, a skinny one. What a funny place to keep... "

"What!?" The smile vanished as if by magic, and she reared up like an alarmed tarantula. "What did he do? What did he do to you?"

"Nothing, Mum," I answered, surprised by her reaction. "He just opened his coat and showed us this funny pink..."

"Chris?" she shouted. "Chris, where are you? Chris!"

Poor Fred the Flasher. His thunderflash had proved to be a damp squib!

One day I saw two dogs behaving in a way that made me doubt my eyes. They were standing in the middle of the street, panting and leering obscenely. Well, nothing remarkable about that. What was strange was that they were standing back to back like Siamese twins or a pair of gothic book-ends with no books between. I gaped, trying to make sense of what I was seeing. Then I rushed into the bar. "Mum, come and have a look at these dogs!"

"What dogs, dear?"

"There are two dogs in the street and they've got their bums stuck together," I cried.

"Ssshhh! I can't come now. I'm busy with the customers." For some reason her face had turned cherry red.

"But, Mum," I was shouting now, my faith in the rationality of the universe teetering, "their *bums* are stuck together!"

I had a long wait before this mystery was explained.

☙❧

3

Cigarette Cards, Horses and People

The cul-de-sac and the immediate environs of the pub soon palled, and I began to wander farther afield. Fascinated by the stalls and the bustling crowd, for a time I frequented the Chapel Street market. I also took to accosting men: "Got any cigarette cards please, Mister?" I had found another interesting activity, one that I pursued until I was almost twelve. My favourite pitch was the exit of the Angel Underground. This disgorged passengers from a large, somewhat rickety lift into a well-lit area. I wasn't so stupid as to approach men in shadowy places. Most smoked then and were usually good-humoured about being pestered by small boys. Soon I had hundreds of cards. Eventually, thanks to Pauline, I had to throw most of them away. While I was out, she had inspected them, covered them with jam, and left them scattered on the floor.

I managed to save some, though, a few sets mounted in albums. My favourite set was "The Kings and Queens of

England". Reproductions of famous portraits, the cards are of fine quality, with vivid colours and a brilliant finish. To this day, I cannot read history without recalling the faces. Beaumaris Castle? I see Edward the First, Hammer of the Scots, a stern man with a short beard. Bannockburn, favourite topic of the Scots when they want to needle the Sassenach? There is Edward the Second, a sissy with curled whiskers. How could you expect *him* to win a battle? The Glorious Revolution? James II, with a blond wig and a thin smile, manages to look sly and constipated at the same time. All the kings and many of the queens of England from a resolute William the First to a bemedalled and bestarred George the Fifth are there. For me, those cigarette cards injected colour and real people into history.

Another set, not quite complete, is of warships, some of which were to be sunk in the second War, including, alas, *H.M.S. Hood.* When I was twelve, I modelled some in Plasticene, with matches for guns, and mapped out a naval action in the Mediterranean between the fleets of Britain, France and Russia on one side and those of Germany and Italy on the other. The remaining two are "Military Uniforms of the Empire" (shades of Gary Cooper in *Lives of a Bengal Lancer*!) and "Aircraft of Today". Of the latter, my favourite was the Hawker Fury II fighter, a silver biplane with spats. Biggles would have loved it. Nothing I had on cards, though, or have since seen in the air, has ever equalled the sight of a great airship flying low over London. Outlined against the clouds, its fluted hull bright silver in the sunshine, it sailed the sky with all the majesty of a great ship. Compared with the airship, the blimp is merely an elongated balloon. As for aircraft and rockets, no matter how beautiful, they are but noisy machines after all.

As at *The King Alfred*, I enjoyed leaning out of an upper-floor window to watch the world pass by. There were fewer cars then, and most of the traffic consisted of commercial vehicles, many still horse-drawn. Some buses had open tops, as did trams. These were ideal for viewing the city – unless it was pouring with rain, and then one had to cower beneath a black oilskin attached to the rear of the seat in front. Most of all I admired the brewers' drays. Driven with careless ease by burly draymen in leather aprons, they were drawn by teams of great horses, matched giants with shining coats and plaited manes and tails. How splendid they looked in their polished harness and gleaming brasses! How proudly they arched their necks and lifted their shaggy, iron-shod hooves! My father once seated me on one. Splay-legged on its warm and massive back, I sensed both gentleness and strength.

One day, to have a better view of the world, I sat on the window sill, dangling my legs over the street. Passers-by waved and shouted friendly greetings – or so I thought, until a drayman shook his fist and then went in to tell Dad. I did this not from bravado, but naturally, for I felt at home in high places. In time I was to dangle my feet from trees and mountains. Obviously the monkey in me.

People were interesting to watch, too – hundreds of them and each one different. Sometimes they were weird, like the man with the "balloon", but I was used to the occasional drunk, or down-and-out, or man with a billboard that read "Prepare to Meet Thy Doom". However, late one evening I saw something that made me doubt the sanity of grown-ups. Distant shouting, unlike the usual revelry by night, brought me to my bedroom window. A column of men was approaching from the direction of the Angel. Tramping out of the gloom carrying placards, shouting unintelligible slogans, and shaking fists, they passed on into the night like a rabble of noisy ghosts. I couldn't imagine what they were up to, as the street was otherwise deserted. Individual oddness I was used to, but that a group should behave in this way was something new! There was no mention of them next day, and so I don't know who they were. They appeared too angry to have been hunger marchers.

❦

4

The Voyage

Spring passed into summer, and August, 1933, brought me excitement of a different kind. Together with a Mrs. Braithewaite and her daughter, Mum, Pauline and I crowded into a taxi early one morning and were delivered to Tower Pier, where a liner awaited us – *The Crested Eagle*. To the tune of "Mama, dear, come over here and see who's looking in my window", played loudly over the ship's loudspeakers, we embarked with a cheerful, chattering throng. Then came the great moment. With a couple of hoots from its siren and a cheer from passengers, our ship slipped its moorings, stood off from land – and then we were steaming downriver with the great paddlewheels churning and the morning sun glinting on the grey water. I was off on a great adventure. We were on our way to Clacton.

It was only a day excursion, of course, and the air I sniffed so appreciatively had as much of sewage as of anything else in it, but for me it was my first sea voyage. There is much I recall of that day on the river. As the Tower and Tower Bridge fell astern, ancient brick warehouses crowded the banks and eyed us blankly through begrimed windows. Clumsy barges lined the shores or, deeply laden, trailed behind tugboats like strings of waterlogged rats. Smoke belching from its stack, its stern squatting in the roiling water, another tug surged across the river with a bone in its teeth. A Thames Police launch hurried through the chop as if on an urgent mission. Small ships, even sailing vessels, lay unloading at wharves, and here and there old riverside pubs appeared. Miles of dockland stretched along the banks, the basins marked by the funnels and masts of bigger ships and by tall cranes that stood in rows like giant, skeletal giraffes. Then, downriver from the Greenwich Naval College and the welcome green of the park, larger ships appeared, steaming out on the tide, and Thames barges, sedate in suits of rusty sails. Past Woolwich and its steam ferries we churned, past the liners in Tilbury docks, past the ghost of the Nore lightship – and out to the open sea.

I suppose we went ashore to sample the delights of Clacton for a few hours. I don't remember; nor would I choose to, for it had to have been an anticlimax. Nor do I remember the voyage back, except that the laughter was louder and the sun sparkled on glasses of bitter as well as on the water. It is the voyage out that remains in memory. "To travel hopefully is better than to arrive"? Yes, that is sometimes true, though it may mean only that journeys often end in disappointment – a dash of cold water, perhaps, or, worse, the realization that one has returned to where one began and that nothing much has been accomplished after all. At the end of a voyage, as at the end of a rainbow – not a pot of gold, but a cry of "Gardy loo". I have had several round trips of this kind, physical and psychological, and the experience can be bitter. Still, we have no cause for complaint when life fails to conform to our hopes. It has its own purposes. "Blessed reality", as Graham Greene calls it, is there to puncture our illusions and keep our feet on the ground – perhaps to keep us from going altogether mad. Nevertheless, although I felt dissatisfied even then, felt, young though I was, that something was lacking, I treasured my first voyage – for I had felt something stir within me.[3]

༺༻

5

Notes from the Subconscious

Dreams fascinate us. Psychologists recognise that they are a way the mind has of communicating with itself and that the subconscious often uses symbols, archetypal or otherwise. Some people think that dreams may even portend future events. I can't pretend to interesting dreams. Most are boring or frustrating, and only once for a brief period have I recorded them. However, twice I have had recurrent dreams, each in a sequence of three on consecutive nights. The first happened at *The Lady Owen Arms*, and the three were identical. *I am climbing the stairs to my bedroom, two floors up, feeling increasingly apprehensive as I go. Then, as I open the door, a large cupboard facing me explodes open and a huge white hand as large as myself reaches out to seize me. In a panic, I hurl myself down the first flight of stairs. At this point, I awaken.* When I told Mum about the dreams, she said that she had been frightened as a girl by finding an uncle's artifical hand in a cupboard. "That's what caused your dream, darling." I was not so sure. My dream was more frightening than that. Whatever the truth, when I was ten years old, the hand was to catch me.

---

[3]   On May 29, 1940, *The Crested Eagle* found what was lacking – a higher purpose. Attempting to clear Dunkirk with a full load of troops, she was hit and set ablaze by enemy fire. Her master managed to beach her, so that most of the troops escaped on other ships. It was a fine end for the old paddlewheeler.

Twenty years after the first, I had the second recurrent dream, one that despite my age I found more frightening. After supper I had settled down for a nap before an evening of study. *As I drift into sleep, I find myself slowly falling backward and downward into a black void and have the dreadful feeling that, if I let myself go, I shall never get back. Unlike in the earlier dreams, in these I don't awaken with a start but have to fight to escape.* Most disagreeable. When I had the same dream the following evening, I began to feel apprehensive. On the third evening, the dream changed significantly. *As I fall helplessly into the void, a disembodied face, black with white markings, swims out of the darkness and approaches until it fills my field of vision. For what seems an eternity I am held there, suspended in pure terror. Then with chilling menace it hisses one word at me – "R e m e m b e r r r!"*

In a panic, I fought my way back and awakened in a sweat. Like Kipling's man with the spur, I was now afraid to sleep. I also recalled M. R. James's ghost story "The Mezzotint" and didn't fancy a progressive nightmare at all. For a week I skipped the evening nap, and the dream never returned. Four years later I had a breakdown. I believe now that the dreams were related, that the hand and the face in a sense were one. But many years passed before I came to that realization.

The subconscious can speak to us in our waking state as well. One winter afternoon, hearing someone at the piano in the saloon bar, I ran in. It was Mum playing, probably to cheer her customers – there were only two or three of them, each one nursing a beer and alone with his thoughts. Head on arms behind the bar, I remained to listen. After a while I noticed a ruck in Mum's cardigan, one side having caught up on the bentwood chair. Staring, I became fascinated as the ruck shifted, changed form, and then grew charged with hieroglyphic meaning. Then a sudden rush of love and anguish pierced my being, and I burst into wails of grief. Alarmed, for I was not given to crying, Mum was beside me in an instant, "What is it, darling?" But how could I answer? I didn't know myself. Later I knew. For the first time I had perceived her as vulnerable and had experienced love as pain. It had been almost too much to bear. When Mum died, a lifetime later, I did not weep. I felt only relief that her suffering was ended. I shed my tears for her while she was alive – then, as a boy, and sometimes later, as a man.

Meanwhile, Dad had been using his initiative. Business was good, but why work for the brewer when you can work for yourself? And so, raising every penny that he could, he leased a property on the other side of the road and turned it into a licenced private club. Not long after the above event, we moved in. It was to prove a disaster.

CHAPTER FIVE

...and Violence

1

An Augury

Although our new home had four floors, we had to make do with less living-space than at the pub. A printing shop occupied the front of the basement, and our beer cellar took up the rear. The club was on the ground floor – two bars with room for tables, piano and dartboards. With its bentwood chairs painted gold and tables covered with red-checkered cloths, the bar at the rear was quite attractive. Even more attractive for Mum was the fact that kitchen space was adequate only for preparing snacks and a limited number of lunches, far from the nearly two hundred meals that had been her daily treadmill at the pub. It was a modest establishment, one that suited my parents' purpose. But as fitting out and stocking the club left insufficient money to furnish all the remaining space, the top floor was left bare and we lived in the one below. We were comfortable enough, though, and I was delighted to be given a small bedroom at the rear to myself.

Now, what to do with the unused floor? It seemed a pity to waste it. Perhaps the ghost of a peasant ancestor whispered in Dad's ear, for he bought half a dozen chickens and allowed them the run of the top floor and a small roof area on the adjoining building. Fresh eggs in return for a little feed and water seemed like a good idea. Of course, the chickens didn't last long. Now and again one would flap its wings, launch itself bravely into space, and then plunge squawking into the traffic below. Few survived to make a second flight. When all were gone and Dad had harvested the droppings, I explored the empty rooms, thinking they would make a grand place to play – until I found my bare legs covered with black specks and beat a hasty retreat. Instead of producing eggs we had raised thousands of hungry chicken fleas! Dad should have taken it as an augury.

During the first months, though, things went well, for many of the staff and regular customers at *The Lady Owen Arms* had migrated with my parents and new "members" soon joined. In fact, when Pauline reached her fifth birthday, our parents felt sufficiently confident of the future to take her from her nursery school and enroll her in the private *Lady Owen School*. The weathercock of our fortune seemed set fair.

⚜

2

Open Sesame

For a long time now I had been starved for books. Save for Christmas or birthday presents such as the *Boy's Own Annual* and *Coral Island*, I had to get by on magazines like *The Wizard, Adventure, Hotspur* and *The Rover*. And I had few of those, for each cost tuppence and wiped out a week's pocket money. A boy has to have some sweets, and so I was forced to badger Mum for more money. One day Dad caught me reading one. "Hmph, blood and thunder! What do you want to read that muck for?" It never dawned on him that I had nothing else to read. Still, I was soon to be relieved of my hunger, for my eighth birthday was drawing near. Usually birthdays did not excite me. True, they brought presents and a special tea with trifle and cake, but they couldn't compare with the joys of Christmas. However, this birthday was special. I would now be old enough to join the public library!

February 13, 1934, came at last. School seemed an eternity and I nearly choked myself at teatime – but then I was off,

56

running through gloomy backstreets to the nearest branch of the library. I knew the way, for I had scouted it well ahead of time – and more than once, just to make sure it hadn't disappeared. It was in a house basement on the corner of Skinner Street, just off Rosebery Avenue. Skipping down the area steps, I entered it, bubbling with anticipation. Crammed into one small room, the library smelt of books, and Ali Baba in his cave couldn't have been more dazzled than I at the sight of hundreds of them. While I gave the librarian my particulars in return for the precious card, the wireless on the counter played "The Music Goes Round and Round". It should have been the "Hallelujah Chorus". Then I was let loose among the books. Bless the public library! It did more to light my mind than any school I ever attended – except for the one that taught me to read in the first place.

After delighted browsing, I found the children's section, tucked away in a corner of the far wall. Two or three shelves down was a row of books by G. A. Henty. These seemed promising, like Ballantyne's books, I thought. Then I noticed another row, all edited by Andrew Lang: *The Green Book of Fairy Stories, The Red Book of Fairy Stories,* and on through the rainbow with some other colours thrown in. Fairy stories? Sounded a bit sissy. Choosing one at random, I opened it – and was lost, enchanted by the illustrations of H. J. Ford. The princesses were lovely sylphs, like Burne-Jones's Beggar Maid; the witches, satisfyingly ugly; and the dragons, winged and scaly monsters that appealed more to the imagination than to sentiment or fear. After happy dithering, I selected *The Purple Book of Fairy Stories* and hurried home, clasping my treasure tightly to me. The famine was ended. The world of books lay all before me, which to choose for my delight, with chance and personal preference my guides – yes, and Providence, too.

"Fairy stories" is perhaps an unfortunate name for the genre, one that suggests Tinkerbell or Disney. In fact fairies rarely appear, and those that do are the full-sized, somewhat sinister medieval ones. Traditional fairy stories are really folk tales from nearly all parts of the world; and though many are hundreds, some perhaps thousands, of years old, most were not written down until recent times. Like the folk ballad and the folk song, they are part of an oral tradition passed down the centuries and modified on the way. In the process, just as the rough ballad has become poetry, the tales have become profound with the wisdom gained from generations of life experience. Like "collective dreams", to use the words of Richard Adams, they speak to the child on many levels. Only a fool would deny them to a child on the grounds that they are fantasy and contain frightening elements. The child's world *is* often frightening, and so are some of the things he finds in his mind and his dreams. The tales deal with his fears and inner problems by projecting them into a safe setting. Dragons, ogres, trolls, djinn, giants and wicked witches clearly live in an imaginary world, a world where animals speak and magicians ride flying carpets – the world of faërie, in other words. No normal child could mistake it for the real world, or believe that the way to deal with a nasty old lady is to push her into an oven and bake her.

Moreover, the world of the tales – in Andrew Lang's collection, anyway – is a moral one. The hero, often a youngest son or daughter with whom the child can identify, receives help on his quest from those he has himself helped – from animals he has spared, from a poor old woman he has fed who turns out to be a fairy godmother. The prince who inherits his father's kingdom, the hero who wins the princess, or the heroine her prince, is the one proved most worthy in a test of wit, courage, and faithfulness. Even seemingly amoral tales usually have a moral underpinning. The hero wins by using his wits, even by trickery, not by victimizing kindly old farmers or poor widows but by outwitting ogres, witches or dragons. The tales are effective because they do not preach or point a moral, like the fable, but present the lessons simply and dramatically: behave like this, and you will succeed in your quest and live happily ever after; behave like that, and like the arrogant elder brother you may be turned into a toad, only to be saved by the hero's generosity. Of course, in the real world the arrogant elder brother is the one who sometimes becomes wealthy and powerful and marries the princess – but he is nonetheless turned into a toad.

Would fairy tales appeal to today's teenagers? In the 'Sixties, discovering that Lang's books had been reprinted in paperback and with the original illustrations, I immediately had a complete set placed in our school library. A few months later, as I wandered around the stacks pulling books at random to discover what my students were reading, I noticed that a distressingly large number of books had been signed out rarely or not at all. However, when I came to Lang's rainbow, I found the books had been borrowed so often they were almost falling apart! As our students ranged in age from thirteen to seventeen or more, I had my answer.

෴

3
"The Naked Truth"

My need for books was taken care of. Now another was beginning to stir, one as yet almost too faint to be noticed:

The Naked Truth
Goswell Road, 1934

So the common dandelion,
growing through the paving cracks,
turns its gaze towards the light
and bares its being to the sun.

A thunderclap had wakened him,
a crash that shook the darkened house
and set the windows rattling,
and then teeth-jarring thuds,
as though a hill had tumbled down
and then gone trundling through the town

As lightning flashes turned his night
to ghostly, intermittent day,
the boy climbed quickly from his bed,
wrestled the stubborn window high,
as high as it would go, and then
looked out upon the world of men.

A sea of roofs, all gleaming dark,
with rows of chimney pots, he saw,
and gutters that were cataracts
from slanting rain that bustled down
yet, oddly, seemed to hang in space
like drifting veils of finest lace.

While peals of thunder rent the air,
wild lightning seared the livid clouds
and scored each roof and steeple stark
or forked a blazing blue to earth
as if the fabric of the night
had cracked before the power of light.

Eyes open wide, the boy stripped bare,
then sat upon the sill, entranced....
"What are you doing *there*, old son?"
His father took him in his arms
and gently tucked him back in bed.
"Watching the storm, Daddy," he said.

Well, yes, it was the barest truth,
but to the question never asked
he *had* no answer. Anyway,
the boy already was asleep
and with his body warmly curled
had set off for another world.

Dad's tenderness is not poetic licence. Although he was not normally demonstrative of his love, he showed it here. Probably he thought I had been sleepwalking again!

֎

4

Moreland Street School

When I read about the boys of Greyfriars and laughed at Billy
Bunter for sneaking a meal in the dorm or stuffing himself
with cream buns at the school tuckshop, it never occurred to
me to compare their school with mine. We had no dormitory
or tuckshop, we spoke differently and had no uniform, and the
teachers wore no gown and mortarboard. Ours was an ordinary
day school. From the time we moved to Islington, I had been
attending *Moreland Street School,* between Goswell Road and City
Road. It was a small backstreet elementary school, built of brick,
with the usual asphalt playground but with walls that were
neither too high nor topped with broken glass. A photograph
taken, I think in 1933, shows my class with our teacher, a Mr.
Jones. Despite the Depression and the area in which we lived,
we are fairly presentable. Several of the boys are wearing suits
and quite a number have collars and ties. Another, taken in 1935,
shows some boys without socks. Yet we all seem reasonably
clean. I recall only three of the boys: Bert, because he was a
friend; and Edwards and Brown, because they were thought to
be the toughest boys in class. Edwards won his reputation for
his surly, unsmiling mien, and Brown, for his ferocious scowl.
One day, when I ventured to tease Edwards, he told me to stop
or get a punch in the nose. I didn't stop and I did get a punch
in the nose. There seemed little point in my getting angry and
hitting him back. I had found out what I wanted to know and
respected him for it. As for the other tough, he came up to me
one day and said wistfully, "I wish I could read like you." Poor
Brown, his scowl came not from ferocity but from unhappiness.

Every normal child enjoys listening to stories and wants
to read them for himself; and there is a period of readiness
when learning to read seems as natural and easy as learning
to speak or run. But if the child is ill or unhappy during that
time, the window of opportunity closes. Then he is faced with
an uphill battle and may never reach that magical state where
print dissolves into an inner world – a world with sound, colour,
three dimensions and the pleasure of safe participation. If at

first you don't succeed, you are not likely to, or at best will find it difficult. It seems unfair, and it is. Could it be that "blessed" reality is trying to tell us something?

If Mr. Jones is the first teacher whose name I can recall, it is not because of the photograph, but because of a lesson in geography he gave one day. As I sat gazing at his wall map of the Americas, thinking how pleasant the Amazon Basin must be because it was such a lovely green colour, he said, "Today I am going to tell you how to put out a grass fire on the Canadian prairies." Why this should stick in my mind I don't know. It was hardly the kind of information likely to prove useful to urchins in Islington, where blades of grass were outnumbered by chimney pots. Still, one never knew, and I found it interesting. Only in one other lesson was I jolted out of the protective, semi-conscious state most students assume in class. Our science teacher had been droning on and on. "Of course," he said, suddenly lapsing into English, "man himself is just an animal." Man an animal? Galvanized into wakefulness, I threw up my hand so violently that I almost bounced off my seat. "Please, sir," I cried, my voice betraying all the indignation of one basely insulted, "man is *not* an animal." Observing my intensity, he wisely decided not to argue the point – which was just as well, because I had exhausted my powers of reasoning. He was right, of course. But perhaps I was, too.

&Y&

5

The Fight at the Kensitas Cigarette Factory

Summer holidays were come and the day was hazy and hot. Freed from school, children played in the afternoon sun, mongrels lay panting and scratching their fleas, and sparrows scuffled in the gutters, ignoring traffic and passers-by. At such a time, people in Spain would sensibly be taking a siesta, and those in Alabama might be shooting each other; but this was London, so the inhabitants merely sweated and muttered a bit. Taking the stairs two at a time, I burst in on my mother as she was trying to relax. "Mum," I panted, "could I have a cup of weak tea?"

"Whatever for, dear?" she asked, taken slightly aback. "Why not have a nice ginger beer?"

"No thanks, Mum. It has to be weak tea."

"But why must it be weak, dear?" she persisted, puzzled.

"Well…I just fancy it, that's all. Could I, please?"

She sighed and got up. "Oh, all right. You're a funny boy. I just can't make you out sometimes."

This was one of several stock sayings she used with me. She had last used it when I spent three ha'pence on a bowl of soup: "Pea soup it was, Mum, with black pepper – delicious!" When she got upset, for the café catered to down-and-outs and the owner might suspect she was starving me, I decided not to tell her about the penn'orth of cat's meat or the dog biscuits. As a change from sweets, I had been sampling some of the street's cheaper gustatory delights. Another stock saying was "You dirty little bugger. Look at the tide mark around your face! Come here." This was always followed by a vigorous scrubbing. Oh well, we can't all be perfect. Less common was "You aggravating little sod!" The truth is that I could be a dreadful tease at times. I teased Edwards to test him and had my nose punched. I teased Pauline, though not often for it could be dangerous. She sometimes reacted either by jumping up and down and screaming or else by launching a murderous assault – and all that jumping had given her muscles of steel, slight though she was. The idea of teasing Dad was ludicrous. That left poor old Mum. "You always hurt the one you love…."

There was no spite or malice in my teasing, only puppy playfulness. Unhappily, small boys and puppies do not know when enough is enough. Sometimes, after teasing her, I would widen my eyes to make them as sincere and innocent as possible and promise faithfully not to do it again. Then, if she seemed persuaded, I immediately *would* do it again. One day she became so exasperated she threw the first thing to hand, a small round breadboard. As I ducked, it skimmed over my head like a frisbee and out through the window, which was closed at the time. Once she bought a small cane and flicked me across the legs with it when I tried her too far. I wasn't happy, but I was fair-minded enough to wonder if I had deserved it. Then she made a mistake. Instead of putting the cane away, she left it on view in the corner and warned me, "Now you know what to expect." Well, that was different. How could I choose to be a good boy with a threat hanging over me? So I sulked for the rest of the day. The next morning the cane was gone, for ever. "He's a good boy," my mother said when outsiders were present. And I was, I was! Well…most of the time. However, all this is by the way. Although I couldn't tell her the reason for my odd request, it was a perfectly sound one. I was in training for my first fight. Somewhere I had read that boxers in training drank only weak tea. One cup should just about make me fighting fit, I thought.

At noon the next day – oh, very well, high noon – my friend George and I strolled arm in arm into the open garage on the ground floor of the Kensitas cigarette factory, and there we squared off. I was about to defend my sister's honour. The insult had been offered a few days previously. I was with some friends, local boys like Bert, the son of a shopkeeper, and George, who was rumoured to be German. We were big boys now, aged eight and nine, and no longer wanted girls around; but on this occasion my sister had decided to join us. As we stood chatting and laughing, she munched on an apple and peered at us from beneath her bangs, eyes slightly narrowed as if she were thinking deeply. Suddenly, judging she had been ignored long enough, she threw the core right into George's face. Yes, he was a handsome devil. But when he accepted the compliment gracefully, by promptly returning it in the same friendly manner, she burst into tears. I sighed. She had asked for it, but I couldn't have boys making my sister cry. Rats! Was there to be no end to the trials of an elder brother?

"You'll have to fight me now, George," I said.

George brightened up immediately. "When?" he asked.

"In a few days. I've got a bad thumb right now."

We met later and decided upon the factory at noon the following day. The drivers would be at dinner or out delivering and we were not likely to be interrupted. We didn't want grown-ups or a mob of screaming kids around. This was a private matter. It was then that I galloped up the stairs to train on weak tea.

George halted and turned around. "Ready?" he asked. He was facing the road, giving me the advantage of the light. On the other hand, he was a little bigger and older than I. That evened things up.

"Yes," I said – and gave him a good solid left to the nose. Very satisfying. I was about to follow it up with a smart right, but thick yellow snot came streaming from his nose and put me off. He gave a long, bubbling sniff and returned the blow. Then we went at each other, slugging it out toe to toe. We had not discussed any rules ahead of time. We didn't need to. We knew the code: hitting below the belt was dirty, and kicking was beneath contempt. All our blows were to the face – and with no charging or dancing around, either. We just stood our ground and fought….

"Hit him in the belly, Phil." It was the voice of Chummy, our head barman.

"No, that's not fair," I gasped. Both of us were sweating and breathing heavily now.

We exchanged a few more blows. Then, "Hit him in the belly!" shouted Chummy again. Risking a quick look over my shoulder, I was astonished to see that a small crowd of men had gathered at the entrance and were watching. Where had they come from? By this time my arms were like lead and neither of us was doing any damage. We were an even match.

A little later, hands descended on our shoulders and pulled us apart. "All right, boys, you've done enough. You've had a good fight." Then the man added, slapping George on the shoulder, "I declare you the winner." Not wanting to argue with a grown-up, for they knew best, I accepted the verdict. But I knew I hadn't been beaten, either.

"Over here, boys." A man in a white apron was beckoning. "Come with me." As he led us into the café next door, most of the men followed and several clapped us on the back. Our fight had emptied the place! The man in the apron smiled, "Sit down a minute, lads, and I'll get you something." Then he returned with a mug of strong tea and a cheesecake for each of us. As we bit into our cakes, relishing the icing and the coconut shreds, George and I grinned at one another. Perfect happiness!

6
My Father Pays Me More Attention

Our head barman, Chummy, had moved with us from the pub. He was about the same age as Dad, in his late thirties, and about the same height, though perhaps a little heavier. He was clean-shaven and wore his thinning hair, already turning grey, brushed straight back. Seldom one to laugh, but with a ready smile and mild grey eyes, he was a quiet man whose presence gave the impression both of strength and kindness. Pauline and I called him "Uncle Dick" and we loved him more than any of our real uncles, whom we rarely saw. In contrast to my father, who up till now seemed to me a remote, sometimes menacing figure barely aware of my existence, Chummy always had a kind word and a smile for me. He had followed my parents out of loyalty to my mother. Like others, he didn't like the way Dad treated her, and he lent her quiet moral support. In the coming months, he was to prove himself a staunch friend to us all.

Whether it was because business was flourishing or because I was older I don't know, but Dad now began to pay me more attention. He took me to see the first picture I remember, *Below the Sea*. After we had taken our seats, he fiddled with something for a moment and then handed me a small tin of condensed milk. "Here, this should keep you quiet. Don't spill it." Settling myself comfortably, I sucked away as Ralph Bellamy fought a giant octopus. Ah, bliss! Later, we all went to see the air display at Hendon. Strangely, I recall nothing of it now but a vast area of grass with hundreds of parked cars. We must have hired a car for the occasion, for we never had one of our own.

Summer also brought a swimming "lesson" in the form of a visit to the public baths. Here Dad made the mistake of allowing me to have a changing booth to myself. Though not overfond of washing, I had enjoyed splashing about in the sea and was not to be overawed by a mere swimming pool. Besides, after the voyage to Clacton I was a seasoned seaman. Fumbling in my eagerness, I stripped speedily and climbed into my swimming costume. Then, as if shot from a catapult, I burst from the booth, uttered a loud "Wheeee!" and made a great jump – right into the deep end. Of course, being composed mainly of skin, bone, and a little gristle and having just expelled most of my breath, I sank right to the bottom and remained there in a green and watery surprise. Fortunately, my joyous leap had been performed under the nose of someone posing on the diving-board; and by the time my father emerged from his booth, resplendent in his water polo costume and wondering what all the fuss was about, I had been fished out and landed coughing and spluttering at his feet. Slightly dampened in spirit as well as body, I was banished to the shallow end with the other little boys. I had miscalculated, too, for I had no idea how to swim.

There were more outings, but only one stands out now – a visit to the dogs one chilly evening late in the year. This was a special treat both for me and Dad, as gambling was not a weakness of his. Apart from an impression of crowds, noise and a general air of excitement, only two scenes remain in my memory. Under high lamps, we stood warming ourselves before a coke brazier, one of many scattered around the grounds like the campfires of an army and each encircled by a group of mufflered figures. I was gnawing away at a Mars bar that seemed to last forever. Suddenly, loudspeakers crackled, sounded a fanfare, and a voice started barking. Dad took my hand, "Come on, son. It's about to start." Once seated on an icy bench, we watched the greyhounds being paraded for the first race. When the last dog came abreast of us, it stopped and began defecating. Put off by the sight of its undignified, humped straining, I declared confidently, "I bet that one doesn't win." Of course, it did, handsomely. I couldn't pick even a loser, where the odds were in my favour!

Perhaps it was a warning from the gods not to gamble, one I wish I had heeded. My first bet was a winner. At the club one day I was challenged by a customer to a game of 101-Up at darts. The stakes were high – one penny. No doubt he intended to let me win and so give a small boy a boost and a penny at the same time. If so, like many a Samaritan he ended with egg on his face. I got off on a double with my first three darts and finished on a double with the second three, the fastest game of darts I've ever had. "He *beat* me!" he cried in comic dismay.

I should have quit while I was ahead. However, in later life, when I should have had more sense, I was twice tempted by greed to dabble in the stock market. Needless to say, I displayed an uncanny ability to choose losers or buy and sell at the wrong time, and I lost more money than I care to think about. Wishing to give my students the benefit of my wide experience and demonstrate the folly of playing the market, I gave one class a major assignment in trading stocks. All of them began with the same theoretical sum of money and had to wind up their portfolios by a specific date. To ensure there was no cheating, I demanded proper buy and sell orders and charged brokerage fees. Then, confident in the purity of my intentions, I sat back, as it were, to await the desired result. Need I say it? To my chagrin, every one of my students made a profit!

☙

7

Crime and Punishment

Business was good, quarrels were rare, and family life was happier. But those halcyon months of 1934 proved to be only a taste of what might have been. Some of the more obvious of society's parasites had smelt fresh blood and were closing in. At first there were only hints of coming trouble – such as the theft of our radiogram while my sister was in the empty bar dancing to the music. Then a pair of thieves approached my father with a proposition. If he would let them store their loot in the cellar, he could have a share of the proceeds. The existence of the club was becoming known to the local underworld and it was only a matter of time before more sinister figures should appear. This was something Dad hadn't foreseen. A public house has the wealth and power of the brewer behind it, and police keep a sharp lookout for trouble. A private club, on the other hand, is more vulnerable to bribery or intimidation by criminals.

Inevitably, a gang decided that our club would make a fine hang-out. With a legitimate business as cover and access to both front and rear, it was perfect. They began with blandishments. If Dad would turn a blind eye to their activities, they would look after him. Of course they would. When he declined their generous offer, they resorted to threats and demanded protection money. But Dad was not one to knuckle under to threats, either, and refused to pay. Knowing him, I should imagine that he expressed his refusal bluntly. And so, slowly at first, began what must have been a nightmare for my parents.

For a while, the gangsters contented themselves with threats. They knew well enough that verbal intimidation is preferable to open violence as it attracts less attention. When it became clear that Dad was not going to give way, they went to work on Mum as well. Then, when that didn't work either, though Mum was naturally frightened, the violence began. Ruffians descended on the club to provoke fights, smash things up and alarm the customers. Not knowing them all, Dad couldn't keep them out, for the gang was careful not to invite police action by operating too openly. Soon, another gang became involved and elements of both sometimes used the club as a battleground.[4]

Pauline and I were not aware of what was going on, of course, as our parents never discussed their problems before us. But they could not protect us all the time. Returning home together one day, we heard what sounded like a riot in the front bar and I ran in to see what was going on. There were men fighting everywhere, with fists flying and faces bloody; and right in front of me towered a man with a heavy wooden bar stool raised over his head and about to bring it smashing down on someone sprawled at his feet. Then hands grasped me gently by the shoulders and propelled me towards the stairs, "Come on, son. This is no place for you." The maniac with the stool remains vivid in my memory, frozen as in a tableau.

As 1935 turned to the ebb, so did our family fortune. The club was now losing money. Dad might refuse to give up, but many

---

[4]   My mother always claimed that the main gang involved was the Sabinis, one of the major mobs in England at the time, and that the other was a rival gang, the Islington Boys. If that was true, my parents were lucky to get away so lightly. Organized gangs in England then were heavily involved in gambling, bookmaking and racing. They seldom used guns, as penalties were severe. Favoured weapons were blunt ones – iron bars or knuckle-dusters; or sharp ones – broken glasses and bottles, or razor blades inserted around the peak of the cap. Whatever the truth of the matter, the parasites that infested our club were not ordinary street hooligans.

regular customers had become intimidated and stopped coming. Most of the staff had also had enough. Where were the police? Weren't they aware of what was going on? Of course they were. But drunks fight and bar-room brawls will happen. It is difficult to prove they are the result of a campaign of intimidation, especially as witnesses are understandably reluctant to come forward.

In the club one day, a man overheard Dad speaking impatiently to Mum. Leaning across the bar, he sneered, "You don't know how lucky you are to have a wife like that. You don't deserve her. I'll get you for this." There may have been some truth in what he said, but it was not his place to say it. And "get" Dad he did. Finishing his beer one day, without warning he broke his glass on the bar and thrust the jagged edges into my father's face, narrowly missing his eye.

This was no brawl but a vicious assault with intent to commit bodily harm. At last the police could act. The detective in charge knew the offender only too well, as our knight-errant was wanted for many similar offences. Unfortunately, the police had never been able to find a witness willing to testify. Promising police protection, this time the detective was able to persuade Mum to act as witness – and then the villain was arrested.

By the time the case came up at the Old Bailey, Mum had had time to think things over, however, and in the witness box "admitted" that she hadn't actually seen the incident. On hearing this, the accused smiled, for it meant a reduced sentence. The detective was enraged, of course, and bitterly accused her of letting him down. The reason for her change of heart was simple enough. A kind lady had warned Mum that police protection lasted only until the trial was over. How would she like her own face slashed afterwards? And didn't she have young children? When one considers how brave the League of Nations was in standing up to bullies, who could blame Mum for changing her mind?

With all the persistence and compassion of flies, the gangsters continued to plague the club. To defend themselves and protect Mum, Dad and Chummy kept heavy brass spigots under the bar. As they were now short-handed, help arrived from the family in the person of Uncle Mac, Doll's father. Tall and strongly built, but a little stooped and balding, he must then have been in his late sixties. He could serve in the bar, but could hardly be expected to engage in brawls. Nonetheless, he kept a short iron bar handy, reserved, he told Mum with a smile, for anyone who dared try to harm her. He meant it.

It couldn't go on. The courage was there but not the money. The business was losing heavily, debts were mounting, bills and taxes were coming due. In desperation Dad turned to crime. A small fire in the club and a claim for insurance might keep the bailiffs at bay. He left a candle too close to the curtains – and the deed was done. A fire there should be quickly noticed. If not, and it threatened to get out of control, he could raise the alarm himself. Not surprisingly, he was as successful in his brief life of crime as he had been in keeping chickens. In rapid order the alarm was raised, the flames doused and the cause determined. This time, witnesses being unnecessary, the law acted with most commendable speed, and my father found himself arrested, tried, and sentenced. The crime had been amateurish and his care not to burn the entire place down obvious, but to prison he went, though mercifully for months rather than years. Perhaps the gangsters found this turn of events amusing. If so, they soon had another occasion to laugh, for Mum now had no choice but to close the club and declare herself bankrupt.

In January of 1936, as the old king lay dying and smoky old London had never seemed greyer or colder, while my father languished behind the bars of his prison, the rest of us found ourselves lodged in a stinking, rat-infested house on City Road. We were destitute.

CHAPTER SIX

"Come, Lassies and Lads"

1
On the "R.O."

Children are resilient. Pauline and I had little idea of what had happened, of course, nor did we remark the absence of our father. We had seen little of him in the preceding months anyway. And so we soon became used to our new home. It consisted of one small room on the second floor and overlooked the busy City Road. There was a little furniture – a small table, several cheap wooden chairs, a double bed for Mum and Pauline and a single for me. A built-in cupboard served as pantry for food and storage for our few possessions. As for the kitchen, that consisted of a gas stove and a small sink on the landing. There was also a cupboard there; but because of scurrying rats, it was used only to hold our pots and pans.

Soon Mum had scrubbed out the room and made it tolerable. She continued to feed us well, and with the aid of a small galvanized bathtub made sure we kept clean. However, she could do nothing about the stink in the house. Stink! – a better description would be a stomach-turning stench, compounded of rotting cabbage, boiling offal, and general filth. We sought to fend it off by keeping our door closed as much as possible and stuffing the cracks with paper. When we used the passageway and stairs between our room and the outside world, Pauline and I held our breath and ran.

Unfortunately, Mum could not do the same. She didn't have the breath to hold. For some time now she had been suffering from asthma. She had seen a number of doctors, but tests for allergies had proven negative and little could be done. Apparently no one had considered my father a possible allergen. Now, because of the strain of the preceding months and anxiety over her present desperate situation, she became subject to severe asthma attacks, and a ritual began that was to last on and off for the next ten years. In an effort to find relief, she would burn a little heap of "Potter's Asthma Cure", a herbal remedy, and inhale the smoke while I pounded her back for minutes at a time as she fought for breath. Later, she would instead roll the herbs into cigarettes. Although she was never to be free of her affliction, serious attacks became less frequent a few years after she separated from Dad.

Where had money for rent, coal, and gas come from? Probably from the same source as our food – the Relieving Office. Today, when social assistance is perceived as a right, it may be difficult to understand the humiliation Mum felt when she had to ask for help. The Relieving Office, or "R.O.", was the last safety net before the street or the dreaded workhouse, and to seek help there was considered almost as great a disgrace. To make matters worse, when Mum presented herself before the Relieving Officer, clean and neatly dressed as she was, he proved to be one of her old customers. And as the help offered came in the form of coupons, very soon the local business community also knew of the depth of our fall. But damaged pride was the least of her worries. A few weeks after we moved into our room, she became very ill and had to take to her bed.

She was not abandoned during her ordeal. Bearing gifts of food, Chummy often came by to see how she was; and if he couldn't get away from work, he sent a mutual friend. As for the person who came every day without fail, who nursed my mother, checked behind my ears and bathed us kids, cooked our dinners, and taught us how to light a coal fire with one match – a useful skill, for kindling cost money – that Samaritan was Uncle Mac. Hobbling about with an infected foot swathed in bandages but with his grey eyes twinkling, he made everything seem like a huge joke. But despite his efforts, Mum's condition grew worse and he had to call a doctor. The diagnosis was double pneumonia. She was critically ill.

A few days after my tenth birthday, an ambulance came and took all of us away, just as we were. Shortly afterwards, Pauline and I found ourselves by a bedside in Highgate Hospital, looking on as Mum was made comfortable. She gave me a worried smile, "Look after your sister, won't you, Duck. Promise." Taking Pauline's hand, I replied, "I will, Mum." But it was a promise I was unable to keep. The two of us were returned to the ambulance and borne off, this time to a children's shelter, where we were immediately separated. In the following six months we were to see each other only once.

❧

2

Banstead

It was raining and dark when we were admitted to the shelter. I recall sitting silently on a wooden chair in a room with other small boys. The middle-aged woman minding us had been studying me for some time. Suddenly, she leant forward and spoke, "Are you fretting?"

I looked at her. "What does 'fretting' mean?" No, I wasn't fretting. I was feeling a blankness. I knew Mum was ill, but not how ill. I did not know where Dad was. And no one had warned Pauline or me that we would be taken away and separated. It was something that had just happened, and I didn't really know what had happened let alone why. It was as if the world had suddenly ceased to make sense. According to Pauline, we were there about two weeks. If so, I have no memory of it except for that one scene. However, her memory of the first night is more vivid. Writing to me at the age of sixty-five, she recalled:

I was undressed and put to bed in a room where some children were sleeping. They didn't turn on the lights, for fear of waking them. The sheets were stiff and icy cold. There was a streetlight outside the window, and it must have been raining for I could see the light reflected on the ceiling. I had been taken from my mother and even from my brother and I have never felt more miserable and alone in my life. There is a streetlight outside my bedroom window today; and if I wake in the night, that same feeling sometimes comes over me and I am that lonely child again. It never goes away. And it still hurts.

She was not yet seven, one lonely and frightened child among numberless others, before and since, who have found themselves in a similar position, or worse. Yet we were luckier than we knew, for we were soon to find ourselves in a remarkable children's home in Surrey – Banstead Residential School.

Apart from a wooden clock ticking away on the mantleshelf, the house was quiet. I was having tea and cake in an airy kitchen, with sunlight streaming through the windows. Across the table, her arms folded, sat a large, grey-eyed lady. Although she was only middle-aged, her hair was almost white, cut short below the ears, and she was big-boned and strongly built – rather like an aging Brünnhilde in a starched white apron. As I enjoyed my simple meal, she questioned me, nodding now and then and revealing even white teeth in a kindly smile. At ease herself, she had done her best to make me feel the same. I decided I liked her.

She leaned forward, "Have you had enough?"

I nodded, "Yes, thank you."

"Come along, then," she smiled. "I'll show you to your dormitory."

I followed her up polished wooden stairs, along a polished corridor and into a large dormitory with two rows of beds lined up like soldiers on parade. Everything was neat and clean, and smelt of polish.

She stopped, pointing to one of the beds, "This is yours. Now, while you are here, you will have to make your own bed. So I'll show you how. Watch closely and then you do it. See if you can get it right the first time."

I watched as she pulled the bedclothes off and then remade the bed with a hospital tuck.

She looked at me. "Do you think you could do that?"

She pulled it to pieces again and I set about following her example as best I could. After I had finished, I looked at it doubtfully. The tuck didn't look right. Still, it was neatly made. Satisfied, I stepped back and looked up at her. I don't know what I expected – but what I got was a meaty smack across the face that rattled my teeth.

"That's not the way I showed you," she said calmly. "Now, we'll go through it again."

Welcome to Banstead.

Later, I understood. It was her way of establishing dominance, and I was going to get the slap no matter how I made the bed. The message was clear enough: this is what you get for being slow – just imagine what will happen if you are naughty! It was effective. There was no indiscipline in the house, no rowdiness at mealtimes or in the dorm, no bullying; and yet there was no atmosphere of fear, either, and I never witnessed any other punishment. She and her fellow housemother, a rather younger woman with brown hair and a slight hunchback, looked after us well. The house was immaculate, we were kept clean and well clothed, and the meals were generous and well cooked. Unfortunately, there had been a price: she had slapped me after being kind and gaining my trust. I had been willing and knew I hadn't deserved it. Such treatment might have engendered respect of a kind, but it did not kindle affection. Had she saved the slap for when it was deserved, the effect on discipline would have been the same – and she might have found that most boys would not have needed one.

After more than half a century, I find it difficult to be precise about Banstead now. It seemed laid out in the form of a village, with an infirmary, a school and a church in the centre. Lining the streets on either side and set well apart were detached houses, each of which had two housemothers[5] and about twenty children. I assume the houses of the girls and the boys were on opposite

---

[5]   Thanks to the Great War, many widowed or single women were then available for such positions.

sides of the centre; though how they kept us apart when we could roam freely, I don't know, for the only time I saw girls was during May Day celebrations.

The "village" was set in spacious grounds, with trees and acres of grass. It was rumoured that Gypsies sometimes occupied the nearby heath and woods. Pauline tells me she kept close to the bigger girls because she had been warned that Gypsies sometimes made off with children. And Gypsies there were on Banstead Downs, for I remember watching a group of boys baiting one as he sat by his campfire. After enduring this for a while, he made for us, swearing loudly, and we scattered like chickens. In all, Banstead was a fine place to be. Only one thing was lacking, of course – the love of my own family. No matter how kind people are, it is not the same thing.

☙❧

3

Wildflowers

For a week, I was miserable. I missed my family. Our housemothers were kind, but I remembered the clout and kept my distance, which I would have done in any case as I was no clinging ivy. As for the boys, ranging in age from about nine to thirteen, they seemed a collection of isolates – or perhaps it was just me. It is a curious thing, but there seemed to be little interaction among us, either pleasant or unpleasant; and in the six months or so I was at Banstead, I made only one friend, Archie, a frail boy who attached himself to me for a while. Whatever the reason, a few days after arriving there I felt despondent enough to write Mum a self-pitying letter that I was ashamed of even then. I am glad to say I never sent it.

No matter how I felt, I had to go to school, and there a science teacher introduced me to collecting wildflowers. I now gained a new interest, one that absorbed me throughout the spring and summer. Whenever free, I roamed the woods and Downs looking for specimens. After pressing the flowers between sheets of blotting paper, I spent my evenings mounting and

77

identifying them in a special collector's book; and by summer's end I had nearly a hundred varieties. It was an occupation that gave a focus to my life. I had little time to pity myself or get into mischief, even had I wanted to. As for school, I vaguely remember only the science class and the school assemblies, where we were addressed by the headmaster, Mr. Raynor, a tall, slender man with a moustache and a military bearing.

As I look back on my childhood and youth, I can see that I was often possessed by a passion, in which state I would live and breathe in the world of my interest. I had collected cigarette cards not to possess, but out of interest in the worlds depicted – of aircraft, of ships and the sea, of uniforms and monarchs and the realm of history. When I was ready for more information, there were always books. Some passions were brief. Blue Bugattis screaming around corners in a cloud of exhaust and smoking rubber, white Auto Unions bellowing down the straights, wheel to wheel with snarling red Maseratis – these were exciting mental images, but two or three books on Grand Prix racing were enough. Other passions, such as mountains, were to go beyond books and last for years. And some – music, poetry and history, for example – would be lifelong.

So I entered the world of plants. Hitherto I had casually noted grass, trees and flowers. But grass was just grass, mostly manicured or straggling in corners, and trees had leaves or needles. As for wildflowers, I could name dandelions, buttercups and daisies – about all that Plumstead and Islington could boast of. Now interest led me to pay closer attention, to become aware that there are many grasses, many trees and flowers, although my interest was focused on flowers. I did not have the approach of a botanist, nor would my power of observation have impressed Louis Agassiz. Rather, it was a matter of attention and openness, the attitude of one meeting new friends, noting each form, each colour, scent and habitat by the way, but trying to grasp each as a whole, as an entity. Squatting for a closer view brought an intimacy and revealed beauties I hadn't noticed before: wild strawberry, with runners and fairy berries; toadflax, like miniature snapdragons; and the humble yarrow, with a fragrance all its own.

In such a state, of attention combined with openness, with preconceptions and the critical faculty set aside, we sometimes learn more subconsciously than consciously. The object of attention enters our being and becomes part of us to a degree we are not always aware of. Many years later, while climbing alone in British Columbia, as usual I had music haunting my mind. But it was unfamiliar. Where had it come from? The answer came months later, while I was listening to Brahms' Second Piano Concerto. The music, a few phrases enfolded in the first movement, leapt out like an old friend. And then I remembered. The previous winter I had played the same recording a number of times. Although I had not then consciously noticed those particular phrases, my subconscious mind had – and later selected them to suit my mood as I was climbing.

This invasion of one's being, as it were, takes place in less pleasant circumstances, too. I have been aware of this for most of my life, only I have experienced the invasion as an "atmosphere". If I find such an atmosphere uncomfortable, I move and avoid it thereafter. If moving is not possible, then I remove my attention instead and fasten it on something more pleasant. I can understand why a prison, with its explosive atmosphere of frustration, suspicion, fear, rage, hate and despair – a miasma compounded of all the negative feelings and thoughts one could imagine – is almost guaranteed not to rehabilitate the inmates. In fact it is more likely to have a negative effect on the staff.

> Stone walls do not a prison make,
> Nor iron bars a cage;
> Minds innocent and quiet take
> That for an hermitage....

I rather doubt that Lovelace would find a modern prison conducive to meditation. He would probably have to assault a guard to get himself placed in solitary. A friend of mine, a healthy-minded Yorkshireman, once worked as education officer in the British Columbia Penitentiary. He did his best for inmates who wished to take courses, even going so far as to invite an occasional parolee to his home. However, at the end of three years he quit. When I asked why, he said that the atmosphere of the prison was getting to him, was beginning to infect his own life.

My fascination was with the living plants not with the faded, flattened shells in my book. Yet identifying them brought something else – an awareness of their names. "What's in a name? that which we call a rose by any other name would smell as sweet." To one not familiar with English, maybe. What if we called the rose "thorny ratbane"? We know well enough that names have power to affect the way we look at things. So now, as I became enchanted by the names of wildflowers – scarlet pimpernel, cowslip, yarrow, harebell – unconsciously I was learning that words have a beauty and power of their own. When on May Day we were freed from school to take part in a celebration with folk songs and country dancing and to watch girls dancing around the maypole -

> Come, lassies and lads, take leave of your dads
> And away to the maypole go

- then wildflowers, their names, folk music and dancing came together in a world that exists only in imagination – like that of Shakespeare's songs, of *A Midsummer Night's Dream*. I knew nothing of that world then; but when I did enter it, I found myself in a familiar country. So now, when I smell the humble yarrow, hear a choir sing "You spotted snakes, with double tongue", or read

> I know a bank whereon the wild thyme blows,
> Where ox-lips and the nodding violet grows;
> Quite over-canopied with lush woodbine,
> With sweet musk roses and with eglantine....

I find myself back at Banstead – or, rather, back in the world of my imagination then.

4

Different Worlds

"Charrge!"

Startled, I looked up from where I'd been contemplating a flower. Running across the grass towards me with a grin on his face was Archie, leading a small army of younger boys. A war! Entering into the spirit of the game, I uttered a fierce cry and launched a counter-attack. But as I wrestled Archie to the ground, to my dismay he burst into tears.

"I was pretending," he wailed. "I wasn't going to do anything."

Hastily I rose to my feet. The small boys had stopped in their tracks and were looking at one another uncertainly. "But, Archie," I said mildly, "I was playing. I was pretending, too." I was beginning to feel like a bullying brute.

But he wasn't listening. Nothing could persuade him that he hadn't been cruelly assaulted. Poor Archie, so pale of skin and hair as to seem almost an albino, he was frail not only in body but in spirit as well. As he stumbled away disconsolately, still sobbing, I wondered how he had reacted to the ritual smack across the face.

I thought of Archie years later, when I was teaching in an inner London school. One class consisted of bright, high-spirited boys in the top band of the first form. After a couple of weeks of my quiet, good-humoured teaching style, several began to try me on. Mild rebukes having little effect and believing threats a waste of breath, I brought a slipper to class and whacked three backsides, quite against the school rules, I must say. As each boy walked back to his seat ruefully rubbing himself, he was consoled by the thought that he had taken his punishment like a man. The class felt better, for they saw that he hadn't got away with anything, and I felt a little better, too. The third boy was a little disconcerting, however. After every stroke, he wriggled his rump and clucked like a chicken. How to deal with that? When he started to rise after the sixth one, I asked him to bend down again – and then I gave him one more, extra hard. "There, that one is a freebie, because you seem to have enjoyed the others so much." That class was a joy to teach. I had them for two years and never had to use the slipper again. Actually, at the end of the first term, one of the boys pinched it! I hope he kept it as a souvenir. Another class consisted of remedial students, there because of language difficulty or virtual illiteracy. Although unqualified to deal with them, I was supposed to teach them history. I would not have dreamt of laying a finger on any of them. In fact I had to be careful how I spoke, for just one sharp word might arouse one to rage or reduce another to tears like poor Archie. Blake is right: "One law for the lion and the ox is oppression." How to reconcile that dictum with the principle of fairness sometimes requires the wisdom of Solomon.

Our bodies may inhabit the same locality and time, but we live in different worlds. Collecting wild flowers was only a small part of my life at Banstead. Like everyone else, I spent most of my time on the daily round. But routines occupy only a small part of our minds and we perform them mostly in a semi-conscious state. As a result, they seldom remain clear in the memory. If flowers and their names bloom so large in my memories of Banstead, it is because they engaged my imagination. I wonder what Archie's memories of Banstead were like?

My sister's memories are not happy ones. She was years younger than I and insecure to begin with. As might be expected, separation from family revived the old bed-wetting problem. She was a "dirty little girl" and was punished by being given bread and milk instead of the regular tea. "I *hate* bread and milk even today," she wrote me. Before long she became ill and was placed in the infirmary. When she showed no signs of improvement, the school authorities tried to transfer her to the same hospital as our mother. Unfortunately, there wasn't room and she was sent elsewhere:

> Because I never had a visitor, I hated visiting hours and I would put the sheet over my head. One day, while I was sitting in my tent, I heard, "Pauline, I have come to see you." It was darling Chummy! He told me he had visited Mum and had brought from her the smallest jar of home-made jam and a card. He also said he had arranged for me to visit her when I was better. Later, when I saw her, she looked so ill and dark around the eyes. I remember taking her back her jar of jam, as I had nothing else to give her and I wanted to give something. It was lovely seeing her again. When I left, she gave me a sachet of lavender. I love lavender to this day. It reminds me of Mum and love.

"Darling Chummy" – he had also come to Banstead to check on me.

When well enough, Pauline was transferred to a convalescent home. Soon after her return to Banstead, it was arranged for me to see her. She looked like a waif – pale, thin and unsmiling, with bangs and granny glasses. She had had every care – the bread and milk, like my slap in the face, being only an idiosyncrasy of a housemother – but she lacked her mother's love. It might have helped had she seen me more often. Splitting the sexes is an understandable administrative convenience, but the school would have done better to facilitate regular visits between brothers and sisters. "My mind to me a kingdom is"? An adult may claim that. But what if the mind is injured before one is sovereign of it? That was the case with Archie and my sister – and is with many a child. The world is hardest on the vulnerable.

⊙Ⴟ⊙

5

School Journey

"Smith, Bloggs, Jones, Condon...." The teacher was handing out mail, to the lucky ones, that is, those not completely alone in the world.

My jaw dropped. Instead of the usual letter, I had a parcel! As I fumbled with the string, I suddenly became aware that the other boys in the dorm were approaching, eyes fixed on my parcel. It was the first time they had noticed my existence, as far as I knew.

"What have you got?"

"Is it sweets?"

"You've got to share!"

Yes, it was sweets, and chocolate bars, and copies of *Beano*, *Dandy* and *Comic Cuts* – not exactly my favourite reading material, but better than nothing. A parcel from Aunt Lil. "All right," I said. I could hardly sit scoffing the lot myself. Besides, they were mostly older and bigger than I. Hands reached and grabbed. What a rotten way of sharing, I thought – then I had to grab as well. "Could we swap comics, when you've finished reading yours?" I asked, ruefully contemplating the one chocolate bar and tattered comic I had managed to save. So far as I remember, no one swapped, but each clung to his comic like a limpet. Pauline says she also received a parcel, a large chocolate Easter egg, but she didn't grab fast enough and ended with nothing. So much for communism. I wasn't upset over the "sharing", though. I had too much to be happy about. It was a teacher who handed out the mail, because we were all on a school journey to the Isle of Wight – twenty boys and twenty girls, with three teachers. At about the time Pauline was in hospital, I was enjoying myself immensely.

On May 22, 1936, I mailed a post card to Mum, addressed to St. Benedict's Hospital, Tooting:

> Dear Mum,
>
> Will you send me some money because I have spent most of it on a photo and post card and stamps. Love and wishes from Phil
>
> x x x x x
>
> You will notice my face in the Photo.

Not one word to ask how she was! Self-centred little beast. Still, I suppose the message is on par with most written by ten-year-old boys to their mothers. How she managed to find the odd shilling to send me remains a mystery. On the front of the card is a photograph of our group posed formally before our guest house – "Oakland House", as far as I can make out – in Sandown. It is interesting, not because my face adorns the bottom left hand corner, but because it shows how well we were cared for. Despite a warm sun, which is making most of us squint, the male teacher is wearing a suit, complete with waistcoat. The two women teachers look fresh, one in a dress and the other in a white blouse and skirt. Their hair looks newly permed, but sensible. All the girls are wearing navy blue gym slips, with snowy blouses underneath. Their hair, too, is tidy. We boys are wearing grey flannel suits with short trousers and white shirts with ties. Our socks are firmly pulled up and our hair, like the male teacher's, is parted on the same side and gleams in the sun. In short, we all look scrubbed, groomed and polished. Compared to us, most of the boys at Moreland Street School looked like scruffy urchins. In fact we looked almost as if we belonged to a mixed version of Greyfriars.

Our fortnight's visit to the Isle of Wight was planned to the last detail. Each of us was given a booklet, run off in three colours, containing our itinerary with interesting information, maps and a few poems. Prepared with care to make it as attractive as possible, it was something I treasured. Much of our itinerary has faded from memory now, but some remains. Perhaps the least interesting visit was to Osborne House. Though Queen Victoria's house was far grander, I felt as if I were wandering around Nanna's, looking at knick-knacks. A visit to an island pottery proved much more interesting. Clustered around a potter at his wheel, we exclaimed with amazement as we watched his skilled hands convert a blob of wet clay into a shapely vase. It seemed magical.

We also enjoyed two trips to the mainland, the first of which was to Southampton docks. And there I had to revise my estimate of the *Crested Eagle*, for we were given a tour of the old *Berengaria*, once the *Imperator*, pride of the pre-war German liners. I don't know what the others thought, but I was staggered that so vast a structure could float. And though I had been rather bored by Queen Victoria's home, I was impressed by the luxury of the first-class lounge and dining-room. Ashore again, we passed one of the screws from the *Olympic*, sister ship to the *Titanic*. Either name would have suited it better than "screw" or "propeller", for its huge blades would have served us as satisfactory slides. Then we halted, with gasps of wonder. Behind the *Berengaria*, its bow towards us, towered another, even more majestic liner. It was the *Queen Mary*. Fresh from her sea trials, she was being prepared for her maiden voyage across the Atlantic. As we gaped up at the bow soaring above our heads, marvelling that so tall and relatively narrow a ship could remain upright, I couldn't know that one day I would take passage in her myself. She would then be an old lady, worn in the service of thousands of passengers and troops; but I would then have less appreciation of her size, for I was to be cooped up in the tourist section. I would also have the good fortune to sail in the *Ile de France*, the old *Aquitania*, and the *Queen Elizabeth*. One does not have to have traveled first-class to mourn the passing of the great ocean liners.

The following week, we visited Portsmouth and trooped aboard *H.M.S. Victory*. Compared to the *Queen Mary*, Nelson's ship seemed small, but I was nonetheless impressed by the thick rope cables and the mighty spars. On the gun decks, though, even I had to duck my head to avoid braining myself on the beams. Were seamen all midgets in those days? I wondered. But what I recall most vividly is the area outside the dockyard entrance. Lined with sooty brick hovels and one or two squalid shops, the streets were strewn with rubbish and layered with dust and filth. Compared with those streets, Goswell Road was a shining highway. And playing on the foul pavement were grey, ragged children – little girls in thin, grimy dresses; and boys in tattered shirts and short trousers, some with torn seats revealing their naked buttocks. None wore socks, and most had no shoes either. But what shocked me most was the children themselves. Their odd grey appearance came from dirt, dirt that was clearly the accumulation of unwashed weeks. Here, within hailing distance of the blanco, polish and swank of a major base of the Royal Navy, chief arm of a proud, still mighty Britain, were children whose condition would have disgraced the meanest native village in the Empire! As we orphans and temporary orphans passed by in our immaculate crocodile, did those children, secure in the arms of their loving families, think we were scions of the rich and privileged? And what would they have made of the *Berengaria*'s first-class lounge?

◑◐

6

I Nearly Make a Friend

About the time I set Archie crying, I came upon two older boys slugging it out toe-to-toe in the manner of my bout with George. Although I once enjoyed watching a good boxing match, I have never liked watching a fight. It's not the fight that bothers me, providing it is fair, so much as the ugliness of the emotions displayed, sometimes by the fighters but more often by the baying crowd. In this case, though, there was no one else in sight. It seemed a pity to deprive the combatants of moral support. And so I galloped up, formed a ring around them and cheered. But my generous encouragement received an unexpected welcome. As if by agreement, they stopped fighting each other and began to knock me about instead. It was the ingratitude that hurt. I knew that it wasn't personal, that they were using me merely as an excuse to end their own fight, and I thought them rotten sports.

Although a bit dishevelled, I did not have to explain my state to the housemother. For some reason I had been on my way to the infirmary and was able to clean up there. Afterwards, I found myself in a waiting-room with a boy I had not seen before. About my own age, perhaps more slightly built, he had dark hair, blue eyes and a face that bespoke sensitivity and intelligence, qualities that our brief conversation confirmed and that attracted me immediately. He was not a new boy, apparently, but had been ill and was awaiting discharge from the infirmary. Here, I thought, was a kindred spirit, one with whom I could share interests. I could have done with a friend, for I had little in common with Archie. Many a time I had longed for a brother my own age – perhaps because I had been one of twins, but my fellow had been stillborn. However, the new boy belonged to another house and I was to see him only once more, at church the following Sunday. During the service, a young chorister stood up to sing a solo. It was my friend. His singing staggered me. I couldn't believe such purity of tone could come from a boy – or from anyone. For the first time I had become aware of beauty in the human voice. A boy soprano, folk music, Brahms' "Waltz in A Flat", "Dancing Cheek to Cheek" (several of us had been taken to see *Top Hat* as a special treat) – it was at Banstead that music ceased to be background entertainment and began to move me.

In August, I was told to pack my things. I was going home. I was taken to the administration building, and there, waiting in a taxi, was Mum! I was overjoyed to see her again and looking so well.

But I was almost sorry to leave Banstead.

CHAPTER SEVEN

Return to Plumstead I

1
"…where our fate,
Hid in an auger-hole, may rush, and seize us…." – Macbeth

Why Pauline was not collected from Banstead at the same time I have no idea. Perhaps fate wished to give another turn of the screw, for when her day of deliverance finally came and she was expecting to meet Dad, he failed to show up! So she had to unpack and wait again, more sure than ever that she was not wanted. Apparently there had been a misunderstanding about the date. Still, by September, 1936, our family was re-united in our new home at 29 High Street, Plumstead, a house belonging to Gran. Though we would have to sub-let part of it, we were together again and nothing else mattered.

For Pauline the period following our removal from City Road had been traumatic and had reinforced her basic insecurity. But what of me? I had bounced back, found new interests and enjoyed life to the extent that I remember Banstead with affection. Bounced back from what? Although I did not think about it, I had been shaken by the suddenness of the removal to the temporary children's shelter and by the feeling I had then that the world had ceased to make sense:

And because I am happy and dance and sing,
They think they have done me no injury.

Like Pauline I had been injured, though to a lesser extent, by the criminals who had ruined our parents. It was not personal – merely mischance, like a road accident or a disease. However, it soon became evident that I had been made vulnerable.

School was well into the first term; and after a brief respite for visiting family and exploring my surroundings, I had to go. I didn't particularly like school but accepted it as a necessary nuisance, part of the natural order of things. And as Mum often reminded me that it was important to do well – she always wanted me to become a customs officer – I did my work conscientiously, though I could not always see its relevance. Now I was to be shaken again.

"Come along, darling," Mum said. "I have to take you to your new school." Where could it be? We walked along the High Street and then turned south. Ahead of us rose Beasley's brewery with its familiar sweet smell, and then Lakedale Road and Plumstead Common. Perhaps I was going back to Timbercroft Lane School, I thought. But instead of going up Lakedale Road, we turned right into Conway Road. Suddenly, I felt sick with foreboding. There on the right was the high brick wall, topped with broken glass, and behind it the school that looked like a prison. I began to drag my feet.

"Come on, dear. Whatever is the matter?"

"Do I have to go to that school, Mum?" I wailed.

"Of course you do. It's the only one nearby."

As in a nightmare I found myself dragged through the gate with the black iron bars. And echoing in my mind were the words that I had uttered so confidently nearly four years before: *One thing I am sure of – I won't have to go to that school.*

"Do you give homework?" Mum asked. "I want my son to do well."

The headmaster smiled, "Of course, in almost every class."

At this, I burst into tears.

Surprised, both of them turned to look at me. "Darling, you know you have to do homework." Mum shook me gently. "I don't know what's come over him," she apologized. "He's not normally like this."

No, indeed. And they weren't the only ones surprised by the tears. The last time I had cried had been in the bar at *The Lady Owen Arms* three years previously. A new school held no terrors for me; after all, this was my fifth. But the cruel coincidence had shaken me, that and the school's appearance. With the mention of homework, I felt as if the school were reaching into my home as well, that bars were beginning to clamp around me.

I had been frightened by a phantom, of course. Although the co-incidence seemed significant at the time, it was not surprising under the circumstances. What could be more natural than that we should move back to Plumstead to be close to the family?

Shown to my first class, I found a roomful of boys studying a blackboard inscribed with hieroglyphics. "Do you know what this is?" the teacher asked me, pointing to the board. "No, Sir." "Long division in algebra. Have you done any algebra?" "No, Sir." The teacher turned to the class. "Smith," he ordered, "take the new boy to the corner and show him what algebra is." (Some of today's math teachers might well smile ruefully, for I have heard complaints, on two continents, that many students come to high school not knowing even their times table.) In science class later, we were each given a blunt scalpel and a cow's eye and told to dissect it. However, I soon settled into the school routine. Though I can recall little of Conway Road School now, I liked the morning assemblies, for we sang the hymns with gusto. My favourite was by John Bunyan:

Who would true valour see
Let him come hither;
One here will constant be,
Come wind, come weather;
There's no discouragement
Shall make him once relent
His first avow'd intent
To be a pilgrim.

Soon a little more discouragement came my way. I was beaten in a fight and found myself crying again. My wily opponent had rejected fisticuffs and slipped behind to get me in a full nelson. Until a woman stepped in to stop it, I was pinned to the ground with my face in the dust, completely helpless. At Banstead I had taken a thumping from two older boys in my stride, and yet here

I was snivelling over a little humiliation. What was the matter with me? Was I getting to be like Archie? Yes, for the first time in my life I found myself psychologically vulnerable. The events of February and the coincidence of the school had softened me up well for what was about to happen.

I am running home through a back street. Although it is afternoon, it is deserted – no traffic or people, not even a child or a dog. At a corner I cut across by the pumps of a small petrol station.

"Gotcha, you little bastard!"

Two powerful hands had seized me by the lapels. They twist, lift me onto my toes, and a great blue-jowled face thrusts itself close to mine. Like a butterfly seized by a mantis, a rabbit by a stoat, I am paralyzed by the suddenness of the shock. *Where had he come from?* Dimly, I realize he had been hiding behind the last pump. My fate had leapt upon me like a spider from an auger-hole.

Blue Jowls tightens his grip and shakes me, snarling, "I've been waiting for you."

Waiting for me? Why? I've done you no harm nor your rotten garage. I've never even seen you before.

It would be an amusing conceit to say that "his eyes looked most powerfully down into mine and mine looked most helplessly up into his", but it wouldn't be true. I wasn't even aware of his eyes, only of that terrifying face, still thrust to within inches of my own. As for my eyes, I know exactly what they looked like, for I was to see their expression later in the eyes of a young man under my own hand. They were staring, with the pupils so dilated that the irises almost vanished.

"D'yer know what I'm going to do with you?" He shakes me again. "Do yer?" His gruff voice is swelling with power and menace.

I cannot imagine what he is going to do, or why, and I await his pronouncement with infinite dread. I am in a curious state. The world has gone still and quiet, as if nothing exists but myself and that face. And some part of my mind seems to have drawn aside and is quietly but helplessly observing what is happening, while the rest of it is flooded with terror.

"I'm going to call a policeman..."

I begin to feel relief: *Policemen help you. They show you the way home if you're lost.*

"… and have you locked up."

It is then that I begin to scream and beg. But he keeps his grip, and his face continues to fill my field of vision for what seems an eternity. Was he enjoying my terror, or was he merely puzzled by it?

Suddenly lifting me higher and thrusting his face even closer, he hisses, "Remember." Then he throws me roughly aside.

As I ran off, the "observer" was still haplessly surveying my disoriented inner state; but by the time I reached home, I seemed whole again. Had the ruffian merely knocked me about, I should perhaps have been all right. But the irrationality of the attack made the world seem meaningless again. In such a world, to be taken away again and locked behind bars for no reason at all seemed entirely possible. Though this experience may not appear as frightening as Pip's encounter with his convict – after all, my attacker had not offered to cut my throat or threaten me with a terrible young man – yet the effect on me was more profound. Pip had merely been terrified for a while, whereas the shock of being seized out of the blue had traumatized me. And while Pip's convict reappeared later, he came as a kindly, albeit embarrassing, benefactor. My Face also reappeared: first, to fill me with unreasoning terror in a recurrent nightmare; and, later, to burst into my life again with all the devastating suddenness of the original attack. And with exquisite precision, fate once more timed the irruption to inflict the maximum damage. Yes, I would remember. Then, of course, I knew none of this. When I reached home, I said nothing to my parents about the attack, and by next morning it had apparently vanished from my mind.

❧

2
Of Films and Books

December brought our first Christmas together since 1934. As usual, preparations and anticipation brought as much enjoyment as the great day itself. That there was so little money for decorations and presents didn't matter. We were a family once more. In any case we made our own decorations and Pauline and I spent hours pasting strips of coloured paper into festive chains, while Mum added twisted strips of red and green crêpe paper. Done to the accompaniment of Christmas carols on the wireless, this was much more fun than putting up ready-made decorations. There was no tree, but a few sprigs of holly and mistletoe made up for the lack. I also spent hours rubbing my nose against the windows of the brightly decorated shops. The bicycles fascinated me, but at a price of five guineas or more they might as well have been Rolls Royces. I also gazed longingly at model steam engines and Meccano sets and at the working models that could be contructed from them. Hornby train sets and fine German models of Grand Prix racing cars – these, too, were beyond my dreams; but it cost nothing to look. As for the Christmas board, for the first time I made my own contribution, a bottle of ginger wine – non-alcoholic, of course, but it showed the right spirit. For me, as for most people in England, Christmas was the focus of merriment and celebration. New Year's Eve served only as a period to the season, and the wonder vanished with the decorations. Ahead lay school once more, and an eternity until the next Christmas.

There had been one shadow on our celebrations. For the only time I can remember, I badgered Mum for a toy. Normally I was content with what I got – usually a book, with the Christmas pillowcase plumped up with nuts, fruit, sweets and the lucky piece of coal. Now for some reason I set my heart on a model aeroplane and whined and badgered until, exasperated, Mum gave in. "It's a waste of money. You'll play with it for five minutes and then you'll throw it aside." She was right. It was a cheap, nasty toy made of painted tin, a poor reproduction of an airliner, and the only thing you could do with it was push it across the floor. It was more suitable for a boy of six than one nearly eleven. It appears I was going through a regressive stage.

I think my intelligence also slipped a few notches around this time. For a while that winter Pauline and I would go to the pictures together. As the cheap seats in regular performances cost fourpence ha'penny, we instead attended Saturday morning children's matinee at the Woolwich Granada. With admission so cheap (tuppence, I think) nearly every seat was usually filled. I have been told that howler monkeys are the noisiest animals on earth. If so, we are their close cousins, as the noise produced during those matinees by the young of our species may only be described as shattering. Most, like Pauline and me, would remain in their seats, chatting or gazing about them; but a minority, possessed by a demonic energy, would exhibit the incessant, purposeless movement displayed by hysterical monkeys and fill the air with screams, catcalls, forced laughter, weird animal noises and flurries of missiles – paper aeroplanes, orange peel, apple cores and the like. Some boys would come equipped with short lengths of rubber tubing through which to blow loud farting noises and spray saliva on those in front of them. Others would come with less innocent instruments, for Pauline once returned home minus several locks of her hair. And one soon learned that to sit beneath the edge of the balcony was to become a target for bombs – gobs of spit and even hard objects.

As lights dimmed, this bedlam would increase to a crescendo and abate only with the beginning of the cartoon; but at no point would it stop altogether. I used to strain my ears trying to make sense of the serial and the main feature. The latter, usually a western starring Ken Maynard, Buck Jones, and the like, had a plot which consisted largely of cowboys galloping furiously about a parched landscape and shooting at each other. I see now that I'd have shown more sense had I brought my own length of rubber tubing and blown loud farting noises at the screen. Still, I make up for it today by swearing at the telly from time to time.

This weekly descent into one of the noisier circles of hell soon lost appeal and I ceased to go, although I attended regular performances as often as I could. Pictures such as *King Kong* and *Tarzan* were a joke, of course; and my cousin Peter and I sometimes amused ourselves by snarling menacingly like King Kong or charging down Bowman's Hollow alarming birds with imitations of Johnny Weissmuller. But pictures such as *Hell's Angels, Things to Come* and *The Four Feathers* were thrilling; and after seeing Gary Cooper in *Lives of a Bengal Lancer* I considered him my hero, although he annoyed me by getting himself killed so often.

Still, though some pictures set imagination flying, there were too few to satisfy an active mind. Fortunately, Plumstead had a well-stocked public library, much larger than my old Skinner Street branch. Having been deprived of books since leaving Goswell Road, for I do not remember books at Banstead, I now made up for it. From the end of 1936 to the outbreak of the War, I read two or three a week, mostly fiction. It was then that I laughed at the adventures of William Brown and Ginger, at Bertie Wooster and the inimitable Jeeves, at the colourful characters of W.W. Jacobs. I competed in Grand Prix races with Nuvolari; fought the Hun with Biggles; and explored Africa with Alan Quartermain, the jungles of India with Mowgli, and the oceans with Captain Nemo. I sighed with relief when Nayland Smith thwarted the detestable Fu Manchu, and I enjoyed the discomfiture of other villains at the hands of Sir Percy Blakeney, Bulldog Drummond, Arsène Lupin, the Saint and Sherlock Holmes. I slipped backwards in time with Scott and Sabatini, forwards with Verne and H.G.Wells, and relished every ghost story I could find, although I did not discover the master, M.R. James, until my teens.

The only "serious" book I read at this time was one I borrowed from Gran, an ancient copy of John Bunyan's *Pilgrim's Progress* with yellowing leaves and many a squashed moth and silverfish. And there, attracted by the gothic illustrations, I met Christian, Faithful, Hopeful and Mr. Worldly Wiseman. I doubt whether I understood much of it, but in the years to come I was to skirt Vanity Fair and tread the Delectable Mountains – only to fall into the Slough of Despond for far too long and take a fall or two from Giant Despair. Sometimes I have felt like one of the moths in Gran's book. I was not a precocious reader – no Trollope, Dickens, Austen or Hardy – but I was an able one, and I romped through books happily. A new ritual now began at home:

"It's time to go to bed, dear."

"All right, Mum. Just let me finish this chapter."

Fifteen minutes after going to my room: "Phil, are you reading under the bedclothes again?" I usually was. And every few weeks: "I can't understand you. You've always got your nose stuck in a book!"

3

Encounter with Another "Strange Man"

Mum's complaint was understandable, I suppose, but not altogether accurate. I did other things too. I did my homework faithfully enough and listened selectively to the wireless, usually both at the same time. At weekends and on long summer evenings I would be out and about. Sometimes I would visit my cousins on Plumstead Common. John was now in his teens and had his own friends and interests, but Peter and I would play cowboys and Indians on the common, engage in friendly pebble fights down the 'Oller with other kids, or wander over the common to Bowman's Hollow and Bostall Woods – always keeping a sharp eye open for the brown-uniformed keepers, who were as deeply suspicious of small boys as we were of them.

On several occasions Peter took me to a gang who used to hang out on Fanny-on-the-Hill, just beyond the Woolwich cemetery. They were not really a gang but rather a shifting assemblage of boys with time on their hands. And they used to hang literally, for the clubhouse was a large tree, and during any given "meeting" half the gang would be clambering about its branches like a troop of monkeys. On our way there one day Peter and I happened upon a pair of older boys playing by a ditch. Suddenly, the devil leapt upon my shoulder and chattered in my ear. "Pete," I suggested, "Let's get those boys to chase us and we'll lead them to the gang." Pete thought the idea brilliant. Needless to say, it didn't occur to either of us that the boys could be members themselves or that the gang might not be there to rescue us. Luckily, all went as planned. A few choice insults, raspberries and rude gestures soon convinced the two that there could be nothing more enjoyable in life than to push our cheeky little faces into the mud – and they came for us. Laughing ourselves silly, we hared off through the bushes. Yes, there was the gang, and there our leader, a sturdy youth. "There are some big boys chasing us," I gasped, feigning distress as we leapt for the tree.

Seconds later our pursuers burst into the clearing, scarlet from exertion and righteous indignation. Upon seeing the crowd of boys, they skidded to a halt – unhappily for them, right before our leader. A few sharp words, a clout about the ear, and our unfortunate dupes left as fast as they had come. Perched in the branches high above, Pete and I exchanged looks and giggled. Before long, however, Nemesis arrived in the form of an angry mother. Labouring into the clearing, she advanced upon our protector and then, after lashing him with her tongue, she whacked him over the head with her umbrella. At this, I felt a twinge of conscience. And my career as an *agent provocateur* ended.

More usually I was alone. Sometimes I would wander about the Plumstead marshes down by the river. It was my late return from one of these expeditions that earned me the belting from Dad. On Saturdays, I would often walk to Woolwich to look at the shops and the market or spend hours riding the free ferry. The busy river fascinated me, as did the ferry's engine room with its hissing steam and the oiled gleam of its Wellsian pistons. Like many of the older generation, I have a certain nostalgia for the age of steam, especially for the great locomotives and ships that crossed land and sea trailing plumes of steam and smoke. It's a feeling possibly not shared by retired firemen and stokers.

For a while I wandered much farther afield in company with Terry, a young man who occupied the top floor of our house with his mother. He was about twenty-five, with ginger hair, merry blue eyes and a ready smile. What he did for a living I don't know. Though his muscular build, tattooed arms and seaman's roll suggested years spent at sea, I suspect now that the swagger was assumed and the muscles came from weightlifting. He had me lifting weights one evening, using only the bar. Once was enough. My slight frame could have done with some muscle, but I found the process tedious.

Much more interesting were the Saturdays we spent together. We took to going on long walks, fueling our way with still lemonade and Lyons fruit tarts. Usually we explored the countryside around Bexley and Chislehurst, although we were never able to escape from the sight of terrace houses and chimney pots. I enjoyed those modest excursions. Terry was a pleasant companion with none of the condescension adults often show the young. Instead, we joked and laughed together as equals.

One day Terry beckoned, "Come outside. I've got something

to show you. There," he said, when we reached the street, "what do you think of her?" Parked by the kerb was a Royal Enfield motorcycle, a gleaming beauty smelling of petrol and hot oil.

My eyes widened and my nose twitched appreciatively. "Is that yours, Terry?" I asked.

He grinned. "Would you like to go for a spin?"

"Gosh, may I?" I had never ridden a bicycle before, let alone an exciting monster like this.

Throwing his leg over the seat, he kicked down on the starter and revved the engine. "Hop on. Now, put your arms around my waist and hang on tight." And with the wind whipping my hair, off we rode up the High Street and on to Bostall Woods. At first I was apprehensive, especially when he threw the bike around corners, but soon I gained in confidence and began to feel an exhilarating sense of freedom.

After a few spins like this, I could reel off most of the better-known marques – Norton, Triumph, AJS, BSA, Matchless, Douglas, Ariel, Velocette. Save for Grand Prix racers, cars did not excite me, although I did admire the MG roadster and the Riley sports saloon. One Saturday, after packing sandwiches, towels and swimming costumes, we roared off to the coast, savouring the freedom of the open road and riding the rolling Downs as effortlessly as an albatross skims the waves. Except on bank holidays, the expression "open road" meant something then.

It was almost the last time I saw Terry. By next weekend both he and his mother were gone. My parents were not over-protective; and, unless I did something wrong, they allowed me a remarkably free rein. Nonetheless, very little escaped Mum's watchful eye. She knew that Terry had been spending a lot of time not only with me but also with Pauline. On one occasion he was even allowed to take her to the Elephant and Castle for tea and then a picture at the Trocadero. If my parents harboured any suspicions, they kept them to themselves. However, one morning Pauline said, "Can I move into your bed after you get up, please, Mum?"

"Of course you can, dear."

"Mum," Pauline added, "can I lock your door afterwards?" It was then that the alarm bells went off. Under close questioning, Pauline told her that Terry had recently developed the habit of visiting her in the morning, giving her wet kisses and calling her his little "wifie". Understandably, she didn't like it.

That evening Dad called Terry down and ordered him to leave. "And if you've done anything to harm my children, I'll have your bloody guts for garters!" At this, Terry rushed up the stairs, tearing the bannister from the wall in his rage, and so disappeared from our lives.

"He's really quite harmless," apologised the mother just before leaving next day. And perhaps he wasn't. There had been a progression in his attentions to Pauline. It was as well she didn't tell Mum what she only recently revealed to me – that Terry had taken her to his own bed that morning. "He was wearing his briefs and he only cuddled me, but I didn't like it and I was afraid." Terry was a paedophile. Unable to relate comfortably to adults, he preferred the company of children, with a specific interest in little girls. It was sad, for he was otherwise a pleasant young man, but he could hardly be considered harmless. Thanks to the alertness of our mother, Pauline had had a lucky escape.

❦

4

Of Guardian Angels

Returning home from Woolwich one day, I was again tempted by the devil and bought a penn'orth of stink bombs from a dingy novelty shop. Now, where to use them? The chance came in the evening, when I was sent across the road for some groceries. While being served, I looked around carefully. Yes, there were other shoppers, a few women. No one could possibly guess who the culprit was. Covertly, I dropped a bomb onto the sawdust and then stepped on it as I left with my purchases. Cleverly done. The shop was less than a minute's walk from our house, but I loitered. Already bored with stink bombs, I tossed the other into a noisy pub and then spent ten minutes or so admiring the bicycles in the window of an adjoining shop.

When at last I burst into the living room with my purchases, Mum looked me directly in the eye for so long I began to feel nervous. Then she snapped, "What's this I hear about you throwing stink bombs?" I almost fell down. One doesn't need the little grey cells of a Hercule Poirot to work out how she knew, despite there being no telephone, for we were regular customers at the grocery. But at the time I was dumbfounded and thought Mum was psychic. In my brief excursion into crime I had been caught as speedily as Dad had in his.

If we have guardian angels, the chief duty of mine surely has been to administer a swift kick the moment I stray too far from the strait and narrow. Months after this first warning boot, I thought it an amusing prank at my sister's birthday party to pull a chair from under a girl as she sat down. When she began to howl, I was told she had a bad back. And in a classroom many years later I once seized one of my pupils by the arm, exasperated by his squirming inattention. He, too, gave a yelp. It was then that I recalled reading a notice in the staff bulletin that we should watch out for this boy as he had injured his arm. Unfortunately, I was too new to the school to know who he was. As there were fifteen hundred boys there and I had a choice of arms, the odds in my favour were three thousand to one. With my guardian angel, those were not safe odds.

Lest I be suspected of paranoia, let me say that these are not the only instances. But I shall tell of one more only. Some weeks prior to my flight from the blue-rinsed Amazon on the *Oronsay* I strayed from the path of chastity with the wife of a friend. We had got our signals scrambled, a circumstance that must have made our guardian angels laugh themselves into a feathery flurry. When her husband came home – and while I was still there, feeling like Judas decked out in cap and bells – my partner in sin whisked him off to another room and proceeded to tell him all about it in grossly exaggerated detail! A novelist could never get away with that. Such things happen only in farces and real life.

5

Plumstead Central School

In September, 1937, I prepared for my new school, Plumstead Central.[6] I had failed my "Eleven-Plus" exam, as we thought, which meant I would have to leave school at age fifteen, instead of eighteen. Despite a natural disappointment at my not securing a place in grammar school, none of us thought it a tragedy. The idea of my going to university had never entered our minds. In the event, it didn't matter, for the War disrupted my schooling anyway.

The week before I was due to start, Dad took me aside for a chat. "You're going to senior school this time, and I have some advice for you. First, if you get into trouble and a teacher gives you a walloping, don't come home and tell me – for I'll give you another one. Next, if you have trouble with another boy, even if he's bigger than you, don't come crying to me about it. Just make sure you get the first punch in." Well, this seemed sensible, manly advice. The only thing that puzzled me was why he felt he had to give it. I can't speak for the first five years of my life, but since then I had never burdened my parents with problems of that sort. I hadn't even told them about my terrifying encounter with Blue Jowls, the Face. Still, when Dad went on to stress the importance of getting a good education, I appreciated his interest.

As it happened, I missed the opening days of school, thanks to a mouthful of ulcers that made speaking and eating difficult. Frequent rinsing with a solution of alum and water soon dried them up. However, Mum had become convinced they had been caused by "impure blood". Determined that we should eat well, no matter how short the money, by practising economies and buying produce in season, she provided us with excellent meals: brown stew; Irish stew (my favourite); rabbit pie, with a porcelain volcano spouting gravy; roast leg of lamb on Sundays, or roast beef with roast potatoes, Yorkshire pud, carrots, parsnips and greens according to season; cold cuts, pickles and bubble-and-squeak to follow on Mondays; shepherd's pie or curry to finish off the scraps on Tuesdays; sometimes roast pork with crackling

---

[6] A central school came between ordinary senior school, leaving-age fourteen, and grammar school. Its advantage over the former was slim – an extra year of schooling, with French added. Neither fish nor fowl, in short.

and apple sauce; stuffed heart, steak and kidney pie, toad-in-the-hole, or liver and bacon; roast chicken or turkey only for Christmas, as poultry was dear, though rabbit (wild) was cheap; haddock and chips once a week, and not from the fish and chip shop, either. Then there were "afters": suet pudding and treacle, fruit and custard, treacle tart, prunes and custard ("Tinker, tailor, soldier, sailor") – the list was endless; jelly or trifle on birthdays; and, for Christmas, mince pies and a fine fruit pudding with a thre'penny bit for luck. For tea we had buttered bread and jam and sometimes home-made cake. "You're lucky," Dad observed on more than one occasion, "When I was your age, we had to be satisfied with bread and butter *or* bread and jam." I took that with a pinch of salt. Now and then, usually on Saturday evenings in winter, we were treated to high tea – a boiled egg, a piece of smoked haddock, a kipper, or herrings dredged in flour and fried. Delicious! Thanks to the Great War, North Sea fish stocks had recovered. Fish was cheap, and herring in season could be had for three ha'pence or tuppence a pound. We had no French cuisine or exotic dishes, just plain English food – but, oh, I did not realize how good a cook my mother was until I left home!

Despite all this care, Pauline and I resembled skinned weasels, and Mum had been supplementing our diet with liberal doses of Radio Malt and cod liver oil. However, my mouth ulcers now caused her to become obsessed with the idea that we needed "purifying". She began with sulphur tablets, to purify our blood, and Exlax, to purge us – not bad, rather like sweets. Then, becoming fascinated with the subject, she experimented with a range of laxatives in a regimen that lasted for weeks. Exlax was followed by syrup of figs (sickly, but tolerable), cascara (bitter), castor oil (nasty), a tea made from senna pods (cat's piss), and finally powdered liquorice in water (vile).

One morning Pauline came late for breakfast. She looked pale. Not waiting for the usual inquisition, she said tiredly, "I've had my lungs well opened, Mum." Perhaps the ensuing belly laugh brought Mum to her senses, or perhaps her obsession had run its course, but the reign of terror was ended. It was time. Pauline and I must have been the most purged and purified children in Christendom!

Plumstead Central, I am pleased to say, was a good school, with competent and in some cases good teachers. There were one or two duds, of course. The French teacher, unsmiling and grey of face, spoke in a whisper and seldom left his chair. Clearly ill, perhaps dying, he soon disappeared. Our cadaverous science master was burnt out. Dull-eyed, he intoned his lessons in a spiritless, mechanical way that bored us all silly. Although interested in science, I can recall nothing except doing things with litmus paper. But these were exceptions. One teacher, nicknamed "Old Poll" because she resembled a cross between a maenad and a parrot, I recall well. Slight and short, with her black hair, streaked with grey, brushed carelessly back, she was one of the least favoured women I have ever seen. Her face was pallid and blotched and dominated by a great hooked beak and a mouthful of crooked yellow teeth. When she spoke, she sprayed saliva. If we felt no affection for her, she at least had our respect. There was no nonsense in her music class. She *made* us sing, and sing, not only in tune, but with gusto and enjoyment. Two songs I especially liked were "The Oak and the Ash" and "The Road to the Isles". The former, with its haunting melody, still fills me with nostalgia for a "north countree" that exists only in my imagination. As for the latter, I never did climb in Skye, but I have glimpsed the Cuillins from afar and in the Highlands found myself at home. The energy Old Poll threw into her lessons was awe-inspiring. Of course, like most students, we thought that when our lesson was over, she had nothing else to do. But she expended energy like that five hours a day throughout the year. No wonder she was meagre of frame.

Our morning assemblies were impressive. To a lively march from our small but able string orchestra, we would file quietly into the hall class by class and sit cross-legged on the floor, girls on one side and boys on the other. There we would listen to notices and an address by the headmaster, Mr. Bishop, before standing to sing the daily hymn. Quiet as mice during the address, for no one wished to be skewered by the headmaster's finger, we more than made up for it when we sang. Most impressive of all was the assembly on Empire Day. Then over four hundred voices belted out "Land of

Hope and Glory" and "Jerusalem" with enjoyment and a swelling pride because we were English and at the centre of a mighty empire. Happy little imperialists, to be so proud of belonging to a whole in which we had so humble a part! I've no doubt, though, that most of the older boys played a rather fuller part during the War. Old Poll was not responsible for assemblies, of course, but she had much to do with why they were so impressive. I still have a love for choral music, and when listening to Last Night of the Proms am instantly carried back to my schooldays.

Another memorable teacher was Mr. Obee. Unsmiling and with a pair of pale blue eyes that nailed you to the spot, he had the ability to reduce us to absolute stillness by his mere presence – the quality, for us anyway, that Renaissance Italians called *terribilità*. He taught us English and Euclid, and taught us well. In proving theorems, we had to line up equal signs, underline each stage of reasoning in red, and give proofs to the right. The conclusion and the *quod erat demonstrandum* were underlined twice. This training in methodical work has served me well, and not just in geometry. I haven't taught mathematics; but as a substitute one day I was dismayed to see how juniors went about their work. They scribbled figures anywhere, used a calculator for everything and were interested only in the answer. And if theirs was wrong, they were reluctant to discover why. In my own subjects, English and history, I set out work in a consistent and orderly fashion, both on the board and in printed notes, and I demanded that my students did likewise. But it was an uphill battle. Such training in order and method is best done early, before students become teenagers and think they know better. Sloppy work is not limited to students, of course. I have seen teachers whose work could best be described as disgraceful. Training children to work methodically while paying attention to detail may be dull compared with encouraging creativity, but it is nonetheless vital. In the real world, carelessness costs lives. "For want of a nail...."

Despite his severity, Mr. Obee was my favourite. However, he was not perfect. One day he interrupted his lesson to regard us with disdain. Some boy had farted, perhaps, or the body odour was stronger than usual. Then, after a pause that made us squirm, he said, "What you boys should do is have a run before breakfast and then follow it up with a cold shower." We gaped at him. Run? What for? We already did most things at the trot. As for a shower, few had a bathroom in the house. And why a cold shower? In winter we were half frozen anyway and had chilblains from trying to warm ourselves before a fire while draughts whistled about our ears. We slipped between cold, damp sheets at night and awoke to a freezing house in the morning. Bedroom fires were lit only in the case of serious illness. But most teachers then were middle class, I suppose, and knew little of the vast unwashed. Perhaps, though, he had another reason for his suggestion. He may have detected a boy masturbating. Such things did happen in class, I know, for I once saw a boy in the next seat going at it with enthusiasm.

Mr. Obee fell from grace, in my estimation, at the same time as I, and over the same incident. He strode into class one day and in the usual ensuing hush declared loudly, "If there is anything I detest above all else it is a boy who is a sneak." He said nothing else on the subject and in the tense silence his eyes rested on no one in particular, but all knew he was referring to me. There was enough truth in the charge to make it sting; but it was not the whole truth, and I felt he had kicked me while I was down. A day or so previously, a boy had tormented me in metal-work class with a red-hot iron. When he refused to stop despite my protests, I simply ignored him – until I smelt cloth burning. Then I went for him and tried to punch his nose. But he was taller than I and brushed aside my punches with ease. By the time I returned home I had forgotten all about it.

"Oh, look at your coat. It's burnt at the back," Mum exclaimed. "How did that happen?" I should, I suppose, have claimed it to have been an accident, but I was not in the habit of lying to Mum. She was psychic. And so I told her the truth. "You have no idea how much I've had to scrimp and save to buy you that uniform," she complained. "I don't have the money to buy you another." Then she added angrily, "I want you to take a letter to the headmaster. I want that boy punished."

I was aghast. "No," I blurted, "I won't do it."

"Then I shall go and see the headmaster myself."

105

Checkmate. Though I knew that nothing but ill could come of it, I finally agreed. Better I be made to feel a fool than Mum. And so the next morning I found myself reluctantly climbing the stairs to the head's study, noting with interest on the way that the teachers' common room contained a full-sized billiards table.

"You say he was larking about and burnt your coat," snapped the head at the inquest. He looked at the other boy, "What's your story?"

"It was an accident, sir. I wasn't doing anything."

The head turned to the teacher, "Do you know anything about it?"

"My book shows I took both boys' names for creating a disturbance."

"Ah, now we have the truth! You were both making a nuisance of yourselves instead of working." His moustache bristling, Mr. Bishop glared at me with distaste. "I find that forty percent of the blame is the other boy's and sixty percent is yours."

Such nicety of judgment! I could have pointed out that the disturbance came after the event, not before. Instead, I remained silent, not expecting justice but wishing only for the ordeal to end.

"Well," Mum demanded, "did you give him my letter?" When I nodded, she added, "And what did he do?"

"He gave the boy a good ticking-off, Mum," I answered. It was forty percent of the truth, anyway.

Visiting England some twenty years later, on my way to see Aunt Mary I saw a crocodile of small boys approaching. In the lead was a familiar figure, grey, seemingly shrunken, but still erect. It was Mr. Obee, still teaching after what seemed a lifetime! At first I wanted to speak to him, but then I reconsidered. How should I recall myself to his memory? "I am the little sneak you detested so much"? There was probably nothing else about me he would remember. And so regretfully I passed by, reflecting on how a few ill-considered words could stand as a barrier long after any hurt had passed.

I have dealt with this trivial incident at length to show that I was, and am, thin-skinned. I remember chanting "Sticks and stones may break my bones, but words will never hurt me" in response to the sort of insult children cheerfully hurl at one another, but I knew that this was not true when the speaker was someone I respected. I never feared physical punishment, but I could be shamed instantly by a reprimand – by an accusation of rudeness, for example. While I have always been ready to make an apology, I have often been baffled by the reactions to it. "It's too late to apologise!" for example. When should one apologise – before the offense? There's a place for that, perhaps, but hardly if the offence is unintentional. "I'm sorry. I didn't mean to be rude." "That's no excuse! It was unforgivable." Again, bafflement. Or even, "Never apologise. It's a sign of weakness." I can only suppose that someone who holds this opinion sees an apology as self-abasement instead of concern for another's feelings. Still, although it is never too late to apologise, one may apologise too soon. Sometimes it is best to remain silent and allow one's victim a cooling-off period first. Part of my problem, I think, is that I tend to give too much weight to the words people use, assuming that they mean what they say, or say what they mean. It was relatively late in my life before I realized we often use words the way a dog uses its bark – to express our feelings of the moment without considering the meaning. That is why I appreciated the scene in *Shogun* where our Elizabethan hero, after shouting "Piss on you!", finds himself being pissed on by his Japanese captor. It was a sharp reminder that words have meaning and a fine juxtaposition of tongue and penis, those two boneless members that cause so much trouble. Most of us, I fancy, might benefit from a spell in a Trappist monastery.

Generally, I was content enough at school, although I didn't like science (litmus paper) and arithmetic. I found the latter boring, as the answer always seemed to involve calculation to several decimal places – intended, I suspect, to keep us busy. But my favourite classes were woodwork and metalwork. Here I could escape from paper and ink for a while and lay hands on something concrete, actually make something. Although the only useful things I ever took home were a toasting fork and a small book rack, I was proud of those.

Sport did not particularly interest me, but I found it a welcome break from classwork. On sports afternoon, we would usually be taken to the common for cricket or football, or to Bostall Woods for a cross-country run. Although I played with spirit, I invariably found myself, rightly, with the more inept athletes. For some reason I have trouble hitting balls – even when they are standing still. At other times we used the schoolyard. For cricket we then used a solid rubber ball which seemed to have a core of lead. No matter how hard we hit it, we were lucky to reach the wall. In all these activities, teachers provided shouts of encouragement – but no coaching whatever.

Swimming I taught myself at the public baths, beginning with a breaststroke with head clear of the water. ("He who teaches himself has a fool for a student!") Eventually, I managed twenty lengths, mostly on my back. The overarm stroke was less effective, as I could never work out what to do with my legs. So mine was a sort of dog paddle that consumed much energy but produced little progress.

As a "swimmer" I one day found myself in an inter-school competition. (We were short of volunteers.) I hadn't a chance of winning, of course, but I could do the required distance, one length free-style, and so thought I would at least not be humiliated. Sure. At the last minute my swimming costume went missing, and Mum hastily modified Dad's old one, the kind with shoulder straps and leggings. And so the line-up exposed to public gaze a wretch with arm holes reaching to the waist, a sagging seat and leggings covering the knees. A whistle blew, spectators screamed encouragement and thankfully I plunged out of sight. Turning onto my back, I began stroking and kicking like a galvanized frog, the costume billowing about me. Unhappily, around the half-way mark it suddenly ballooned into a drogue and not only reduced my speed to near zero but threatened to part from me altogether. Desperately flipping into a sidestroke to keep at least one shoulder strap on, I finished the last quarter in solitary ignominy. "Why did you change style?" someone shouted as he hauled me out. "You were keeping up well until then." Clutching my sagging pride about me, for it was reaching now for my ankles, I tried to explain – but hadn't the breath.

6

The Way It Was

Before 1936, our parents were in the bar mid-day and evening every day of the week, so Pauline and I saw them only at odd hours, and seldom together even then. Apart from a fortnight during the War, when Dad had embarkation leave, after 1939 we would never be together again. And so those three years were the only time we four lived as a normal family. It is for this reason that I cherish this period in my life. Even so, Pauline and I saw little enough of Dad. During the week, he was gone to work by the time we awoke in the mornings; and at weekends and most evenings he worked as a bartender, not arriving home until after we had gone to bed. In fact, the only time we had dinner together was on Sundays. Why, in spite of the hours he worked and our sub-letting parts of the house, we were short of money I don't know. I can only suppose he was paying off his debts. At least he drank less now, except for the Sunday skinful. However, although I remember no family squabbling during this time, I don't think Mum was any happier with him. She still suffered from asthma. While she was out shopping one day a severe attack rendered her so helpless, struggling for every breath, that passers-by had to hail a taxi for her.

Sundays, as I have said, I loathed. After breakfast, the papers and the rotten Hawaiian music, Dad would send me to Gran's and then leave for his three hours of bartending and elbow-bending. Visiting Gran was not my idea of fun, for she was then over eighty and bed-ridden, but I was under orders. Dad had been her last child and her darling. Now I was the object of her love, for she never asked to see Pauline. After a cup of Aunt Mary's Camp coffee, I would go into the parlour, where Gran had her bed. "Ah, there you are, darlin'," she would exclaim in a resonant voice. "How are you? Come here and give your old Gran a kiss." This would be followed by a surprisingly strong hug and a great plonker. Despite age and failing health, she radiated strength and loving warmth. Then I would sit on the bed chatting and playing Chinese chequers with her for an hour or so. It was a duty I am now grateful for, as it gave me the chance to know and love both her and Aunt Mary. Gran was one of life's brighter spirits.

The one meal our family shared every day was tea. We always sat at the table together, even if we had only bread and jam. Of course, high tea was better. Even now, I have only to smell fried herrings or smoked haddock poached in milk to be immediately carried back to this happy time. At this meal, Dad hadn't been drinking and was almost amiable. It was then that the sense of family oneness was most strong. This and the evenings were the times I loved best, especially in winter, when the rain and the fog and the world were shut out and the living-room was made cosy with a cheerful coal fire. What did chilblains and a few draughts matter, anyway? That we could hear trams rattling by every few minutes, for our house fronted directly on the street, only reassured me that all was well with the world.

As for many families then, the wireless became an increasingly enjoyable part of our lives and we bought the *Radio Times* to plan our listening. I always made sure I was home in time for *Children's Hour*, which had fine programs like a serialization of Conan Doyle's *Lost World.* Generally, I preferred *Dick Barton, Special Agent* and other B.B.C. dramas to the pictures, as they allowed my imagination free rein. Our favourite programs were *Monday Night at Eight o'Clock*, with "big-hearted Arthur" Askey and Richard "Stinker" Murdoch, and *In Town Tonight*, which followed the news at nine on Saturday and consisted of interviews with interesting people. Except when there was a program the family wanted to hear, I would tune in to B.B.C. concerts. I liked shorter classics such as "Marche Slav" or "Pavane for a Dead Infanta", but I listened to longer pieces as well, even chamber music. I knew nothing then about different kinds of music and little enough now, but I knew what I liked and was willing to listen, even if the piece was not immediately attractive. I also liked the popular music of the day, of course, but found jazz less appealing. My long-suffering mother found chamber music a little too much, though. "I can't understand what you see in that closet music," she complained mildly. As with the public library, the B.B.C. was a blessing. Today, I have a wide choice of radio and television stations, both Canadian and American. Except for some specialty stations and the publicly-funded ones (which commercial interests would dearly love to strangle), they air too much rubbish.

For all its smoke and fog, I loved London as it was then. I loved its bustling streets and markets, its busy river, and the humour of its cheerful, quick-witted people. The trams, with whining electric motors, were fun to ride. So were the buses, especially if one had a front seat on top. Although they seemed underpowered and tilted alarmingly at corners on the steeper hills, they always got you home safely. Street-criers and vendors still abounded then – the muffin man with his handbell; the knife-grinder; the rag-and-bone man, his cart piled high with junk and drawn by a shaggy pony; and the Walls' Ice Cream man, with his tricycle and tinkling bell. (What an evocative song is Lionel Bart's "Who Will Buy?"! It is like hearing once more the voices of the dead.) With their horse-drawn carts, the milkman and the baker still called, as did the window-cleaner, the chimney sweep, the gas man for the pennies in the meter, and, yes, the rent man.

For a boy with tuppence burning a hole in his pocket, a visit to a tobacconist and confectioner's was a treat. There, amidst the aroma of pipe tobaccos, one could scan with mouth-watering anticipation row upon row of glass jars filled with sweets of all kinds – humbugs, acid drops, pear drops, Sharp's toffees, Pontefract cakes, Maynard's wine gums, Fox's Glacier Mints (Mum's favourite), Basset's liquorice all-sorts, Rowntree's fruit pastilles, and on and on.

Even an errand to a corner grocery could be a minor adventure. In contrast to the superstores of today, with their air-conditioning and piped music, each family shop had its own character and a variety of visual and olfactory experiences. One such shop, which I soon came to know better, was Cook's, next to *The Woodman* on The Slade. Built into the parlour and hallway of a terrace house, it had room inside for only three customers at a time. Others had to wait outside. This diminutive shop was crammed with a thousand-and-one items; and no matter how long you waited to be served there was plenty to look at, including little surprises tucked away in odd corners. Moreover, you could stand there savouring the smells – of paraffin, measured into whatever container the customer had; of cedar, from the small bundles of kindling stacked on the floor; of bacon, from flitches slung from hooks in the ceiling; of cheeses, cut from the round; of York ham, cut from the bone; of butter, cut from a block, weighed and patted into shape with wooden paddles; of teas, coffee beans, spices and goodness-knows-what-else that filled the dozens of little green drawers that lined the walls. Mr. Cook was tall and lean, not given to idle chatter, and the best his pale and rather melancholy face could manage was a faint half-smile. I never saw a Mrs. Cook or any younger Cooks. Perhaps they did not exist.

At the centre of this world, a world now largely gone forever, was the one who made my appreciation of it possible – my mother. My father worked and earned the means to keep us; but it was she who created the home, who made it a clean and loving refuge. At its heart was her unselfish love. At the time, of course, too often I took her for granted; but on those rare occasions when I came home from school or play and found she was out, I felt an emptiness in the house, regardless of who else was there. When she returned, life entered the house and it became home again. She *was* the home. Poverty is most unpleasant; but worse for children, for adults too, is the absence of love. I can understand women wishing to have careers, but I cannot understand those who feel that they must apologise for being "only" a housewife or home-maker. Of what consequence is a brilliant career or social life – for men too, for that matter – if the family is miserable?

As for Dad, I saw little of him, but I knew that he loved both Pauline and me. Though he rarely demonstrated affection, I recalled his gentleness at Goswell Road when he found me perched on the window sill, watching the storm. Now I was to have further proof of his love. One Saturday, while Mum and Pauline were gone shopping and I had the house to myself, I began playing a nasty game of tossing a penny into the air and swearing to kill myself if I failed to catch it. I soon stopped, for I knew it to be wrong. Besides, I had more than a suspicion that I wouldn't keep my oath. Suddenly, this gave me the idea of playing dead. No sooner thought than done – and I slid to the floor, face down, making myself seem limp and lifeless. At that moment I heard the front door open. Foolishly, instead of getting to my feet, I remained "dead". I heard someone enter, stop, and then come rushing over. Strong arms lifted my still limp body and a voice said brokenly, "Ah, my son…." It was my father. *Well, I thought, good old Dad! Who'd have believed he could enter into the spirit of the game so well?* Then I opened my eyes and laughed.

I didn't laugh long. Strange expressions were chasing across his face in swift succession. Then he went a deep red, dropped me with a thud, and rushed out. As he pounded up the stairs to his bedroom, taking them two at a time, it dawned on me that he hadn't been playing make-believe. *Blimey,* I thought, *he'll kill me.* With some trepidation, I sat to await his return. He came down about ten minutes later. Taking my face between his hands, he forced me to look into two steady grey eyes for longer than I would have wished. Then he spoke briefly and with finality: "Don't you ever, *ever,* do anything like that again!" No, indeed, and I felt suitably sheepish. But I have never forgotten the love and anguish I had heard in his voice that day. David, mourning for Absalom, may have expressed his grief with more poetry, but not with more feeling.

I was happy at home and my mind had enough to chew on, but nestlings become fledglings. I was beginning to chafe at physical restraints. I had the commons to roam and Bostall Woods, it's true; but they were mere patches of greenery surrounded by buildings, and the presence of keepers made me feel I was there on sufferance. Half consciously, I was becoming aware of a longing for the countryside, a longing teased, not satisfied, by long walks to Bexley and beyond. Over the next ten years it would develop into a hunger for mountains, for the swing of the sea, for wilderness.

Mum, Age 18, 1918   Dad, Age 18, 1914

Dad in France, c.1915   Dad in N. Ireland, 1941

Linda, R.N. 2006

My niece, Linda, 1966

Pauline, c. 1996

Our Mother, c. 1969

CHAPTER EIGHT

Evacuee

1
Distant Drums

After a short illness, in January of 1939 Nanna died. She was sixty-three. As she lay in her coffin, I could only stare at her dumbly, the silence and stillness of death an enormity beyond my understanding. Hers had been a quiet life, with much work and little play. Though most of it had been spent in the shadow of a rather sour, dominating husband, she had kept her sweet nature to the end. Her memorial was the love of her children and grandchildren and the gap her passing left in our lives. Her death affected us in another way. A few weeks after the funeral, the four of us moved into Grandpa's house on Plumstead Common. He would continue to pay the rent and in return my mother would care for him and provide his meals. It was an agreement that suited all – except for the fact that Dad and Grandpa detested each other. However, each kept the peace by the simple expedient of ignoring the other's existence.

By the time of our move, Dad must have worked his way out of debt, for with my thirteenth birthday came a pair of roller skates and soon I was trundling uncertainly but happily over the pebbly pavement. It was then that girls entered my life. More accurately, it was one girl, sister of a classmate but a year older. She was cycling regally around Wynn's Common when I first saw her and the vision dazzled me and set my pre-pubescent heart thumping. Of course, I didn't dare talk to her. Content to worship this goddess from afar, I would detour past her house on my way to the library in the hope that she might look out and see what a fine fellow I was. Puppy love may occasion a condescending adult smile, but it can be intensely felt, nonetheless. This was a curious but bright exception to my normal relationship with the opposite sex, for I had ignored girls before and was to ignore them afterwards – until I was about nineteen, that is. I had too many other interests. After 1939 I was to see her once more, twenty-five years later, when I spotted her walking along The Slade. Although she was then thirty-nine, I recognized her instantly.

About the time of the Munich Crisis, Dad joined the Territorial Army and began attending regular parades at his local depot, near *The Star* on Plumstead Common. He was forty-three and a married man with two young children. As conscription was not introduced until 1939, and then for men aged from eighteen to forty-one, I can only suppose that he had joined from motives of his own. It is not difficult to guess that they were a combination of boredom and a nostalgia for the cameraderie of army life. Whether or not, in spite of Chamberlain's scrap of paper, he sensed the inevitability of war I don't know. In any case, one consequence was that he was required to attend training camps in 1939. I accompanied him to two of them. The first was held near Okehampton, Devonshire, where Mum and I gorged on clotted cream while the troops manoevred on the moors. One day, Dad took me to a pub with some of his mates and allowed me to join them in a glass of local rough cider. After a sip, they grimaced and left their drinks unfinished; but I, not willing to waste anything and wishing to impress, determinedly finished my half pint. Pride was rewarded. I felt horribly sick for hours afterwards. Fortunately, it did not put me off drinking for life. When the time came to leave, Mum returned by train; but I was privileged to go with Dad, riding in the back of one of the convoy transports and feeling myself one of the troops.

The second camp, held somewhere on the Downs, proved even more fun. Here I messed with the troops, shared one of their bell tents, and lined up with them for morning inspection behind our neatly folded bedding and kit – although my kit, a battered suitcase and a butterfly net, rather spoilt the uniformity. Needless to say, I was not allowed to join in the manoeuvres. Instead, I spent the days chasing butterflies, hoping to net a rare specimen or two for my cousin's collection. While the men trained for battle, I played touch with butterflies! It was a portent of the future. I was not to know that the cresting tidal wave of war, whose approach even now was touching our lives and whose desolation already was afflicting millions, would wash me into quiet backwaters and bring the happiest years of my life.

ॐ

2

Encounter with the Church

Between these unlooked-for holidays, my cousin Peter and I had joined a boys' club run by Father Cox of the Church of the Ascension. Our clubhouse, grandly named Ascension Hall, was a small wooden building on the corner of Wynn's Common, only yards from the gas streetlamp around which the 53A buses turned before retracing their route from London. Here we played ping-pong and billiards and did a little boxing, all of which I enjoyed. One evening I was matched with a young Mohammed Ali. Although no boxer, I was spirited enough and normally landed my share of punches, but I couldn't put a glove on this boy. In contrast, he could hit me whenever he wished, which was depressingly often. Also, as a special treat, Father Cox would sometimes entertain us with ghost stories, while we sat on the floor with our mouths open. These were a great hit.

Of course, the club was not operated just to entertain us and keep us out of mischief. There were our souls to consider. Soon I found myself being instructed in the catechism and attending church; and one day, in fear and trembling, I presented myself for my first, and only, confession.

"Bless me, Father, for I have sinned."

"What sins have you committed, my son?"

I steeled myself. "I have played about with those parts of my body I shouldn't play about with." *Whew! That was the hard one.* "I've not always been as willing to help my mum as I ought to be." There was a long pause.

"Yes, my son?"

"I have not always told the truth." *That was safe enough. I must have told some lies. Now what? What other sins are there? I must have committed dozens.* But imagination failed me. Obviously my education had been badly neglected. "I can't think of anything else, Father." Of course not. I was far too young to know what has taken me many years to realize: that there is only one sin – not loving enough. From that one failing all others come, like foul things breeding in a stagnant pool. After receiving absolution and penance, I left the church light of heart and foot.

One day, Father Cox called at the house and introduced himself to my mother. Fortunately, Dad wasn't in. He was not fond of priests and ministers, an animus no doubt resulting from his service in France, where padres held officer rank, were seldom seen near the Front and were much more likely to inspect the men's feet than to wash them.[7] He had, however, a surrogate – my little white dog, who growled and clamped her teeth on Father Cox's cassock, perhaps confused by a man wearing skirts. With a black patch covering one ear and a skewed excuse for a tail, poor Smutsie had been bought for sixpence down and tuppence a week. I had thought her a fox terrier puppy, but her pedigree proved doubtful, for in the year that I had her she refused to grow an inch. She disappeared shortly thereafter – not for the attack on Father Cox, but because there was no place for her at Grandpa's, especially as I had been away

---

[7]   Padres were banned from the Front. Many, usually Catholics, ignored the ban, but most did not. See Michael Moynihan, ed., *God on Our Side: The British Padres in World War I*, Secker and Warburg, London, 1983.

so often and was not there to give her runs on the common. And so she was sold, cheap. Now, *there* was a sin I had forgotten: I had not really looked after her as I had promised! However, there was to be compensation for her coming loss. Father Cox's call was not merely a social one. He had come to suggest I attend a camp during the summer holidays. And so, together with Peter and hundreds of other boys, in the latter half of August I found myself enjoying my third holiday, at a Church of England camp in Ashdown Forest.

How had this encounter with the Church affected me? The boys' club was fun, and I liked Father Cox. As for the Sunday service, I was impressed by the ceremonial – the procession, the swinging censer, the prayers in Latin, the celebration of holy Communion, the robes of the officiants, the sound of organ and choir – and I loved singing the hymns, or most of them. Yet when I knelt to pray or recite the creed amidst the smell of furniture polish and incense, I felt nothing – nothing, that is, except a vague unease because I was not sure that I meant what I was saying or that I even understood it. Each of us is drawn to God in his own way, I suppose, and my way has proved not to be through the Church. I state that as a fact – not with pride, but with a sense of loss.

☽☾

3
"You're a lucky little girl."

On September 1, 1939, the great evacuation began. Knowing war to be imminent and fearing immediate air raids, perhaps even gas attacks, the British government set in motion its long-prepared plans. Like many thousands of other children, my sister was taken from her school to a railway station, whence, labelled and carrying her rucksack and black-snouted gas mask, she was taken with her schoolmates and teachers to the safety of the countryside. She wept bitterly at having to leave home yet again, this time without even her brother, but her safety took priority over feelings and leave she did. She was ten years old. A few hours later she found herself in Boughton Monchelsea, a quiet hamlet on the North Downs some five miles from Maidstone. In this idyllic setting she found herself plunged into a child's nightmare more suited to the world of *Oliver Twist*. Years later, Pauline described the experience for me:

Carrying my rucksack with my rubber sheet, I assembled with the other children in the village hall. After a while, we were split into groups and taken around the village. Now and then my lot was halted before a house and there made to parade like animals at a market while the woman of the house made her choice. "Don't want a girl," one woman said, looking at me. "They're too much of a nuisance." If anyone looked as if she might choose me, she quickly changed her mind when the billeting officer said, "This one's a bed-wetter, I'm afraid."

When it became clear no one wanted to take me, I was returned to the hall and there left on my own. Some time later, two men entered. "That was a good job," said one. "We got rid of those kids quickly." It seems I was not only the last in my group, but also the last one in the school! When the other motioned to where I was sitting, quietly hugging my rucksack, he added, "Why hasn't she gone?"

"Well, she's a difficult one. She's got a rubber sheet – wets the bed." They were discussing me quite loudly, as if they thought I was too young or stupid to understand.

"Oh I see," said the first. "Just a minute." Then he dashed out and in no time at all he was back. He had found a place for me with an elderly couple only a few doors away.

The house, as I recall, was tiny, smaller than Grandpa's. When you entered it, you stepped right into the living-room, where a flight of stairs led to the second floor. The kitchen was at the back of the house and the lavatory in the yard. The old couple, both into their seventies, had the front bedroom, while an equally elderly brother slept at the back. The house felt damp and smelt of tomatoes and cucumbers.

"You're a lucky little girl," the old lady told me. "It's not easy to find a home for someone like you."

I didn't feel very lucky when I found I had to share her bed. Oh God, instead of my lovely, sweet-smelling mother, I had to sleep

121

with a grey-headed old witch who had long whiskers growing from her chin. As for her husband, he had been booted out to sleep in the other room with her brother. Because she didn't want me wetting the bed, she would nudge me from time to time during the night and make me use the chamber pot. Several times, when her niece visited her and stayed the night, I had to sleep under the window. The floor was hard and it was draughty.

One Sunday, on our regular visit to the cemetery, I whistled as I helped her tend a grave. When she told me sharply to keep quiet, I cried out, "I hate this place and I want to see my mum." Of course, I was told that I was an ungrateful little girl. That night I wrote to Mum, telling her how miserable I was and that I wanted to come home, but the old lady found my discarded rough draft. A couple of days later, I found my things packed and I was taken away.

Out of the frying pan.... The next place was worse, terrible in fact. When I was taken in, I could see that it must once have been an old beerhouse, for I found myself in a large room that was paved with cobblestones and had a double trapdoor to a cellar. I remember seeing little else there, except for a cooker and, in one corner, a small stone sink with a single tap. At the rear of this sort of indoor courtyard, a doorway led to a dark and dismal room which was furnished with a table, a couple of wooden chairs and a bed. This was where the woman of the house lived with her child.

I was taken upstairs to a rear bedroom, and there I was left with some other evacuees – a Plumstead woman and her two children, a girl of about six and a boy of about three.

"You're a lucky girl," said Plumstead, as her kids ran all over the room in their wellington boots, jumping on the wooden chairs and the bed as well. "You will have a whole room to yourself. Do you want to see it?"

"Yes, please," I answered. I noticed that she didn't try to stop her kids from trampling the bed.

I could see that no effort had been spared in preparing my welcome. My bedroom floor, like the stairs, consisted of bare boards. Hanging from a nail by the one small window was a dirty towel, and in one corner of the room was a camp bed on which lay a coarse sackcloth palliasse. There was nothing else – no pillow, sheets or blankets. I looked at this emptiness for awhile, and then I quavered, "But what will I put on me at night?" Meanwhile, her brood had charged in and had begun to trample all over my bed too. They were followed by a kitten and a dog with sores. Both, as I soon discovered, were walking flea-colonies.

"Throw your coat over you," the woman replied, as if this were quite normal. When I mentioned that I wet the bed and that I was afraid of going out into the yard in the dark to take a pee, she disappeared downstairs. "Here, piddle in this," she said when she got back. It was a battered enamel wash-basin. Ah, the comforts of home!

That night was bloody hell. I never got up to use the wash-basin, as I could hear mice or rats gnawing away and scampering about all over the floor. And so I wet the bed instead, as I did nearly every night. At six the following morning, she sent her kids in to wake me up. I had to wash them and myself in the sink downstairs and then make their porridge for breakfast. After that I was free to go to school. At noon, I didn't come back to the house. Instead, I had a cooked lunch at the school. This was just as well, for about all I ever got in the evening was a cup of tea and some broken biscuits, bought cheap. That was the pattern for the days that followed, except that on the second night I was sick all over my coat. I did my best to sponge it clean, but I was only a little girl of ten.

As the days passed, I began to stink of urine and vomit; after all, I had not had a bath or a shampoo since leaving home. My hair grew unkempt and was crawling with lice. My clothes were no better, for nothing was ever washed. As for my nighties, they had been piddled on and dried so often that they had all the colours of an oily rainbow. No one seemed to notice my condition at school; and no one, neither teacher nor billeting officer, ever called to see how I was being cared for.

This purgatory seemed to go on forever. In fact it lasted a little over two weeks. Then rescue arrived at the door in the person of Mum. She had received a letter from me, requesting sheets and blankets. She thought this odd enough; but when she read it again, she realised that, although the handwriting was mine, the words were not. The letter had of course been written by my kind hostess and I had been persuaded to copy it. Now highly suspicious, Mum at once decided to come down and see what was going on. Grandpa came too, because Dad had already gone into the Army.

When I saw her, I burst into tears and threw myself into her arms. She told me long afterwards that she could hardly bear to hold me, as I stank so much. She was even more horrified when she saw the conditions I had been living in. Right away she got in touch with the billeting officer and demanded I be moved at once. To Grandpa she said, "If my son is living like this, I'll take them both back to London, war or no bloody war."

The woman of the house was in tears when the billeting officer came to fetch me – but not because she was sorry to see me go.

We must feel a certain sympathy for the elderly trio at the first billet. In their situation, it would not have been easy for them to make a small girl happy, even had they been kinder. Nonetheless, there is a touch of Pumblechook about the old lady. As for the energetic duo at the second billet, they seem to have deserved each other. They remind us that poverty existed in the country as well as in the cities, but that it is not solely responsible for slums. Some people can turn a mansion into a slum, and they are not necessarily ill-educated, poverty-stricken peasants either. One of the dirtiest houses I have visited – cat urine and faeces all over a gritty kitchen floor, a week's accumulation of unwashed dishes filling a reeking sink and piled upon a filthy counter, an overflowing garbage pail – was a detached residence belonging to a married couple, both well-paid university professors! In contrast, one sees photographs of African children sent to school with shining faces and snowy linen in spite of living in a ramshackle township with no power or running water. Like crime, slums do not come from poverty alone.

Pauline's unhappy experience does not cast a favourable light on her teachers or the billeting authorities; but, to be fair, one must concede that both were under considerable pressure to accomplish a great deal in a short time. In any event, Pauline's third billet seemed like paradise after the others:

> My next billet was the home of Mrs. Startup. When I was taken there, I found a hot bath waiting for me and I was scrubbed from head to foot. Then I was dressed cleanly and given tea: bread and jam and a delicious Dundee cake, with pretty yellow cups and dishes all laid out on a beautiful white tablecloth. Instead of telling me how lucky I was, she told me that I was the little girl she had always wanted! She was a wonderful woman. Mr. Startup was a kindly man, too. Though they had two young boys of their own, they looked after me well. I was happy there.

And there Pauline stayed for nearly a year. Mum and Grandpa came to check on me as well. She looked at my scruffy appearance and then at my billet, which seemed almost buried in bushes and trees. It was a red-brick house, about three-quarters the size of Grandpa's, with four rooms but neither power nor running water.

"Are you all right, darling?" she asked anxiously. "Are you happy where you are?" When I replied that I was, she looked doubtful. "Are you sure?"

Wondering why she was worried, for I knew nothing of my sister's experience, I reassured her, "I really am, Mum. Honest." Unfortunately for Pauline, perhaps, for it meant neither of us would be taken home, I considered myself to be on my fourth holiday of the year. In fact, I was having the time of my life!

◉✜◉

4

The Garden

When the air raid sirens first sounded in London, fortunately a false alarm, I was still at camp in the Ashdown Forest, near East Grinstead. I remember little of it now, except that some boys spent a lot of time hunting snakes and that it was there I played my first game of golf. Golfers might be interested to learn that we were equipped with one club and one ball each, that our course was a farmer's field, with rough fairways and non-existent greens, but that in compensation the holes were of sensible size – half-barrels sunk into the ground, in fact.

Two incidents at camp created a minor stir. One Sunday, amid a clatter of overturned chairs, I performed a spectacular faint during Holy Communion. Peter, and perhaps some of the other boys, thought at first that I'd been struck dead by an irate God. A rather more interesting incident was the beating of a boy for writing rude words on the side of the swimming pool. Like crows attacking a fledgling, two priests struggled to belt him as he fought back and shouted obscenities. I didn't know priests could be so physical!

The news that war had been declared set us all chattering. Now that *was* different! War might be exciting. We had as much idea of war, of course, as lambs have of the slaughterhouse. Told our stay was to be extended until new arrangements were made, we were delighted. Gosh, things were happening already! About ten days later, I said good-bye to Peter and climbed into a car with another boy. We were being taken to Kent.

The road from Maidstone to Staplehurst runs over the North Downs and down onto the Weald. On this final slope lies the village of Linton. Our car descended through this village, turned right into a narrow road at the foot of the hill, and there we were left at the house of the local billeting officer. We had reached our destination. As its name suggests, the flat, low-lying Weald was once a great forest, the haunt of outlaws, and travellers feared to cross it. But it has long since become a region of farms and orchards so productive that it is has been called the Garden of England. I was in real country at last.

Evacuee
Linton
Autumn, 1939

"The school is full," she said.
   Then, businesslike, no time for niceties,
"The couple we have placed you with
    work on the farm, and so must you."
And so I did – but I
   found work a holiday.

The house, two up
   two down of weathered brick,
stood beside a lane that wound
   through orchards and a woodland rise;
   and like the trees that crowded close,
it, too, seemed rooted in the earth,
   with pluming grass and wildflowers round.
We drew water from a mossy well
and lit our nights with burnished lamps,
   and the hiss of their burning seemed to me
   the breath of the house.

Oh, at one bound
I was translated from a world of grey,
   of dusty pavement,
   soot-blackened brick
   and endless chimney pots,
to one where colour was new born;
and the tread of feet, the din of traffic
were but a dream, fading, then lost
in the ever-new chorale of birds
– the thrush's song,
   sweet blackbird's carolling,
   the skylark's gloria, and
   laconic caw of rooks.

The way to work passed sun-kissed banks
  where grasses jostled for the light with flowers
  – campions, red and white, and yarrow,
    yellow hawkbit, and pink mallows -
all courted by sun-dusted bees
  and by the powdered butterflies,
  those antic cavaliers of flight;

through orchards then,
  where gnarled retainers clad in green
  bowed low with offerings of fruit
  – sweet Worcesters and Victoria plums;
and then beside a rushy stream,
  where beetles dived with silvered legs,
  and minnows swam, and sticklebacks,
  beneath their strange half-silvered sky;
  there, linking worlds with perfect rings,
  pondskaters danced on silvered feet,
  while dragonflies flashed overhead
  like living jewels with silver wings;

over at last a bridge of planks
  and down green-shaded earthen aisles,
  hung, as for harvest festival, with bines
  whose fragrant incense never cloyed.
And there,
  midst cheerful East-End banter,
I worked, if work it could be called,
  stripping the bines with
  nimble fingers
  and watching the hops and
  pennies mount.

At sunfall, home before the rooks
for supper and the wireless;
  and then a quiet read in bed,
- or else a venture in the night
  to share the moon and glowworm light

with hooting owls and cricket choirs,
to watch the bats' erratic flight
and stare in silence at the stars.

And so day followed shining day.
Far off, a nightmare had invaded time;
while here,
I slipped into eternity a spell
for harvest-home in Eden.

I was not alone. The other boy shared the billet and we stripped hops into a shared bin. But we lived in different worlds. In the evenings and on Sundays I would walk the lanes on my own with a spring in my step, often with the *March of the Little Lead Soldiers* running through my mind, for I had my own Sony Walkman long before it was invented. It mattered little to me that our foster parents were cold and our lives spartan. I knew nothing of what was happening elsewhere. While my sister endured her lice and Warsaw died to the strains of a Chopin polonaise, I had become acquainted with joy for the first time.

Not everything in the garden was perfect. When my companion and I managed to catch colds, we were given some camphorated oil to rub on our chests and backs. We considered this a lark, and in the giggling process of helping each other managed to deposit an oily handprint on the bedroom wallpaper. This brought down on us the wrath of our foster parents. A tedious inquisition was held as to who was responsible – as if it had been done intentionally. We were then coldly informed that any repetition of our behaviour would result in expulsion. The young couple looked after us well enough and made sure we had a bath once a week. With both of them working, coping with a pair of frisky boys must have been trying at best. However, there was a distance in their treatment of us, a lack of real human contact. Far from feeling part of the family, we knew we were there on sufferance. In consequence, I cannot even remember their names, though I am grateful now for their care.

Also, my companion and I eventually had a falling-out. Why,

I don't know – perhaps I had been teasing. He shortly told me to stop, or he would punch my nose. "And you know I can do it, too," he added. I did know, as he was none other than the young Mohammed Ali who had outboxed me with such insulting ease at the club. The threat, made seriously, was unfortunate. Not having the instincts of a toady, I felt that now we could not be friends. I reacted by treating him thereafter with cool respect but dismissed him from my mind. We would doubtless not have become friends anyway. I was living too intensely with my inner experiences for that. Curiously, I cannot recall his name, either.

There was also the question of books. As nights were drawing in, I needed something to occupy my mind. There were but two books in the house, and I was allowed to borrow one – Zane Grey's *Riders of the Purple Sage*. Of course, I galloped through it and wanted more. The problem was solved with my very first earnings – a munificent sum of about sixteen shillings, earned from the bushels of hops I had picked. Having been advised to buy a pair of rubber wellingtons, one Saturday I took a bus to Maidstone and seized the chance to visit a book shop. There I discovered pulp westerns. "Buy two of those," said the dealer, "bring them back when you've read them, and you can have two more for the price of one." How resist a bargain like that? And so, for the remainder of my stay at Linton, I devoured cowboy stories for tuppence a week plus bus fare. My favourite author, I recall, rejoiced in the name of Harry F. Olmstead. I always read his stories first.

During this time I was not completely cut off from family. There had been Mum's visit. Then, when she sent me Pauline's address, one Sunday I walked over the Downs to visit her, for Boughton was only a couple of miles away. Pauline's billet stood in a hollow, overlooking a pond with ducks swimming. It was quite large, a farmhouse I thought, but really it consisted of two cottages combined into one. On entering, I found myself in a clean, airy living-room with a cheerful fire blazing in the hearth. Mrs. Startup, a warm and friendly woman, made me feel at home instantly. It would be pleasant to record that I gave Pauline a hug and a kiss, but I did nothing of the kind. I may have fought for her a couple of times, but at that age I would have gone to the dentist rather than kiss her. Over tea and cake, we chatted for a time to satisfy ourselves that the other was all right; then I returned to Linton.

One sunny morning Mum and Dad arrived in a taxi and took us to Maidstone, where we had lunch and some shandy in a pleasant garden behind a pub. Dad had been given leave. Both looked younger. Dad was uniformed as a sergeant in the Royal Artillery, while Mum had turned herself into a blonde! Afterwards, we visited the zoo. This proved a disappointment. I remember only two enclosures now. The first was a dirt pound where dingoes trotted restlessly to and fro beside a fence. Their water trough, I saw, contained only dust. The next was a large brick shed. Inside this dim prison, with one hind leg chained to an iron stake, a solitary elephant was swinging its trunk and swaying from one foot to the other – the kind of unceasing movement sometimes performed by the mentally ill. The animal was bored half to death. Pauline and I glanced at one another, both upset, while Mum was audibly outraged. From this moment, born out of compassion and shame, grew my aversion to animal acts and zoos. In spite of the shadow cast by this unthinking cruelty, our family reunion, brief as it was, was a happy one.

As that glorious autumn wore into October, the leaves began to turn. The hop harvest was in, and the pickers, cheerful East-enders mostly, had gone home. As for my fellow evacuee, he had gone too. Instead of doing piecework, I now worked on a variety of jobs for fourpence-ha'penny an hour. Picking apples was a delight. Amidst the leaves and branches, I felt almost part of the tree. I was less sure about leading a horse up and down a field while men loaded his cart with sacks of potatoes. "Watch old George don't step on yer feet, now," a man warned. Suspecting old George of malicious intent, I at first held his halter at arm's length, but I soon saw he was both docile and guileless.

The first intimation that farmwork was not all fun came early on a chilly morning, when my hands grew slimy from pulling onions and the bones began to ache. Harvesting cob nuts was tiresome too. Ordered to pick them from the ground, not off the bushes, I had to work bent from the waist, as the nuts were too scattered to make squatting worthwhile. After a few hours of this, I began to understand why older farm workers were knotted and bent. Then the weather turned. I awoke one morning to find dark clouds scudding low and wind-driven rain lashing the trees. *Crikey*, I thought, *I'll get soaked*. But farmers have plenty of work reserved for bad weather. Taken to an earthen cellar beneath a barn, I was ordered to sort seed potatoes, a task that involved going through dozens of wooden trays to ensure the potatoes had their eyes uppermost. And there, with rain bucketing down, I spent the day with the mice and spiders, relishing the earthy smell and now and then peering out at the sodden farmyard, where a few bedraggled hens lacked sense enough to stay inside. Like a hobbit in his hole, I was content.

☙

5

Marden

"We had to leave you there," remarked the driver, as he turned the little Austin onto the Staplehurst road, "because there were no billets left where the school is evacuated." He looked at me. "I hope you didn't think you were forgotten." My driver, tall and grey-haired, was a teacher from Plumstead Central School.

"No, sir," I answered. Well, that was true. I had been so wrapped up in my new life that I hadn't thought about the school at all. "Where are we going, sir?" I asked. "Is it far?"

"Ah," he said, "There is a minor difficulty. There were too many of us for one village and so we had to split the school between two. The boys' school is at Staplehurst and the girls' at Marden." Looking at me again, he added, "You're going to Marden. It's not far away." *To the girls' school?* My face must have mirrored my dismay, for he laughed, "It's all right. You'll find other boys there. There's no more room at Staplehurst, you see."

Pondering my fate, I stared out the window. Orchards had given way to more open country dominated by oast houses, but the hop fields were empty of all but the poles. Summer was long gone, the harvest was in, and the yellow and russet leaves were drifting to earth. I, too, was returning to earth

– only to find myself surrounded by females at a time when I lacked all interest in them.

After taking a right fork, we soon afterwards crossed over some railway lines and parked. "Here we are," he said. "I'll take you to your new billet." Grabbing my case and gas mask, I followed him through a gate and along a cinder track by the railway lines. Before us stretched a short row of terrace houses, each no larger than the one I had left. A small sign announced, "Railway Cottages". Stopping before Number 6, my guide knocked at the door, which was promptly opened by a slight woman in her forties. She had evidently been watching for us by the window. "Mrs. Obbard?" he enquired, removing his hat. I had been delivered to what was to be my home for the next nine months.

We were at the table, enjoying a well-cooked Sunday dinner. Observing my eye on him, Mr. Obbard paused as he was about to take another mouthful. Then he pulled a face at me and with mock scorn jeered, "Yah, Plumstead!" "Yah, Chequers!" I shot back, entering into the spirit of the game. At this, Mrs. Obbard and Bob, their son, almost choked with laughter. My riposte, made instantly and unthinkingly, had found its mark. Like my father, Mr. Obbard enjoyed his pint or two, though I never saw him drunk or surly; and of course *The Chequers* was his favourite pub. Putting his knife and fork down, he stared at me for a moment, his eyes a little bloodshot. Then, satisfied there had been no malice on my part, he grunted and resumed his dinner.

I had become one of the family, the junior one, for Bob was four years older than I. Initially, he had resented sharing his bedroom with a stranger and on the first night had subjected me to a long, unpleasant monologue, the substance of which was that I was not wanted. I heard him out in silence for awhile and then said quietly, "I'm not listening to you any more, Bob. It's no use going on, because I'm putting my fingers in my ears." He left me alone after that. Although he soon found I wasn't a nuisance, we did not become friends. The age gap was too wide and we had little in common.

Mr. Obbard was a railwayman and walked with the easy grace

of one long used to physical labour. A tolerant man, he always had a ready smile and a bantering word for me, although he could hardly be called talkative. His eyes were his outstanding physical feature. They were cornflower blue and usually abrim with secret amusement. I liked him. Like Dad, he was rarely at home.

Mrs. Obbard came to be like a second mother to me. Possessed of a slightly sallow complexion, she hung her head slightly and pursed her rather thin lips as though she were sulking or disapproving. I soon found this not to be the case. Her characteristic expression stemmed in fact from shyness and masked a warm-hearted, generous nature. As the nights drew in, we spent a lot of time together in the evenings, for Bob and her husband often went out after tea. While she sat knitting, we would listen to the wireless or she would regale me with stories of her childhood. Once more, books disappeared from my life; and as I had to have something to do in addition to homework, I took up knitting. I began by copying some of the girls and braided wool through a cotton-reel. When Mrs. Obbard saw this, she suggested I learn to knit properly, and soon the two of us sat knitting together. She was very patient when I made a snarl of things. Eventually, I knitted two scarves, one for myself and one for Mum as a Christmas present.

It was a cold winter. At one time we were cut off by snowdrifts several feet deep. Apart from frozen pipes, this caused little hardship, as most locals walked to work and the railways were soon running again. The cessation of road traffic also made little difference. Save for the odd bus, farm vehicle or doctor on his rounds, the roads were mostly empty anyway – a factor which made the war years a fine time for hiking or cycling. As the only snow I had seen before had been in London, where rare falls soon turned to slush, I found the winter landscape magical and happily ploughed through the snow in my wellies, although it seemed almost sinful to ruin the pure line of a snowdrift by trampling on it.

The war seemed remote. Apart from exciting news about the Battle of the River Plate and the rescue of British seamen from the *Altmark*, little seemed to be happening. This was the so-called Phoney War, with "patrol activity" on the Western Front and leaflet raids on Germany. We heard little of Poland, and broadcasts about the Winter War in Finland were vague. The silly songs we sang, "Run, Rabbit, Run" and "Hang Out the Washing on the Siegfried Line", perhaps suited the time. The only thing I recall of Christmas, 1939, is a quotation read by the King in his Christmas Day broadcast:

> I said to the man who stood at the Gate of the Year, "Give me a light that I may tread safely into the unknown."
>
> And he replied, "Go out into the darkness and put your hand into the hand of God. That shall be to you better than light, and safer than a known way."

Like many others then, I found the words moving, and they became engraved on my memory. I also remember part of another speech from that first year of the war – the one made by Chamberlain in April, when that unhappy old gentleman claimed that Mr. Hitler had "missed the bus."

My school, or rather the girls' half, was in the Memorial Hall, a short walk past the church and *The Chequers*. To my relief, I found other boys there, including former classmates. As for the girls, I ignored them. Why, I don't know. It wasn't as if I were pre-occupied with other interests as at other times. On the contrary, my mind seems to have gone into hibernation, for I had nothing to read and school provided little challenge. Instead, I concentrated on outgrowing my old uniform until I felt ridiculous. Fortunately, the headmaster preserved my dignity by finding another jacket for me. Considering that I had been smitten by "love" only the year before, my attitude to girls was odd. Several of them told me one day that a local girl was "sweet on me." I was outraged. What cheek! I even stopped the unfortunate girl in the street and ticked her off. Later I was told she was thrilled I had spoken to her. Perhaps my rebuke had been a little incoherent. Let's say I was going through a phase, one in which girls were an irrelevance.

My attitude did not pass unnoticed. While fighting a boy in the school yard one day, I became unnerved by the behaviour of the girls, who milled around us in a ring, screeching encouragement – all, as far as I could tell, in support of my opponent. And many screamed very specific instructions as to where to kick me. I usually got on well enough with schoolfellows or at worst was ignored by them. Now I had to endure widespread unpopularity. Those around me at the time had need of much patience, I fear. In contrast, one boy fell in love with a different girl almost every week. We could tell his latest fancy by the way they played netball – passing and re-passing the ball between them and all the while grinning at each other like apes. It was sickening.

School made little impression on me. All the science teachers being with the boys' school in Staplehurst, I found myself taking typing and bookkeeping instead of physics. As it happened, my ability to type has proved most useful. In English, I felt the first stirring of interest in poetry. I especially liked some of the Elizabethan lyrics.

With spring came mobility in the form of a bicycle that Mrs. Obbard borrowed for me. A heavy antique that shimmied alarmingly at speed and once pitched me off onto my face, it nonetheless enabled me to explore the countryside. One expedition, to pick primroses with Mrs. Obbard, reminded me of Banstead. And another, to an arboretum with the headmaster, brought me my first sight of a rhododendron tree in full bloom. Standing before the astounding glory of its pink blosson, I felt like Moses before the burning bush.

֍

6

War Comes Closer

May brought endless blue skies – and a brutal end to the Phoney War. Reports about the campaign in Norway had been confusing enough, but event now crowded event in bewildering succession. In Holland, German parachutists were dropping from the sky disguised as nuns, it was said. Rotterdam had been bombed. The Germans had invaded Belgium and our troops were advancing to meet them. Terrified refugees jamming the roads were being strafed unmercifully by German planes. It all seemed remote, almost unreal. Listening to the voices of B.B.C. announcers, who would soon begin identifying themselves by name, even I became aware that something was wrong. And my father was over there!

Hearing a stir outside, I looked out. Neighbours were talking together excitedly and pointing. Other people were hurrying towards the station. A train was standing there, one of many that had been shuttling back and forth for days. The Dunkirk evacuation was under way. Galloping onto the platform, I found the train crammed with weary soldiers – French poilus in blue-grey and British troops in baggy khaki battledress. I decided to practice my French. "Bonjour, m'sieur," I said politely to a young French soldier. He looked tired and needed a shave. "Comment vous portez-vous?" The French we were taught was somewhat formal.

He smiled, "Je suis fatigué." When I looked puzzled, the word not being familiar to me, he placed his palms together against his cheek.

Fatigued – of course! "Ah, oui. Vous êtes fatigué." Running out of conversation, I stood there grinning at him.

"Hey, son!" A haggard Tommy was beckoning from an adjoining compartment. "Would you post this for me?"

I looked at what he handed me. It was a buff card with an address on one side and printed statements on the other, one of which he had ticked. "What is it?" I asked. "Does it need a stamp?"

"It's a field card. You don't need a stamp. Just put it into a letter-box." Seeing me hesitate, he explained, "It's to let my family know I'm safe."

"Yes, all right," I said. "What was it like over there?"

He looked at me sombrely. How explain the reality to an innocent? "Bloody awful. We've one man dead here and two without their legs."

Several more handed me field cards. Well, *there* was something I could do – and I passed along the train calling for them until I had a wad inches thick. The way the Post Office operated then, I should imagine most of the cards were delivered the next morning.

When I arrived on the platform, only a few villagers had been there. But more had been appearing all the time, and soon the platform buzzed with chatter and activity. Housewives hurried up with plates of cake and hastily-cut sandwiches. Some brought glasses and a jug of lemonade. The dairyman trundled a milk churn onto the platform, and the baker came by with trays of cakes and buns. It was all spontaneous, and only a few of the troops received refreshments in the time the train was there; but after what they had been put through, the peace of the English countryside and the welcome of the villagers were no doubt refreshment enough.

It was as close as I came to the catastrophic events of that spring. My father had been far too close for comfort. In the scramble to escape encircling panzers, he had guided his battery through the chaos in Lille, as he remembered it well from the first War.[8] Upon reaching Dunkirk, he had been made guard commander at a bridge with orders to prevent vehicles crossing and cluttering up the town. It was feared they would attract dive bombers. But the Stukas came anyway. "I was there three days," he told Mum, "and I was sure I had been forgotten. Then I was relieved and allowed to take my place in the embarkation lines." Perhaps he had been on one of the trains that had passed through Marden. Upon his return, he had been posted to Conway, North Wales, and Mum had joined him. In the meantime, while the war receded from us, France was enduring the agony of defeat.

In late July, as I was ambling across a field enjoying a glorious summer day, a dozen pneumatic drills suddenly opened up behind me. Startled, I turned – to see a Spitfire apparently leap from the ground and roar off in a steep climbing turn. It had appeared from behind a low rise less than a mile away, but what it had been firing at I didn't see. The Battle of Britain had begun, although as yet most of the action was over the Channel. At Linton, I'd had a strong feeling that I would see nothing of the war, not a German soldier nor a German aircraft. It would prove to be true. In the first week of August, as the Luftwaffe was about to shift its attack to the airfields of Fighter Command

---

[8]   While Dad was in France during the Great War, his father died. He lost his mother while he was in France in World War II. Two retreats in France and the two deaths of his parents – he must have had a sense of déjà vu!

and turn the skies of Kent into a battleground, I found myself packed, labelled and deposited with my sister into the maroon carriage of an LMS train. "Don't forget," said the teacher. "You have to change at Crewe and Llandudno Junction." We were on our way to Conway to rejoin our mother.

PART TWO

The Hills of Youth

1940 – 1944

Chapter 9 Conway   143

Chapter 10 Of Books, Mountains and Stars   175

CHAPTER NINE

Conway

1
Reunion

Brakes squealing, the train slowed to a halt with a great sigh of steam. A loudspeaker crackled into life: "This is Llandudno Junction Station. The train arrived on Platform Two is for Deganwy and Llandudno. Will passengers for Conway, Penmaenmawr, Llanfairfechan and Bangor please board the train on Platform One." What strange names! The enunciation was clear but the intonation alien, musical. "Come on, Pauline," I said. "This is where we change." Clasping her hand, I led her over a footbridge to where our next train stood waiting. There were only two carriages, but we found an empty compartment and settled down comfortably. Doors slammed, a whistle shrilled and our train began to glide slowly ahead, clattering over the points. Suddenly the view opened up and I could see a river, small craft at their moorings, mountains – then a tunnel swallowed us, though a hollow metallic sound immediately proclaimed it a bridge. Emerging by a high stone wall – at the foot of the castle, I found later – we soon drew into a little station.

There was no sign, of course, because of fears of invasion, but an announcement soon put us out of doubt. We had reached our destination. Leaning out the window, I peered anxiously at a handful of people on the platform. We had not seen Mum for almost a year. *Has she still got blonde hair?* Then someone waved and I heard a familiar musical cry, "Phi-il!" It was her!

Emerging from the station, we found ourselves in a square with shops, a police station and the inevitable cenotaph. Conway seemed a quiet little town, with few people and less traffic. But we were not to see much of it yet. Turning uphill, we passed through an archway in the town's medieval wall and before long, chattering away happily, we were walking past Bodlondeb Gardens. It was a warm afternoon at the height of the holiday season, with the sun shining from a cloudless sky. Only there were no holidaymakers – at least, none I could see. At the foot of a hill, we crossed over by a diminutive shop, Dougherty's, and then continued past a union workhouse. Where the road veered under a railway bridge we turned off and before long arrived at what was to be our home for the next few years, 1 Mona Road. Clad in dirty grey stucco, it was a small council house on an estate with dozens of others, all identical; but it had three bedrooms and a bathroom upstairs. An indoor toilet, a real bath, hot running water? After years of living in Victorian brick houses with none of these amenities, I considered it the height of luxury.

"Where's Dad, Mum?" I asked. After a tour of the house and the garden we were at table in the kitchen, having our first meal together – a little ham, fresh salad, potatoes, a plateful of bread and margarine and a steaming pot of tea.

"I'm afraid your father's not here, dear. He's been posted."

That was a disappointment! I had hoped we would all be together again, at least for a while. But I soon recovered. "Is this our house, now?" I asked, and then added, "Do we have to share with anyone?"

"No, dear. It's all ours." She smiled, watching me to see my reaction.

"You mean we have all of it to ourselves, just the three of us?" I persisted, incredulous. When she nodded, Pauline and I glanced at one another. What happiness! Then we set to and demolished the meal. I was eager to explore my new surroundings.

So began the happiest time of my life – a period of four years during which most of Europe and the Far East endured misery, suffering and horror on an unparalleled scale. Peace in the eye of the hurricane! Like a plant, transplanted and well-watered, I grew vigorously – not only physically, but mentally too. If at Marden my brain had lain fallow while I outgrew my clothes, now I became aware, probably for the first time, that I had a mind. Having endured nine bookless months, I hastened to join the Conway public library and, soon afterwards, the Llandudno library as well. I grew in confidence. By the age of sixteen, I had read over a hundred books, left school, been fully employed for a year and become a cadet corporal in the Air Training Corps – the highest rank I ever achieved in uniform.

By the time I was seventeen, I sometimes felt that I could do anything, that if only I had the power I could solve mankind's problems in no time. It was then that I took it upon myself to write to Churchill, advising him on post-War policy. By 1943, of course, after three years of being on the receiving end of a brutal boot, we were clearly on the winning side. As Britain was crowded, and suspecting the Empire would not last indefinitely, I suggested that the government sponsor large-scale emigration to the Dominions and provide free medical attention and family allowances to increase the birth rate at home. One could say that I wanted to ensure *lebensraum* for the master race! Oh well, at least I never suggested stud farms for the Brigade of Guards. As I read the letter now, from a draft faithfully kept by my mother, I cringe – as no doubt I shall similarly regret writing this book. Still, if we feared overmuch to appear foolish, we wouldn't set one foot before the other. We have to make do with what means we have, no matter how modest.

Needless to say, my advice was not taken, although I did get a polite letter of thanks from a secretary. What else could be expected from someone brought up on Kipling, Biggles and "Land of Hope and Glory"? What if I had been brought up on the Teutonic legends and Wagner? Romance can be a dangerous thing. It may sound as if I were a bumptious little ass, full of himself. I probably was. Nevertheless, although as self-conscious as most adolescents, I was not full of myself so much as of my inner experiences. I don't think I particularly wanted to make an impression on anyone. I didn't need to. I was supremely confident and concerned only with *being*. Today, I can smile at the puppy who flexed his strength, which was little enough, and who was so sure of his knowledge and understanding, which were miniscule. As I write this sixty years or so later, my strength is less and my knowledge little more. As for mankind's problems, I cannot solve my own. I am certainly humbler – and so perhaps a little wiser.

The main reason for this blossoming was not the reading of a few books but the security of a loving family, despite the separations. There was another reason. Upon my arriving in Wales I fell in love again, this time not with a lilywhite girl on a bicycle but with something immensely larger and rougher. I fell in love with mountains. They became my passion and filled me "with the joy of elevated thoughts". These two loves would give me "life and food for future years". And when the time came when I needed support, they gave me strength to endure the unendurable, to stand when I felt my life to be in ruins and could sense the abyss yawning beneath my feet. Perhaps because I do not like the man too much, I can look back on the boy with some affection. He was spirited, courageous, eager to learn, even though, to use my mother's words, he could be a "tormenting little sod." He was like the son my wife and I would have loved, but were destined never to have. As for the youth, he was emerging from childhood like a butterfly from its chrysalis – not a fine Swallowtail, perhaps, but at least a Small White. He flexed his wings and rejoiced in his meagre strength, his growing awareness of the world and his new-found freedom. He was romantic, high-minded and full of illusions. I cannot mock him or condemn his ignorance. "Innocence" would perhaps be a better word.

◈

2

Conway Mountain

As we walked to the Morfa that first day, my eyes had been drawn
to Conway Mountain – or Mynydd y Dref, a name I thought more
romantic until I learned that it merely meant "Town Mountain".
Viewed from Bodlondeb, it rises from woods like a broad grassy
ridge, clad in bracken and heather and with a distinctive rock
tower beneath its highest point. From the Morfa it appears more
impressive and rises steeply above the coastal road with an
overhanging precipice at its eastern end. From there to Penmaen-
bach, a secondary summit, it is some two miles long and a mere
809 feet at its highest point. It is hardly a mountain but a low hill,
the last slight rise and fall before Snowdonia meets the sea. But to
me, who had seen only Shooters Hill, it was a mountain.

From the coastal road a few minutes' scramble brings you to
the top and a magnificent view of the Conway estuary. However,
the easiest access is by the broad footpath on the southern flank.
Merely an energetic walk, it is the best way to approach the
mountain for the first time. Then, when you leave the path for the
skyline ridge, the view to the north comes as a dramatic surprise.
The feeling of openness and height is greater than might be
expected. The first thing to attract the eye is Great Orme's Head,
three miles across the estuary. Not as high as Conway Mountain
but more massive, this is the great limestone promontory that
rises above Llandudno and juts out to sea. Immediately beneath
your feet are Conway Sands, extensive enough at low tide for
half a dozen football games, and the Morfa, a sandy area with a
fine golf course and, during the war years, an army camp and a
council estate. On the far side of the river, Deganwy lies at the
foot of a small hill where once stood a castle; and, beyond that,
Little Orme's Head marks the far end of Llandudno Bay.

Upstream, the river widens to tidal flats. Here, where small
craft lie at moorings, a causeway and bridges carry road and
railway across the river to Conway, a walled town huddled beneath
the ruined battlements of Edward I's grim military fortress.
Southward the view is equally fine. The woods and pastures of
Conway Valley are to the left; and to the right is Penmaenmawr

Mountain, its summit scarred by a rock quarry. Directly ahead, the ground slopes down to Sychnant Pass before climbing again to Tal y Fan, a mountain that rises like a great green wave about to overwhelm Conway.

Today, many feet tread Conway Mountain, in the tourist season anyway. But in the fall of 1940 it seemed my personal domain. Pauline claims that I insisted on climbing it even before our salad that first day. I shouldn't be surprised. Over the next weeks it was a rare day when I wasn't on the mountain, usually sharing it with only the sheep and the jackdaws. I was with my family, school was out, and I had a new love. Joy entered my life again and once more my heart began to sing. And when the heart sings, the mind demands music, too, and the body walks with a spring in its step, or runs, dances. Music, like an odour, is often associated with experiences, usually happy ones. Fortunately, except for psychologically scarring traumas, the others tend to fade from the mind. But happy experiences live on to be cherished all our lives, sometimes to be evoked vividly years later by an unexpected whiff of fragrance or few bars of melody. On the rare occasions when I hear "The Music Goes Round and Round", I am taken back to that magical Open Sesame in the library at Skinner Street. A whiff of hops or a few bars from "March of the Little Lead Soldiers" – and I am at Linton once more and feel the spring return to my step. One cannot summon up such feelings at will. The music, the odour – or the taste, if one is like Proust – must be encountered by accident. Then, if it comes at all, the remembrance of things past comes unbidden.

And music filled my mind. A visit to the Conway cinema impressed me with the beauty of Deanna Durbin's voice, and for a few days "Love Is All" monopolized my mental gramophone. Happily, for that song is somewhat limited, Mozart, Jerome Kern and Cole Porter came to the rescue with the "Turkish March", "All the Things You Are" and "Begin the Beguine," music that was to accompany my exploration of Conway Mountain. I seldom whistled, hummed, or sang. That was too limited and, besides, I didn't want to alarm the sheep. Instead, my mind provided the full orchestra, sometimes fortissimo, sometimes very quietly, a hint in the background. In ensuing years the music changed, and there were times when the mind became altogether quiet and I seemed to hear the music of the mountains themselves, as some claim to have heard the Northern Lights or the Music of the Spheres.

So, like the spirit of the place, the *genius loci,* I haunted this, my first mountain. I dangled my feet by the side of the precipice; sat on a ledge watching wheeling jackdaws and envying them their freedom of flight; climbed the horn and inserted an old penny in a crack, where perhaps it is still; blessed the sheep for sharing their little paths with me, paths that followed the contours of the mountain and provided the foot with the restful bliss of level lodgement; or just sat quietly on the sheep-nibbled turf, inhaling the fragrance of grass and heather and feeling at one with the mountain and nature. Then Tal y Fan beckoned. Before long, music, mountains and stars came together in harmony with my inmost being – and the universe seemed to smile.

ᏬᏝᎧ

3

I Mona Road

I suspect that 1 Mona Road became a house of ill repute in the minds of some of our neighbours, none of whom we got to know in the years we were there. Before leaving for Northern Ireland, Dad had asked some of his mates to watch out for his family. As a consequence, soldiers for a time became frequent visitors to the house, sometimes several coming at a time and bringing girl friends, wives. Rations being meagre and a sergeant's pay not generous, entertaining, if only for tea, could have strained our resources. However, the troops often came bearing gifts, usually little packets of sugar, butter or tea, though one winter day we received a load of coal, delivered gratis in an army lorry. None of this was official, of course, but in the time-honoured army tradition of scrounging. This attention flattered Mum immensely, and she kicked up her heels perhaps more than was good for her. But it was wartime, the soldiers were young, and the detested husband was far away. Besides, she was forty, peroxide mutton disguised as lamb, and not getting any younger. And so she was off to the pubs a couple of nights a week to enjoy a few drinks and a social whirl.

Sometimes the troops brought a few bottles of beer and enjoyed home entertainment; after all, they could go to a pub anytime. On a couple of occasions, we spent hours playing "spooks" with a pack of alphabet cards and an upturned glass. I thought it foolish at first, as we sat solemnly around the table, each with a finger on the glass; but when the glass began to move, I felt my hackles stir. "Hello, Friend, do you have a message for us?" Yes, there were messages – but they were in code, for they made little sense.

Another time, bored with pubs, perhaps, or broke, one of the soldiers remained with me instead of going off with the others. We chatted awhile, watching the houseflies zig-zagging around the light. "Damned flies," I said at last. "Look at them. Must be dozens." Rising to his feet, he snatched one in mid-flight. "Can you do that?" he asked, grinning. I could. Then, feeling a passion for the hunt, "Let's see how many we can catch," I suggested. And for the next hour or so we tormented the flies for a change, casting our prey into a bowl of water until by the time we tired of the chase we had dozens of soggy little corpses.

"What did you two get up to while we were out?" asked one of the girls later. "Pooh," she said when we told her, "little things please little minds." Her sharp eyes spotting one of the survivors, she made a sudden grab. "Look, easy!" She shook her fist vigorously and held it to my ear so I could hear the fly's frantic buzzing. Then, opening her fist slightly until the dazed fly appeared, struggling to get free, she mashed it slowly with her thumb.

Flies were not the only pests we had to contend with. We soon discovered that we also shared the house with wolf spiders, mice and cockroaches. We clouted the spiders with newspapers, boarded cats to take care of the mice, but never rid ourselves of the cockroaches. The first of us to enter the house after dark would reach gingerly into the living-room and flip the light switch. Immediately, there would be a rustling as cockroaches by the hundred scuttled for cover with amazing rapidity. Although we would all pile into the room and do a frantic tap-dance, we never managed to kill many. Fortunately, they emerged only in the dark and restricted their activities to the kitchen and living-room. One would think buildings could be designed to keep pests out. Still, even if they were, contractors are not noted for perfectionism. I have worked on construction – and noted the habit some have of cutting corners.

After a while, the stream of soldiers dried up, as one by one they were posted away. Their place was taken by refugees from the London Blitz and occasional lodgers. Mum continued to spend a few evenings a week in a pub, but this time to earn extra shillings as a barmaid. Was there any hanky-panky going on, carefree fornication? With two exceptions, I doubt it. Pauline and I were around most of the time, and she shared Mum's bed at night. If Mum got up to anything, she was very clever about it. The only soldier to put a foot wrong was a medical officer, who arrived one day in an ambulance to offer his services. As the services he had in mind were not the professional kind, he was sent away with a flea in his ear.

The first exception came in 1941 with the arrival of our first lodger, a woman in her late twenties who claimed to be an actress. With her coming, men appeared in the house again, civilians this time. One I recall was Bert, a dough-faced, humourless fellow with a permanent drip on his pointed nose. He took it upon himself one evening to lecture me on the need to get a trade – carpentry, plumbing, something useful. His advice was sensible enough, but at the time I could think of little else but mountains, books and "getting in on the war". Besides, I instinctively disliked him. As a result, I became cheeky and goaded him until he lost his temper. I don't think he liked me, either – not after that. A week or so later, as I lay in bed, reading late as usual, I heard a rhythmic twanging of bedsprings in the spare bedroom, which adjoined mine. Our lodger had sub-let half her bed for the night to a pudgy civil servant. At breakfast next morning the atmosphere was a little tense, but nothing was said. "I let men make love to me because I feel sorry for them," she afterwards explained to Mum. A little later our compassionate lodger disappeared, by request.

George, an ex-miner and postman from South Wales, was the other exception. He was batman to an officer on the permanent staff and appeared as a regular caller sometime in 1943. His battledress was not the usual shapeless sack but smartly tailored, with trouser creases sharp enough to whittle wood; and instead of regulation black boots he wore gleaming brown shoes. Of medium height with a wiry build, he had wavy ginger hair, grey eyes and a creased, weatherbeaten face that seemed to radiate geniality. I can still see him as he was then – smiling, wagging his head slightly from side to side as though preening himself, and talking in a resonant voice with a hint of a stammer. He had every reason to be pleased with himself, I suppose, although I did not know it then, for he and Mum had fallen in love. A few weeks after I joined the RAF, she wrote telling me that she and George had decided to live together. And that they did, common law, until his death nearly thirty-four years later. They could not have done more had they promised "to love and cherish till death do us part"!

☙☙

4

War Comes to Conway

During our first month or so in Conway, the Battle of Britain was raging over the south of England and the expectation of invasion was growing by the week. After making his celebrated speech about fighting the "Narzzies" on the beaches, in the towns, on the hills and all over the place, Churchill is said to have added, *sotto voce*, "And we shall hit them on the head with beer bottles, for that's all we have to fight them with." But that may be apocryphal. Most of us, ignorant of brutal reality, were filled with the "Dunkirk spirit". We were alone, with no more awkward allies to worry about, and if Hitler landed we would give him a black eye. Local Defence Volunteers, as "Dad's Army" was called then, drilled with sporting guns and pikes, and a joking rumour had it that Boy Scouts and old ladies were arming themselves with knives. When I received a letter from Mr. Bishop, my old headmaster, detailing the exciting times they were experiencing in Marden, with air battles overhead every day, I felt a twinge of regret that I was missing "all the fun".

152

Fortunately, thanks to the R.A.F. and the Navy, the fearsome pikes were never put to the test. Instead, we began to receive copies of our local London paper with casualty lists running to several columns. Entire families were being wiped out and sometimes, it seemed, whole streets. The London Blitz had begun. Although none of the London raids was apocalyptic like the later RAF raids on Hamburg and Dresden, they were unrelenting and went on night after night for months; and despite official reports of the cheerful endurance of Londoners, the nerves of some were becoming frayed. As a consequence, we began to receive temporary refugees. In October, Little Lil arrived with her two boys, John and Paul, and stayed for a few weeks. The boys did not improve our relations with the neighbours, I fear. With all the excitement of the Blitz, they had been allowed to run a little wild. Although I took them up Conway Mountain and tried to communicate some of my enthusiasm for climbing, they proved more interested in the disused quarry buildings and thereafter spent their days scavenging.

Their place was taken my another Plumstead family, a woman and her son Ray, a boy my own age. Occasionally, the husband came up for the weekend as well. They were pleasant enough, but they also contributed to our unpopularity by bringing their dog with them. "Scrap" was a Staffordshire bull terrier with massive jaws, a slavering leer and at times a powerful smell – the last, perhaps the last two, coming from a habit she had of rolling in things long dead. Though gentle and playful with us, she terrorized visitors, and more than once we had to rescue the postman. She was also vague as to our territory and one day treated me to the sight of a neighbour sprinting smartly up his own garden path with her snarling at his heels. With some satisfaction I noted that it was the father of an obnoxious little boy who had plagued me for weeks. He used to jeer and spit at me when I passed him in the street. Apart from an occasional glare, I suffered this in silence. He was only eleven and it was beneath my dignity to do anything else. But one day the little toad deliberately stuck a pin into Pauline. That was a mistake, for she was his own age and had none of my inhibitions. Taking off a shoe, she set about him like a Fury and knocked him nearly senseless. "I didn't want to hurt him," she told me, still seething, "I wanted to *kill* him!" He never bothered us after that. He got off lightly – Pauline might have used him as a trampoline.

Indirectly, Ray contributed to our unpopularity by bringing an air rifle with him, a powerful and accurate one. Tempted, I borrowed it to do some practice shooting from my bedroom window. My first victim was a thrush pecking for worms. After watching its feathery death agony with sick fascination, I aimed at another perched on the wall of a private house next door. One shot sent it toppling into the neighbour's garden. It was enough. Feeling suddenly ashamed, I put the gun down and returned to my mountain. From there our house was clearly visible. If Mum wanted me, she used to hang a tea towel on the line as a signal and I could be home within minutes. As I sat musing on what I had done, I saw the neighbours emerge and examine something by their wall. My crime had been discovered – and my cheeks burned.

Answering a knock at the door that evening, I found the neighbour standing there with a dead chicken cradled in his hands. "I want to speak to your mother, please." He was ashen-faced. "Your son," he accused when she appeared, "has been shooting my chickens from his bedroom window." He held up the corpse for her inspection then thrust it towards me. "Here", he said, pointing in evidence to a minute nick on its comb. Then he demanded ten shillings. Mum paid without demurral, while I stood by in silence. I hadn't shot at his chickens, of course. Mum knew that without my having to tell her, as we couldn't even see them from the window. And it wasn't a ricochet, for I had fired two shots and killed two birds. Yet I felt like a murderer. As for the chicken, we didn't even get to keep it! A pity – it would have made a fine stew.

So there was some justification for our unpopularity with the neighbours, I suppose. But these were only isolated incidents. We were not noisy or disruptive. Perhaps it was enough that we were strangers from the "big city" and so obviously enjoying life. I found later, after starting work, that the local people were almost invariably pleasant. I have happy memories of Conway and its people.

In the spring of 1941, while we were between refugees, Dad came home on embarkation leave and for two weeks we were a family again. I don't know how Mum felt about it, but I was happy. Naturally, I couldn't wait to tell him about my interest in mountains. Would he like to come with me one day? "Tal y Fan is a nice climb, Dad," I urged, adding, "Its not difficult and it's only ten miles there and back." How could he resist such a tempting offer? After a pause he nodded, "Hmph. All right." Not exactly enthusiastic – but he had agreed.

Sunday morning we were off – over Conway Mountain, across Sychnant Pass, and then up the long incline to Tal y Fan. After a while, we stopped for a breather. While Dad lighted a cigarette, I looked up to the summit. Another hour should see us there. I took in deep breaths of the sweet air. The morning had been cool, but the spring sun was now warm and lambs were skipping. I felt like skipping myself. "All right," Dad broke in. "This way." Snapped out of my reverie, I turned. He was pocketing his watch and pointing toward a farm track that led down into Conway Valley. "No, Dad," I said. "This is the way to the top." He shook his head, "No, this way." Then he started down. Of course, the watch! It was almost opening time. Half an hour later we were enjoying a glass of bitter in Henryd. With an unerring eye, he had located the nearest pub.

As we all sat together in the living-room the night before he was to return to his unit, I suddenly rushed out and wept. They were the last tears of my boyhood. As for my father, I would not see him again until after the War – and by then the family had broken up.

The sirens began to sound at the beginning of May, 1941. The London Blitz had become intermittent now, for the Luftwaffe had for some time been extending its favours to other towns. Although it had hit Liverpool several times already, now it had decided to give the city a thorough pasting. Some of the German bombers, if not all, found their way there by flying along the Welsh coast. At least, I think ease of navigation was the reason, as I doubt whether the bombers feared our flak or night fighters at that period of the war. And so every night for about a week we could hear their bombers flying overhead. Lying in bed listening to the throbbing of their unsynchronized engines, I felt a chill at the thought that the crews could rain down bombs at the touch of a button without my being able to do anything about it. But I also knew they would do no such thing.

Late Saturday night, having walked home from Llandudno as usual, I let myself in and then stopped in astonishment. The furniture in the living-room had been up-ended and piled around the table. My mother was standing there and soon heads popped out from under the table. Ray and his mother had returned for another respite.

"Hello," I said. "Playing tents?"

Mum spluttered, "There's been an air raid!"

I stood there, grinning. I could see there had been no damage.

"A bomb, they dropped a bomb!" She was almost shouting.

"Yes, I know. I heard it go off while I was in Llandudno. But that must have been two hours ago."

"It's all right for you to stand there like a fool with that silly grin on your face, but we might have been killed." She was becoming distinctly annoyed with me.

"Oh, well," I answered soothingly, "they're not likely to drop another. Obviously that one fell by accident. There's nothing here worth bombing."

So war came to Conway. It was to return indirectly in 1943, when part of the Mulberry Harbour was built on the Morfa, although we had no idea what it was then. The solitary bomb had come fairly close to our house, falling between the council estate and the mountain and narrowly missing a farmhouse. It was the only bomb to fall on that part of Wales during the entire War. Thereafter, Conway returned to peace. The rest of Britain soon enjoyed a breather, too, for Hitler now turned his attention to Russia. But that was to be a different war.

☙❧

5
I leave school...

"Condon, the headmaster wants you in his study. Run along now." *Now what?* I thought, hastily reviewing my behaviour as I ran along.

"Ah, yes, I did send for you," said Mr. Pierce-Jones when I

identified myself. "Let's see. You've just turned fifteen, haven't you?"

"Yes, sir."

"Well, the local Food Office informs me they need an office boy. Are you interested?" When I hesitated, he added, "You'll be leaving anyway in July, and there's little more we can teach you here."

Inspired by the Battle of Britain like myriads of other boys, I intended to join the RAF as soon as I was old enough, but I had given no thought as to what I should do in the meantime. I had to do something. "All right, sir," I decided.

"Good," he smiled. "Well, report there at nine in the morning." Then he leant over and shook my hand, "Good luck."

So, without fanfare, ended my formal schooling. I had attended Conway Central, my seventh school, for a little over four months.

What influence my schooldays had on me is difficult to assess. I have mentioned only a few memories of school, but all of them together don't amount to much. The truth is that the main influences came from outside – from family, from books and increasingly from music. This implies no criticism of either my schools or teachers. If my formal education was limited, it was the fault not of the schools but of the system, and of circumstances beyond the control of either. Banstead and those backstreet London schools served me well, instilling in me many of the habits, attitudes and values that make me what I am, and no doubt influencing me by many "nameless, unremembered acts Of kindness and of love".

Yet when I look back, with one possible exception I feel neutral about my schooldays – and having spent half my working life as a teacher I say this with a certain wry reluctance. Neither dreading nor liking it, I found school something to be tolerated because "getting an education is important". The one exception, of course, was Banstead. But that was not only a school but also a home, one which cared for me well, and the passion for wildflowers that I developed there colours my memory of it.

A curious aspect of my school days is that I formed no close ties with any of my fellows. I suppose the only close friends I had in my boyhood were my cousins, John and Peter, and I saw little enough of them. Although there were times when I longed for a brother, it would not be true to say that I was lonely. I was generally too caught up in my interests for that. Nor would it be true to say I was an isolate. True, at Marden I was unpopular with the girls, but I usually got on well with boys. Though diffident and not given to thrusting myself on others, I was approachable enough, certainly not standoffish. However, I was not a follower, not one to attach himself to another merely to have someone to hang around with. If there were "in" groups, far from seeking to join them, I was usually unaware of their existence. As for peer pressure or attempts at manipulation, if I detected either, I tended to be like the dog – he might be friendly, but he will quietly resist being pushed or pulled to where he does not wish to go.

In short, I'm an introvert, not a social animal, and have gone my own way largely unconscious of the effect I might have upon others. Later in life I was to form close friendships, even – though only after a struggle – to become married, but I have never had an active social life. Generally, friends accept my peculiarities with tolerant good humour. Only rarely has one shown justifiable impatience with my lack of sensitivity to the social graces. "Really," exclaimed an old friend one day, "for years I introduced him to some really lovely women, and he didn't even notice them!" That was news to me. Nonetheless, she was not quite right. I had noticed them, but had thought them fellow guests, not potential matches. I had wondered why one of them had seemed so irritated with me.

6
... join the work force...

After threading the needle of Telford's bridge, westbound traffic turned sharply to avoid the castle and then bore left into a small, irregular square with two side roads. To the right was Castle Street, Conway's main business centre, while to the left the other road dipped behind the castle and then continued up the Conway valley. On the corner of the latter road stood the town hall, a modest stone structure in the Gothic style with its entrance facing the bridge. Here, in the shadow of the castle, was housed the local branch of the Ministry of Food.

Our office occupied a lofty chamber with a public counter by the entrance and a large, arched window overlooking Castle Street at the other end. Much of the chamber was taken up by filing cabinets and a long table around which sat most of the staff, eight or so women clerks. To preserve the dignity of our superior, the Deputy Food Executive Officer, beneath the window a small corner office had been partitioned off with plywood. Between this office and the staffroom door stood three small tables, two for the typist and another for the office boy. At this humble work station I was to remain for almost three and a half years.

My pay was thirteen shillings a week, less than I had earned on the farm. Still, the hours were reasonable – nine to five, plus Saturday mornings. At first I was set to counting, sorting, rubber-stamping *(Do you think you could make a little less noise?)*, filing and water-boiling. Later I also did some typing *(Why didn't you tell us you could type?)* and other things.

Filing could be perplexing, as the main file, which contained a card for every person in the district, revealed that half the local population shared ten or so surnames. When the Crown forced its Welsh subjects to adopt surnames, no doubt to facilitate the collection of taxes, officials must have ground their teeth when they were faced with such a proliferation of John Joneses, Hugh Hugheses and William Williamses. If so, it bothered the Welsh not a whit. They simply continued with the old custom of identifying one another by place (Williams Ty Gwyn) or occupation (Jones the Fish) – a custom, along with patronymics,

159

that antedates surnames and of course is the origin of some of them.

Before long I was permitted to attend the public and deal with some of the simpler routines myself. Although the last thing one could expect from a Food Office was food, one such routine was the regular issue, free of charge, of a bottle of cod liver oil, orange juice or rose hip syrup to expectant mothers and mothers of young children. This was a practice that, together with the slender but balanced rations, no doubt helped make the wartime generation of children so healthy.

On the whole, meeting the public was a pleasant duty. Mostly the language used was English, although now and again someone would ask for a Welsh-speaking clerk. One day a minister came in who would speak nothing but Welsh to me. "You would think a minister would be able speak some English," I commented when he left. "After all, he is an educated man." "Oh, he can speak English all right," one of the women replied. "But he's a Welsh Nationalist and refuses to." I thought this a bit odd – not that a nationalist should feel so strongly, but that a minister should be a nationalist.

One group that none enjoyed serving was a family bombed out of Liverpool. Though not ragged or obviously dirty like the children I had seen outside Portsmouth dockyard, they brought with them an acrid body odour, and their ration books appeared to have been polished with black lead. I suspect they had something in common with Queen Isabella of Spain, who was rumoured to have had but three baths in her life – when she was born, when she was wed, and when she was laid out! But that may be an old English slander.

After buying my first bicycle on the HP[9], made possible because I was paid three and six extra a week for its use, I was often freed from my desk to run errands. In addition, I delivered "monthly returns" to every caterer, food retailer and confectioner in the district – which included Deganwy, Tywyn, and Llandudno Junction as well as Conway. These were packages of forms that had to be completed to keep the Ministry of Food happy. One such return, addressed Dickensian fashion to "The Master of the

---

[9]   Hire Purchase, as buying on credit was called then.

Workhouse", invariably brought into my mind the words of the traditional ditty:

'Twas Christmas Day in the Workhouse.

The day of all the year.

The paupers were eating their Christmas pud

And drinking their Christmas beer.

When in strode the Workhouse Master,

And echoing through the halls,

He wished them, "A merry Christmas!"

And the paupers shouted, "Balls!"

And wasn't there something about what he could do with his Christmas pudding?

This duty provided a day's outing and made me a familiar, albeit unwelcome, sight to the local business people. However, although my appearance meant hours of annoying paperwork for them, they were invariably kind and not one offered to kill the messenger. In general, I was content to be an office boy. If my duties were neither challenging nor well paid, at least they were varied enough to preclude boredom, and the hours left me ample time for outside interests. Moreover, I liked the people I worked with.

At this remove I remember only some of them now. The chief clerk was Mrs. Black, an attractive brunette in her late twenties or early thirties – as were Mrs. Jones and Mrs. Rees. Then there was Mrs. Parry, a kindly, grandmotherly woman, I thought, though she was probably only in her fifties. Perhaps the one I remember best was Miss Knepler, the typist, for we shared the same corner. A plump young woman with ginger hair and a fresh complexion, she spoke little and smiled less; but when she did speak, it was in a frank, matter-of-fact manner. I fear I must have tried her patience often. Office boys are an exceedingly low form of life. One who carried himself with assurance, who looked you in the eye and tended to speak as an equal, who chattily shared stale information as though he were the original discoverer – such a one must at times have been irritating, to say the least.

This tendency to share generously the treasures of my mind – an indication, surely, that I was born to become a teacher or else was born a fool – one day led me to drop a large-sized clanger. "Did you know," I asked, addressing fellow workers as they sat around the table smoking and sipping tea, "that Hore Belisha is a Jew?" This pearl, carelessly cast into a pause in staffroom chatter, created the desired effect – stunned astonishment that a Minister of the Crown should be so perfidious. Then one of the women raised a warning finger to her lips. "Shhh," she said, "Don't you know that Miss Knepler is Jewish?" This unexpected intelligence silenced me – effectively for a change – and as I sat there with my mouth open, no doubt looking extremely doltish, the chatter was resumed.

Doltish I may have appeared, but my mind had been spurred from plod to gallop. A question framed itself, *What is a Jew?* I scanned my memory. *Rebecca in* Ivanhoe, *or was it* The Talisman? *Shylock. Wait a minute – the Bible. Jews lived in the Holy Land. Foreigners. Christ was one – a Jew, that is. King of the Jews. Then what were they doing here, becoming typists, Ministers, speaking English like natives? Well, why not? Many foreigners settled in Britain. Guthrum and his damned Danes. William the Conk. (Poor old Harold!) Come to that, the English had been foreigners. Booted the Welsh into the mountains.* Here I glanced at my companions. *Then why did I ask such a stupid question?* But after much feverish rummaging, I was forced to give up. I really didn't know why! Then a picture forms:

I'm playing in Goswell Road with my friend Bert and other little boys. Then a boy I don't know sidles up to me and whispers, "Did you know that Bert's a Jew?" "No!" I exclaim, feigning shock and casting a look of suspicion in Bert's direction. I've no idea what a Jew is, but the boy's furtive manner has implanted a worm in my mind. Keeping this a secret – whatever it was – must mean only one thing, I think vaguely. Bert must belong to a kind of secret society, like those men who ran around in bedsheets and pointy hats. What are they called? Oh yes – the Ku Klux Klan. And there the picture fades.

Contemplating this preposterous residual maggot, I smiled to myself and then cast it from me. I still might not know exactly what a Jew was, but one thing was clear. If Miss Knepler was one, then there could be nothing much wrong with Jews. Not a scientific conclusion, perhaps, but nonetheless right. Mentally, I heaved a sigh of relief that she had not been in the staffroom to witness my stupidity. Though she never encouraged chat, she was kind and never talked down to me. Not for anything would I have wanted to hurt her. In fact all the women were kinder and more tolerant than I deserved, and only rarely did I get a rap over the knuckles.

It was not so with our male superior, Alderman A.T.S. Smith. With more than a passing resemblance to the actor John Le Mesurier, only larger and unsmiling, he walked with a heavy tread and habitually wore an expression of great weariness, as if he were ill or burdened with deep sorrow or crushing responsibilities. As his face had a yellowish cast to it, I incline to think that he was not well. In any case, for some reason he usually avoided even looking at me. And on those rare occasions when he had to notice me, he addressed me formally, sighing as if the effort added to his burden:

Mr. Smith:	Why were you not at work yesterday?
Me:	I didn't feel well, Mr. Smith.
Mr. Smith:	Ah, so you were sick?
Me:	Oh no. I was ill, sir.
Mr. Smith:	[*Testily*] Then you were sick!
Me:	No, I wasn't sick, sir. I just felt ill.

[*Sighing heavily, he turns away with an expression of suffering. Several of the women suppress grins.*]

At the time, I thought "being sick" just meant "vomiting".

After the first year, these rare exchanges often ended with the refrain, "You are more trouble than you are worth." As I knew I was doing my work competently and was rarely late or absent, far from being abashed by this I took it in the same spirit as I once had taken my father's threats to "kick my arse". Nevertheless, I was curious as to why Mr. Smith should feel this way. Surely it couldn't have been the smashed washbasin? Anyone can drop a kettle. Nor could it have been my lying about my age and volunteering for the RAF at the age of sixteen. That cost him only an exchange of letters. What of the solicitor I had angered, a large, elderly gentleman much respected for having hurled an insolent younger man down his office stairs? Sent to arrange an appointment with him for one of our women clerks, I had been subjected to a brusque cross-examination.

What was my name? Where was I from? When did I come here? Why? Where was I living now? What was the street number? At first I had thought him deaf and, while answering his questions, I kept repeating that the appointment was not for me but for Mrs. Jones. But he had ignored my increasingly loud explanations and continued to rap out questions. It was the last that moved me to say, "I can't see what all this has to do with Mrs. Jones's appointment." This mild objection had brought about an explosion of rage and some remarks that I considered somewhat rude. Perhaps he had complained about me. Could that have upset Mr. Smith?

Another explanation suggested itself later. One day, I found myself summoned with my mother to Bodlondeb, temporarily the townhall, there to present ourselves before the Food Executive Officer, Mr. Ralphs, who also happened to be the Town Clerk. A slender, birdlike man, he seemed tense and nervous. Hunching his narrow shoulders, he leant forward over his desk and directed his beak towards my mother. For some time he had been hearing complaints about me, he informed her. Hearing this, I felt my heart sink. But he hurried on without being more specific. It was a state of affairs that was not satisfactory and it really couldn't be allowed to continue. Here he looked at me. Surely, if I was not happy at the office, I might like to do something else? For example, work was available at the factory in Llandudno Junction and the pay was good. He would be glad to put in a word for me. In fact he could arrange for me to work there.

I don't know what Mum thought as he carried on in this vein, but I felt confused. The "complaints" I discounted. Other than Mr. Smith, who had little enough reason, I couldn't think of anyone who might want to complain about me. I was polite and cheerful enough with the public and local business people. Why was he trying to get me to leave?

At last, after Mum had exclaimed "Well, I don't know. I really don't know what to say" a number of times, while I merely stood looking at him, he became agitated. "You've no idea of the black looks I've been getting from some mothers because your son has that job," he complained, throwing up his hands. "They think the position should go to a local boy. It's making life very difficult." Ah, understanding dawned, although I was surprised that anyone should covet so menial a position. Then the dog in me asserted itself. No, I was perfectly happy at the office, I told him truthfully. As for the factory, I wasn't interested, nor in the extra money. And there I fell silent. If he wanted to get rid of me, he would have to sack me. But he had no cause. Rising from his chair and flapping his arms in the manner of Chaplin's *Gold Rush* chicken, he exclaimed, as much to himself as to us, "Well, I've done all I can. I can't do any more!" The interview was over. And an office boy I remained until the RAF decided that they wanted me.

❧

7

...make a friend and prepare to do my bit.

On Saturdays, my invariable routine after dinner was to catch a bus to Llandudno, there, if the weather was reasonable, to stroll along the seafront or wander about the Great Orme before dropping in at W.H. Smith's to gaze longingly at their selection of books. (Eventually, I even bought a few, the first hardcover setting me back two and thre'pence, new!) Then, after visiting the public library and the cinema, I would pick up some chips to fuel my return home. Despite the black-out, a five mile hike by way of Conway Road and Tywyn hill presented no problem, although I had to navigate darker winter nights by sensing the road with my feet and keeping my gaze fixed on the sky, where I could vaguely make out the tops of trees and buildings.

It was in a Llandudno cinema that on two successive Saturdays I had my last (I hope) encounter with a strange man. While watching the screen, hands in lap, I suddenly became aware that a finger had gone dead, for when I squeezed it there was absolutely no feeling. Glancing down in some alarm, I discovered that it wasn't mine at all but belonged to an old man in the next seat. He had managed to insert his forefinger furtively among mine without my noticing! I had a glimpse of a fleshless face, wattles, a nose like a hooked beak. Then, as if stung, I leapt to my feet and moved to another row. Later he approached again, and again I had to vacate my seat – rather like musical chairs in slow motion. What could he be up to?

Understandably, when I entered the cinema the following week, it was with antennae quivering. Would old "Thin Nose" be there? Yes, he would. In the half-empty cinema I had no difficulty spotting him several rows ahead, and thereafter kept one eye on the screen and the other on him. When he arose to leave during intermission, I covertly studied him. Wearing a long scarf and an open jacket reaching almost to the knee, he was round-shouldered and stooped, with a body like a baggy, overripe pear. He must have been at least seventy-five. Here he interrupted my musing by suddenly turning into my row. His antennae had been active, too! As he plodded towards me, I found myself looking into a raddled face, dull-eyed, expressionless. *Bloody old fool ought to be made to wear a bell,* I thought angrily. Then, my flesh crawling, I moved to another section. It was the last I saw of him.

This unpleasant interlude aside, I looked forward to my weekly visits to Llandudno. Normally, I am not fond of seaside resorts. The very term brings to mind vague childhood memories I prefer to forget: of acres of mostly unprepossessing flesh baking in the sun or goose-pimpling in a breeze (Let's have less of body and more of soul, say I!); of endless amusement arcades, pubs, ice cream parlours, fish and chip shops, cheap restaurants, and souvenir shops with lettered rock, unfunny postcards of fat women, and shoddy trinkets; of the funfair, with its lights, screams, shouts, rackety machinery – all dominated by the noise from the steam organ (Who misappropriated poor Calliope's name for that awful instrument?); of the smell of the "sea", which on closer analysis seemed compounded from fish and chips, toffee apples, sour beer, rotten seaweed and sewage. Not that I haven't at one time or other enjoyed some of these delights, but encountering them all at once is stupefying. Mass tourism eventually spoils the very amenities that attracted it in the first place.

Llandudno was not such a resort then, fortunately. (Nor is it, unless it has changed greatly since my last visit in the 'Seventies.) Though all the above amenities were there, they were not concentrated along the front but sprinkled around discreetly. Moreover, the funfair, banished to the less fashionable end of the promenade, was silent and rusting, and the acres of semi-nude bodies were absent from the beach. The promenade itself, fronted with clean-looking hotels, was spacious and dignified, as were most of the main streets in the downtown area. It was a resort more likely to appeal to, shall we say, the more staid members of society.

Shortly after starting at the Food Office I met Philip Noel Williams, whose parents ran *The Bluebell* on Castle Street. With mobile features and a ready laugh, he was much the same height and age as I, but looked older because of the moustache he was cultivating. As he, too, was an avid reader, we discovered that we had plenty to talk about and became friends. There were our names, of course. We agreed it would be idiotic to call each other "Phil"; and because neither fancied his second name, "Noel" and "Alf" were out. In a moment of inspiration I therefore called him "PN", and he reciprocated by dubbing me "The Colonel", although why I don't know.

When he could be spared from helping his father manhandle beer barrels, he often joined me on my Saturday excursions to Llandudno. To anyone who cared to look we must have presented quite a contrast. PN was heavy-set and marched with a purposeful, springy stride as if to a soundless drum, whereas I swung along loose-limbed fashion. With my physique it could be no other way. His company pleasantly shortened the walk home – too much, in fact, for our chatter, as he usually accompanied me to my garden gate for another half hour of it before turning back to Conway. "You were never noisy," said Mum years later, "but as I lay in bed I could hear you talking and laughing outside, though what you found to talk about all that time I can't imagine. And the squeaking as you swung that damned gate almost drove me mad." Typically, she never complained at the time.

As 1941 unwound its dismal train of military disasters, I gave some thought to readying myself for the RAF. This was going to be a long war and I wanted to play my part. The obvious first step, PN and I agreed, was to join the Air Training Corps, or air cadets. Accordingly, one evening we walked into a dusty wooden hall in Tywyn and there presented ourselves before a grizzled warrant officer. "What do you want to be, boys?" he asked as he took our names. "A pilot," I declared promptly. "That's right, lads," he said. "Aim high." Ah, but a boy's reach should exceed his grasp!

We found ourselves in a flight with about two dozen others, all local boys save for one refugee from the Nazi-occupied Channel Islands. Soon, decked out like the rest in smart uniforms, we were being initiated into that solemn male ballet known as parade-ground drill. This I liked, especially when we took part in public ceremonies and marched proudly through Georgia to bugle and drum – though I doubt whether any of us had heard of Sherman or knew where Georgia was. But we had little other instruction. True, we practised recognizing aircraft from silhouette cards and learned morse, but we had nothing on theory of flight and meteorology and only one lecture on navigation. This last was eventually given by a yachtsman, Mr. B. Lenthall, but the natives grew restive. It was too much like school and they began to chat. By then corporal, I admonished them mildly, meanwhile glaring at the sergeant, a leading culprit.

Because of this lack of interest, Mr. Lenthall gave no further lectures. Instead, he offered to provide tuition at his home for those who wished it. PN and I jumped at the chance and soon were learning how to determine courses by allowing for magnetic variation and wind drift. Before long, we were tackling problems in interception, something I never got around to in the RAF. Our mentor even outlined in general terms the principles of astral navigation, although we lacked the math skills for practice. Being fascinated with astronomy anyway, I decided to learn the major constellations and chief navigation stars. This I accomplished by plotting their positions on a planisphere, using co-ordinates taken from *Norrie's Nautical Tables*. Meanwhile, conscious of weakness in arithmetic, I worked through *Aircraft Mathematics*, a text for air cadets. There was no doubt about it – I was in grave danger of becoming a Keen Type.

Our commanding officer, pale and angular of face, was an elderly civil servant masquerading as a flight lieutenant. At least, that's how we viewed him at first. In fact, he was well on the right side of fifty, with medal ribbons and a military bearing that hinted at service in the Great War. His rare, laconic utterances, given in a husky, strangulated voice and often accompanied by a faint smile, suggested a diffident nature. As he generally kept to his office, leaving us in the hands of his second-in-command, he therefore tended to merge with the background. But there was more to him than we knew. As we strained and grunted through an exercise in rope-climbing one evening, the old man suddenly sauntered from his office, seized a rope and with insulting ease hauled himself up to the ceiling in the jackknife position. Then, as we stood boggling, he let himself down smoothly in the same manner and promptly vanished again. A veritable Spartan! After that exhibition, I suspected that the PT was his idea and that the smile was prompted not by diffidence but amusement.

Doubtless it was his idea to import the boxing gloves and have us flail away at one another. To my surprise, I won my bouts – a result due not to skill or strength but to style. Mindful of Dad's advice always to get the first one in as you might not have the chance later, instead of prancing about like Alec Guinness's Herbert Pocket, I would attack immediately with every intention of hitting, a tactic that disconcerted most of my opponents. However, it didn't work with the shortest boy. Having noted my style, he turned the tables by attacking first with such ferocity that he drove me from the hall altogether! Forced to give ground before this onslaught, I backed up until my heels caught the doorsill. "Hold it!" I cried, throwing arms wide in an effort to preserve my balance. But he was a little deaf and instead knocked me sprawling amidst a crash of overturned dustbins. He later threw in the towel, though, exhausted by his efforts, perhaps, or disheartened by the sight of a grinning Phoenix rising from the wreckage.

PN was not called upon to take part, which was just as well, for his confidence in the use of his mind was equalled only by his uncertainty in the use of his limbs. I was once foolish enough to entice him up the North Ridge of Tryfan, a climb far too easy to merit a rating. I say "foolish" because I had to help him over the drystone wall at the foot of Milestone Buttress and should have abandoned the climb there. Instead, we persisted. As a result, he got stuck on the one steep section that calls for the use of hands as well as feet. Casting his eyes wildly over a profusion of generous holds as if they were mere rugosities fit only for flies, he broke into a sweat. "I think...I don't think...I seem to be having a little difficulty," he gasped. There was nothing for it but to help him down, which I did by taking charge of his feet while he devoted his attention to his hands. It wasn't fear of heights that proved his undoing. It was having to give attention to all four limbs at once. Later he cheerfully accompanied me over Carnedds – but there he had only his feet to consider.

That his ability to box was also limited he had revealed during some friendly sparring. Standing square on and ignoring footwork, he had pumped out lefts and rights with metronomic regularity – a tactic both unique and useless, as the punches were designed not to hit but merely to keep danger at bay. The thought of him in the ring was too painful to contemplate. An opponent could almost whip out a cigarette and enjoy a smoke while waiting for him to exhaust himself!

My own lack of skill was made only too apparent by the arrival one evening of a boxing instructor, an older man who appeared disturbingly springy on his feet. "Right, lads," he said cheerfully, "who's going to be first?" We lads looked at one another – and then several turned to look at me. Rats! Resignedly pushing to the front, I pulled on the gloves. "Well, lad," he said, performing a shuffling dance and taking a defensive stance, "let's see what we can do." What we could do was to step forward, unleash a straight left, and land a jarring punch full on his nose – all in one smooth movement. Then, not having the killer instinct, we stood politely by as he snorted, shook his head and blinked away the tears. Now began the boxing lesson. Blocking our further punches, he proceeded to beat out the Anvil Chorus on our right ear until, growing bored, he moved in and did the the same for our ribs. At last, we patted his behind, the only part of his anatomy we could reach. The lesson was over. Oddly, there was no further instruction.

In the event, all this did nothing to prepare us for the RAF. As I discovered later, boxing was discouraged, among aircrew anyway. Let Commandos and the like knock one another silly. We, the Cream, were to be coddled. This ruling from Olympus came not out of tender concern for our persons, of course, but from the knowledge that one punch could send several thousand pounds' worth of training down the drain.

Our interest in boxing soon waned, and the problem of how to keep us occupied must have taxed our superiors considerably. The idea of putting on a variety show probably came from our flight commander, a pilot officer in a virgin uniform. A young farmer with a remarkably pretty wife and an even more desirable green MG, he was popular with us because he was outgoing and carried his authority lightly. Almost before we knew it, we were plunged into the exciting world of show business and found ourselves rehearsing humorous skits and warbling such stirring songs as "Coming in on a wing and a prayer". Later, with all the blithe courage of innocence we went on tour, with Corporal Condon as Master of Ceremonies – a well-merited reward for failing to rein in his tongue. The "tour", to a couple of RAF stations, with a grand finale at the Pier Pavilion in Llandudno, was moderately successful. The airmen, accustomed to superannuated ENSA artistes, were tolerant; while the Llandudno audience, inflated by the presence of numerous relatives, was almost convincingly enthusiastic.

Though some of the troops may have perceived it as unmerited punishment, our entertainment of them was in the nature of a "thank you" for their entertaining us. An unlooked-for bonus for joining the ATC was that we were entitled to another week's holiday, with pay, so that we could attend camp at an RAF station. Presumably, the idea was to give us some experience of service life and work us up into a lather of enthusiasm. Needless to say, we eagerly looked forward to this annual event, though I suspect harassed station personnel were rather less enthusiastic. What we hoped for, or what most hoped for, was a flight, of course, but the RAF had better things to do than provide joy rides to cadets. In fact at my first camp, RAF Llanbedr, set in idyllic country on the west coast of Wales, our presence was ignored totally, and we spent the week swimming and swearing.

The following year, RAF Hawarden proved more forthcoming. It was there I had my first flight – in a Link trainer. This early flight simulator, a boxy parody of an aircraft used for practicing instrument flying, had zero inherent stability, and flying it demanded the skills of a juggler on a high wire. The instructor began by demonstrating the use of stick and rudder. Easy. Biggles taught me that. Then he identified the instruments. "This one is the ASI, or airspeed indicator. This is the artificial horizon. For straight and level flight you must keep the image of the aircraft centred on the line and the wings parallel. Over here is the rate of climb or descent indicator, marked off in feet per minute. On the bottom are the altimeter, gyro compass and turn and bank indicator. You'll find that you will have to pay attention to all of them." Well, that's straightforward, I thought doubtfully, looking askance at the turn and bank indicator, which had one needle pointing up and the other down. As yet, all the instruments were reassuringly steady.

"Right, it's all yours." He dropped the cockpit canopy, sealing me off from the world. "Now," his voice resumed over the intercom, "let's try some straight and level flight." Then he switched the beast on. As soon as the instruments came alive, the artificial horizon tilted and assorted needles began to wander. Hastily, I attempted to centre the aircraft image. "Your wings are not level. Notice the turn and bank indicator. The needle shows you're sideslipping." Which one? I thought. There are two. "Now you have dropped the nose and are losing height. Pick it up." I did, overcorrected, and dropped a wing – and so porpoised and skidded through the imaginary air.

"All right," he said, when I had at last achieved a semblance of straight and level flight, "Let's try a gentle turn to port. Now, a little left aileron, a touch of left rudder and a slight pull back on the stick." I did my best to follow his directions and felt the beast tilt over with a sigh. All the needles were moving now, wagging admonitory fingers in different directions, and I could hear asthmatic little gasps, whether from me or the beast I wasn't sure. "No, you have too much bank and your nose is too high. Look at your ASI. You're losing speed. Any more and you could stall!" Desperately ignoring everything but the artificial horizon, I dropped the nose, took off some bank, and eventually managed to achieve a wavering, drunken sort of turn. I was beginning to sweat.

My tormentor's voice broke in again, "Straighten up when you come to a heading of 135 degrees." Thankfully, I resumed straight and level flight – and then felt a moment of panic. Something was wrong! The artificial horizon told me I was flying more or less straight, but my body told me I was turning to the right. Again that remorseless voice, "No, keep to the heading of 135. You may feel that you are turning the other way, but that's just your inner ear fooling you. You must trust the instruments. You can't fly by the seat of your pants here." Five minutes later I emerged from the hut feeling exhausted and chastened. Damn Biggles. He hadn't prepared me for that purgatory.

By the summer of 1944 I had been wearing my RAFVR badge for almost a year. Having volunteered for aircrew, this time without having to lie about my age, I'd been summoned to Chester, where I'd received a medical and had to write an essay. After an interview, I'd been sent on to RAF Padgate for testing. The result was the coveted badge.

My last camp was at RAF Valley, on the island of Anglesey. It was there that, browsing through copies of *Tee Emm*, a periodical training manual for aircrew, I became acquainted with the ineffable Pilot Officer Percy Prune. Like the good soldier Schweik, Bill Hooper's button-eyed creation is an embodiment of willingness and stupidity, a disaster with legs. There resemblance ends, for Schweik only pretends to be an idiot as a cunning aid to survival, whereas Prune is a natural clot – and an outrageous "line-shooter" to boot. Committing every sin known to pilots, he saunters away unharmed from one pranged aircraft after another and onto the pages of history as a winner of *The Most Highly Derogatory Order of the Irremovable Finger* (Motto: *Dieu et mon doigt*). In time his fame spread even to the Luftwaffe! His popularity with readers came, I suspect, from an amused recognition of their own "pruneries".

And it was there, at RAF Valley, that I had my first real flight. As I walked towards the aircraft, carrying my parachute, I saw with some disappointment that it was an old Avro Anson, a relic numbered among the cigarette cards of my boyhood! Still, a flight was a flight. Moreover, when a second pilot climbed into the passenger seat, I began to entertain the hope that this wouldn't be a mere "circuit and bump". It wasn't. Taking off, we climbed away from the airfield, with the co-pilot energetically winding up the undercarriage. Where were we off to? A trip around Snowdon, perhaps? Contentedly I relaxed, enjoying for the first time the sensation of flying. The air was a bit lumpy, perhaps, but that only made the sensation of flying more real. Hell of a lot better than a Link trainer, I thought. I hope a real aircraft is easier to fly than that.

"Is your harness good and tight?" The pilot was addressing me over his shoulder as he levelled out. Touched by his concern, I assured him that it was, but I gave the straps an extra tug to reassure myself. Suddenly, the earth tilted to an angle of about sixty degrees and began slowly to rotate. At the same time I felt my face sag and my assorted tripes begin earnestly to enquire of my sphincter as to the adequacy of its muscle tone. G-force, I recognized, deciding that I didn't enjoy the sensation at all. Just as I was beginning to feel concern for the well-being of my breakfast, we flipped over into a steep turn in the opposite direction, straightened out into a shallow dive and then zoomed upward, apparently headed for outer space. *He's not going to loop an Anson, surely?* But no – just at the point where my stomach caught up with me, we winged over in a stall turn and left it behind again as we plunged back to earth. There followed a fine exhibition of low flying among pastures and hills, with an occasional climbing turn over a hill and down into the next valley – turns so close to the hillside that I suspected the pilot of trying to goose the scattering sheep with his wingtip.

"Faithful Annie" rolled to a stop on the tarmac and her engines were switched off. Releasing his harness, the pilot turned and grinned at me. "Enjoy the flight?" Beneath his wings was a row of fruit salad. An experienced operational pilot! That exuberent display of flying had not been merely for my benefit. He had been letting off some of the steam generated by his duties as an instructor. "Yes thank you, sir," I replied politely. Well…perhaps that was an understatement. G-forces aside, I had found the experience exhilarating. Wot larks! And as the three of us walked away from the aircraft, I felt I belonged.

I was ready.

CHAPTER TEN

Of Books,
Mountains and Stars

1
Books: The Old "New Age"

Although a guideless, ill-educated lover of books can waste much time reading the second-rate, he may also find himself exploring curious byways. So it was with me. I was delighted by Dornford Yates and the lunatic world of Thorne Smith, and ghost stories continued to entertain me (Sheridan Le Fanu, Bram Stoker, Arthur Machen, M. R. James, for example), but I read mostly non-fiction now. From Dennis Wheatley's *The Devil Rides Out*, I learnt of Satanism and embarked on a reading binge through the occult: Eliphas Levi's *Transcendental Magic*, Madame Blavatsky's *Isis Unveiled*, Gurdieff, Steiner, numerology, witchcraft, poltergeists, ghosts – in short, every book I could lay my hands on of the kind that today crowds the shelves of "New Age" bookshops. But none fired my imagination or caused me to lose sleep. The only book to chill me was one on Jack the Ripper. This was no demon masquerading as a spider, or a white thing leaping through the woods at night, but a human being. For the first time I had glimpsed the sickness some people carry in their heads and found it disturbing.

Two books that fascinated me for a while were J. W. Dunne's *An Experiment with Time* and Oliver Fox's *Astral Projection.* Both were concerned with dreams, but for different reasons. Dunne recorded his for years because he suspected they might draw on future as well as past events. Could the mind be outside of time, with only the conscious mind being subject to the clock? The idea seemed preposterous. How could the mind, subconscious or otherwise, perceive something that has not yet happened? True, to make sense of the present we must not only remember the past but also anticipate the future; but that future is only a predicted one, and the accuracy decreases rapidly the further we try to see. Listening to a symphony for the first time, we might anticipate the next few bars, but not the next movement. So, to account for dream perception of the future, Dunne expounded a theory of time in a later book, *The Serial Universe.* But this left me no wiser. Time was stranger than I had supposed. Today, having been informed that time varies with speed and gravity and can cease to exist altogether, I am still at a loss. Time is odd. Like the universe.

Fox, on the other hand, used dreams as an aid to achieving out-of-body experiences. He called them "astral projections", a term fitting in nicely, I thought, with Madame Blavatsky's "astral plane". His method was to seize control of a lucid dream – a dream in which one knows one is dreaming – and then convert it into an astral projection. Simple. Finding the idea of flitting around in my astral body attractive, I decided to give it a try. But the "Aha, I'm dreaming" invariably relapsed into nonsense, and far from recording my dreams I soon wanted to forget them.

Many people claim to have had an out-of-body experience while asleep or under an anaesthetic. Patients who have undergone surgery have sometimes confounded operating room staff by afterwards describing their operation and repeating staff conversation. Such claims are not necessarily the work of crackpots or liars. The experiences are no doubt genuine. However, that does not prove the existence of astral bodies. The mind has powers that we do not normally notice. Even in the deepest sleep, part of the mind remains alert in order to keep the body functioning. A mother can sleep through thunderstorms yet awaken at the slightest cry from her baby. And the mind seems to have a built-in clock, allowing us to awaken at the regular time or even at a time of our choosing. We use alarm clocks for insurance.

Pigeons have a homing instinct. Dogs have been known to find their owners from hundreds of miles away – even when the owner has moved to a new town. Whatever the explanation, do we have similar powers? "Really, you men are afraid to ask someone for directions!" my sister has more than once exclaimed impatiently to me. Well, no. Unless time is a factor, I prefer to follow my nose. It's more fun that way and I usually get to where I want to go. In London one evening to see a particular picture but not knowing where the cinema was, I decided to leave it to my nose. From Charing Cross, I strolled in a northwesterly direction – Leicester Square, Soho ("No thanks, dear."), Oxford Street, Regent Street, apparently heading for Regent's Park and casually taking in sights on the way.

Suddenly, as if a switch had been thrown, the thought came, "Wait a minute. Aren't you looking for something?" Halting, I looked about me, consciously seeking the cinema for the first time. And there it was – on the other side of the street! As well as I could in that jumble of streets, I had made a bee-line for it, a place whose location I did not know, though I may have noticed it subconsciously, of course. Whatever the truth, this peculiar faculty seems to work only when I am afoot.

We have more than five senses. If we fail to notice the others it is because they are usually drowned by the vividness of the five. The "recognition" experiences I described earlier were real enough. So was the feeling I had on first meeting Jan. I felt as if I had known her for years and received the distinct intimation that she would become my wife, as in fact she did. Love at first sight? Not exactly. It was dark and she appeared only as a shadowy outline. We all notice that we can feel neutral, comfortable or uncomfortable in close proximity to a stranger. The feeling can be strong. I once encountered a young man who projected a wave of aggression so powerful that I felt it almost as a physical blow. "Bad vibes" in hip vernacular. We'd had no eye contact and his face was expressionless. That my feeling was not illusory he proved later when someone provoked him into a temper tantrum. Never before have I seen so sustained an outburst of rage and hatred.

This sense may have some bearing on the phenomenon of crowd behaviour – the hysteria of a crowd of young females, the violence of a mob of men. People in a crowd seem to feed on one another and behave in ways they would not normally dream of alone. For this reason, I prefer to avoid crowds, even friendly ones. And if I am part of one, I usually watch the crowd rather than the focus of its attention.

Places, too, can have a "feel" to them, an atmosphere. Twice, for no apparent reason, I have felt uncomfortable in a particular place, first in a castle tower in Wales and later in a dreary inn north of Inverness. On both occasions my companions were more disturbed than I. In the latter case there was no possibility of suggestion. My companions then were my sister and her family. The husband and I shared one room, and Pauline and her daughter the other. It was not until the next day that I learnt that Pauline had also felt uncomfortable and that her daughter, then nineteen, had been apprehensive enough to insist on sharing her bed. The atmosphere of the inn was not so much evil as unclean. An illusion? I don't know. The trouble with experiences of this kind is that they happen so rarely, to me at least, that before long one comes to doubt their reality.

Can we communicate telepathically? I doubt it, which is just as well, thank heaven. But we may do so at an unconscious level. One day I ran into an acquaintance whom I hadn't seen for years. "You've no idea who I saw downtown today," I remarked to my wife when I got home. "Bert", she replied instantly. As I stood there with my mouth open, her lips began to quiver with repressed laughter. "How on earth did you know that?" I finally spluttered. But she never answered me. I know why. She didn't know how. It may have been mere guesswork, as he had been a mutual acquaintance, but her answer had been too immediate to allow time for reflection. My wife often demonstrated a disconcerting ability to knock me off balance with the unexpected.

In any case, I have performed the same "trick" myself. I had arranged for a professor to deliver a lecture to our senior physics class on his advertised topic, "How many dimensions does the universe have?" On the day of his lecture, he was ushered into the classroom a few minutes after the bell. "I'm sorry I'm a little late," he apologized, after we had been introduced.

"That's all right, Professor," I reassured him. "While we were waiting, the class and I were discussing your topic. We decided that there had to be eleven dimensions." Was it my imagination, or did he start a little?

He delivered his lecture a little nervously, I thought. It proved highly abstruse, being concerned with the sequence of events during the early seconds of the Big Bang. Calculations evidently showed that the four dimensions of space-time were not enough to account for the sequence. More were required, some spiraling in on themselves like winkles. I doubt whether any of us made much sense of it.

The professor paused, then he said, "In the end, we concluded that for our model to work there had to be eleven dimensions."

It was my turn to start! The class and I had not discussed dimensions at all. I'd merely introduced the topic of cosmology and briefly described the "No Bang", "Big Bang" and "Bang-Bang" theories. My little pleasantry, intended to put him at his ease, had been made on the spur of the moment. In fact, when I began my statement, I'd had no idea how it was going to end. No wonder he had seemed nervous. He must have thought he was lecturing to a class of geniuses. It might have added to his confusion had I told him I was not the physics teacher but a teacher of English.

Come, you spirits that tend on mortal thoughts.
- Lady Macbeth

Finally, there is the matter of "spooks". Seated with me around the table were my mother, my sister and my mother-in-law, Kathy. The year was 1976 and my mother and sister were visiting me in British Columbia for the first time. Just returned from a motorhome tour of Banff and Jasper national parks, we were spending the last few days of their holiday with Kathy at her home in Victoria. It was

Pauline who suggested that we play "spooks". As we each placed a finger on the glass, I resigned myself to a rather tedious hour or two. I remembered the sessions in Conway so many years before. There the glass had sat motionless for minutes at a time; and when it did decide to move, it had done so hesitantly and spelt out gibberish.

But I was in for a surprise. The glass immediately began skittering around the table so fast that we had difficulty keeping our fingers in place! I could feel the force of it.

"Welcome, Friend. Do you have a message for us?" (A silly question. It would hardly say "no". Not polite, either. We should have asked "it" to introduce itself first.)

YES

"Who is the message for, Friend?"

KATHY

"Who is the message from?"

LES (Kathy's husband, who had died a few months previously.)

"What is the message, please?"

HE IS WORRIED BECAUSE YOU ARE DRINKING TOO MUCH

As one, we turned our heads to look at Kathy. "But it isn't true, it isn't true. I'm not!" she protested, her voice and face filled with dismay. "I don't, do I, Philip? she appealed. Hastening to reassure her, I suppressed a giggle. Whatever it was had a sense of humour. Les was the one who had been overfond of the bottle.

There was no message for my mother, but Pauline and I were targeted next. We each would soon meet someone and form a romantic attachment. Though we took these "messages" with a pinch of salt, we perked up a little – especially me, for I had been a widower for many years.

YOU MUST GET IN TOUCH WITH EDITH The glass was whirling around the table almost angrily.

"Why is that, Friend?" (Edith, then in Hawaii, was a close friend of Kathy's. Neither Pauline nor my mother knew of her.)

HER BROTHER PAUL HAS BEEN SERIOUSLY INJURED IN A CAR ACCIDENT IN THE STATES

After the crack about the drinking, we decided to take no action on this. It was just as well, for all the "messages" were false. They were not malicious so much as mischievous. Before the session ended, our messenger identified himself as "Harry" and claimed that he had been killed in a fall from the Matterhorn.

What staggered me was the energy with which the glass had moved. Moreover, the messages had been unhesitating and coherent. The usual explanation, that one or other of us had been subconsciously pushing the glass, seemed highly unlikely. A session the following evening perhaps provided a clue.

Again the glass began its dervish dance almost immediately. This time we began by asking it to identify itself.

JAN

Now everyone looked at me. But if they expected an emotional reaction they were disappointed. I felt cold, not with a supernatural chill but with anger. The thing lied. Had it been my wife I was sure I would have felt her presence. As a result, I resolved to set a test by asking it something only my wife and I knew. On the morning following our wedding night, Jan had accused me of flirting with the attractive blonde hostess at our honeymoon lodge. "What are you talking about?" I exclaimed, astonished. "I've only seen her once, and that was at the desk last night." "It's no use denying it," she replied. "I caught you red-handed. You were reeling in her trout." I gaped, uncomprehending. Then I noticed her lips quivering. She was doing it to me again! "Yes," she continued, controlling her lips with an effort, "I dreamt I was walking along the beach – and there you both were...."

"If you are my wife, what did you accuse me of on the morning following our wedding?" Carefully raising my finger a fraction so it only seemed in contact with the glass, I at the same time attempted to mask my mind – no great trick for one given to too much introspection. The glass remained still for a few seconds and then, hesitantly this time, spelled out

SOMETHING ABOUT A FISH

Not only was it not my wife, but it was rather stupid. Harry up to his tricks again? "Well, you're not my wife, are you," I stated. I paused, then asked, "What do you do on your side?"

181

No answer. I tried again. "Why do you attend these sessions?" The glass spelled out slowly

WE LIKE TO READ YOUR MINDS

While I have never been so sure of myself or the universe as to dismiss the paranormal or the supernatural out of hand, neither do I accord belief without evidence or personal experience of some kind. I prefer to keep an open mind. When one electron seems to know what another is doing, when physicists theorize about many dimensions and parallel universes and talk as if quoting from ancient Buddhist scriptures, when the more we learn about the universe the more wonderful it appears – then there seems at least a possibility for some psychic phenomena to be part of reality. In other words, some aspects of the "supernatural" may be a part of the natural order not yet understood.

This reading binge was not a waste of time. After all, a natural curiosity is healthy. However, although at first I thought I was "on to something", before long I realized it was only a byway. Apart from the experiments with "astral projection" and playing "spooks" – and I can recommend neither as a practice – I have never been tempted to dabble in the occult, certainly not in witchcraft or Satanism. The latter is dangerous, if only because it might lead to contact with unhealthy minds. Reading about the occult and paranormal revealed to me much to be taken on trust or authority but little for which there was evidence. Moreover, I found myself repelled by secrecy, by initiations, oaths, magic rituals, adepts, secret Orders, mysterious Great White Brotherhoods. It was like playing with shadows – interesting, perhaps, but not worthy of much attention.

This healthy conclusion was instinctive, not reasoned. After all, the reading of a few books hardly constitutes a firm basis for sound judgment. Years later I learnt that some Hermetic philosophers had a high purpose, that the Philosopher's Stone was not something created by magic rituals but was a symbol for the spirit, that spirit which could transmute the base metal of fallen human nature into the gold of spiritual being. But even there I see little reason for secrecy. One could shout spiritual truth from the housetops, or preach sermons from a mount, yet much of it would fall upon deaf ears.

There was, however, one idea that I seized upon, something gleaned from Gurdieff that I felt to be true: that we possess more than one level of consciousness. We may have no control over the incoming stream of sensory impressions, but we can choose which to give our attention to. Similarly, our minds are filled with a stream of thoughts. But that is not the sum of our consciousness. There is an observer who can evaluate the thoughts, choose which to entertain and which to reject – or else choose to think about something else altogether.

In other words, we no more have to be captive to our thoughts than we do to a television program. In both cases, we can simply change channels. Or switch off altogether. (Switching off thinking while retaining full awareness may be more difficult but it can be done.) According to Gurdieff, if we allow ourselves to be engrossed in our senses and thoughts, then we remain at a lower level of consciousness – a sort of waking sleep. To be truly alive, we should keep the observer awake as much as possible.

This I attempted to practice, not as a discipline, but whenever the thought came to me. I found self-awareness came naturally when I was alone on the hills. Occasionally, in a cinema I would recall where I was – seated in a darkened room with hundreds of others, all engrossed in a shadow-play on a screen. I could see clearly that this was a form of sleep. As might be expected, I found awakening from this sleep much less frequent when I was at work or involved in social activity.

And so I tried to monitor my thoughts. "Evil," says Milton, "into the mind of God or Man May come and go, so unapprov'd, and leave No spot or blame behind" – a curiously passive statement for such a "wayfaring Christian". If one is healthy-minded, one dismisses such thoughts. But it is not always easy. My grandfather, though not noted for a sense of humour, once defined the height of cheek as a small boy piddling through the letter-box and then knocking on the door to ask how far up the passage it had run. My mind, I fear, can behave like that. From time to time it tosses up an offensive thought or image, and then, despite its rejection, piddles through the letter-box again, as it were, and again knocks on the door. In defence I tried substituting another image for the offending one. For example, I'd picture myself climbing a ridge

183

of pure snow. It worked. But this technique is less effective with painful memories of real events. Those are scored too deep.

This monitoring was not part of a program of self-improvement. It was not a conscious impulse to become pure or good, for I am neither. I rarely thought of God, whom I associated with religion, and I had no clear idea of the meaning of "spirit" or "spiritual". What I did have was an aversion to ugliness and meanness of all kinds and a dread of shame. In addition, I had two powerful influences working in me – the love and joy I had experienced. I had not only the love of my family but also my love for them. Being loved, though primary for the child, is not enough. It is loving that is essential. It is that which works the real magic. These influences, joy and love, prevented me from becoming obsessed with the occult. Ghosts, demons, magic (weeping statues and flying monks, come to that) are mere shadows in the light of their reality.

⚬Ϯ⚬

2
Books: The Great War

"But what good came of it at last?"
Quoth little Peterkin.
"Why that I cannot tell," said he,
"But 'twas a famous victory."

- Robert Southey

In an attempt to follow the course of the war I decorated my bedroom wall with maps. In this way I learned much about geography – the whereabouts of places like Smolensk, Benghazi, Crete, Guadalcanal – but little about the war itself. All I had to go on, of course, were newspapers, the newsreel at the cinema and B.B.C. broadcasts ("This is the B.B.C. Home Service. Here is the news and this is Alvar Liddell reading it." Or, as the cast of "Beyond the Fringe" later put it, "Here is the news of the latest disaster.") So I began reading about the First World War. Great and terrible events cast long shadows before and after. Born in the shadow of the first great Slaughter, I grew up surrounded by its memorials – the ubiquitous cenotaphs, men with faded medal ribbons but lacking an arm or a leg. (Only much later did I learn that, throughout my boyhood, hospitals wards were still filled with their broken comrades.) I became familiar with the songs of that War: "Tipperary", "Keep the Home Fires Burning" and "Roses of Picardy", my father's favourite. Then there was that November day in the early 'Thirties when to my surprise the traffic slowed to a halt, men removed their hats, and everyone stood in silence for what seemed like hours. Although I did not know the reason then, for it was the first Armistice Day I recall, so simple yet solemn a demonstration of respect came to have more meaning for me than all the speeches I have heard since.

Beginning with a weighty volume of the Official History, for several days I peered at faded sepia photographs and laboured through curiously bloodless prose, struggling with unfamiliar military terms and a proliferation of unit designations. Finally I gave up. It presented as clear a picture of the War as a textbook on anatomy does of a living human being. Chance put the next book into my hand. Guy Chapman's *Vain Glory* is an anthology of personal anecdotes from almost every theatre of the War. The details may have faded, but the overall impact of the book has remained. For the first time I perceived the horror that man sometimes has to face and the magnificence of spirit that he can display, although decades passed before I realized that man creates the one from the other. It was not the courage and suffering alone that moved me, but also the prodigal waste of men. Britain's professional army, largely destroyed by 1915, was superb; but "Kitchener's Army" of volunteers, though spirited and disciplined, were poorly trained. As a result, their casualty rate was appalling. In his book *The Battle of Loos*, Philip Warner describes the fate of two divisions of inexperienced innocents thrown into the battle without adequate artillery support and with the enemy wire still intact. Out of ten thousand who began the assault, more than eight thousand were killed or wounded, including members of "Pals" battalions, units composed of post office workers, university students, professional men, public schoolboys, or artists, – all enlisted as privates.

This and similar early disasters were no doubt responsible for the German comment that the British Army was an army of lions led by donkeys. Certainly imagination was rarely the strong point of Imperial staff officers. Though there was no doubt plenty of creative thinking among frontline officers, little of it filtered up. Men did not last long in the trenches and in any case commanders are not noted for consulting junior subordinates. In his poem "The General," Siegried Sassoon portrays the general as a genial old gentleman – but his plan of attack nonetheless proves disastrous. Perhaps it was the same expansive, well-manicured gentleman – or one like him, complete with red tabs, baggy cavalry breeches and gleaming riding boots – who discouraged the digging of deep dug-outs because they might affect the troops' "offensive spirit", or who opposed the use of parachutes because aircrews might jump rather than fight. But I must not be unkind. It might have been he who actually visited the Front in person to see why the offensive had stalled before Passchendaele – and then burst into tears at what he saw there. Not that the tears did much good, for the battle was allowed to drag on for three months, long past the time when all hopes of a breakthrough had drowned in mud and blood.

But it is easy to criticise after the event, especially when one is free from responsibility and seated in comfort by one's own fireside. Not every general can be a Wellington or a Zhukov, and it is pointless and unfair to condemn those who aren't. Besides, generals are not always free to choose. Though the Third Battle of Ypres was ill conceived – given the climate, the terrain and the fact that the Germans could observe all the preparations, it was almost bound to drown in mud – Haig had little choice in mounting the earlier Somme Offensive, as the French were stretched almost to breaking point at Verdun. Moreover, offensives require detailed planning, complex logistical support, and once launched gain momentum of their own, rich with opportunities for the unexpected. The poor communications of the day – vulnerable telephone lines and runners – rendered staffs half blind and made changing course in mid-battle difficult, if not dangerous. As for calling an early halt, the "offensive spirit" was against it. As with Hector, the very courage of the combatants brought disaster upon them.

Despite initial successes, even major German offensives like that at Verdun and the March Offensive of 1918 ended with the exhaustion of the attackers. The fact was that for most of the Great War a resolute enemy, well entrenched behind barbed wire and defended by artillery and machine-guns, was bound to make any offensive costly. As with the medieval castle before the advent of cannon, the defence had a powerful advantage, for attackers had to expose themselves to a storm of fire and steel. That defenders also lost dearly doesn't alter the truth of that, for many of their losses resulted from their counter-attacks. It is no wonder that the bloodiest battles sometimes assumed the awful inevitability of Greek tragedy.

I have read of other wars since. Who could remain unmoved by the gallantry of Lee's ragged, half-starved Army of North Virginia, by the savagery of the fighting at Kohima and Okinawa, by the titanic struggle in Russia? Yet it is the Western Front of the Great War that haunts me, that blood-drenched landscape of mud, shell-holes, splintered trees and rubble – all strewn with barbed wire, lit by flares and heavy with the stench of gas and corruption. In this vile desolation men endured lice, rats, cold, incessant sniping and shelling, and a "normal wastage" of thousands of casualties a week – all during "quiet" periods between offensives. Despite the most heroic efforts to achieve early victory, it seems as if everything – circumstance, duty, courage, sacrifice – combined only to prolong the war and inflict the maximum suffering on the nations most involved, nations that had been at the peak of their power and confidence. As with the sinking of the *Titanic*, the gods seemed intent on punishing hubris, and in this case ensured that even the weary victors should feel they had suffered a defeat.

And what good came of it at last? Though the Powers who went to war in August of 1914 had what they thought were good reasons, they were nothing compared with the cost. When war was declared, what are now called innocent civilians cheered; and some, together with politicians, bayed for revenge when it ended – thus ensuring a second round twenty years later. But the soldiers, whether clad in khaki, blue or field grey, had no hate; or, if they had, it was reserved not for the enemy who shared their misery, but for the artillery and the lice – with perhaps a little left over by way of good-humoured contempt for some "innocent" civilians. What soldiers gained is the knowledge, true because it was writ in blood, that some men are magnificent in action and that none can deny the love of one who risks his life for another.

How much my consciousness of the Flanders poppy and all it stands for has influenced my life I find difficult to estimate. Reading about that and other wars has shown me, at second hand, thank goodness, part of the topography of hell. More importantly, it has revealed some of the astonishing dimensions of the human spirit. In the process I have been given a criterion for judgment. Whenever I am tempted to feel sorry for myself, as a I have on several occasions when I have felt crushed, I seem to hear the words that echoed in my mind when I first listened to Benjamin Britten's *War Requiem* – the disconcerting words that conclude Wilfred Owen's "Apologia Pro Poemate Meo": "These men are worth your tears. You are not worth their merriment." And when I contemplate the antics we get up to today and wonder what the men of the Somme would think of our brave new world, I seem to hear the sound of distant laughter.

❧

3

Books: The Spirit of the Hills

At the beginning of 1941, bed-bound with 'flu and short of reading material, I asked Pauline to pick up a book from Conway library. "It's called *Careers*," I informed her. "It's quite small and has a whitish cover. You can't mistake it."

Upon her return, she handed me what appeared to be the right book. "Here you are, Phil," she said. "I couldn't find the book you wanted, but this one has a white cover just like it."

I glanced at the title, *The Spirit of the Hills*, by F S. Smythe. "Blimey," I laughed. "I ask for a book on careers, and you bring me a fairy story!" Looking a little hurt, she stamped out of the room. Idly, I opened the book and began to read.

It is, of course, not about fairies but mountains. Nor is it a simple narrative. Writing of the hills he had climbed, hills ranging from the green Downs of his childhood to the icy Himalayas, Smythe focuses on his love for the hills and on his physical, mental and spiritual relationship with them. Absorbed, I read far into the night. Afterwards, pulling aside the blackout curtains, I stood looking towards Conway Mountain. I was not alone! Others climbed mountains, too – with nailed boots, ropes, ice-axes. Much more significantly, they *loved* the hills as I did. A door had opened. A-mountaineering I would go! Providence had guided Pauline's hand to select not the book I wanted but the one I needed.

Wanting to know more, I began reading everything on climbing that I could find, from Edward Whymper on. Meanwhile, equipment. Beale's was the place for rope, one book informed me, and there was a maker of fine climbing boots on South Molton Street – but both were in London. There was another drawback. I had not yet begun work and had little money. Forget the rope. There was no one to climb with anyway. Boots? I could make my own. And so, buying a pair of cheap boots and some hob nails, I was soon hammering away at a cobbler's last. When I had finished, I looked at the result critically. My nails would not be as effective as clinkers or tricounis, but the boots would have to do. At least they would prevent me from slipping and their weight might help keep me anchored in a high wind. Clothing? An army battledress blouse was what I wanted. At my request, Mum ran one up from an old blanket. Though unlined and a trifle thin, it was a well-made facsimile.

Towards the middle of February, issued forth one morning the compleat mountaineer, equipped with satisfyingly noisy boots, a map of Snowdonia and a thick corned beef sandwich. ("Take care, dear, won't you?") Just fifteen, I was off on my first mountaineering expedition – an ascent of Foel fras, a three thousand footer in the Carnedds. I peered at the sky, a thick overcast of dark grey clouds. Not very promising. Still, it wasn't raining and there was no wind to speak of. Having almost been blown into the sea while running along the beach before a strong gale, with vortexes whirling spray hundreds of feet into the air, I had a healthy respect for its power.

A little later I stood on Conway Mountain, looking south. Fresh snow mantled the hills down to the 1500 foot level, but there seemed little threat of further precipitation and the cloud base was well clear of Tal y Fan. It was on! And so, filled with a sense of high adventure and the sound of music, I descended to Sychnant Pass and began the long, gentle climb of Tal y Fan.

On the summit about two hours later I brushed the snow from a large rock and parked myself. Time to eat, I decided, wishing I had a thermos of hot tea. Fishing my somewhat crumpled sandwich from my pocket, I took a large bite and began to study the route ahead. Before me the ground fell some six hundred feet to a bwlch, or pass, over which ran an old Roman road. From there it rose again fairly steeply to the two thousand foot level before easing off and then climbing another five hundred feet to the bald dome of Drum about three miles away. Though there were no difficulties, under the iron sky the way seemed bleak, uninviting, not at all like the grass and heather of Conway Mountain. I shivered. Suddenly, I became aware that I was cold. With neither hat nor gloves, and with only a thin woollen jacket, I had to keep moving or freeze. Rising to my feet, I set off again at a brisk pace, finishing my sandwich on the way. Of the road trodden by Roman legionaries almost nineteen centuries earlier I saw no sign.

On Drum I found myself in a world of snow under a louring sky, with both Conway Valley and the coast now lost in gloom. Before me stretched a broad, high ridge that rose to the rounded humps of Foel fras and Foel-grach and was linked to lesser peaks by snowy saddles. Farther away reared the impressive bulk of Carnedd Llywelyn, its 3485 foot summit shrouded in cloud. Beyond that, I knew, were Carnedd Dafydd, Pen yr Oleu-wen and the Nant Ffrancon Pass. As I began the slight descent from the summit of Drum, a distant movement in the snow caught my eye. Three climbers were descending towards Aber. They were already on their way home, while I was still outward bound!

Reminding myself that February days are short, I began to move with some urgency. Foel fras might be little more than a mile away, but there were still seven hundred feet to climb before I could turn for Aber. Moreover, close overhead now and pressing down with almost palpable weight, the dark grey overcast was beginning to give me a feeling of claustrophobia. Was it my imagination or was it sagging lower? Half an hour later, my arrival at the summit of Foel fras confirmed my suspicion, for advancing rapidly towards me was a dense grey wall. Already it had swallowed Carnedd Llywelyn and Foel-grach and was now less than a mile away. There was no time to lose. Without pausing to admire the view further, I turned and began to descend, thankful that the snow was firm enough to provide good footing. A few minutes later ghostly grey tendrils reached around me, and then a chill fog reduced my world to a patch of snow. I had been taught that my clothing was inadequate. Now I was to receive another lesson – that a map is of little use when you cannot see. Successful navigation also requires the use of watch and compass.

Unsurprisingly, by the time I scrambled free from cloud at about the 2300 foot level I was somewhat disoriented. I continued to descend nonetheless, peering ahead to locate a small lake, Llyn Anafon, and the rough track which begins nearby. But after several hundred feet I began to feel disturbed. Where was the lake? I stopped and consulted the map again. The contours seemed to fit, there was the stream – but Llyn Anafon stubbornly refused to show itself. Slowly it dawned on me that it wasn't going to. I was in the wrong cwm! In the swirling murk I had somehow borne too far to the left and as a result was headed not for the lake but for Aber Falls.

Falls – that was ominous! Looking at the map closely, I saw clearly marked a band of cliffs extending the full width of the cwm. With a sinking feeling I realized I was in a hanging valley. How steep the cliffs were I didn't know, nor was this the time to find out. The gathering gloom was not the result of the dense clouds only. Somewhere beyond all that overcast the sun was setting – and I had no torch. Dismayed, I turned aside and forced my tired legs to climb back until, just short of the clouds, I reached the shoulder of the intervening mountain. To my relief I found myself looking into Cwm Anafon and could see safety 1300 feet below. Twenty minutes later I was on the trail to Aber, scout-marching the remaining miles in a race against the dark.

Riding home in the darkened bus, I reflected upon my day with some satisfaction. I had done what I set out to do, in the process hiking fifteen miles over the Carnedds in winter and climbing more than four thousand feet. Although I had felt anxious at times, especially while descending blindly through the cloud, I considered the experience an adventure. However, I knew I'd been lucky. What if the wind had picked up? What if it had come on to snow? If the cloud base had gone down to a thousand feet? As these and other unpleasant possibilities presented themselves to my imagination, I felt a chill at the nape of my neck. The Carnedds are remote, desolate, bare of shelter. Given my equipment, or rather lack of it, I had no business wandering about them alone in poor conditions, especially when no one knew where I was.

"Ah, there you are," exclaimed Mum as I clumped in. "I was beginning to worry about you, dear. It's been dark for so long. Did you have a nice day?"

"Yes thanks, Mum," I smiled. Then, to ease her fears, "I had to wait quite a bit for a bus." Henceforth, I decided, as I wolfed down a large plate of stew, the Carnedds would see me only in fair weather.

I returned often that year, climbing to the accompaniment of "My Russian Rose", "The Polovtsian Dances" and other selections from my internal juke box. I swore at the flies, greeted the sheep and admired the clouds. But never again did I see another climber there. Like Conway Mountain, the Carnedds seemed to become my personal playground. And if the weather was too bad for them, I explored Snowdonia on my bicycle, enjoying roads virtually free from traffic. As for another winter traverse, that had to await a time when I had adequate clothing and a companion.

4

I make no apology for this digression into the realm of books, for they have been a major influence on me. In the course of a lifetime one can expect to encounter only so many people – relatives, teachers, friends, casual acquaintances – all of whom, if one is alert and willing to learn, may serve as conscious or unconscious mentors, exemplars or object lessons. Reading broadens one's acquaintanceship, provides more choice. And if one chooses wisely – that is, with the intent of seeking what is true and good – one may encounter fine minds. One may even gain a little of what one is seeking.

Smythe's *Spirit of the Hills*, for example, made a major impact upon me. It did not determine my feeling for mountains, although it may have conditioned my attitude to climbing, making me something of a purist, I suppose. What it did do was to confirm the validity of my experience on the Welsh hills, to give me an encouraging nudge on the way, as it were. As much as anything, perhaps, it was the book's title. It resonated in my mind.

The impulse that drove me to climb had been given long before – on the night when a boy of eight had bared his being to the thunderstorm. The world "means intensely, and means good," says Browning. Is that what I sensed, subconsciously, so early? Was it that which led me to take such delight in wildflowers at Banstead? to seek escape from the sight of chimney pots even though I loved London? to experience joy when I succeeded first at Linton and then on the mountains of Wales?

It is not surprising that I should have felt at home in the Kent countryside and on the Welsh hills. Every city-dweller feels the need to stretch his legs in the park from time to time, to keep a dog or cat, potter around the garden, feed the birds. Those not fortunate enough to have a garden or a nearby park make do with window boxes, potted plants, perhaps an aspidestra and a caged canary; and a prisoner in solitary confinement might even make friends with mice and spiders, like Byron's Bonnivard. The city is largely an artificial environment, like a zoo for humans, only they are not caged in – not obviously, anyway. It may be pleasant or not, depending on the city and the circumstances of the person, but it is still a zoo. The most confirmed city-lover feels he must escape sometimes, if only for a day or a week or so, to plunge into the sea, paddle along the beach, walk barefoot through the grass, stare at the sheep and cows. Consciously or not, we feel the need to keep in contact with something living, something other than our own species.

One reason is not far to seek. We know now that the earth and every living thing on it are composed of elements created within massive stars that exploded like stupendous seedpods and cast them into space. "A leaf of grass is no less than the journeywork of the stars," wrote Walt Whitman in the 1850's, expressing a belief not confirmed as true until this century – a fine example of poetic vision anticipating scientific discovery. We are the offspring of stars, nurtured and shaped by our foster mother the earth, and in a real sense the distant cousins of the plants and the animals. "You never enjoy the world aright till the sea itself floweth in your veins, till you are clothed with the heavens, and crowned with the stars." Traherne knew what he was talking about, as did the author of "Genesis" when he wrote that the "Lord God formed man of the dust of the ground". That does not necessarily mean that God squatted on his haunches and made mud pies, of course. He must be permitted to create in His own fashion. Through nature. ("A tip of the hat to you, brother monkey!") We are part of nature, and we ignore that reality at our peril, as we have at last begun to realize. At least, our *bodies* are. Traherne again: "You never know yourself till you know more than your body. The image of God was not seated in the features of your face but in the lineaments of your soul." If one believes in God, there need be no conflict between the theory of evolution and creation – unless we insist on remaking God in *our* image.

I can imagine a cynic nodding agreement here, perhaps a little impatiently, but going on to suggest that on the hills I was merely a romantic, frolicking lamb, healthy and full of the juice of youth. This is true, but not the whole of it. I was well aware, or thought I was, that nature has a darker side – that men and animals are subject to disease, that I would not likely feel quite so much at home in a leech-infested and fever-ridden swamp, for example, and that some creatures, like the ichneumon fly, have extremely unpleasant habits. But what I felt on the hills was more than a mere sense of physical and mental well-being. There was something other. What it was, I couldn't say. I knew that I felt at home on the hills in a way I never did in London. I knew that the rewards of climbing outweighed the effort, the occasional discomfort, the risk. In fact these were part of the attraction, a price that was not only paid gladly but welcomed. "The true success is to labour," says Stevenson. Yes. It is not the summit that is the goal. One could get there by mountain railway, chairlift or helicopter. It is the attainment of it on one's own feet.

I knew more. At times, as I trod the hills in solitude, I felt that there was more life about me than that in the grass, the sheep, the birds. Sometimes it seemed as if the hills, the clouds too, in some way were alive. In his autobiographical poem "The Prelude", Wordsworth writes of having experienced a "sense Of unknown modes of being... huge and mighty forms, that do not live Like living men." Could hills and clouds be living entities? Could the earth itself? In one of his strange novels Olaf Stapledon suggests that even the stars are living entities – a preposterous idea, surely. Teillard du Chardin might not have thought so, for he advanced the proposition that consciousness is inherent in the universe – even in rocks and atoms, though to a far lesser degree than in man, of course. Nor would the Bushman think it so. *In The Heart of the Hunter,* Laurens van der Post records that for the Bushman, an aborigine once hunted like an animal by Whites and Bantu alike, the stars are great hunters with voices that could be heard. For him the sun also has a voice; and as long as the Bushman could hear it, he felt at one with life. Not to hear it was a sign of his alienation. Perhaps he would then, in his own way, echo Wordsworth's lament, "Where is it now, the glory and the dream?" Does the Bushman know something we do not?

Why not push the idea to the limit. Could the entire universe in a sense be a living, evolving organism, aware in some way of what is going on everywhere? This is not so ridiculous an idea as it may seem. Thanks to Einstein's staggering equation, we know the universe to be composed of energy, some of which happens to be arranged as matter. Modern physicists sense, perhaps reluctantly, that maybe the universe "communicates" with itself at speeds far in excess of the speed of light. And when, in his book *Cosmic Consciousness,* Dr. R. M. Bucke writes of his received perception of the universe as a "living presence," he is echoing the experience of at least one medieval saint.

But this last is to introduce a note of mysticism, anathema to many. Nevertheless, the universe is odd and, as J.B.S. Haldane suggests, probably odder than we can imagine.

This sense of "something other" was not with me all the

time, needless to say. It came only occasionally, during periods of silence on the hills. I can best describe it as a sense that I was in the presence of invisible magnificence, of something behind the awe-inspiring beauty of the hills, the cloudscape, the stars. It was a feeling dim, but real. I felt like a blind man who senses the presence of someone or something in the house with him but who strains his ears in vain to detect it.

That the feeling was real and not a passing fancy is indicated by its effect on me. On several occasions I experienced joy, a momentary feeling, one or two seconds at most, when something stirred within me and struggled to burst free, to hurl itself out into the universe with a great shout of delight. Though momentary, it had after-effects. The most immediate, although brief, was an incredible sense of well-being, as if I were so charged with life that my skin could barely contain it. And for a while I was left with a feeling of moral uplift, a feeling of reverence and a sense of the pure. The purity was not within me, needless to say, although something in me was drawn to it, but associated with the unseen magnificence. More lasting was the "renovating virtue" of the memory. I was twenty-seven before I came to read Wordsworth, and then his poetry exploded in my mind like a star. Much of what I and others have experienced was there. He, too, had experienced it all, only he had been able to render it into superlative poetry:

> And I have felt
> A presence that disturbs me with the joy
> Of elevated thoughts; a sense sublime
> Of something far more deeply interfused,
> Whose dwelling is the light of setting suns,
> And the round ocean and the living air,
> And the blue sky, and in the mind of man:
> A motion and a spirit, that impels
> All thinking things, all objects of all thought,
> And rolls through all things.

One cannot breathe this rarefied atmosphere for long. Mostly, I was merely happy (!) on the hills. Only once did I descend in a sombre mood, ironically after spending a midnight hour on Conway Mountain in a scene of astonishing beauty:

In The Blackout

Midnight on Conwy Mountain, 1943

How clear
the silence on this hill!
How radiant the night!

With streets deserted, blackouts drawn,
the towns below seemed lost in sleep
- and yet the darkness brimmed with light,
spilling splendour everywhere!

The Bear bestrode the northern sky,
its faithful beacons burning clear;
recumbent in a silent sea,
the Great Orme nuzzled at the shore
with pallid limestone flanks agleam;
and small craft moored by Conwy's walls
had swung to greet a shining tide.

Southward, bright clouds thronged the sky;
floating in the sapphire night,
dappling hill and valley floor,
they brushed the crest of Tal y Fan,
swirling, dissolving as they came,
then drifted by like languid ghosts
and, sinking, vanished in mid-air!

How beautiful they are!
How lordly their unhurried pace!
Like outriders,
heralds liveried in light,
they ride the air with soundless horns
– as if proclaiming to the night
a coming Glory!

In congregation with the pines I watched,
    rapt in the shadow of their passing.

The play of moonlight and cloud
        – type of that beauty Shelley spoke of,
        flaming forth from hidden fire -
and yet, for one long, breathless moment,
        almost…an expectancy!

Was it mere fancy,
        born of beauty and solitude?
Or was there something more
        – the seed-leaf stir, perhaps,
        of some blind, buried need?
I know only, when the moon drew clear
        – full moon, the one which, poets say,
        moves lovers, lunatics and poets -
I felt…an emptiness,
        a sense of something lost.

Still I stood,
        staring at that ravaged face;
then, suddenly chilled, I turned away
        and dogged my shadow down the hill,
            down to the empty road below,
                and into the shadow there.

I don't wish to make too much of these experiences on the hills of my youth. There was no epiphany. I remained much the same amiable youth, with all his faults and with a distressing tendency to make a fool of himself. But not quite the same. Like a barque navigating a confused sea, imperceptibly I had altered course a little – with my sails and rigging, as it were, strengthened for any trials that lay ahead. But the star I steered by was invisible to me.

⊙⊦⊙

5

Idwal

By the end of 1941 I had explored the Llanberis and Nant Ffrancon passes on my bicycle. An attempt to climb Snowdon by the Pyg Track had to be abandoned as I feared I might run out of time and didn't fancy cycling home in the dark. I had no lights on my bicycle, of course. Of the long list of equipment I didn't have, the item whose lack I felt most keenly, especially on the Carnedds, was a watch. Having nearly been overtaken by darkness there the previous February, I had no desire to repeat the experience. Still, if Snowdon was too far, whether by cycle or bus, I had discovered Idwal and had instantly been drawn to Tryfan and Idwal Slabs. During the course of the year I had chanced upon an old guidebook to Lliwedd, written by the Abraham brothers. After poring over this for days, enjoying the climbs in my imagination, I knew that I had to do some rock-climbing. And so I began to haunt Idwal.

Though I knew experienced climbers frowned upon the practice of wandering about the mountains alone, most of the time I had little choice in the matter. I climbed alone or not at all, and the latter was unthinkable. What I could do was to be careful; and as I had a keen eye and was as sure-footed as a cat, I considered I could keep the risk at an acceptable level. In fact the only time I nearly killed myself in Wales was in Llanfairfechan. Used to having the road to myself, I made a sudden turn on my cycle and nearly ended up under the wheels of a car. The driver must have been an army officer on leave, for his expert dressing-down made me smart for days.

Solo rock-climbing, though, was a different matter. Given the equipment of the time, it was thought irresponsible. Still, scrambling on easy rock could hardly be considered rock-climbing, could it? And so I was soon amusing myself on the North Ridge of Tryfan, including, but only once, the obligatory leap between Adam and Eve, the monoliths on the summit. Then I usually continued up Bristly Ridge to the Glyders. I would also climb Introductory Gulley, now called the Idwal Staircase, and lounge on a rock ledge to gaze enviously at the handful of climbers sporting themselves on the slabs below. From there I would continue up Glyder Fawr, where one could scramble almost anywhere.

I succumbed to temptation once. Having bought the Climbers' Club guides to the area, I decided that climbing only moderately difficult routes would not be irresponsible. Now, where to start? Studying the guides, I decided upon the Ordinary Route on Milestone Buttress. But here I had an unexpected setback. The holds were plentiful enough, but many had been so rounded by countless bootnails that in my clumsy boots I felt anything but secure. If this was only a moderately difficult climb, what must the harder ones be like? After finishing the climb, I therefore decided that solo rock-climbing was out, and thereafter restricted my solo climbing to scrambling around Idwal, with occasional traverses of the Carnedds.

About a month before my sixteenth birthday, one wintry morning found me plodding up the main street of Bethesda, my footfall muffled by fresh snow. For once, I'd had the Bangor bus almost to myself; and even Bethesda seemed deserted, with its inhabitants either at work or sensibly haunting their firesides. Under its mantle of snow the chapel looked drearier than ever. "The spirit of God," says Donne, "is not a dampe." No, but unlike the Gothic church or cathedral, whose very stone seems to take a joyous leap heavenward, the typical Welsh chapel, with a name such as "Sion" or "Bethel", resembles nothing so much as a boxy mausoleum. The singing within may be joyful, but the architecture is an emphatic dampe. Use of the local slate for the roof, sills, lintels and austere adornment may have something to do with it. The mauve slate is particularly funereal.

Despite this dampener and the cold, I was in high spirits, for the snow had magically transformed the hills into a miniature version of the Alps, with only the glaciers missing. I was off on my second winter expedition, this time Tryfan by the North Ridge. My earlier decision, not to climb alone in poor weather conditions, applied only to the Carnedds. The Glyders are safer, in that nowhere is more than half an hour from the road. Besides, I had booked for the night at Idwal Cottage youth hostel and wouldn't have to worry about time. My cold-weather gear was much improved, too. In addition to my blouse, I now sported a raincoat, fingerless woollen gloves and a cheap trilby. This last had been inspired by photographs of alpinists in porkpie hats. Very fetching they looked, too. I knew exactly how I looked – like a standard lamp. But if that's what real mountaineers wore.…

At the head of the pass the snow was more than a foot deep, and crossing the boulder field to the Milestone proved wearisome, even though I was following someone's tracks. The fresh powder offered too little resistance to my feet, and before long my hands had become cold from having to steady myself against boulders. An ice axe, even a walking stick, would have been useful.

Fortunately, the going improved beyond the wall, and a half hour or so brought me to the crest of the ridge, where I paused for a breather. The road below was deserted, and save for the smoke from Idwal Cottage there was no sign of life in a world of white. Yet some climbers were about in addition to those whose tracks I was following. About five hundred feet below, I spotted three figures in navy blue floundering in my wake. Cadets from the training ship *Conway*, I guessed.

Emerging from a gulley a few hundred feet higher, I suddenly came upon my trail-breakers, two climbers enjoying a smoke at their ease. I grinned at them, "Hello. Beautiful, isn't it?" Then I added, "Mind if I join you?"

For a second or two they stared at the apparition in raincoat and trilby that had arisen before their eyes. Then one spoke, "All right. Are you alone?"

"Yes," I answered. "Thank you." Plopping down with my back to a rock, I hauled out a large cherrywood pipe and began to fill it. They had ice axes, I noted, gloves, windproof jackets, thick woollen balaclavas. Mentally, I made a note to consign my hat to the dustbin and obtain a balaclava as soon as I could.

"Here, have one of these," said one, offering me a cigarette after watching me try vainly to light my pipe. I accepted gratefully. My fingers hadn't been able to grasp the matches.

Pleased to have company for a change, I followed them up the ridge; but when we reached the steep section where handholds were required, I found to my dismay that I could go no farther. "I'm sorry," I said, "but I'll have to turn back."

"What's up?" The man above was looking down.

I waved my hands at him. "I can't hold on. I can't feel the rock."

"Will you be all right?"

"Oh yes," I said, "I won't need handholds going down."

Finishing my meal with a sigh of satisfaction, I filled my pipe and was soon wreathed in smoke. Seeing this, two girls exchanged glances and giggled. More kindly, the men affected not to notice.

"It seems we have a problem." It was the hostel warden. "We may have to send out a search party in the morning. Two climbers reported that someone who joined them on Tryfan got into trouble and had to turn back. He hasn't been seen since."

I pricked up my ears. "What did the climbers look like? Did they have ice axes and balaclavas?"

"Yes, why?"

"Oh well, that would have been me. My hands became too cold for me to hang on, and I had to turn back near the top."

"Are you sure? I thought you had just walked in."

"I did. But I felt too cold to wait for you to open," I explained, "and so I walked down to Bethesda with three boys from the *Conway*. They had been forced back, too."

It was not until I got home that I discovered one of my fingers was still pellucid to the first joint. It had never occurred to me to examine my hands the previous day. Frostbite on British hills simply didn't happen, I thought. Fortunately, the tissue hadn't been frozen and the blood returned. Nature is not kind to fools. But something there is that occasionally takes pity on a young one.

First Day on the Rope

It took pity on me again the following year. In 1943, wearing a balaclava from Black's and with my old boots now edged with clinkers, I lounged up the path to Idwal Slabs for the umpteenth time, intending to survey the climbing from my usual eyrie before continuing over the Glyders. Though the Slabs were deserted, two climbers were standing by the shore of Llyn Idwal. They seemed to be arguing.

"Hey, there!" One of the two came galloping up. He was

tow-haired, slender, perhaps a year or so older than I. Grey eyes. "Would you care to join me in a climb or two?" He spoke with a Manchester accent.

Would I care to...? With an effort I restrained the urge to leap into the air and cheer. "Yes, I'd love to."

"Good! Name's 'Arthur', by the way." He fell in beside me. "My mate doesn't feel like climbing today," he explained, adding scornfully, "All he wants to do is lounge by the lake and soak his feet."

Arthur and his mate, it emerged, were Bevin Boys, conscripts assigned to the coal mines. I thought of the Kentish colliery I had visited in 1940. At the coal face, I had seen where colliers had to work an eighteen inch seam with pick and shovel while lying on their sides in a space three feet high. Like rats in a hole. I shuddered. The mere idea of it made me a feel claustrophobic.

Suddenly, I was startled by a terrible noise: "DI DI DI DAH – DI DI DI DAH – DAH DAH DI DI DI DAH!" My companion had begun bellowing from Beethoven's Fifth and was waving his arms as if conducting an orchestra. Mountains and music! I grinned at him. I was beginning to warm to Arthur.

At the foot of the Slabs we halted, and Arthur began uncoiling his rope. Like his clothes and boots, it was well worn – thin and chafed, in fact, and little more than a clothes line. I felt a momentary twinge of apprehension but instantly dismissed it as unworthy. My friend was clearly an experienced climber and no doubt knew what he was doing.

"Done much rock-climbing?" he asked cheerfully.

"Not on a rope. Scrambling. You know – easy stuff."

"That's all right. Can you tie a bowline?"

"No, I can never remember which way the damned rabbit goes around the tree."

"Here, I'll show you." In one smooth movement, he passed the end around his waist, rotated his wrist around the rope and pulled the end back through. Then he repeated the demonstration slowly. "There. It's easy. Try it."

He was right. Now I could tie three useful knots.

Charity proved a marvellous climb. With the rope freeing me from all sense of irresponsibility, I thought it a romp and like Oliver wanted more. "What next?" I asked, looking up at the Holly Tree Wall.

"Up there." Arthur was pointing to the right. "The Wall Above. It's rated Vee Diff and I'd like to try it."

The wall was different. Starting from a wide ledge, it was only about twenty feet high but nearly vertical, and as Arthur started cautiously upward I could see that the holds were somewhat thin. With no need to belay, I observed his progress critically. He was careful with his handholds. Very proper. His footwork proved most interesting, though. Glancing down at a foothold, he scratched away at it like a chicken until his boot caught. As I watched this unorthodox procedure, the vague outlines of a doubt began to form. Suddenly, there was a wild scrabbling, a screech of nails, and then Arthur landed back on the ledge with a thud.

"Gosh," he exclaimed, rising to his feet unruffled. "That's a hard one. I don't think I'll be able to make it."

"Shall I give it a try?" I tried to sound casual.

"Yes, have a go," he said, dusting himself off.

It was hard. And as I inched upwards, pressed close against the wall, I took great care in placing my feet.

Afterwards, we sat in silence on the ledge above, dangling our legs and enjoying the view. Arthur's mate had disappeared and we had Cwm Idwal to ourselves. I could not have asked for a better first day on the rope. My leader, though somewhat less than expert, was a kindred spirit; and conditions were perfect, with a cooling breeze and puffs of cumulus lazing in a blue sky. There were none of the flies that could be so exasperating on the slopes of the Carnedds. Gradually, my mind became like a still, clear pool.

"What I'd like now," Arthur broke in suddenly, "is to have a look at Suicide Wall. No one's been able to climb it."

My pool promptly developed ripples, as if Arthur had heaved a rock into it. Suicide Wall? I'd never heard of it, but a climb with a name like that didn't inspire enthusiastic anticipation, not after the performance on the wall. "Where's that?" I asked cautiously.

"The other side. Come on." Arthur rose to his feet and led me across the Slabs to a wide terrace. Here we knelt and peered carefully over the edge. What we saw made my testicles draw back nervously – a nearly vertical cliff that ended with a slope strewn with boulders. Although little more than a hundred feet high, it was slabby and hadn't a comforting belay in sight. I could understand why no one had been able to climb it.[10] Surely Arthur wasn't thinking of trying?

"Interesting," said Arthur. "Let's rope down and have a close look."

Rope down? "I haven't done any abseiling," I objected mildly. I was keen enough to learn, but preferably somewhere else.

"That's all right," he said airily. "I'll walk you down on the rope and rappel down afterwards."

"Yes, we could do that, I suppose." I was trying not to think of the chafed rope. In silence, I watched as he belayed and then braced himself in a sitting stance. Providing the rope held, he was secure enough to hold someone twice my weight. From Arthur the rope ran at an angle to the cliff for about fifteen feet and then around a smooth bulge. When I stepped down to the edge, the bulge hid Arthur from my view. "Ready?" I called.

"Half a minute." There was a long pause, and I could hear him moving about. Then, "O.K. you can go now."

"Right. Here I go." I gave the rope a firm tug. It was reassuringly steady. Then I leant backwards over the void….

A split second later I found myself gyrating gently on the end of the rope. I had fallen about ten feet. In films, a climber usually falls to his death with a satisfying scream. Had the rope not held, I can say with authority that I would have plummeted to mine in silence, feeling mild surprise all the way to the first bounce, as that is all I would have had time to feel. Now, as I rotated slowly on the rope's end like an undernourished spider, I attempted to collect my scattered wits. When I went into freefall, I hadn't felt the rope give way. I had felt no resistance at all!

"Are you all right?" A head had appeared over the edge and was peering down – Arthur, looking anxious, his tousled hair standing out against the sky like an antic aureole.

"What the hell happened?" I shouted, feeling a little aggrieved.

"Ah, well, I felt it would be safer if I passed the rope behind

---

[10]   It was climbed two years later, on October 7, 1945.

a boulder," he explained, far too cheerfully for my liking, and then he added unnecessarily, "but it slipped off." At this point I might have been forgiven for entertaining bloody thoughts. But in fact a quite different thought was tugging insistently at the edge of my attention: if that was Arthur up there, indulging in accident analysis, what was happening at the other end of the rope? Hastily, I made a grab for the rockface and began to clamber back….

Here memory fails. Did we try again? Or did I hurl myself upon my leader and attempt to strangle him? No, it couldn't have been either. I'd have remembered. We must have walked off. I liked Arthur. He was a fine, carefree spirit. But two falls in three climbs suggests he was also a careless one. I hope he survived the coal mines to enjoy many years of climbing.

For me, there were to be other mountains, but fate allowed few more rock-climbs. A month or so after my frolic with Arthur, I was invited to join a party on the Holly Tree Wall, where the leader offended my purist soul by using the tree as a hold. Finishing with the Groove Above, it was a fine, airy climb on perfect rock. It was then rated "severe", but I found the only difficult move to be the first one, an awkward mantleshelf. In 1948, after trying him out on sandstone cliffs in Kent, I lured my cousin Peter to Idwal for a weekend. By then transformed into a muscular ex-paratrooper, he impressed me with his delicacy of style on Charity and with his fine command of soldierly language in the bowels of the Monolith. Finally, in 1964 I spent a week rock-climbing in the Rockies – for old time's sake, as it were, and to dislodge some of the chalk dust from my bones. But all the climbs together amounted to no more than could be done by any active party in a week. No matter. The number of climbs is not important. I had scaled more than mountains.

PART THREE

Royal Air Force

1944 – 1947

Chapter 11 "What Did You Do in the War, Daddy?" 209

Chapter 12 I Sprout Wings...   231

Chapter 13 ...Spread Them Confidently...   241

Chapter 14 ...And Have Them Clipped.   260

CHAPTER ELEVEN

"What Did You Do in the War, Daddy?"

1

Scarborough

It was a fine afternoon in July, 1944. Allied armies were hammering their way out of the Normandy beachhead, and Hitler had begun a second blitz on London with buzz-bombs, or V1's. But that was far away. For me, cycling home in the warm sun, the world seemed peaceful. The sound of air-raid sirens was only a distant memory, and even the strange concrete structure on the Morfa was gone. I was thinking of the next Sunday. Our ATC flight had converted a farmer's pasture into a suitable gliding field. The equipment – a motorized winch and a Dagling glider – had arrived, but all we had done so far were ground slides. I wanted a flight. Resembling a ski with wings, the Dagling dispensed with trifles such as a cockpit and placed nothing in front of the pilot except a stick and a rudder bar. Such splendid exposure made the prospect of even a low hop exciting. But it was not to be.

"There's a letter for you, dear," my mother said as I entered the living-room, and she handed me a buff envelope marked OHMS. Tearing it open, I scanned the contents, aware that her eyes were searching my face.

"It's my call-up," I said. I had been expecting the notice for months, but expectation and reality are not the same. Now it had come and a hand seemed to have gripped my vitals. As I stood before her, each of us regarding the other soberly, I had the curious sensation that part of me was already gone and that we were fading into phantoms. "I have to report to the RAF at Scarborough next week."

⚅

For me, as for most cadets in my flight, I imagine, the first days at Scarborough remain but a blur in the memory. With fifty others I found myself part of 34 Flight, "E" Squadron, 36 R & C Wing, billeted in the Prince of Wales Hotel on the esplanade. After answering roll-call and choosing a bed – hereinafter variously called a "wanking pit", "wanker" or simply a "pit" – we were rousted out again and marched off to a warehouse to be kitted out. There we filed along a counter and collected the following:

> boots and socks
> underwear, shirts, collars
> PT strip and running shoes
> battledress, best blue and greatcoat
> forage cap, a white flash (to distinguish us as cadets)
> sleeveless pullover,
> cap comforter (a sort of scarf that could double as a hat)
> webbing, small pack, large pack, kitbag
> housewife ("hussif") and sundry odds and ends.

Changing into battledress, we marched back to our billets, stowed our gear and then tumbled out for drill. I emerged from the equipping in fair shape. True, my uniforms and PT strip hung loose about me, but the boots and greatcoat fitted. However, over the next year I grew over two inches, put on twenty-five pounds, and soon found I could wear the greatcoat only by hunching my shoulders and breathing like a canary. For reasons known only to themselves, equipment sections were willing to exchange anything *except* the greatcoat. In consequence, I had to endure the last two winters of my RAF service without its benefit – except when ordered to wear it, and then I resembled one of David Langton's cartoon "erks".

There followed a whirl of activity. To the barber, to be shorn. To the dentist, to be drilled. "All these fillings have to come out," said the dental officer lugubriously, poking about in my mouth and surveying a decade of accumulated metalwork. Unless memory plays me false, his drill was powered by a foot-treadle; and for the next hour or so the poor fellow had to slave away, scraping, drilling and pedalling, while I sat in white-knuckled comfort watching evil-smelling smoke spiral past my nostrils. I almost felt sorry for him. Thence to the medical section where, like plucked chickens in a food-processing plant, we were chivied through a series of rooms to be scrutinized, stethoscoped, probed, prodded and interrogated. Later, we trooped along the production line again, this time to face the dreaded needles for assorted scratches, jabs and shots. Many accounts of service life make altogether too much of this ordeal. We, brave lads, endured it stoically, although some made rather too much show of their nonchalance.

These rites of passage culminated in our first FFI (Free From Infection) parade. Dressed in PT strip, all fifty-one of us were herded into a large room, lined up in two rows facing each other and ordered to drop our drawers. Averting our eyes politely – though no doubt some furtive glances were made for the purpose of comparison – there we stood, like two chorus lines of discouraged flashers, while the medical officer inspected each man, peering closely at his collection, inserting a finger slightly to the northwest of each right testicle and requesting a cough. It took forever. In an unguarded moment, I asked my neighbour what they were checking for. "Why, crabs, clap, the pox," he said, looking at me as if he had never seen me before. "Where've you been?" I sought to know no more. I could guess, but I wasn't overly shocked. I had long recovered from any outrage I had felt at discovering the universe cared little for human dignity.

Why was the FFI conducted as a group activity, and why were the rows made to face each other? Because there is safety in numbers, for both inspector and inspected? Or because it was a tradition intended, like parade-ground drill, to cement group solidarity? 'Twas a mystery.

For those who survived medical screening, attention shifted to our eye, mind and muscle co-ordination. Were we to be trusted within a hundred yards of an aircraft, that was the question. As future training depended on them, we took the ensuing aptitude tests seriously. Ham-fistedness might result in selection as a flight engineer. Who wanted to spend his time in the air peering at dials? Or worse, one might be remustered into the infantry, the coal mines, even the cookhouse! It was hard to decide which would be the most dreadful fate. Afterwards, we questioned one another eagerly.

"How did you do?"

"All right, I think."

"Piece of cake."

"Stuff me, I couldn't get all those pegs turned in time!"

"I bet I did better than any of ye." This last was delivered with a husky laugh. We turned to stare at the speaker – Jock, a ruffian "frae Glesga" with steel muscles and whisky-marinated vocal cords.

"What makes you think that?"

He flashed an engaging, gold-toothed grin. (How come he had kept *his* fillings?) "Easy," he replied. "I cheated." Then he proceeded to tell us exactly how he had managed to cheat on nearly every test. As we listened, impressed, I'm sure I wasn't the only one to make a mental note to avoid being in the same crew with him. I doubt whether cunning availed him much. Judging by what I saw of him and by reports about his subsequent activities, I suspect he was destined for the glasshouse.

Having successfully leapt all these hurdles, I began to feel that I was "in" – one of the brotherhood. But no, like neophytes in a mystery-religion we had to descend into the underworld and submit to a final ordeal before re-emerging into the light of day purged, purified and reborn as full initiates. A dusty lecture room, curtains drawn, lights put out. A film-projector whirrs into life, tinny music. The flickering light on the screen resolves into a title, *Venereal Disease*, and then dissolves into a shot of servicemen and girls drinking, laughing, chatting one another up. "This innocent scene," announces a portentous voice, "could be the prelude to unpleasant consequences." Illustrations follow – extreme close-ups of pubic hair teeming with wildlife, an assortment of male genitalia, blotched and pimpled from generous doses of some ghastly infection. The voice drones on.....

This is rather more detail than most of us want. I feel my palms becoming clammy. Around me I hear haunches shifting uneasily in seats, feet shuffling. The atmosphere is becoming tense.

"All these consequences," continues the voice, "can be avoided by exercising restraint. If not, they may be prevented through proper use of prophylactics." These are neither explained nor illustrated. The intent of this film is not to impart information but to arouse dread.

A hoarse whisper, "What the fuck are profferlacticks?"

A hissed reply, "French letters, you clot."

"Shut up there!"

"...Should you become infected, however, the treatment can be rather painful." The camera zooms in to show a large, throbbing penis in extreme close-up. It is scabbed, knobbled, whelked. Like the face of Chaucer's Summoner, it is a sight of which we children are aferd. A long, thin instrument of stainless steel then materializes. It is slightly curved. The voice now assumes a certain relish. "Here, for example, is an instrument popularly known as 'the umbrella'. The tip opens rather like an umbrella, hence the name." A demonstration follows. The flange appears wickedly sharp. "This is inserted into the urethra in the closed position. The tip is then opened and the instrument slowly drawn..." But the rest of the commentary is drowned by a dismal, universal groan.

It would be an exaggeration to say that men had to be assisted from the room in a half-fainting condition, but many of us were decidedly pale. It is not surprising. Despite protestations to the contrary, most of us were still unsullied virgins. As for me, for weeks afterwards whenever I saw an attractive girl approaching, I felt an almost irresistible urge – to march smartly to the opposite side of the street.

Meanwhile, there was training. Lectures, of a sort, on gas drill, fire drill, RAF law and administration, the Browning .303

machine-gun (*This is the sear spring retainer, and this 'ere's the sear spring retainer keeper*) filled a binder with an inch-thick wad of printed notes but left my mind disturbingly empty. No matter how much I studied it, the material drifted off, leaving not a rack behind. When careful enquiries elicited that we were not going to be tested on any of it, I decided to ignore the notes. Whatever I needed to know I could learn as occasion demanded. My instinct was sound – I never had to consult them again.

A visit to the range for an introduction to the use of weaponry confirmed my belief that I was not suited for the infantry. Several rounds from a revolver, an antique model of great weight (*Hold the revolver at arm's length, slowly lower your arm until you are lined up with the target, and then squeeze – squeeze – the trigger*). I've no idea where the bullets went. Ten rounds from a .303 Lee Enfield, with more damage to my bony shoulder than to the target. A spray of bullets from a Sten gun, a nasty little machine-gun apparently bought from Woolworth's (*Keep your 'and away from this 'ere slot, or you'll lose your fingers*). The only weapon I used effectively was the Browning machine-gun, perhaps because it was pre-aimed at a large sandbank and secured. All I had to do was to depress a lever.

Like the course of lectures, our training in weaponry was not to be taken seriously. Nor was our training in unarmed combat. We had two short sessions of this. In the first, my shoulder was nearly dislocated by an over-enthusiastic partner; and in the second, my ribs were punched violently by an ungrateful corporal when I obligingly tried to strangle him at his own request. These incidents confirmed the wisdom of my choice of service. If I had to fight great hairy Germans or Banzai-shouting Japanese, I preferred to do so seated behind a bank of machine guns.

These amusing activities were mere time-fillers, thrown in for variety. The main aim of R and C Wing was to screen us and turn us into reasonably fit facsimiles of servicemen, which meant that most of our training consisted of PT and drill. The PT, I must say, was reasonable, consisting mostly of running and prancing about, with some chin-ups and push-ups thrown in. It was designed to make us fit, not turn us into supermen. As I was fit to begin with, I managed not to disgrace myself. My only embarrassment came in the first session, when we were lined up in our singlets and baggy drawers to be inspected by a sergeant instructor, a gentleman resembling Charles Atlas. Passing quickly along the ranks, he paused when he came to me, slowly looked me up and down, and then shook his head with an expression of infinite sadness. I could almost read his thoughts as if they were inscribed in a cartoon balloon: *Oh ah, we've got a right one here – a youth misspent on smoking, billiards and wanking, possibly all three at the same time.* It was not true, of course. I hadn't played billiards for years. Still, I couldn't blame him. I stood over five foot ten yet weighed little more than 120 pounds, or eight and a half stone.

Though our PT would probably have been derided by paratroopers as physical jerks for fairies, our standard of drill would have done credit to the Brigade of Guards. The drill instructor responsible was Corporal Collinson, a square-shouldered, muscular man with the rugged good looks of a lifeguard. Though his bronzed complexion suggested hours spent sunning himself on the beach, flexing his muscles at the local talent, he proved to be a paragon among DI's. It's true, he tore strips off us distressingly often (*This room is like a shithouse. Clean it up!*), but he did so impersonally, without malice. In drill periods, his instruction and orders were clear and his demonstrations impeccable in timing and style. Not for us the extremes of the casual, somewhat theatrical style of the Americans, who seem unsure what to do with their arms, or the arse-splitting goosestep of the Germans, designed to turn men into robots. No, our drill sought the golden mean: a cadence of a hundred and twenty paces to the minute, arms swung waist high, and with none of the boot-stamping and arm-quivering often encountered in the British Army.

Under Corporal Collinson's tutelage we achieved such a degree of proficiency – in drill quicktime and slow, with rifles and without – that we were given practice in continuity drill, a series of manoevres performed on the receipt of just one order. Chorus girls would doubtless scoff at so simple a routine; but we performed without music and needed good timing. Thereafter, further drill being pointless, we spent much time on sport or on marching about the countryside, alarming wildlife with lusty renditions of "Tipperary," "Abdul the Bul-Bul Emir" and "Green Grow the Rushes, O".

At first, not wanting to attract unwelcome attention, most of us adopted a low profile. But inevitably some were thrust, or thrust themselves, into the public eye. One such unfortunate was Arthur. A quiet, moon-faced youth with a broad rump, he drew the eye with his utter lack of co-ordination and his style of locomotion, a rather bouncy ploughman's plod. Whether he was in step or not mattered not at all, as his unvarying cadence was some twenty paces slower than that of the rest of us. The result was chaos in the ranks. Ordered to change step one day, he gave an elephantine hop but unhappily failed to change his arm-swing and for a few paces waddled along like an enormous blue duck with painful haemorrhoids. Poor Arthur vanished shortly afterwards, no doubt remustered into the cookhouse or the mines. I doubt whether even the Pioneer Corps would have wanted him.

Although on the whole we were an amiable lot, some could ill tolerate irritating thrusters. John, a gangling, pimpled youth with an unhealthy pallor, became just such an irritant. Usually accompanied by a grinning minion, he took to wandering around trying to impress people by boasting in a hectoring manner. Perhaps he believed it made him intimidating, but anyone could see it was mere bluster. As one might guess, one day he went too far. "Right," a voice brayed, as we were marching off for some mayhem on the sports field. "I can tell you this. If anyone hits *me* over the head with a hockey stick, he'll be bloody sorry." Well, we were only too familiar with that voice. Foolish youth! He had huffed and he'd puffed and he was now to be punctured. Five minutes after the game had begun, John staggered off the field with a bleeding head. He was quiet thereafter.

And then there was Jock, Jock of the engaging, gold-toothed grin, he who had boasted of his ability to circumvent tests. Perhaps because he was, or seemed, older than the rest of us, he had been made cadet flight commander – a position designed in theory to give cadets experience in command, but in practice intended to give DI's the chance to slope off for an hour or two. In any case, it was a position that Jock filled well enough. At first. Before long, however, we noticed that, except on formal parades, he was usually invisible. If someone was required to march the flight off to the beach for some touch-rugby or even, as on one occasion, to take it on a cross-country run, then Jock, like Macavity, wasn't there, and the task fell to his deputy. As skiving on such an admirable scale could hardly have excaped the notice of Corporal Collinson, one must conclude that, in addition to his other virtues, Jock had the skill to worm his way into the indulgent good graces of superiors. He was a sly and able thruster.

The deputy cadet commander, who was also made right marker, was a slender youth for whom the daily shave was a mere formality. Had he wondered why he had been selected for such high offices, as I'm sure he had, then he might have concluded in his innocence that it was because those in authority recognized the aura of a leader when they saw one. But this was not in fact the case. The truth is that he had been the only one fool enough to report for duty in his A.T.C. uniform, and this had marked him out as a Keen Type. Nevertheless, the flight tolerated him, partly because he was both competent and obviously harmless – a thrustee, if ever there was one – and partly because no one else wanted the job. Need I say more? Dressed in a little brief RAF authority for the first and only time, the victim was I. As for my aura, if I have one, it was a tender shade of green.

⚜

2

Skellingthorpe

Summer declined into autumn. The winds from off the North Sea were growing chill, yellow and russet leaves had begun drifting to earth, and we were bored. We should have finished square-bashing and been posted off to points unknown by the end of August. Yet here we were, still mucking about in Scarborough in the middle of October. There was no question of obtaining relief by painting the town red. At the rate we were paid, three shillings a day, the best most of us could manage was a pastel pink, and that on fortnightly paydays only. The other evenings

217

were spent mostly on our pits, polishing our boots and buttons, writing letters, reading or chatting, with the only excitement a visit to the Naafi for tea and wads. There was clearly a hold-up somewhere. The reason was not far to seek. France and Belgium had been liberated, the Luftwaffe nearly cleared from the skies, and the Wehrmacht everywhere in retreat. Even we, with little access to the news, could see that the collapse of Germany was not far off. It seemed likely that we would not be needed as aircrew after all, but instead have to face an eternity of being marched hither and yon. And so, when the admirable Corporal Collinson one day called for volunteers to do some potato-picking for a while, I stepped forward. A spot of work on a local farm should come as a welcome change.

Several days later, I was mildly surprised to find myself on a train as part of a mixed squad of cadets committed to the care of a tall, dough-faced corporal. We had been posted on detachment to RAF Skellingthorpe. It transpired that my fondly imagined local farm was in Lincolnshire. "Never volunteer for anything", the received wisdom of old sweats, was a maxim I was aware of but ignored, as I had a low threshhold of tolerance for make-work and boredom. I should have listened to the old sweats. When a bottleneck is cleared, authority sheds the burden of idle louts first and useful volunteers find themselves at the end of the line. It took me two years to realise that truth.

As our train trundled sedately across the Yorkshire countryside, a grey overcast with low clouds pressed in from the North Sea. By the time we had passed between the ancient battlefields of Marston Moor and Stamford Bridge and on through York – one can hardly take a step in Britain without barking one's shins on history – the sky had become gloomy and a thin rain had begun to fall. The fine weather we had taken for granted was ended. Gradually, woods and pastures gave way to a blighted landscape – row upon row of grimy terrace houses; acres of foundries and factories set amidst stunted vegetation and sludge ponds filled with vile effluents; and a forest of brick chimneys, towering vomitories spewing dense smoke that trailed roiling in the wind to merge with the clouds scudding low overhead. We were coming into Sheffield. As we had to change there, some took the opportunity to wander around to view the sights. With the rain drizzling through the smoky gloom to lie upon the roofs and squalid streets like cold sweat, it seemed more like twilight in November than an early afternoon in October. The sounds of pedestrians and traffic were muffled and the few lights shining wanly in the shops offered scant cheer. It was as if we had stepped into one of the more depressing drawings of Gustave Doré.

After Sheffield the sky brightened perceptibly; and less than two hours after remarking the twisted spire of Chesterfield in the distance, we drew into Lincoln. Here we piled into the back of a waiting MT, an RAF lorry, and were driven off through the narrow, ancient streets. Sometime later, after jouncing along a maze of country roads, the transport slowed, turned sharply into an entrance and halted at a guardhouse. We had arrived.

RAF Skellingthorpe proved to be an operational bomber station, one of many in a swathe of eastern England stretching from East Anglia into Yorkshire. It was then home to 50 and 61 Squadrons, both equipped with Lancasters. Here were no squads of marching rookies, no DI's barking orders or prowling with eyes alert for slovenly skivers. Instead we saw a hive of purposeful activity. In and around the hangars, fitters clambered over the great planes like ants ministering to a queen. Tractor-drawn trains of trolleys snaked by, laden with bombs from the dump. And farther along the perimeter track, where bombers crouched at dispersal like dark birds of prey, petrol bowsers and armourers were at work refueling, loading bombs, and checking machine-guns and ammunition. This was the business end of the RAF. No one informed us that we were there under sufferance. There was no need. We knew exactly what was expected of us: to do what we had come to do and to keep out of the way.

Peripheral we may have been, but our needs were seen to with quiet efficiency. After a visit to the bedding store to collect blankets, another to the equipment section to receive coveralls and rubber boots, we were driven to the far side of the airfield. There we carried our gear to our billets, a group of Nissen huts scattered among conifers and about as far from the business of the station as was possible without being off the station altogether. Our MT then took us to the messhall for an evening meal. We had to hike the mile or so back to our huts. MT was provided to save time, not legs.

That evening, upon hearing engines being revved up, a few of us wandered over to the airfield to watch the bombers take off. At the far end of the field, a line of planes zigzagged around the perimeter like giant winged ants about to swarm. Then, engines roaring, one after another they accelerated down the runway towards us and laboured into the darkening sky. A group of officers stood waving them off, the C.O. and his staff, probably, and no doubt they would be present to count the bombers on their return. Which city were they going to raid? How many would not make it back? Losses, I knew, could be severe. I remembered my dismay the previous March on hearing the BBC announce that over ninety planes had failed to return from the night's operations. That was from just one raid, one operation among many hundreds over the years, one small part of a process which Churchill once whimsically described as lugging loads of bombs into Germany but which in fact was a hard-fought and mutually costly battle.

I tried to imagine what it must be like to be one of the crew, winging through the great deep of night in a cocoon of one's own noise, unable either to see or hear the encompassing danger – of a collision, of uncomfortably accurate flak, of the nightfighter sliding up from astern and the sudden shock of cannon fire. I tried to imagine being coned by searchlights, blinded, the aircraft desperately manoevring to escape, to imagine seeing other aircraft exploding or falling through the night in arcs of fire like Milton's rebel angels. But it was useless. The images came, but only reality could provide the feelings. Fortunately or not, depending on how one looks at it, fate decreed that I would not have to experience that particular reality. As for reality itself, I was shortly to learn that that, too, could seem unreal.

After breakfast the following morning, we were transported across the flat Lincolnshire countryside and deposited beside a large field where a farmer was already churning up potatoes with a horse-drawn digger. Quickly split into teams, one for each side of a cleared centre section, and assigned pitches, we were set to work on the exposed potatoes. By the time we caught up with the digger, it was time for lunch – packed sandwiches and a smoke. All too soon for us, the farmer remounted his infernal machine and began once more to churn up the ground, cannily maintaining a speed calculated to keep us working steadily. By mid-afternoon, backs were complaining and so were we. Plaintive appeals to give the horses a rest falling on deaf ears, one wag cast himself down, kicking and screaming, into the team's path. But the farmer's nerve proved steadier, and the horses didn't miss a step. Perhaps our antics amused our stolid employer. Perhaps not. In any case, crops left in the ground would not feed a population short of food nor put money into the farmer's pocket. We were made to earn our keep.

As days passed, sometimes we let off steam with an occasional potato fight or a little group psychodrama:

A falsetto voice: *What did you do in the great War, Daddy?*

Roared chorus: *Picked fucking potatoes, that's what!*

As it grew colder, we supplemented lunch with potatoes baked in the hot ashes of a small fire. But, in general, the first day set the pattern for the weeks that followed. The discovery that the coaches we had noticed carried Italian prisoners, bound like us for the fields, only heightened our self-mockery. It seemed appropriate, somehow, that our former enemies should be borne to work in upholstered comfort while we were carted along in the back of a draughty lorry.

Life in our free time also became circumscribed. The preparations for raids faded into the background, bombers thundered off unwatched, and even trudging through the dark to the Naafi was often too much of an effort. Apart from weekends, when we sometimes played basketball in the gym, and paydays, when we hiked to a country pub to drink ourselves silly on watery beer, we became bound to our woodland Nissens. With no wireless, little to read, not even cards or a chess set, we were thrown upon our own resources – and before long a squad of smart cadets had degenerated into a rabble of bored peasants.

Only once did we attract attention. Around 1100 hours one Sunday morning, footsteps sounded in the passage of our Nissen and then the door flew open with a blast of light and cold air to admit a spruce orderly officer with a bright-buttoned sergeant in attendance. Not even the sudden materialization of the Archangel Gabriel could have created more consternation. But the surprise was mutual. Halting as if he had run into a wall, the officer gaped disbelievingly through the fug at a nest of scruffy herberts, all – save for one semi-clad specimen who had been morosely poking the fire – still stinking in their pits and now frozen into a state of suspended animation. There was a prolonged, strained silence as the officer, Adam's apple bobbing, struggled to find words to fit the enormity of the crime he had uncovered. At last he found them. "This is definitely wrong," he spluttered. Then he turned and marched back out again. What a rocket was there given! When we had finished laughing, we debated our likely fate. The consensus was that we would soon be spending our free time peeling the potatoes we picked by day. But nothing further happened. With better things to do than chase us, authority wisely decided to let sleeping erks lie.

⚜

Green grow the rushes, O!

"D' ye wank?"

"Eh?"

"Dae ye wank?"

"Of course," I replied, surprised by the question. Tossing a shovelful of coal into the stove, I gave the fire another poke. By chance (or was it by chance?) I was alone in the hut with Jock, who now lay sprawled on his pit, the one closest to the stove. Our erstwhile flight commander, he of the gold-toothed grin, was not a companion I welcomed. He was usually friendly enough – at least, he smiled a lot – but he was crude and manipulative. Apparently unable to endure his own company, he had become the increasingly noisy centre of attention in our hut, and with his coarse voice and loud laughter had threatened to become an intolerable nuisance. Luckily, he was given to frequent disappearances, no doubt driven by his personal demons to seek mischief elsewhere.

"How often d' ye dae it?"

I began to feel irritated. Masturbation was not my favourite topic of conversation. As for its practice, I found it shameful. I was subject to the same sexual urge as everyone else but generally found it a nuisance, one to be disposed of as simply and directly as possible. My chief interests were elsewhere. "Oh, about every ten days or so, I suppose. Why?" I asked, glancing up.

His hands clasped behind his head, he was staring ruminatively at the ceiling. Then he raised himself upon one elbow and looked at me. "How d' ye dae it?" he said, ignoring my question. His manner was friendly, inviting confidence.

How did I do it? What kind of silly bloody question was that? "With my hand, of course. What did you think?" I rose to my feet. This conversation had gone on long enough.

He flopped back on his pillow with a gusty sigh. "Now me, I like to climb into a warrm bath, with the top o' ma pecker just clear o' the watter. Then I pull the wings off a blowfly and let it run aroond on it." He laughed huskily.

I froze, then felt a wave of revulsion. "Well," I remarked, as I walked out of the hut, "it shows imagination, anyway."

I made very sure I was never alone with him again.

He, however, was not finished with me. Some days later, after an evening spent swilling beer at our regular hostelry, a small group of us lurched merrily into camp and dispersed. For the first time since I had tried to poison myself with Devon rough cider, I was drunk. It was dark in the hut, and the smoky fug resonated with snores as I tiptoed into my corner, which was enclosed on three sides and resembled a scruffy monk's cell. Fumbling, I divested myself of my boots and uniform, pulled my tie over my head and then crawled under the blankets. To hell with my shirt and socks. But sleep wouldn't come. The head of my bed was sinking into the floor and my brain had begun to spin. Breaking into a cold sweat, I flopped onto my stomach and tried again. As I lay there, fighting well-merited nausea, I felt someone leap onto me and begin bouncing me up and down. What kind of stupid clot would lark about at this hour? Didn't he realize my stomach was not constant? "Gerroff," I groaned.

"It's a' reet. It's a' reet." The words were whispered huskily almost in my ear. It was Jock, his voice thick, urgent.

Anger and a sudden imperial summons impelled me to action. "Get the fuck off!" I shouted. Arching my back violently, I hurled him to the floor and staggered outside.

"Faugh!" exclaimed Dennis, wrinkling his nose. Just returned from his morning ablutions, he was digging his ears out with his towel. "Who was the dirty sod who threw his ring up outside?"

Lifting my head carefully from where I'd been contemplating my boots, I said, "That would have been me." Suddenly, I became aware that the hut had grown oddly still and that everyone was staring at me curiously. Jock, I noticed, had performed one of his disappearing acts. "Well, what did you expect," I added defensively, "with bloody Jock bouncing around up there." Why were they all staring like that? Anyone could get sick on that rotten beer.

"You could have gone farther away," said Dennis at last.

I grinned. "You're bloody lucky I managed to get that far."

Unlikely as it might seem, several decades were to pass before mature reflection suggested to me exactly what Jock had been up to, "bouncing around up there". Is there anyone else, I wonder, who has taken quite that long to realize he has been sexually assaulted?

❦

Whoever degrades another degrades me.   – Walt Whitman

"DAH DI-DI DAH, DI-DAH DI-DAH." Boots hammering the floor, Jock was at full bore, bending the poker with his bare hands and bawling snatches of song in a hoarse voice deliberately made uglier. He seemed pleased with himself. The reason was soon evident. Suddenly stopping his caterwauling, he exclaimed, "Eh, I had a guid time last night. After a few wee nips, I like nothing better than to bash a Yank." He chuckled, looking around for approval.

"Why a Yank?" someone asked.

"Look how they treat their Blacks. Who the fuck do they think they are?"

Jock, the noble defender of the downtrodden! Where did he find Americans? Lincoln, probably, certainly not at our local. Although I had noticed his absence from the potato fields by day and from the hut most evenings, I had never wondered where he got to. In any case, I wasn't impressed by his explanation. I knew he liked to pick a fight when he'd been drinking. His preferred victim was usually the last one who had annoyed him. Failing that, the nearest fellow Scot would do – or anyone.

As fate would have it, there was another Scot in our hut. For reasons that will become apparent, I shall call him Riever. Muscular, yet softly spoken, he usually had little to say; but when Jock was absent he tended to rabbit away.

"I'm getting fed-up with Riever," remarked Dennis to me one day. Like Jock, Dennis had also been a member of my flight at Scarborough.

"Why?"

"Oh, he's always going on about what a great athlete he is. Claims he's a champion wrestler. I wish he'd shut up."

As if bragging were not enough, Riever tempted fate further by demonstrating his athletic prowess in a basketball game. Bounding all over the court like a manic Springheel Jack, shouldering lighter players out of his way, he soon had some of us muttering. "Leave him to me," Dennis reassured us. "I'll fix him." A few minutes later, Riever retired from the game, clutching his groin and looking unhappy.

Perhaps he was a slow learner, or just stupid, but one quiet evening Riever decided to push an argument with Mike into a fight. The rest of us, three bods sprawled on their pits in a state of stupefied boredom, immediately perked up, curious, yet ready to intervene, for Riever outweighed Mike by at least three stone. We needn't have worried. Mike, the quietest and shortest of us, had no intention of fighting on Riever's terms. Instead, clasping his hands behind his head, he lay calmly on the floor and kicked out with his boots whenever his burly opponent came near, a novel defensive tactic that at first didn't seem promising. However, when the champion wrestler showed no sign of hurling himself from a great height to tie a flattened Mike into knots, we leant against our bedding and prepared ourselves to be entertained.

What followed was a fight reminiscent of the boxing bout in *City Lights,* only in this case there was no physical contact whatever! Mesmerized by the lashing boots, Riever circled the imperturbable Mike, looking for an opening. Round and round he went, making tentative little rushes and then leaping back with exaggerated caution as if he were a large but timid mongoose facing its first deadly cobra. After a few minutes of this unprofitable tactic, he began to wave his arms in exasperation and make little whimpering noises. Then, casting his eyes around wildly for inspiration, he rushed across to his bed and began to pelt Mike with biscuit mattresses. "Thanks," said Mike, seizing the first as a pad for his back and booting the other two out of the way. It was now that Riever made another mistake. Maddened by frustration and by our laughter, which was now bordering on hysteria, he seized the broom and made to hit Mike with it.

"Hey!"

"No you don't!"

As one man we had sprung to our feet. We weren't laughing now. His eyes brimming with tears of rage and humiliation, the inept champion obediently threw the broom down. The great fight was over.

Someone must have told Jock. The following evening, as I lay reading, trying to ignore his usual racket, a sudden disturbance made me look up. Jock was having a go at Riever, his fists pumping out like pistons. For his part, Riever was retreating, making no effort to strike back but simply trying to fend off the blows. Suddenly, he threw up his hands. "I give up, Jock," he bleated. "I've had enough."

But not nearly enough for Jock. "Take your clothes off," he rasped.

Now on our feet, the rest of us stared with astonishment as Riever hastily stripped off, even to his socks, and then stood before us like a great white ghost.

"Come here!" Jock seemed to be swelling with power and menace.

Nervously, Riever began to edge towards the door.

"Where are ye going?"

"I need to take a shit, Jock."

Without hesitation, Jock kicked the coal bucket towards him. "Shit in that!"

It was time for someone to put a stop to it. Yet not one of us moved. Instead, we stood around like slack-jawed yokels at a sideshow.

Riever complied instantly, squatting on the bucket and staring up at his tormentor with absolute attention. With his great moon face, he resembled a huge, terrified little boy on his potty.

Shadows seemed to gather and deepen. The atmosphere in the hut was becoming unendurably oppressive, as if charged with dreadful import. Again, no movement from us, not a word of protest. We were as if spellbound.

"Pick it up." The tormentor's voice was now quiet, speculative. No one needed to ask what he meant. "Now grease your lips with it."

It was enough even for Jock. He ordered the pale wretch before him to empty the bucket in the latrines and then told me to see that he did it. Without protest, I walked out, his victim babbling by my side like a lunatic.

Even had he been coherent, I doubt whether I could have grasped a word. I was shaken, stupefied. What had happened had blown up so suddenly, order and compliance had followed one upon the other so swiftly, that the whole incident had seemed a like a single appalled glimpse into a Boschian hell. Since the first punch, no more than two minutes had elapsed. Riever hadn't been beaten into submission. He had collapsed into terrified servility after a mere scuffle. Sensing that he had been incapable of helping himself, I felt not condemnation of him but only horrified puzzlement. Here was something I could not understand. As for imagining how he must feel, that I shied away from. I did not wish to know.

Nor could I understand his tormentor. Although I knew him to have the instincts and confidence of a practiced bully, I found his domination of events, of us all, incredible. It was as if he had plotted and scripted everything beforehand. And what devil had prompted him to make his victim strip naked? Above all, how could he wax so fat with pleasure and power from another man's degradation? Here was something alien, another whose mental world I had no wish to enter.

And then there were the bystanders. We had leapt to the aid of Mike. Why did we – why did I – not intervene this time? I knew that I should have done. The fact is that I did not. What I did understand, and understand clearly despite a sense of unreality, was that something terrible, irremediable, had happened – that, in less time than it takes for sand to run out in an egg-timer, a man's life had been destroyed and all of us degraded.

It is perhaps ironic, and would be of no comfort to him, that Riever should be the least culpable of us all. As for me, the day would come when I would understand only too well what had happened to him. Since then, for my failure to act I have paid to the last farthing. At least, I hope I have. But one never knows. Like the Ancient Mariner, I may have penance yet to do.

☙❧

December's arrival drove us from the fields with a sharp frost, the first bite of the most bitter winter of the War. What the others then did with themselves I have no idea, for the farmer wanted volunteers to continue working and I was one of the few to step forward. The inducement was money – to be paid now to us instead of to the RAF. It was something I could do with. As I allotted part of my pay home, I was having to scrape by on one shilling and ninepence a day. This time the farmer provided the transport – an open two-wheeled trailer of the kind used to carry sheep or pigs to market. In this luxurious conveyance we were deposited shivering onto a frosty field at first light and carted back to camp in the same state in the evening. Nonetheless, we worked with a will. It was too cold to do anything else. It was the first fall of snow that brought our frosty harvest to an end. It also brought very few shillings, and we cursed the farmer for a skinflint.

Almost my last memory of Skellingthorpe is of a group of us trudging through the snow in the last drear light of day. We were on our way to the Naafi. Haunting my mind were the strains of "Lili Marlene", perhaps the one song of World War II that approached the emotional impact of "Tipperary" and "Keep the Home Fires Burning" in the earlier War. There was none of the usual purposeful activity on the station. In fact, apart from us, it might have been deserted. The hangars, huts, and control tower were all dark, the windsock hung limp, and the bombers squatted silently on their pads, staring blindly at a leaden sky. Ops had been scrubbed again, and anyone with any sense was inside trying to keep warm. The foul weather providing cover for the Germans in the Ardennes was also giving our bomber crews a welcome break.

Suddenly, a hut came to life, as a crowd of laughing, chattering aircrew burst out to board a waiting crewbus – off, no doubt, to savour the joys of Lincoln nightlife. But they were not to escape so easily. As the last man, an officer, prepared to board, from out the gloom flew an unerring snowball to explode its challenge on his cap. The chatter ceased abruptly as they all peered out to discover the perpetrator of this cheeky outrage. Who was that mob of scruffs? Then, noticing the scruffs' preparations for battle, and perhaps their rather grubby white flashes, they gave a great shout and tumbled out to the attack. And the air filled with snow and laughter, wails of mock dismay, triumphant shouts – in one brief, joyous encounter among the boys we all still were. Then, honour satisfied, they were gone. It was the only contact we had had with them.

The following day I was summoned to the orderly room. There I was given a leave pass and railway warrants, with orders to report to RAF Brough in January. I would be home for Christmas.

⊙⦿⊙

Postscript

A month or so after leaving Skellingthorpe I bumped into Dennis again. After exchanging greetings, he said, "Things really blew up after you left, you know."

"How do you mean?"

"You remember complaining about how little you got from the farmer? Well, we discovered that Jock and that tall streak of a corporal had pocketed at least half the money between them. And that's not all. One night, Jock came back drunk and stole a transport from the MT section. The SP's were chasing him all around the airfield just as the bombers were coming in to land."

"Bloody hell! He must have run amok. What happened to him?"

"I haven't a clue," Dennis replied, "but I know they had him up on about thirteen different charges."

"A busy bugger, wasn't he," I said. "I hope they sent him to the glasshouse."

Then I dismissed him from my mind.

CHAPTER TWELVE

I Sprout Wings...

1
Brough

RAF Brough was on the Humber, near Hull, but when I reported to the guardroom in early January, it might have been on the snowbound coast of Labrador. It was bitterly cold and a sly easterly from off the North Sea tweaked my nose and thrust icy fingers through my uniform with insolent ease. Sniffing and blinking away tears, I could vaguely make out the shapes of wooden huts looming out of a dense, bone-chilling fog. Massed frost feathers clung to every surface exposed to the wind and even to the snow itself, where they lay like clotted cream on milk. This dismal weather, which had provided cover for the Ardennes offensive, had persisted for weeks. It was to last for another fortnight.

Bundled up in greatcoats and wearing our cap comforters as scarves, my flight spent much of the days that followed being marched from hut to hut, to whichever was free at the time and had a fire. The cold was such that – wonder of wonders! – even PT had been scrubbed. The nights were less comfortable. Although more than twice the size of a Nissen, my hut was furnished with only one stove and a fuel supply consisting mainly of coal dust. Far from keeping us warm, the fire had to be nursed merely to be kept alive. As a result, we spent the nights shivering under blankets and greatcoat and awoke in the mornings to find boots frozen to the floor and frost glittering everywhere save for a small circle around the stove. A midnight raid on the fuel compound by two enterprising spirits produced only more coal dust. There was nothing else to be gleaned.

But there were consolations, apart from the obvious one that we were far better off than the troops in the field. The Naafi provided a warm refuge for much of our off-duty time, and we were occasionally treated to a picture. Also cheering was the improvement in the mess. In place of the usual RAF cooking staff, who sometimes steamed the life out of food, a private caterer had been brought in. On the whole, the cooking was better and the mess hall cleaner and brighter.

One evening, as I sat in a warm fug waiting for the picture to begin, George Carey dropped into the chair next to me. George was a native of Goderich, Ontario, although why he was there as a cadet instead of arriving fully trained like most of his countrymen I don't know. After sitting in silence for a while, he leant towards me and said quietly, "You've no idea what I've just been through."

I looked at him. Even under artificial lighting he appeared pale. "Why, what happened?"

"I was visiting a friend at an operational station today," he explained. "While I was there, a bomber crashed as it was taking off on an exercise, and we were roped in to help clear up the mess." He paused, obviously shaken. "Christ, you should have seen it. Bits of bodies all over the place."

I tried not to visualize the scene. "Best not to think of it."

By the end of the picture, however, he had brightened a little. "Hey," he said as we walked out, "I've got an invitation to a nurses' dance. Want to come along?" Seeing me hesitate, he added, "There'll be another guy coming with us."

The only dance I could do was the veleta, which I had learnt at school. Somehow I didn't think that would get me very far. Rats! I'd feel like an idiot. Still, it was something to do and I could hide in the crowd. "OK," I agreed. "Thanks."

I was half right. The three of us began the evening well by finding the hospital, which stood in its own considerable grounds. In view of the fog, arriving only half an hour late was a good effort. It was when we were shown into the reception room that doubt began to creep into my mind. Seated in a row beneath the blackout curtains were about twenty young nurses, chatting quietly among themselves. At our entrance they fell silent and looked at us expectantly. Beside them in a corner stood a long table with refreshments, a large tea urn with plates of sandwiches and cakes; on a card table at the end of the room sat the dance band – a wind-up gramophone with a small stack of records; and on either side of this were seated two middle-aged ladies, evidently the matron and her deputy. It was only when I glanced at the side opposite the nurses that the awful truth became apparent. There stretched another row of chairs – all conspicuously empty! I gulped. Where were the other men? Surely they would arrive soon. Perhaps some over-paid, over-sexed Americans would come to the rescue. No such luck. The crowd in which I had expected to lose myself never materialized. We were not only the first, but the last men to turn up. There had been a snafu.[11]

Any normal red-blooded young male would have felt a warm surge at such a heaven-sent opportunity and have gone flitting from flower to flower singing *It's Tico time for all the lovers in the block*. Well, I was young, male and red-blooded, but what I felt rising within me was not my libido but a feeling akin to panic. What chance was there now for playing wallflower? It being too late for craven flight, I had no choice but to face up to my duty. And so, as record followed record, bravely I tripped the light fantastic – "tripped" being the operative word – desperately trying to make intelligible conversation with my unfortunate partners and punctuating my inanities with apologies for clumsy feet. Eons passed.

Refreshment time arriving at last, the three sweating musketeers grabbed their share and fled to the men's side of

---

[11] In the sanitized version *Situation normal, all fouled up*. Less well known are the comparative, *Sirfu* (*Situation is really fucked up*), and the superlative, *Fubar* (*Fucked up beyond all recognition*).

the floor. But there was to be no sanctuary. Some of the more forward young ladies followed us, drew up chairs and began peppering us with questions. Where were we stationed? How long would we be there? Had we been doing any flying? One brazen wench even placed her hand lingeringly on my thigh. How was a fellow supposed to feed, or defend, himself with a plate in one hand and a mug of tea in the other? And why was the heat turned up so high?

It was the matron who came to the rescue. Pitying our plight, she used the weather as an excuse for declaring festivities at an end. I felt sorry for the nurses. They were underpaid and worked long, hard hours under a discipline as strict as ours. They had deserved an evening of fun. What they got were three boys in blue.

Still, the evening was not a complete loss. Two managed to get dates after all – the matron and her deputy! The following weekend they whisked George and me off to Hull for afternoon tea and an evening at the theatre. They were very maternal. The other innocent I think had had enough.

☙❧

2

Interlude

Huddled close to the stove, I gave the fire another irritable poke. Rats, two days to payday and not even a penny for a mug of Naafi tea. As I sat thus in solitude, pondering the injustice of it all, the door opened to admit a cadet and a blast of even colder air. He looked around and then approached. "You wouldn't know where Jonesy is by any chance, would you?" he asked.

"Haven't a clue," I replied. "At the Naafi, probably."

"O.K. Thanks."

As he turned to go, I did something that surprised us both. Rising from my seat, with no warning I hurled myself at him and wrestled him to the floor! Almost immediately, I sensed something wrong. Instead of crying out and fighting back, he lay supine, apparently unmoving. Disturbed, I relinquished my bear hug

234

and rose to my knees. He was not absolutely motionless. Holding his hands before his chest like a begging puppy, he was making feeble little resisting movements of the kind one sometimes sees in very young children. And his eyes were enormous, black. Looking more closely, I could see that the pupils were so widely dilated that the irises were barely visible.

Alarmed, I placed a hand on his shoulder and shook him gently. "Hey," I said mildly, "I was only larking about." Getting up, I cursed myself for an idiot.

After lying still for endless seconds, he climbed to his feet. He was tall, slender, a complete stranger. For a moment he remained there, wordlessly dusting himself off, and then he turned and walked away.

"I'm sorry," I called after him.

Bloody hell, I thought, watching his silent, retreating figure. Someone must have got to you when you were a child.

Later, thinking back on the incident, I wondered if it had been the shock of my attack that had traumatized him. But I dismissed the horrid thought. True, it had been sudden, but it had been a mere puppy pounce and I had released him at once. Why should I have done such a thing? I did not normally indulge in horseplay. It certainly was not because subconsciously I sensed vulnerability, for in that case my instinct would have been to feel compassion, not take advantage. I can only suppose it to have been an act of extreme boredom, and completely unpremeditated. Otherwise it is a mystery. Years after the event, however, the significance of its effect was to become only too clear.

ళ

3

Tiger Moth

Dawn arrived on January 17 with a silent explosion of light. Gone were the fog and cloud at last, driven off by a shift in the wind, and the sun rose into a clear blue sky. Although it was still freezing, the cold now nibbled only at fingers and nose and stimulated the circulation instead of penetrating to the bone. As we were marched briskly off, the station was springing to life about us. Brough was no mere collection of huts, after all, but a working station, the wartime home of 4 EFTS.[12] Ahead of us, we knew, were twelve hours of flying training, the purpose of which was to screen out promising pilot material.

By the time we were halted at the flights, ground crews had rolled back hangar doors and were wheeling out what appeared to be relics of the last War – biplanes, covered with doped fabric and complete with struts and wires, wooden propeller and open cockpits. Tiger Moths – a pilot's dream! Clad in vivid training yellow but with wartime camouflage on the upper surfaces, they seemed the archetypal flying machine. Even as we watched, mechanics began swinging propellers and engines spluttered into life. Someone had been busy during the fog. Though the countryside was still sheeted with snow, the grass airfield had been largely cleared.

While instructors ran up engines and took the long-idle planes for test flights, we made initial entries in our logs and stowed our newly acquired flying gear into assigned lockers. The big moment for me came after lunch. Wearing full flying kit and carrying my parachute over my shoulder, I waddled out to the aircraft like a stuffed French goose. Though I felt ludicrously overdressed, given the cold and the open cockpit I knew I would need all the kit I was wearing: fleece-lined flight boots, kapok-filled inner flying suit, windproof outer suit, leather helmet, goggles, face mask and three pairs of gloves – silk inners, woollen gloves and leather gauntlets. With goggles down and face mask fastened, the only parts exposed were my cheek bones.

Lesson 1 in the sequence of instruction was familiarization with the cockpit. As I stood peering into it, my instructor, Flight Sergeant Bale, pointed out the instruments and the controls. The layout was spartan, pleasingly simple after the Link Trainer.

"This is the throttle lever," he said, "and this is the friction nut. It's loose right now for easy control while taxying. When you fly solo, though, you must tighten it before you take off or the vibration of the engine will jar the throttle back and cause you

---

[12]   Elementary Flying Training School. The airfield actually belonged to the Black-burn Aircraft Company, which had a factory nearby.

to lose power. Here are the ASI, the turn and bank indicator, the engine speed indicator and the altimeter. Those are the rudder pedals and this" – seizing the stick and waggling it – "is…"

"…the joystick," I said, nodding.

An expression of pain came over his face. "We don't use that term here," he admonished. "We call it the control column."

Oblivious to the phallic connotation of the term "joystick," I nonetheless sensed disapproval and dropped the term. Mostly, though, it was simply called "the stick."

"All right," he sighed, "before we get in we have to check a few things." He led me around to the front of the aircraft. "Make sure the tyres are fully inflated and that the chocks are in place. We don't want to kill the mechanic." He pointed to a device mounted on a starboard strut. "That's the pitot head. Always check to see the cover is removed, or your airspeed indicator won't work. That could be an embarrassment. Now, put your parachute on and climb into the rear cockpit. Try not to put your foot through the fabric."

When he was sure that I was firmly strapped in, he leant over and waggled the stick. "Before we take off, we must check to see that the controls are working properly." Here he ran me through the process. "OK," he said, satisfied, "I'll demonstrate all this in the air. You'll soon get the feel of the controls. Now, fasten your face mask and plug in here. That's the Gosport tube. We'll need it to communicate in the air." That said, he climbed into the front cockpit and raised his hand.

"Switches off,"the waiting mechanic shouted.

"Switches off."

The mechanic stepped up to the propeller, rotated it a few times and then stood with his fingers resting on top of the blade. "Switches on," he called.

"Switches on."

"Contact!" The mechanic gave a mighty heave, stepping back smartly as he did so, and the engine spluttered into life.

"Chocks away!"

Then we were off, taxying to the downwind end of the airfield.

As we climbed into the light – in the full glare of the sun the snow-covered countryside was dazzling – I had a fleeting sense of déjà vu. Seated in the open cockpit of the frail biplane with the helmeted head of the pilot in front of me, I felt tempted to look around for the Hun in the sun. Only the Lewis guns were missing. More to the point, when the instructor handed the controls over for me to get the feel of them in straight and level flight and gentle turns, I found handling the plane to be much easier than "flying" a Link trainer. Although engine vibration made the instrument needles waggle and the plane tended to bounce about, I felt confident at the controls, and from that moment had no doubt that I would be selected as a pilot.

Over the next ten days I made six flights, for a total of five hours. Then foul weather set in again and persisted for a month, with fog, low cloud or high winds making flying too risky or impossible. Just how risky flying a Tiger Moth in a high wind could be was demonstrated by the Chief Flying Instructor on a test flight one day. Throttling back, he amused himself and us by hovering over the station like a hawk. Unable to fold his wings like one, however, he had a struggle to land the plane safely.

Even the most miserable English winter can't last forever. A fine spell set in on February 27 and training began in earnest. Four days later, after a fifteen minute test in which I did one circuit and bump, the examining officer climbed out of the front cockpit. "Feel ready to take it up on your own?" he asked.

"Yes, sir," I replied confidently.

"Off you go, then." He walked away as though he had no further interest, but I knew he would be watching keenly.

After nine hours dual, I was about to do my first solo.

Swinging the aircraft round, I taxied to the downwind end of the field and lined up into wind. Then, after glancing around to make sure no one else was taking off or landing in my vicinity, I opened the throttle. I was allowing no time for doubts or apprehensions to creep in.

Perhaps, I should have done. The engine note increased to a snarl, the aircraft surged forward, and in no time the tail came up. A few bounces on the rough field, and then I eased the stick back. I was airborn. Reaching climbing speed, I throttled back and looked around. So far so good. Another couple of hundred feet and I could begin my climbing turn onto the crosswind leg.

Suddenly, I detected a change in the engine note. A quick glance at the ASI revealed that my speed was dropping off. Something was wrong! I looked at the throttle lever. It was vibrating wildly and gradually closing. Bloody hell! I'd forgotten to tighten the friction nut. Cursing, I rammed the throttle open again with one hand and tightened the nut with the other, at the same time trying to hold the stick with my knees. Had my instructor noticed? A gentle climbing turn to the left, another turn at a thousand feet – and I was on the downwind leg. All was well, and my pulse rate began to drop. The thing now was not to cock up the landing. A turn onto the crosswind leg, throttle back into a glide, keeping a vigilant eye on the speed, and then a final turn into wind. The grass rushed up to meet me. Round out...hold off...a few gentle bumps...and I was down.

If anyone had noticed my minor crisis, no mention of it was made to me; and after making up my log, I went off to the messhall in high spirits.

And there, as I waited in line to be served, I had another surprise, a pleasant one this time. Seated at one of the tables was a flight sergeant with the coveted brevet of an observer. His face looked familiar. What's more, he was grinning at me. My cousin John! Learning of my whereabouts from my mother, he had come down from York especially to see me. It was the first time we had met since before the war. Now he was a veteran, having completed a tour of ops on Wellingtons and Mosquitos with Bomber Command.[13]

Two days later I had my last flight with my instructor. After having me practice spin recovery (*Stick forward...full opposite rudder*), he taught me the steep turn and then allowed himself to be persuaded to do some aerobatics. "Can't make the slow roll too slow," he commented, as I hung upside down in my straps with debris from the cockpit falling past my face. "The fuel system uses gravity feed and the engine is liable to cut out." Here the engine gave a warning cough. "See?" Then, after permitting me to try

---

13   Many years after the war and by then aware of the appalling death rate among bomber crews, I asked him how he had survived. "Don't know how I managed it," was his only reply. Luck – and transfer to Mosquitos probably had something to do with it, as their loss rate was much lower than that of the heavy bombers.

a loop, we landed. "Wait in the cockpit," he said, unbuckling his harness and leaving the engine running. "Someone will be along in a minute to give you the final test. Good luck."

After the forty minute test I was through. In twelve flights, I had completed the last seven hours of flying training in six days.

CHAPTER THIRTEEN

...Spread Them Confidently...

1
At home on the rolling deep

The corvette rose easily to the heavy swell, an unending procession of grey rollers bearing down out of the murk, but a wicked cross-sea slapped spray high over her bridge and made her roll violently. Just as well I didn't join the Navy, I thought, watching her wild gyrations. As a small boy I had once toyed with the idea, imagining myself at the helm of a warship or peering from the crow's nest with eagle eyes alert for enemy ships. Now I could see the reality. Like most of the ship's crew, I would more likely have been battened down below decks, feeling damp, cold, claustrophobic and unpleasantly sick.

I was enjoying these self-congratulatory thoughts while leaning in relative comfort on the rail of the *SS Volendam*, a small troopship ploughing across the Atlantic in the teeth of a moderate sou'wester. It was early June, 1945. Together with returning Canadian servicemen, fellow cadets and a few war brides, I was outward bound for Halifax. Though war in Europe had ended weeks before, the authorities, fearing attack by "pirate

U-Boats," had provided us with the corvette escort and routed us far to the south.

After Brough I had completed ITW (Initial Training Wing) at R.A.F. Bridgnorth, where the study of navigation, meteorology and theory of flight had proceeded side by side with much practice in the uses of morse code, blanco and assorted polishes – metal, boot and floor. The DI of my flight had been Corporal "Stand by your wankers" Purdey, a short man with a potato head and a lop-sided body that terminated in a pair of large, bright boots. He was to die under a train, I heard later, encouraged thither by a surreptitious push. If the rumour was true, I am sorry, for he deserved no such fate. A genial man, he had eased our stay by enforcing Bridgnorth bull with good humour.

Few events at Bridgnorth present themselves to memory now. A fresh April morning when, freed from the lecture room for a cross-country, we had run wing-footed over the Shropshire uplands with all the joy of lighthearted youth. My officer-selection interview, remarkable only for its brevity:

> I present myself before the desk, snap off a smart salute and remain at attention. Ignoring me, the interviewing officer continues leafing through what are presumably my records. Suddenly, he stretches himself full length in his chair and regards me with cool, grey eyes. A flight lieutenant with pilot's wings, he is fair, large of bone and extremely tall, at least six foot three. He speaks:
>> Do you play rugger?
>> No, sir.
>> What subject have you learnt most about?
>> Theory of flight, sir.
>> What can you tell me about the binomial theorem?
>> Never heard of it, sir.
>> That will be all. (*He nods.*)
>
> I salute and march out, feathers only slightly ruffled. I knew a commission to be beyond my reach anyway.

A newsreel, when I had gaped uncomprehendingly at a vision from hell – a bulldozer pushing a pile of grotesque dolls with matchstick limbs into a communal grave, only these dolls had once been human beings. It was my first appalled intimation of the Holocaust. And VE Day, which had coincided with our completion of the course. In the evening several of us had gone to the Sally Ann canteen to celebrate with tea and wads. Upon emerging, we had become aware of leaping flames and the sound of revelry by night. Investigation had revealed the source to be a huge bonfire on the parade ground, fueled by chairs, benches, tables, signposts, doors and sundry other combustibles and around which capered a noisy mob in a wild chiaroscuro reminiscent of children's matinee at the cinema and Disney's "Night on Bare Mountain". After watching this antic scene for a while, we had gone on to our hut.

Shortly thereafter had followed a lengthy passing-out parade in the blazing sun, during which, kept standing to attention, I nearly *did* pass out; two weeks' embarkation leave, feeling immensely rich with my new pay scale of seven and three a day; and then a posting to Heaton Park with the desired rating of Pilot/Navigator/Wireless Operator, a category, veterans had warned, that would keep me there until I took root. Fortunately, they had been wrong. Two weeks later had found me shouldering my kit aboard the *Volendam*.

As might be expected, life on the troopship was crowded, spartan and tedious. Although the cross-sea gave the ship only a slight roll, the swell caused her to pitch considerably, a movement comfortable enough amidships but less so at the bow and stern. Unhappily for those subject to sea-sickness, we were accommodated far forward in a dank steel compartment that ran the width of the bow and shuttled ceaselessly up and down like an enormous lift. Here we lived, a hundred or so cadets, eating our meals at fiddled mess-tables by day, and by night swinging above them in our hammocks like a colony of portly bats. Two large galvanized iron sinks served for washing and puking, though usually not at the same time. The only access to the compartment was by a steep accommodation ladder, the negotiation of which called for careful timing. Depending on the movement of the ship, one flitted up or down the steps like a fairy or else buckled at the knees. Either way was tricky, especially for the cadets detailed to bring food from the galley. It was no place to loiter in unless one had to, and whenever possible we escaped to the open deck to admire the tossing, multitudinous sea and pity (or gloat over) the unfortunate corvette.

Even after three days of heavy weather, with one exception none of us minded. In fact, I'm sure that I wasn't the only naive romantic who secretly hoped to experience a good storm. As for tedium, we were used to it. Far from complaining, for the privilege of crossing the Atlantic to train in Canada we would willingly have stoked the boilers ourselves. The one likely exception was the "Green Ghost", a tall, fair cadet who had attracted our amused attention by turning green and vanishing below even before we had cleared Liverpool harbour. His failure to reappear eventually aroused speculation. The consensus was that he had ferreted out a hole near the ship's centre of gravity and was nesting there in solitary misery.

To keep idle hands from mischief, the ship's authorities assigned duties – swabbing-out, peeling potatoes and like chores for the troops, and guard duties for us. I had two regular watches. Together with another cadet I had to patrol the boat deck for an hour or so after dark. As we were never quite sure what we were supposed to be guarding or guarding against – presumably unauthorized lights – when some wag suggested our main duty was to ensure no one was sampling a war bride under the lifeboat covers, we dubbed ourselves the "anti-shag patrol".

In the afternoons, I guarded the petty officers' heads from contamination by other ranks. This was a fine and private place with regular toilets, partitions and doors; and while guarding it was about as interesting as the love-life of Winnie the Pooh, there was a bonus – no one was there to watch the watcher and so I made use of it myself. I justified this betrayal of trust on the grounds that the alternative would have been a bad case of constipation. Having used the men's heads once, I wasn't anxious to repeat the experience. There was no privacy there, not even toilet seats. Instead, two rows of naked porcelain bowls faced each other for the length of a long compartment, and upon these men perched at their offices like bare-arsed hens attempting to lay directly into egg cups. To compound the indignity the compartment was flooded and the ship's rolling sent a miniature tidal wave of unmentionable composition rushing from one end of it to the other. To avoid having his boots filled, each man in turn was thus forced to salute his opposite number by raising both legs into the air in a grotesque anticipation of "the wave". No, it was not a pretty sight.

After an unusually comfortable night, I came on deck on the fourth day to find the ship steaming downwind under a clear sky. Gone were the grey rollers, their place taken by eager little whitecaps that chased one another across a sparkling blue sea. Gone, too, was the corvette. Flying fish escorted us now, breaking surface from time to time and skittering ahead on iridescent finny wings. Reportedly we were close to the Azores and so not far from the Northeast Trades. As I looked about me, admiring the changed seascape, I spotted the "Green Ghost." He stood propped up against a door jamb, evidently drawn on deck by the easier motion of the ship. Looking paler and thinner, he was gnawing on something and casting mournful eyes around the empty horizon. For a while he stood thus, and then he turned green and vanished below. I never saw him again. I have since wondered whether he deserted in Canada rather than face the ordeal of another such crossing. Not having his affliction, I rejoiced in the elemental waste of sea and sky. As far as I was concerned the longer the voyage the better. In the event, thanks to our re-routing far to the south, the crossing took ten days and gave me a sense of the vastness of the Atlantic not experienced by travellers in today's jet-propelled chicken batteries.

ⓧ

2

23 EFTS, Yorkton, Sask.

After docking in Halifax, we disembarked late the same night to board a train waiting at the dockside. This trundled off into the darkness and we awoke next morning to find ourselves in Moncton, New Brunswick, some hundred and sixty miles to the north. The RCAF introduced itself by providing us with breakfast – fried eggs and bacon with hash brown potatoes, or a stack of hotcakes with butter and maple syrup. This proved to be the regular breakfast and not a special treat! The suppers were equally lavish – fried chicken, fresh salmon, pork chops or T-bone steak. After nearly six years of rationing, we thought we were in paradise. When in addition we were awarded the temporary rank of LAC with the rate of pay of two dollars a day, we began to conceive a high regard for the RCAF.

RCAF Moncton provided me with something else. Intent, late one evening, on visiting a nearby café for a hamburger and a milkshake – as if we didn't have enough to eat – another cadet and I were on our way to the guardhouse. At a point where the path passed within a few yards of the perimeter fence there came a sudden "crack." Simultaneously, something went "phut" by our heads. On the road outside the fence, a darkened car roared to life and then sped off round a corner.

"Hey, Corp," I complained at the guardhouse, "some bugger just took a shot at us."

"What do you mean?" he asked.

Explaining what had happened, I added, "It was a small pistol by the sound of it."

"Probably someone pissed off because one of you guys pinched his girlfriend," the corporal said, grinning. "OK. I'll report the matter."

But we heard nothing further. Not that we cared. *You've got to accentuate the positive, eliminate the negative.* Besides, to immortal youth a miss is merely good fun. It was the only shot fired at me during the entire war.

After about ten days at Moncton, we boarded another train and headed west. Except for a break at Montreal that gave us a chance to wander around downtown for a few hours and practise our schoolboy French, on the train we remained for the better part of three days, a journey broken only by occasional waits at sidings to allow other trains to pass. Most of northern Ontario was wilderness, endless miles of conifers, lakes and fast-running streams, with only scattered settlements. The trees thinned out and habitations became more in evidence as we approached Winnipeg and thereafter gave way to open prairie. By the time we reached our destination, Yorkton, Saskatchewan, we were nearly twenty-five hundred miles from Halifax yet still only two thirds of the way across the country. Canada seemed as vast as the Atlantic and almost as empty.

"Look at that," someone exclaimed, pointing.

We looked, craning necks to peer through the bus windows. "That" was RCAF Yorkton's station HQ, a trim building set amid manicured lawns and weed-free flowerbeds. Freshly whitewashed rocks edged both beds and paths, and an immaculate RCAF ensign flew from a gleaming white flagpole.

"Looks as if bull is thick on the ground here," another muttered.

This suspicion deepened when we were assigned our barracks and given all of the following day to clean them. "You're to wash everything – walls and windows inside and out, floors, shelving, ledges. And don't forget the hallways and ablutions. We don't want them looking like shithouses. When you've done that, polish the floors until you can see your faces in them."

Bloody hell! Even at Bridgnorth we didn't go so far as to wash the walls. The RCAF must be peculiar about cleanliness. Observing our faces, the officer laughed. "We're having an AOC's inspection in a couple of days," he explained, "so do a good job."

At that we relaxed – a flap was something we understood. The next morning we set to with a will, enlivening the proceedings with a water fight. In the event, the RCAF proved highly professional, and we encountered none of the unnecessary bullshit we were occasionally subjected to in the RAF.

Flying began on June 25. Our aircraft was the Fairchild Cornell III, a trim monoplane with enclosed cockpit, fixed undercarriage and fixed wooden propeller. Though its 200hp Ranger engine lacked punch and delivered a cruising speed little faster than the Tiger Moth, the Cornell could do aerobatics and proved easy to fly. We also had the luxury of paved runways, as we did at our emergency landing field at Sturdee, a disused nearby airbase.

In an emergency, though, we could land almost anywhere. The surrounding countryside was prairie, given over to meadow and grain-growing and with no high ground to worry about except for low wooded hills about sixty miles away. Railways and main highways in general ran northwest, but nearly all secondary roads and the large fields were oriented to the cardinal points. Provided one could see, one hardly needed to consult the compass. To make navigation even easier, our flying area contained only three small towns – Canora, to the north; Melville, to the south; and Yorkton itself, about eight miles southeast of us. Two large lakes served as additional landmarks – Good Spirit Lake, between us and Canora, and Leech Lake, immediately south of Yorkton. Moreover, we were bounded to the east by the Assiniboine River, fifty miles or so away. Where it meandered southward across the Manitoba border it broadened into the sixty mile ribbon of Lake of the Prairies. From there, as if drawn by a ruler, a road ran for over a hundred miles due west through Yorkton and on over the horizon. The whole area might have been designed for trainee pilots.

And then the weather. Apart from a brief spell or two, we enjoyed week after week of sunshine, with rarely even a cumulus cloud to break the blue of an enormous sky. With none of the haze common in England, visibility was clear to the horizon, and the light was so overpowering that we had to wear sunglasses. RCAF summer uniforms of light khaki drill made the dry heat tolerable, with the tunic discarded in favour of short-sleeved shirt and tie for working dress. At night, the familiar constellations blazed with rare splendour and the Milky Way appeared as clear to us as it had to the ancient Greeks.

With flying training virtually uninterrupted, we completed EFTS quickly. Nine weeks had been needed for twelve hours flying at Brough. At Yorkton ten weeks sufficed for, in my case, over seventy-seven hours. As about seven out of ten aircrew received their training under the Commonwealth Air Training Plan, one wonders how the RAF would have fared without it.

In retrospect I seem to have spent the whole of that idyllic summer lounging around the flights watching others dice with death, as we lightheartedly called it, or else dicing myself – rather like being a member of a select flying club. It was not quite like that, of course. There were periodic visits to the Link trainer for one thing, ground school too. After going solo, however, I rarely had fewer than two flights in a day; and when we began night flying, I once had eight, for a total of five hours. Soon I was handling the aircraft with confidence. At night, instrument flying proved far easier than on the wretched Link. The aircraft was inherently stable, for one thing, and the air so still one could fly with precision. On my night solo, cocooned in the cockpit in the dim glow of the instruments, I seemed to be suspended motionless beneath the stars. Only the runway lights and the drone of the engine reminded me I was hurtling through the moonless night.

Youthful overconfidence, the confidence of ignorance, was a well recognized danger. "There are old pilots, bold pilots, but no old, bold pilots" we were warned more than once. In truth, some of the dangers of flying were obvious enough. I first conceived sympathy for flying instructors on the day of the Evans bounce. Misjudging his landing, said student had prematurely rammed his wheels into the runway, caromed up and seemed about to attempt a stall turn at thirty feet. Only his instructor's hasty application of full power had averted a crash.

Instructors could make mistakes, too. Not long after the previous incident, my instructor took me up for an hour's dual. As we cleared the end of the runway, the flap lever slammed forward with no warning and our aircraft, deprived of lift, sank perilously close to the ground, barely clearing the perimeter fence. There was a long silence, as two minds absorbed the same sober fact: had that happened a second or two earlier we would have hit the ground in front of the fence. At full power and with full fuel tanks the likely result would have been an instant barbecue. "You know, you really shouldn't have done that," the instructor said at last, his voice tense.

Done what? Released the lever prematurely while he was in control? Did he think me an idiot? I knew what had happened. He had botched his vital actions – actions a pilot must do to ensure safety on take off. One of these was to set a few of degrees of flap to provide extra lift and shorten the take-off run. The flap control on the Cornell is a simple lever that dogs into a ratchet. In setting the lever he had not made sure the teeth were engaged. Instead, they had merely rested on top of the ratchet and buildup of air pressure on the flaps had caused the lever to slip. "I didn't touch it, sir," I replied, nettled. There was another long silence. Now we both knew.

Needless to say, I committed pruneries of my own. Forgetting my vital actions altogether was one of them! Along with landing with one's undercart up this is a major no-no and one more likely to be fatal – as I knew only too well when one day I found myself frantically performing them while roaring down the runway. Fortunately, I was solo at the time and the checklist on the Cornell is a short one. And so I got away with it. That time.

On another occasion my engine suddenly quit while I was on a cross-country exercise. My immediate reaction was to freeze. Then I began to suspect the engine of malicious intent and like Basil Fawlty wanted to climb out and give it a damned good thrashing.

"All right," suggested my instructor calmly, having given me a chance to react on my own, "go through your checklist 'In the event of engine failure'."

Yes. Right. What a good idea! Why didn't I think of that? Let's see. What was the first item? "Check the fuel," I intoned, peering at the fuel gauges. The needle on the left guage was pointing accusingly at "empty". Rats! Angry with myself for not being alert, I leant forward and flipped the switch to the right tank. To my relief the engine re-started immediately. That has happened a couple of times to me since, fortunately in a car, though. I recall, still with embarrassment, running out of gas in the middle of Lion's Gate Bridge in Vancouver….

Not all flying hazards are as obvious. It doesn't take many hours of training to become proficient in handling a small aircraft, but to fly one safely under all conditions is another thing entirely. Nature sets traps for the unwary, traps best avoided altogether, and one day she gave me a sharp lesson in meteorology. Having been signed out for ninety minutes' solo instead of the usual hour, and with the sky an innocent blue to the horizon, I decided to climb much higher than usual and set off to the southwest. Half an hour later I leveled out at ten thousand feet and looked carefully about me. Not a cloud or another aircraft in sight. Below, the ground had resolved into a checkerboard of fields, with the lakes, main roads and railways standing out clearly. Turning south, I practised recovery from stalls and spins and then, becoming bored, amused myself with a series of aerobatics.

At the end of half an hour I called it a day. Now for a nice, quiet gliding descent home. Pulling the nose up in a stall turn, I headed back. The airfield was where I expected, some twenty miles northeast of me. But there was something else – and my heart gave a sickening lurch. On the western edge of the field, looming over it menacingly, reared an enormous thundercloud, its top fanning out into the characteristic anvil and its sooty base nearly dragging the ground. And behind that was another, and another, in a line stretching to the northwest as far as I could see. I gaped in disbelief. Where the hell had they blown up from? And so quickly! Less than half an hour ago I had been looking at a cloudless sky.

Hell of a fighter pilot I would make, I thought, allowing myself to be jumped not by a Hun but by a bloody great cumulonimbus cloud! Now I regretted having climbed so high. I couldn't simply stick my nose down in a screaming dive. Lacking a constant speed unit, my propeller would over-rev and perhaps damage the engine. I could not take the risk. Descending as fast as I dared, I headed for the far side of the field. It would be a race between me and the cloud.

The cloud won. By the time I arrived, its leading edge was covering the airfield. To lose height more quickly without gaining speed, I sideslipped beneath the scud roll and then lined up with the runway to begin my approach. The air was still calm. With any luck I would make it! But as I crossed the perimeter fence, suddenly I was seized as if by a giant's hand and shaken violently. In a moment I found myself fighting for control a few feet above the runway, the aircraft slewing and its wings flipping in the turbulence. For endless seconds I continued the struggle. I didn't dare risk a look at the ASI, but I knew from the engine note that I had sufficient airspeed – too much for the aircraft to settle. What I was trying to do was fly the aircraft down. Even so, I was barely crawling along. Just how strong was the wind?

Opening up full throttle, I did a perilously low turn around the control tower and in no time found myself back to where I had started my approach. I would try again. Perhaps there would be a lull in the wind. Perhaps not – and soon I was struggling for control again. Now a new thought entered my mind. Winds associated with thunderclouds are not steady but extremely turbulent, with vollying gusts. If there were a sudden lull, I would hit the runway with a thud. Moreover, the wind can suddenly shift direction as well. The term "wind-shear" had not been invented then – at least I hadn't heard of it – but I knew the principle. If I ran into that, a sudden and radical shift in wind direction, there could only be one result. Meanwhile, it had become unnaturally gloomy. Swooping towards me, just beyond the end of the runway, was an ominous wall of darkness. I needed no further urging. It was time to go.

Full throttle, another dangerous low turn, and at a hundred feet I headed back towards the only bright spot left in the sky. As I flew clear of the cloud – or perhaps more accurately was flung out from under it – I received another jolt. Where I had been gaily disporting myself less than half an hour earlier, towering thunderclouds now extended far to the south! But there would be no race this time. The emergency landing field at Sturdee was less than ten minutes away and at a comfortable distance from the coming storm. I even had time to climb for a regular approach.

Landing safely in the last of the sunlight, I taxied over to the hangars, parked in the lee of a brick wall and switched off. The aircraft should be safe enough there. After locking the controls and closing the cockpit hood, I then went off to try the 'phone inside the hangar. The line was dead. Damn! Now I had another problem, though a minor one. Taking off again after a forced landing was a no-no. I was supposed to wait for someone to find and collect me like a load of lost baggage. It might take hours, and as it was already near suppertime the searchers would be hungry and unsympathetic.

My train of thought was interrupted by a sudden gust of wind that set the heavy hangar doors clanging and drove a cloud of dust scurrying across the apron. Meanwhile, the sky had grown as dark as doomsday. I had beaten the storm by five minutes. Lighting a SweetCap, I prepared to wait it out.

Another violent gust, another – and then the wind pounced and the empty hangar began to thrum. I could see now that I should not have attempted to land at base in the first place but have gone directly to Sturdee. Going round for a second try had been idiocy. Here, as if to emphasize the point, the heavens delivered a series of brilliant flashes and gut-shaking thuds. Then, as the reverberations died, a torrent descended, with heavy raindrops drumming on the roof and splashing ankle-high off the apron. Within seconds, there was water everywhere.

At least, I reflected, taking another pull on my cigarette and luxuriating in the feeling of being dry and safe, I knew now why I hadn't spotted the clouds earlier. They had arrived invisibly in the form of a cold front. The leading edge of a cold air mass, it had overridden the warmer air below, which had then unpeeled from the ground in giant globules or cells, fed continuously from below. Rising rapidly through the dense cold air, the cells had expanded with decreasing air pressure and condensed the water vapour into cloud. The consequent release of latent heat had kept the process going until the clouds reached the stratosphere some six miles up.

In other words, the clouds had not drifted up from over the horizon at all. Instead, with all the suddenness of milk boiling over, they had materialized out of clear air like malevolent djinn. I had been lucky – quite apart from not killing myself trying to land in a wind that exceeded my landing speed. In less time than I had needed to reach 10,000 feet these monsters had boiled up to over three times that height! Had they formed around me instead of upwind I would have been trapped. Today, weather planes routinely fly through hurricanes, but my light trainer would not have stood a chance. Bailing out would have been no option. I would have been wafted aloft, coated with layers of ice like a hailstone and then released hours later to drift to earth as a human popsicle.

The rain stopped and the sky brightened. The storm front had passed, and I left the hangar to look around. Shoulder to shoulder, still uttering threats, the djinn were trooping off, leaving behind a clear blue sky. The wind, now shifted to the east, had abated to a fresh breeze, sunlight danced on the wet grass and my stomach reminded me of supper. To hell with it, I decided. I would fly myself back. I would deny that I had made a forced landing. Was one permitted to take off again after a precautionary landing? I couldn't remember.

The following morning, when I arrived at the flight, I was ordered to report to the CO immediately. The station commander! My heart slid to my boots. There had been no inquest the previous day. Everyone had been far too impatient to be off for supper. I had made a rotten landing. The sight of about a hundred bods watching me from the tarmac had persuaded my strained nervous system, hitherto under control, to punish me with stage fright. To a chorus of "What happened?" from the crowd of cadets who had galloped up as I climbed from the aircraft, my reply "I landed at Sturdee" had produced a mass groan of disappointment. Silly buggers! What had they expected? In the flight office, instructors had greeted me with stares, apart from a muttered "Welcome back" from one and a bleated "But he's not supposed to take off after a forced landing" from someone else in the rear. Then the flight commander had released everyone. "I'll see you in the morning," he had added to me.

"We were amazed to see you join the circuit properly just now," a mate had remarked on our way to the messhall.

"Why?"

"Well, we expected you to come haring back over the fence. You must have been shit-scared."

"Not much point after the event, is there," I'd replied, grinning.

Now, after saluting the CO, I stoically awaited my fate. But to my surprise he was most pleasant. Instead of giving me the grilling I deserved, he congratulated me on how I had handled the situation. No doubt he had concluded, rightly, that the lesson had been sufficiently driven home by the experience.[14]

<hr />

[14] It occurred to me later (fifty-three years later, to be precise!) that he may have reserved his grilling for someone else. Landing conditions were too dangerous even for an experienced pilot, let alone a student. Whoever was in charge of the control tower should have warned me off with a red flare as I began my first approach. That I received no such warning even on my second try suggests that he had had a spot of finger trouble.

Celebrations

On Friday, August 31st, Course 139, "Last of the Many", was treated to a formal graduation dinner, with the admin. staff and instructors as guests of honor. The main item on the menu was "Milk Fed Young Saskatchewan Chicken". Milk, coffee, cocoa and tea were listed as beverages – but something more substantial was available before and after. Having successfully passed the course, with my logbook endorsed "above average", I felt more than ordinarily pleased with myself. It was, although I didn't know it, the high point in my RAF career.

Yet some of us had mixed feelings. The War was over. Our idyllic summer had coincided with its last bitter stages; and with the loss of Okinawa and the incineration of some of its major cities, Japan had surrendered. It was an occasion for rejoicing, but one tinged with disappointment. We were to be given two weeks embarkation leave, at the end of which we were to report back to Moncton. We would not be going on to SFTS in Canada, and probably not in England either. The chance to win our wings had apparently vanished.

The following day most of us piled into the train for Regina. We had been given a week-end pass to join in the V-J Day celebrations. In the event I saw little of the town and none of the celebrations. Our arrival at Regina's large, echoing station hall rather dampened my spirits. The rows of benches provided for waiting passengers were filled instead with shabby men, men who obviously were waiting for no one and going nowhere. Smoking rollings or chewing tobacco, they watched in silence and without expression as we passed by. It was unnerving. I had seen such men in England on park benches or in the reading rooms of public libraries, but never so many at once. Fall-out from the Depression, I thought.

My spirits were further dampened the following morning, when I awakened in the YMCA dormitory to find that my wallet had been rifled in the night. Whoever the thief, he well knew the difference between having little money and none at all – for he had charitably left me a two dollar bill. As this was insufficient for the bus fare, I blew most of it on a good breakfast and then set out to hitchhike back to camp. The loss of the better part of two weeks' pay was a blow, but the trip back made up for it. With most of the little traffic heading towards Regina, I had to rely on short rides from local farmers, and one of them insisted on bearing me off to his farm in the Qu'Appelle valley to share the mid-day meal with his family. It was my first experience of the generosity one often encountered "on the road" in Canada.

⊙⥎⊙

3

Banff

"Where are you going to spend your leave, Condon?"

"Banff. I want to see the Rockies before we go back."

"Anyone going with you?

"No," I snorted, "everyone seems headed for Niagara Falls and the bright lights of Toronto or Montreal."

"Mind if I come with you?" My interlocutor was Alf Heath, a sturdy fellow with an eagle's beak and rather uneven teeth. Unlike me, he was unusually reticent, as if mindful of the admonition "Better to remain silent and be thought a fool than to open your mouth and prove it." At the same time, however, he looked well at ease with himself. The imperturbable Alf! I had first met him at Bridgenorth.

"Not at all. Be glad of your company."

Though I doubt whether the British Treasury would have approved the expenditure entailed by the extra thousand miles of rail travel, our passes and meal tickets for the train were issued without quibble, and we were given another two weeks' pay.

Banff in September of 1945 would have been easily recognizable to a time traveller from today, although it was smaller then and, except downtown, had unpaved roads. More noticeable would have been the absence of crowds. Only a few passengers left the train with us – probably locals, as none remarked on the elk grazing the lawn in front of the CPR station.

At the recommended B & B the landlady welcomed us like long-lost nephews, plied us with coffee and cookies, and then showed us to our room – twin beds, pine flooring, spotlessly clean. A few minutes later she called up the stairs, "If you come quickly, you'll see a bear going through the garbage cans in the backyard."

We tumbled downstairs and ran out the back, but by then the bear had vanished. "Never mind," she consoled us brightly, "I'll have a friend drive you to the town dump at dusk. You'll see lots of bears there." And see them we did – herds of wandering bears with buns and other titbits. There must have been more bears than tourists in town. Then supper at a half-empty café, listening to the juke box playing hits (*Atchison, Topeka and the Santa Fe, Sentimental Journey*), a movie (*Picture of Dorian Grey*), and thence to bed, shut up in measureless content.

Extending from the Yukon to the Rio Grande, the Rocky Mountains form the continental divide, the major watershed of North America. Run-off from the west side drains into the Pacific, while that from the east finds its way to the Arctic Ocean, the Atlantic or the Gulf of Mexico. As we looked about us the following morning, the reason why they are so named was at once apparent. Unlike British hills, which are clad in grass, bracken and heather with only occasional rocky out-croppings, these mountains consist of great cliffs and ridges of naked sedimentary rock, thrust like mighty reefs above the rolling sea of conifers that engulfs the foothills and laps the scree slopes at their feet. Depending on the orientation of the strata, the peaks resemble great petrified waves, vast ruined pyramids or crenelated and towered castles. On some peaks the stratification is more nearly vertical, as in the serrated Sawback Range, and on others, contorted and folded – mute testimony to the enormous forces that have gone into their making. The Rocky Mountains, in short, appear to be what they are – the exposed backbone of a continent.

Though a little disappointed to see neither glaciers nor snow, I was nonetheless impressed. Here was rock enough to keep a climber happy for decades. Unfortunately (perhaps fortunately) we were not equipped for mountaineering of any sort; and so, advised by our hospitable hostess, we followed the usual trails of the active tourist. We began by ascending Tunnel Mountain, a mere nine hundred feet or so above the town, and then, feeling ambitious, went on to climb Sulphur Mountain. This took us above the tree line and to our first sight of glaciers glinting on the high peaks. That's where we needed to go.

On our way back, a refreshing soak at the hot springs led to a curious discovery. I found I could barely muster the strength to climb from the pool. Even dressing required an effort. Perhaps the fact that I had spent the time swimming had something to do with it – Alf had merely floated placidly by the poolside – but half an hour of being parboiled seemed to have turned my muscles to wax.

The next morning found us in an old Brewsters bus, rattling along the gravel road to Lake Louise and trailing a long plume of dust. Among the handful of other passengers were two girls who sat a few seats in front of us, chattering and giggling and casting sheep's eyes at us over their shoulders from time to time. Oh dear! For some reason they had a more powerful effect on Alf. On our way back to the bus after the obligatory viewing of the lower falls at Johnston's Canyon, he drew me aside and said *sotto voce*, "Listen, let's not get mixed up with them." He was red-faced and his mouth was working strangely. I smothered a grin. There was no doubt about it. Imperturbable Alf was in a lather. But he needn't have worried. It was the mountains I was interested in. In any case, the girls went on to Moraine Lake with the others. We had booked for Lake Louise only, to allow more time for exploration on foot.

Along with the Matterhorn, Lake Louise must now be one of the most familiar and most photographed mountain scenes in the world. But it was new to us. Some 5,678 feet above sea level, it lies in a hanging valley with mountains to each side and the glacier and mile-high wall of Mt. Victoria as a backdrop. The setting is spectacular. But it was the colour of the lake that astonished me. Instead of the cold grey I had expected, I saw an expanse of aquamarine and lapis lazuli – like a patch of April sky seeking the solitude of a mountain retreat. As with the sky, the colour comes from the scattering of light by particles in suspension – fine glacial silt in the case of the lake. Glaciers, like the mills of God, grind slowly and exceeding small, sculpting the high peaks, transporting the detritus, transforming the surrounding landscape – yet all the while adorning the peaks and painting the lakes at their feet. Function and beauty combined – the economy of nature.

For while we stood, taking everything in and clicking snapshots with our landlady's ancient box camera. Then we set off up the trail to Lake Agnes, climbing quickly through a dense forest of spruce and fir with only the bright eyes of whiskey jacks and chipmunks to mark our passing. Ignoring the teahouse, which we knew to be closed, we skirted the lake and continued to the top of the Big Beehive. And there, amid scattered stands of larch, already turning gold at the touch of fall, we rested. We seemed to have the world to ourselves.

As the train reeled off the miles towards Calgary and the bald-headed prairie, punctuating its metrical rhythm now and then with mournful wails, I watched the Rockies recede into the distance. They were snow-capped now. Noting my earlier disappointment, the gods had arranged a surprise for our last day. Several inches of snow had fallen overnight, powdering the hills down to the 5,000ft level. We had expressed our gratitude by climbing Sulphur Mountain yet again, bringing our four-day total to over eleven thousand feet.

I felt blessed. Our landlady had been an angel, and the weather throughout our stay had been perfect. For the first time I had set foot in primeval wilderness, one where the animals not only lived in their natural state but had lost their fear of man. Linton, the Welsh mountains, and now the Rockies – for a brief period I had experienced a third and rougher Eden.

CHAPTER FOURTEEN

...and Have Them Clipped.

1

Into Limbo

Although Bob Christie, our grizzled physics teacher, was not given to talking about his experiences as a US Marine in the Pacific War, he unbent once, when staffroom gossip turned to the topic of slow and reluctant learners. "I'll never forget," he mused, "my first day at bootcamp. Like shorn lambs, with polished boots and new fatigues, we had fallen in for our first drill session. The sergeant called us to attention and paced along the ranks, looking each man up and down. Then he ordered us at ease. 'Before we start,' he asked, smiling, 'is there any man here who thinks he could take me?' There was a long silence, as we considered the import of his words. Then some character, some *idiot*, actually stepped forward." Bob paused.

"What happened?" someone asked.

Bob grinned, "The sergeant beat the *shit* out of him in front of us."

"No slow learners in your outfit, I take it?"

Bob nodded, "You got it. No reluctant ones, anyway."

Whether the good sergeant had the best interests of his men at heart or was merely relieving his frustrations, Bob didn't say. Fear, to paraphrase Dr. Johnson, may concentrate the mind wonderfully, but the sergeant's technique is not likely to be approved for the classroom or tolerated in the British forces, at least not openly. Still, the anecdote does point to the need for discipline, without which there is little learning in class or efficiency in a military unit.

It was a problem I had faced at Scarborough. As I marched the flight back from the beach one day, a cadet had begun needling me from the ranks. The gauntlet had been thrown down and something had to be done. But what? The method used by the Marine sergeant was not open to me. Apart from the fact that most of the flight could have made mincemeat of me, it was not my style. On the other hand, a good-natured appeal to shut up would likely have resulted in mockery. Mere words were useless. Waiting until I was sure of the culprit, I halted the flight, stood them at ease and called him to me. He marched out and stood to attention, eyes front. Very airmanlike – except for the smirk on his face. For a long moment I regarded him coldly. Then, "*You* take the flight back," I ordered. Leaving him no time to react, I at once took his place in the ranks.

Now he had a choice – shut up or play the fool. Needless to say, he chose the latter. Marching us off, he peppered me with idiotic orders and kept it up until the inevitable happened. "Why don't you shut up," growled someone at last. Realizing he was isolated, shut up he did, instantly. I'd had no further trouble.

At Bircham Newton the sergeant in charge of us was not so lucky. It was November, 1945, and there were about thirty of us in the room, all newly arrived and mostly strangers to each other. Supper over, we were writing letters, polishing boots, chatting or lying on our pits reading – a typical barrack scene. Suddenly, the door flew open with a crash and there, like a stage Mephistopheles, appeared a DI sergeant. Having obtained our startled attention, he began pacing into the silence, hands behind his back, chest out, heels thudding into the brown linoleum.

But he kept it up too long. By the time he had taken five paces, there was not one of us who hadn't realized that the dramatic entrance had been premeditated, perhaps even rehearsed.

Stamping to a halt as if he were on parade, he inflated his chest even further. "My name," he boomed, as if he were Ozymandias, king of kings, "is Sergeant Kramer, and I'm the poor sod who…"

A languid voice broke in,"Three cheers for Sergeant Kramer!"

Heads turned, immediately identifying the voice's owner. He was sitting cross-legged on an upper bunk, admiring a sock he was darning. Clad in nothing but PT shorts, a bushy moustache and a thatch of hair that no headgear short of a bearskin could have contained, he invited an immediate charge for his appearance alone. What dire retribution would now befall and from what height?

Unfortunately for the sergeant, none. Visibly deflated and with an expression on his face suggestive of Oh God, it's happening again! he repeated, "I'm the poor sod who's been put in charge of you lot, and I want you on parade outside at 0800 sharp. Battledress," at which he turned and marched out, this time with more speed and considerably less dignity.

0800 found us paraded as ordered. Whether or not the sergeant had managed to have breakfast I don't know. Some prankster had tied his doorknob to a heating pipe during the night and trapped him in his room. And when he wheeled us around the first corner, half the flight disappeared into the woodwork the moment they were out of his sight. What other treats were in store for the unfortunate man I didn't stay long enough to find out.

With reason I had little patience with such nonsense. Banff had been followed by anti-climax. Breaking our journey to view Niagara Falls had proved a mistake. In Toronto, unable to find an affordable bed for the night, Alf and I had ridden streetcars and walked the streets until, soaked in a sudden downpour, we'd sought shelter in a sleazy all-night cinema and steamed away the hours to breakfast. Learning from this experience, we'd booked a room at Niagara Falls – only to arrive late on a Sunday night and have the railroad station locked behind us and see the last of the other passengers disappear into the darkness in the last of the taxis. Finding the hotel had taken over an hour of wandering through ill-lit, deserted streets, each of us with a distended bladder and all the time with the damned falls roaring in the background. They weren't worth it. They no longer thunder away in the wilderness. There are towns there, one each side of the border, and each a tourist trap since the death of Hiawatha. Though the falls are impressive enough, I had found myself thinking of the chained elephant in Maidstone Zoo.

After a brief spell at Moncton and an uneventful crossing on the *Ile de France*, we had disembarked at Liverpool to find ourselves shunted off first to Morecambe and then into a kind of limbo. The War having ended, the return of hundreds of partly trained aircrew had presented the RAF with the problem of what to do with us all. As a first measure, we had been posted singly or in groups to units all over the country, in my case to a small unit outside Cirencester, where my only amusement had been an occasional solitary stroll along Cotswold lanes.

Having arrived at Bircham already bored silly, when volunteers were called for to work on air publications for Fighter Command, I therefore stepped forward. Anything would be better than brain death. A few days later I reported for duty at Bentley Priory, HQ Fighter Command. With me was Alf, who had also volunteered. It was to be my home station for the next fifteen months.

I had expected HQ Fighter Command to be stiff with brass and bullshit – parade grounds, flags, thudding boots and bawling DI's – but apart from a flag or two and the brass, whom I never saw, it was nothing of the kind. It was a working station where wheels turned without fuss; and while it may have been a beehive during the War, in November of 1945 things were quiet. Except for the Priory itself, the demesne of the brass, the station consisted of wooden huts, mostly offices and barracks. Occupying a few small offices in one of the huts was the Air Publications section.

In charge was Flight Lieutenant Milne, an officer who treated subordinates as human beings. "We're reorganizing our procedures," he explained. "Eventually, you boys will be sent to fighter stations, and all mail dealing with air publications will be funneled through you. Your job will be to sort it out, deliver it to the appropriate sections and encourage them to make necessary amendments. It's important that these be done, especially where modifications to engines and airframes are concerned." He smiled. "You'll soon get the hang of things. Meanwhile, you can help us out here." With no parades to attend and with our work proving anything but onerous, we soon blended into the scenery and enjoyed life.

Christmas Interlude

About twelve days before Christmas Alf and I were called into Flight Lieutenant Milne's office. Our first posting had been decided upon: we were to report to RAF Dyce just after Christmas. In the meantime we were to have two weeks' leave.

Much of what had happened to my family since I left in 1944 I was not to learn until years later. Life in Wales had not been as kind to Pauline. Three years younger than I, she'd had to endure that much more of the local school, where she'd been required to learn Welsh. For her, mildly dyslexic and having difficulty enough with English, this had proved humiliating. With no close friends and few interests, she had become an unhappy girl; and when Mum became involved with George, Pauline had once more thought herself unwanted and had run away. Ignoring trifles such as identity card and ration book, she had scraped together the train fare to London and appeared penniless and hungry on Little Lil's doorstep. Lil had taken her to Grandpa, where she was as welcome as toothache, and he had immediately called the police. Two days later she was on her way back to Wales. "When I saw Mum, I dropped my case and ran to put my arms around her," she told me. "But oh! her face was like stone and her voice to match." "What else did you expect?" I said sympathetically. "It's a wonder she didn't strangle you."

Of the postwar reunion with Dad, I leave her to tell the tale:

> We left Wales at the beginning of May, 1945. News that the War had ended was broadcast while we were on the train. George got off at Hitchin and Mum and I continued on to Norfolk to spend a week with Aunt Doll before heading for Grandpa's back in Plumstead. When we entered the house, Dad was sitting by the window, still in his army uniform.

"Hello," we said, just looking. No one stepped forward to embrace. What a homecoming!

"Well, Chris," Mum said, "what do you think of your daughter after all these years?"

"She can take those earrings off. They make her look common."

Well, that was that – and they were only little pearl ones. In the kitchen, as we were getting tea, Mum started to cry. "I can't bear going to bed with him tonight."

I understood what she was saying. She loved someone else and now her husband had returned. That night my bed was the sofa in the front room and I cried myself to sleep – both for myself and my darling. I felt no closeness with my father. As a child I had been terrified of him.

Welcome home, the happy warrior!

Of the situation at home that Christmas I remember nothing. I know only that after a couple of days' leave I decided to head for the Welsh mountains. Donning my Black's anorak, I packed climbing boots, balaclava and toiletry – and was off.

I was shivering when I alighted from the empty, unheated bus in Capel Curig. Snowdonia was in the deep freeze. Snow blanketed the land and had compacted into ice on the roads, massed frost feathers adorned every surface facing the wind, and the only signs of life were a few lights and the smoke rising from village chimneys. At Plas Curig, the youth hostel, I found only two others – the warden, a pleasant young girl, and Joe, an employee of the forestry commission. It was just as well we were few, for the plumbing was frozen solid. Still, the kitchen was warm, and a cheerful fire blazed on the common room hearth.

After tucking away the evening meal and doing our chores, Joe and I settled down in the common room. I filled my pipe with Gold Block and began to smoke, staring into the fire and feeling well content. Then the warden entered. Like Browning's Pippa, she was singing. When she had finished, I exclaimed, "Oh, what a beautiful song! What is it?"

She smiled, "E lucevan le stelle."

"Eh?"

"*E lucevan le stelle*," repeated Joe.

"What does that mean?"

"The stars are shining," Joe said. "It's from Puccini's *Tosca*."

Mountains, music and stars again! Years were to pass before I heard a performance of the opera – and then I was disappointed to hear the song sung by a man. Not a patch on the warden. Her performance had been magical. Before turning in, I asked if they would care to accompany me up Glyder Fach the next day. To my delight the warden agreed. Joe, however, had to work.

The Hills of Youth
Glyder Fach, 1945

"E lucevan le stelle"

Our eyes were shining
as we swung in the wholeness of our youth
along the icy road from Capel Curig.
There would be no romp
on Tryfan's buttresses today,
no nod from Idwal's holly tree,
for all was deep in snow or fledged with frost.
Our hearts were higher, where familiar hills,
solemn now in formal white,
reared heads into a mystery of cloud.
Faint smoke from lonely hearthfires rose like
                                                    prayers;
and, save for the ghosting breath that marked our
                                                    passing,
all else was still.

The snow was firm!
And so, liberated from paths, we left the road
- right for the summit ridge of Glyder Fach.
Kicking steps on printless slopes,
joyously we climbed until,
like hoar-rimmed phantoms in the cloud,
we reached the place

where megaliths were piled, broken,
like some neolithic shrine or tomb
half-buried in snow
- a scene, one might think,
to chill the heart, but not for us.
Here was no ruin of war,
nothing of human making,
but a union of simplicities,
a harmony of elder elements -
rock, and snow, and air – and our youth's ardour.

And my heart sang;
while, far above the grey,
beyond the azure curve of earth's far rim,
still singing in their appointed courses,
the stars were shining.

To adapt Walt Whitman, that wordy yet magnificent poet,
Music, mountains and stars twined with the chant of my soul,
There on a clouded peak and we shadows hoar and dim.
Yes – a hopeless romantic! As I write this, more than fifty years
later, it seems so much nonsense. But the joy and sense of one-
ness were real enough to me then.
The following day I returned home for Christmas.

2

RAF Dyce

Aberdeen, New Year's Eve, 1945 – a gloomy town of sooty granite
and ill-lit, virtually deserted streets. After wandering around
to view the attractions, Alf and I had decided there weren't any
and had repaired to the Naafi club. Naafis were not noted for
sparkle, but this one, perhaps influenced by Aberdonian thrift,
was singularly cheerless, made more so by the absence of women
and the presence of only a handful of other servicemen. Where

were the festive crowds?

"Quiet, isn't it?" Alf said, as we downed our watery beer.

I glanced at the clock. "It's early yet," I said, adding hopefully, "Perhaps it will liven up later. Let's have another pint."

As if on cue, the barman called, "Drink up, please. We're about to close."

I gaped at him. "It's only nine o'clock."

"We close early on New Year's Eve."

"But I thought this was the biggest night of the year up here."

He grinned, "It is, but the parties are in private homes."

Rats! There was nothing for it but to return to camp the way we had come, on foot. The only sign of life on the way back was a shadowy group of youths on a backstreet corner, one of whom shouted something incomprehensible at us. As it didn't sound much like a festive greeting, we ignored them. So much for Hogmanay.

RAF Dyce was equipped with Mark XXI Spitfires – beauties with Griffon engines almost twice as powerful as the Merlin. One might think that I would have wasted no time before hanging my nose over the edge of a cockpit to inspect its layout. But I didn't. Soon after our arrival I had discovered something much more interesting: on the station was a mountain rescue service unit that went on a training climb once a week! Alf and I immediately volunteered.

Soon after dawn the next Wednesday, our MRS convoy, consisting of Jeep, ambulance and a heavy lorry, halted beside Loch Muick, and we set up base camp in an outbuilding of what had been Queen Victoria's hunting lodge. Our target peak, Lochnagar, was shrouded in cloud to the thousand foot level and steady rain slanted down.

After brewing tea, we set off, leaving a man at base to operate the radio and prepare hot soup for our return. The going was steep, and soon I was sweating freely. According to F.S.Smythe, the ideal pace on mountains, one that can be maintained for thousands of feet, is the rhythmic, lounging plod of alpine guides. My companions, obviously not having read Smythe, climbed with all the impatience of youth and by the time we had climbed five hundred feet I was reeling. Only two weeks earlier I had climbed Glyder Fach with ease. I shouldn't be in trouble now. Something was wrong. For a while I considered carrying on until I collapsed. I had, after all, the mountain rescue service to cart me down. But I rejected the idea. Accustomed to making my own decisions on mountains, I wasn't about to change now. "I'm sorry, Scotty," I gasped, addressing the corporal who led the unit, "I'm going down."

He stopped. "What's wrong?"

"I don't know. I don't feel so good."

"Can you manage on your own?"

I nodded and began to descend. What was wrong, although I did not know it then, was that I was suffering from heat exhaustion. Over the climbing gear, I had been wearing a rubberized army ground sheet, and this had rapidly converted itself into a portable steam bath. My decision to turn back had thus been the right one, as I might have precipitated a heat stroke. Of course, all I had needed to do was to remove the ground sheet. But that is to be wise after the event. As it was, I was puzzled to feel perfectly well once I had reached base camp.

Nothing was said when the party returned, but I noticed that Scotty made a point of praising Alf's performance. Next morning, as we were picking up the mail a voice brayed, "You've been found out, then." It was the orderly-room sergeant, a tall streak who had hitherto ignored us. Now he was staring at me with malicious glee. So that was the way the wind blew! For a moment, I regarded him coldly and then I turned my back. His *schadenfreude* was misplaced. I wasn't in the least crestfallen, but I was annoyed by the rush to judgment.

Annoyed or not, I had to endure it longer. After a bitterly cold drive the following week – as junior members, Alf and I had ridden with the gear in the back of the lorry – we arrived in Glen Esk. The sky was clear, snow sheeted the upper slopes, and the summit of Mt. Keen, our target, glowed like a red beacon in the rising sun. Waiting for tea to be brewed, I stamped my feet, eager to start and warm up. We had a new man, I noticed, a wide-shouldered sergeant.

I was mistaken. He was the chief PT instructor, and he had

been brought for a purpose. Throughout the climb, he remained close behind me and at one point drew alongside. "Gosh," he said, pretending to be out of breath, "I felt like giving up a moment ago. But I told myself 'You know you can do it'." Ah, he was there to observe me and stiffen my spine! I ground my teeth and ignored him.

On the descent we used a different route and then had to face a climb of several hundred feet over a spur to return to base. By this time, the packs, containing the radio and emergency supplies, had fallen to Alf and me, and we began to lag behind. After a while, my legs feeling distinctly rubbery, I looked up. Ranged along the skyline about fifty feet above, the rest were observing us. The detour had been deliberate, a final test. Well, bugger them! I looked across at Alf. Red-faced and cursing, he was in no better state than I – and I began to laugh. Nothing further was said. Spine suitably stiffened, I was now a member of the mountain rescue service.

Although my relationship with Scotty remained cool, for I had not appreciated being treated as a spineless liar, I nevertheless enjoyed the following months immensely. Deeside I thought especially beautiful. In Wales I had bought a Bartholomew's map of the Scottish highlands and pored over it, climbing bens in my imagination. Now here I was, and in winter, my preferred season. And there were not only the climbs. No small part of each exercise was the treat to the stomach that followed. After soup at base camp, we would interrupt the drive back for a well-earned pint and chips and then return to Dyce still with appetite enough for the full meal awaiting us.

Two further exercises I recall clearly are an ascent of Beinn A'Bhuird from Tomintoul, a marathon hike of over twenty-five miles, and a visit to the Cairngorms. The latter involved no climbing, as deep snow blanketed the region, but it was memorable nonetheless. The unit had split into two, with the main body leaving early for Aviemore to try a traverse of the Lairig Ghru, the pass that bisects the Cairngorms. The rest of us, led by Scotty, left in the late afternoon and set up base in an outbuilding of Derry Lodge, near the southern end of the pass. By this time, it was dark. However, just as we began to make ourselves comfortable, we were rudely interrupted by the entry of a gillie, my introduction to that dour breed. "What are ye doing here?" he growled. "This is private property. Ye must get oot."

"But we're on an official RAF mountain rescue exercise," Scotty protested.

"I dinna care who ye are," grunted the gillie sourly. "Ye've nae business here. This is private property and ye'll have tae get oot – on the other side of the fence, mind."

And oot we got.

With the aid of our vehicles' headlights, some ferreted among the pines for firewood, while the rest of us pitched tents in foot-deep snow. Then, while the radio operator tried to contact the main party, we sat around a crackling fire, smoking and drinking tea. Scotty meanwhile had set up the small searchlight, brought along to guide the main party in. As he swept Glen Luibeg with its beam, numerous pairs of green eyes stared back – deer, driven from the hills by heavy snowfall. After an hour or so, the radio operator managed to contact the others. Without either skis or snowshoes, they'd been forced to turn back by deep snowdrifts. What a pity! Now we had to eat their stew as well. The night was uncomfortable, for the snow compacted into a hard and lumpy mattress. But the evening had been magical.

A Lousy Life

But for our weekly climbs, life would have been tedious. Provided with our own office, Alf and I found our workload ridiculously light, and we spent much time chatting or riling on our chairs staring at the ceiling. In the evenings we played Shanghai, a round-the-clock dart game. As for Aberdeen, we returned once, to attend a performance of *Il Trovatore*. The cast, clad in moth-eaten pre-war costumes, did their best in the chilly theatre, but I found the plot incomprehensible and Verdi not to my taste.

The only thing resembling stimulation was my campaign against fleas. I was lousy. I suppose I could have accepted them the way cows accept flies – as a reminder that one is alive – but they made me feel unclean. Despite frequent baths, however, each day brought its crop of fresh bites. In desperation, I hung all my bedding in the open air, filled a bath with scalding water and dumped in all I was wearing, even my battledress. Then I took a bath. That would fix 'em. It didn't. Next morning I awoke to find myself scratching a multitude of new bites. Scotland's fleas, like her gillies, seemed indomitable. Sitting up in my bed, I glared around the hut. "Any of you fellows got fleas?" I asked bitterly. "I'm being eaten alive."

The man in the bed opposite stirred. "Yes," he said, "I have."

"Well, where the hell are they coming from?"

"There," he replied, nodding towards the end of the hut, "from the NCO's room."

"Eh?"

"It's being used as a bedding store," he explained.

Ah, so starving replacements were skipping up every night, and as occupants of the nearest beds we were naturally first on the menu. Well, what to do? Complain to the MO? No, this was a personal fight. Let's see. Fleas must track by smell. Right. Now, how to make myself smell unappetizing? The answer came from the MT section in the form of a blanket reeking of petrol and oil. Let's see how the buggers like that, I muttered, draping it over my bed. Next morning, and thereafter, I awoke blissfully flea free.

At Easter nearly everyone, Alf included, vanished on a four-day pass. Seeing little point in wasting half of it on crowded trains, I asked Bill, an Aberdonian member of the MRS, if he would care to accompany me to the Cairngorms. He agreed readily and suggested we spend the night at his home so we could catch an early bus. There, I was introduced to some local colour in the person of his dad, a genial man with twinkling grey eyes who gave me a friendly welcome. At least, I think that's what it was – only I couldn't understand a word. "Does your dad speak only Gaelic?" I asked. Bill laughed, "No. That's the local dialect." And so it was – a form of speech (*Fars this? Fars tha? Fit'll ah diddlum?*) impenetrable to Sassenachs and to many a fellow Scot besides.

The next day we hiked in from Braemar and camped in Glen Derry. With some trepidation I noted that our packs, stuffed with tent, sleeping bags, cooking gear and provisions for three days – mostly in the form of tinned food – were abominably heavy. Sure enough, when we set out for Ben Macdui the next morning I found the going hard and was glad to call a halt at Little Loch Etchachan, where we each had a tin of self-heating soup. With some of the weight transferred from my pack to my stomach, I found the remainder of the climb virtually effortless and suggested we descend to the Lairig Ghru and climb the Devil's Point. This we did, completing a traverse of over four thousand feet of climbing – a fair day's outing considering our packs. After a splendid meal, we climbed into our sleeping bags well content, and the next day made a leisurely return to Dyce.

A few days later I was recalled to Bentley Priory. I did not see Alf again.

ॐ

3

Training Resumes…

Except for a six-week posting to RAF Manston, preserved in memory as a vague blur in the amber of a hot summer, at Bentley Priory I remained for a year. With me, in place of Alf, was Pete Doe, another fellow graduate from Yorkton. Taller than I, with blue eyes and a seraphic smile, he radiated benign cheerfulness. We got on well together. It was during this time that I acquired my first girl friend, Jean, a blonde civilian employee. But I was hardly a satisfactory boyfriend. With little money, no prospects, and blessed – or cursed – with a sense of responsibility that I ignore at my peril, I had no intentions whatsoever, honourable or otherwise. Besides, I wasn't really interested in women. Climbing and flying were my passions. In mating matters, as with most things, I was a slow starter. And so the relationship withered on the vine.

It was at this time, too, that I began to get to know my father. With weekend passes freely available and home less than two hours away via the Bakerloo Line and Southern Rail, I was home most weekends and spent Saturday evenings with him, having a few beers and taking in the odd picture. By now he was living with his sister Hetty, though what the circumstances of the separation were I didn't know and, considering it none of my business, didn't ask. Pauline was with my mother, earning her keep as a hairdresser until she left the following year to work as a lady's maid, and George had reappeared, commuting every weekend from Hitchen. As for Grandpa, who had survived the Blitz and worked throughout the War, he was less approachable than ever. Now retired, he seemed interested only in playing the horses.

Just before Christmas, 1946, Nature assumed a festive mood and decorated the countryside with nearly a foot of snow. A day or so later came the night of the Bentley Priory staff Chistmas party, and by the time my mates and I had hiked to the rented hall we were in a similar mood. It was warm inside, bright with lights and Christmas decorations and filled with laughter and cheerful chatter. The party was well under way.

"Phil," a Waaf was beckoning to me. Daphne. "Here," she said, thrusting a half-filled tumbler into my hand, "this will warm your cockles."

"Thank you. What is it?"

"Whisky and ginger ale."

"Oh good. Well, Cheers!" I said, raising my glass in salute and taking a good pull. I hadn't tasted whisky before and rather liked it. It was pleasantly warming. We wandered off to join the rest of the gang. A little later I had another scotch, and then I sampled the rum punch. There were some remarkably attractive Waafs there and I had a couple of dances. A wizard party! I had been there for about forty minutes and was suffused with a warm glow. All was right with the world.

Not quite. Suddenly, I became aware that I was going to die! With an exclamation I took one step towards the door – and then the lights went out. The next thing I recall was lying face down in the snow with someone tugging at me. "Phil, Phil, get up." Daphne again. But all I could do was groan. I felt hands pull me to my feet, brush me off, and balance me on a chair jammed against the wall. Then my benefactors went back inside, leaving me to the mercy of the elements.

How long was I left in the snow – an hour? two hours? I know only that when they decided to call it a night they found me still stretched immobile and unconscious on the chair. Vaguely I became aware of hands pulling me to my feet and of being supported on each side as I staggered the mile or so uphill to camp – conscious, but with very little going on between the ears. Despite this, I awoke the next morning feeling fine, though somewhat sheepish. Why hypothermia, even rigor mortis, hadn't set in I don't know. Youth, perhaps, and fitness – with help from a guardian angel or the patron saint of idiots.

During my Christmas leave I again made a flying visit to Capel Curig. There was a different warden at the hostel, and the experience proved anything but magical. In the morning I set off to climb Snowdon. This time there was no snow, but a succession of thaws and sharp frosts had plastered the mountain with great sheets of ice. For a couple of hours I carefully picked my way around and over them. But then I gave up. At the speed I was going I would never make it to the top and back before dark and, besides, with soft iron clinkers on my boots it was too dangerous. Descending as carefully as I had climbed, I reached the edge of the last ice sheet and with a sigh of relief stepped onto some grass. Before I knew what was happening, I hit the ground with a thud and at the same time felt a sharp pain in my hip. The grass had masked a treacherous layer of clear ice. Damn! Gingerly I investigated the source of the pain and discovered that my trousers, shirt and underclothes had been cut as if by a razor. So had the skin, and through the gaping wound I could see the blue sheen of muscle beneath. Hastily stuffing a none-too-clean handkerchief into the hole, I continued down to Llanberis Pass and hammered on the door of the Gorphwysfa Hotel.

After a while, footsteps sounded, the door cracked open a few inches and a nose appeared. "What is it?" it asked.

"I'm sorry to bother you, but I've had an accident on Snowdon. Could you tell me where the nearest doctor is?"

"Bettws y Coed," responded Nose – and then firmly closed the door.

Regretting I hadn't been able to thank it for its concern, I limped off. Eventually a car from Beddgelert gave me a ride. It was the only time I hurt myself on the hills – on Snowdon's Pyg track, of all places.

After being stitched up, I caught a bus to Idwal. And there I bumped into Joe. The girl warden was now at the Clwyd hostel, he said, and urged me to drop in for a visit. I understood what he was saying – but there was not the time.

In the spring of 1947, I was reclaimed by Training Command and posted first to RAF North Coates and then, after a side trip back to Bridgnorth for a medical, on to 15 EFTS, RAF Kingstown, just outside Carlisle. In return for continuing flight training, I had agreed to sign on for another five years, with the option of cancelling should conditions not be to my advantage. For a chance to gain our wings, it was a price I and the rest of the flight were willing to pay.

Before going to SFTS, we were to have a refresher course. What this would amount to, we had no idea. I had hoped for fifty to sixty hours of flying time, but I was to be disappointed. By the time we left Kingstown six weeks later I had received less than sixteen hours, only four more than at grading school at Brough. Thanks to the weather, no one flew the first week. We were issued with our flying kit, given a few lectures and spent much time sitting around the flights, playing bridge. Flying began the second week, but my instructor, whom I had not yet seen, happened to be duty pilot and except for a session on the Link I continued to twiddle my thumbs. The third week I spent at home on compassionate leave. Dad had been taken dangerously ill and nearly died. Following my return, I flew only three times in the next two weeks – and after each flight my instructor vanished with an alacrity that suggested he had an ongoing steamy affair with a girl friend. In short, nearly all my flying was crammed into the last five days.

Despite having so much time on my hands, I enjoyed the stay at Kingstown. Discipline was relaxed and it was fun to fly Tiger Moths again. Moreover, Carlisle boasted a justifiably celebrated Naafi club, where we spent hours every week, writing letters, playing games, having a meal or a few drinks, and dancing with Waafs and Wrens. One Sunday, most of us signed up for a tour of the Lakes. The coach, a pre-War relic that ground and strained up the hills, could not quite make the summit of Kirkstone Pass and we had to pile out and push, but it managed to complete the tour and get us home. My impression of the Lake District was fleeting. A one-day coach tour under an overcast sky offers little. One needs to explore at leisure – and on foot.

On May 17 the larger world entered in the person of Field Marshal Viscount Montgomery, who had come to receive the Freedom of the City. As part of a cordon to hold back the cheering crowd, I managed only a glimpse of him as he drove by. But which hat he was wearing – Staff Officer's cap, Tank Corps beret or laurel wreath – I cannot say.

Whitsun arrived and with it the chance to don climbing boots again. Setting my sights not on the Lakes but on Ben Nevis, I hitchhiked to Glasgow on Friday evening and arrived after dark to find it seething with transients – no room anywhere, not even at the "Y" or the Sally Ann. Not fancying the prospect of walking the streets all night, I left my pack at the railway station and sought help from the first policeman I came across, a very large gentleman. Although now six foot one, I found myself looking up at him. His face was broad, his jaw massive and his shoulders such that he probably had to edge through doorways. He listened gravely and nodded. "Weel now, ye can get a bed at the Buchanan Street Guest Hoos." He pointed and then added confusingly, "Ye'll find it on Cowcadden Street. It's no the best place. It's the *only* place."

Thanking him, I turned in the direction indicated. My guide was given to understatement, for the guest hoos proved to be a dosshouse. Upstairs were a series of small dormitories with bare boards and cheap iron cots, most already claimed by somewhat unsavoury characters. Mindful of my experience in Regina, I began preparations for the night. Uniform – folded and under the pillow with my socks, collar and tie. Now, my wallet. Aware that the occupant of the bed opposite had been watching me closely, I decided to put it inside my underpants. Anyone groping around my balls would be bound to start me into wakefulness. Satisfied,

I began to climb into bed.

"Yeer boots!" It was my interested observer, a grizzled ruffian with a week's growth of whiskers.

"Eh?"

"Yeer boots. Put 'em under the legs of yeer bed."

"Never thought of that. Thank you." I did as he had suggested and slid between the sheets. Well, sort of. The top sheet was only about two feet long. For a while I reflected on the kindly thief who had left me two dollars. Now – a Samaritan in a dosshouse! One could never tell. Then, hoping there were no fleas, I drifted off.

In the morning, life, virtue and possessions intact, I had an early breakfast, booked a seat on the afternoon train to Fort William and then wandered around to view the sights of Glesga. "Glesga" – it's odd, but whenever I visit Scotland I begin to pick up the vernacular as readily as I picked up fleas at Dyce. I dinna ken why. Perhaps I was a Scot in a previous incarnation. In contrast, my four years in Wales had no such effect, though I made every effort to pronounce place names correctly (Llanfairpwll...etc. and Drum, for example); and after more than fifty years in Canada, although I now eat with a "fourk" instead of a "fawk", I have only to open my mouth to be instantly recognized as a Limey – and fellow Limeys usually spot the London accent.

After buying a one-inch map of the Ben Nevis area and having lunch at the Naafi Club, I collected my pack and boarded my train at Queen Street Station. Then I settled back, expecting a lengthy vista of dreary suburbs; but in no time at all the greys and soot of Glasgow gave way to open country and soon I could see sunlight dancing with the wavelets on Loch Lomond. After a stop at Crianlarich to allow us off for something to eat, the train trundled on and soon we were crossing the Moor of Rannoch. Here I thought of old Poll and a class of London urchins singing *Sure by Tummel and Loch Rannoch and Lochaber I will go*. Our pace was sedate enough not to diminish the Highlands, and the Cuillin still seemed far – but I knew it to be a romantic illusion. My first view of Ben Nevis came when we passed Roy Bridge – great black buttresses and gulleys choked with snow.

I spent the night at the Glen Nevis hostel and after breakfasting at a roadside café set off up the Ben, adopting what I imagined to be the Alpine guide's lounging pace. Some two thousand feet later I rounded a bend and came across three climbers resting. Perhaps galvanized by the thought of having been caught up, they immediately stubbed out their cigarettes and set off again. Feeling no need for a rest, I joined them. The pace they set was a killing one – at least for me, as apart from the attempt on Snowdon I hadn't climbed for over a year. Nonetheless, remembering Lochnagar, I stayed with them until we reached the summit ridge. And there I had to stop and let them go on. Having pushed myself to the point of exhaustion and beyond, I had begun to feel more and more nauseated. Throwing my pack down, I prepared to rest – but instead found myself casting around the hillside for discarded scraps of food! Of a sudden my fatigue had become overwhelmed by a ravenous hunger. But there were no scraps – and my teeth seemed to grow longer and sharper. Finding a matchstick, I bit savagely on that. Had a sheep come by I felt that I could have launched myself at it and snapped a chunk out of its rump. (*Please, Sir, man is not an animal!*) Years later, out of curiosity I fasted for three days, taking in nothing but beverages. Save for a sharpened sense of smell – my nostrils would twitch if I came anywhere near a restaurant – I experienced no such hunger as I felt on the Ben. It was as if I had pushed myself to the point where some bodily imperative had been triggered.

Still there when the others returned half an hour later, I asked if they could spare any food. One offered a jam sandwich and I wolfed it down shamelessly on the spot. Then I went on to the top. I had learned two new lessons – never to push myself to such a degree again, and never to climb without emergency food supplies.

On June 3 I wandered into the flight after a forty minute solo, my fifth flight of the day, and glanced around. Except for one instructor and a couple of cadets filling in their logs, everyone had left. Suddenly, a thought occurred to me. "This is our last night here," I said. "Has anyone organized a course booze-up?" Ray Carter raised his head. He was fair, about six foot three and combined the chest and shoulders of a basso profundo with the voice of a tenor. "Not that I know of." He looked at the others, who shook their heads. "Well," I said, "wouldn't it be a good idea to have one?" Yes, it would be a jolly good idea. We would meet at the *Crown and Mitre*. The instructor would pass the word to the others and we would see to our own. What about my instructor? Typically, he had vanished immediately after our last session of dual. To make assurance double sure, I phoned the officers' mess. No, he wasn't there and, no, they didn't know where he was. Probably already shagging his girl friend, I thought.

The booze-up was a success. As I recall, nearly everyone was there – except my instructor. At closing time we piled out, awash with beer, and stood in a group discussing what to do next. Carter finished a beer he was drinking and tossed the bottle high into the air. "Anyone who looks up has got the twitch," he challenged. No one did – and we roared when the bottle hit his own head. Having accepted an invitation to the sergeants' mess, most of the gang then returned to camp to change into civvies, while I and a few others who had none paid a farewell visit to the Naafi Club. By one in the morning, the last of the drunks returned to the huts. Carter, however, decided to enter by a window but slipped and with a thud disappeared from sight. Moments later he entered by the usual means, pale as a ghost and grinning like an idiot. "Look what I've done," he giggled, displaying a shin lacking several inches of skin. He seemed accident prone! As I helped bear him off to get bandaged up, I hoped he wouldn't suffer a third mishap. We were flying in the morning.

"Arrrgh!" Startled, I looked up. My instructor was elbowing his way through the subdued crowd in the flightroom. Halting before me, arms akimbo, eyes blazing, he bellowed, "There was a flight booze-up last night. Why wasn't I invited?"

"It was organized after you'd left, Sir, and I couldn't find you."

For a while he remained glaring at me. Then he snorted, "All right, let's go."

Obediently, I grabbed helmet and 'chute and made to follow.

"Aren't you going to put your flying suit on, Condon?" one asked.

I looked out the window. It was a fine sunny morning. "No,

I'll not bother. It won't be cold today."

As directed, after the flight I completed my log to show that I had practised stalls, spins, instrument flying, forced landings and aerobatics. It was almost a complete fabrication. Apart from a couple of spins and a loop, I had practised nothing but restraint. My instructor hadn't. He began by climbing to over 7,000 feet in an attempt to freeze me to death. Then he did a spin and ordered me to do two more. Then he did a loop, told me to do one, and then he did another. What fun! I was beginning to get the message – I was to be punished – but decided to take it in good humour. "Would you mind sideslipping, Sir?" I asked, feigning a need to vomit. He ignored me. "Would you mind not doing any slow rolls, Sir?" He did four, one after the other, and then amused himself by vigorously stirring the stick. I tried once more. Laughing, I seized the stick. "All right, Sir, I have control." "Like hell you have," he growled, yanking it back. Realizing that the bugger had no sense of humour, I decided to do what I should have done from the beginning – ignore him. He seemed to have relented, though, for he headed back to the airfield. However, instead of landing, with refined sadism he flew right by, did three or four more slow rolls, and then launched into an interminable succession of maximum steep turns. Only then, after well over an hour of torment, did he turn the aircraft over to me and allow me to land.

At the flight, he lost no time in telling the other instructors of his little jest, and they pissed themselves laughing. "That'll teach you not to drink when you have to fly the next day," he trumpeted. Such dedication to my better good was commendable – but we both knew his motive to have been more personal than professional. And his triumph was misplaced. Despite all his efforts, I hadn't puked my ring up.

In the afternoon I was sent up for 45 minutes solo – to practise, my log shows, stalls, spins, sideslipping and (*Ha ha*) steep turns. That too is a fabrication. I merely tootled around admiring the scenery.

4
...And Ends.

In the evening, we packed our gear and twittered about obtaining clearance, a tedious procedure that involved collecting signatures from various sections to prove that we weren't attempting to make off with a pair of flying boots or a Tiger Moth but had indeed returned all issued items. Afterwards we were left to our own devices until 0030 hours, when we boarded our train and vanished into the night.

About seven hours later MT picked us up at Grantham and bore us off to RAF Spitalgate, where we dumped our kit in a barrack block, had breakfast and then paraded for a welcoming address by the Officer Commanding #1 FTS. It proved unsmiling and to the point: in order to secure fifty percent discipline in the air, he would demand one hundred percent discipline on the ground. When he left, we expected to be released to settle in. No such luck. We were marched off to sick bay to present our genitals for inspection, and then to accounts to do the same with our paybooks. Thereafter, with a break for dinner, we had pep talks from the chief ground instructions officer (CGI), the chief flying instructor (CFI) and various signals types. Having had little sleep the previous two nights, by the time we were dismissed at 1730 we felt knackered. Reveille next morning was to be at 0625. *Crippen!*

Next day brought more of the same – a parade for the course photo; to stores to receive a parachute and flying helmet; to the flights to be made cognizant of, and to sign that we understood, the standing flying orders; a lecture on the check lists for the Harvard; a return to the flights to be introduced to the aircraft, with a demonstration of engine starting and cutting-out procedures; and an hour's rifle drill to ready us for CO's inspection the next day, Saturday. Our evening, needless to say, involved much polishing of buttons and boots. In the event, the inspection was cancelled on account of heavy rain – but not before we had become soaked awaiting the decision. For the rest of the morning we were set to polishing barrackroom floors. Only then were we free to spend the weekend feverishly boning up the Harvard check lists. Well, almost free. There was to be no lying stinking in our pits on Sunday mornings. We were to turn out for church parade at 1000 hours. Best blue. This intelligence was received with a groan. "Does that include me, Sergeant?" asked one innocently. "You see, I'm a sun-worshipper." The sergeant didn't miss a beat. "Ah, then your service is at sunrise," he replied. "Report to the guardhouse fifteen minutes before dawn."

Flying began Monday and continued in earnest. When not flying – and it was a rare day when I did not have at least one flight – we practised instrument flying on the Link, pranced about on PT and attended ground school, where we practised morse and listened to lectures on R/T procedure, meteorology, navigation, engines, bombing theory and armaments. As for our spare hours, frequent tests ensured that we kept busy reviewing. In short, our flying club days were over and we hitherto privileged gentlemen of leisure were converted into obedient blue-arsed flies!

For one used to the Cornell and the Tiger Moth, the Harvard IIB presented a proliferation of knobs, levers, switches and dials, enough, one might think, for a bomber, but one soon learnt where everything was and what it did. More daunting, at least for me, were the numerous check lists. For the external check of the Tiger Moth, one kicked the tyres, checked the chocks and pitot head, counted the wings and then climbed aboard. For the Harvard there were twelve items. This was followed by a preliminary cockpit check, engine starting (16 items), full cockpit check (24), engine run-up (12) and vital actions (13). After lining up into wind and obtaining a green light, one could take off. Then came an after take-off check at 300 feet (8) and another on reaching required height (6). If one was merely doing a circuit, one then had the downwind check (9) and final crosswind check (6) There were also an engine shutdown list and others in case of emergency – fire (mercifully brief), precautionary and forced landings (lengthy). Many items involved memorizing an array of numbers – speeds, revs, boost, pressures, temperatures. Today, when I have difficulty recalling the names of friends or find myself standing in a room wondering why I'm there, my mind reels at the thought of them. Nonetheless, thanks to mnemonics, I can still recall the vital actions (HTMPFFGGSI) and the circuit checks (BUMPF)!

With a Pratt and Whitney engine, the Harvard had ample power to provide a satisfying shove in the back on take-off and do aerobatics without wallowing. Its characteristic snarling rasp at full power, like the buzz of a demented Brobdingnagian wasp, bothered only the people on the ground. Though it was not fast – it cruised at around 125mph – it gave me the sense of flying a real aircraft at last.

However, though the Harvard lacked vices, one couldn't simply fly around by the seat of one's pants admiring the scenery and singing "Oh for the Wings of a Dove". Handling demanded care and attention at all times, a degree of concentration upon externals that does not come naturally to us introverts. This was especially true on cross-country flights. Unlike Saskatchewan, the east Midlands is not designed for easy navigation. Haze limits visibility even in fine weather, the countryside is a patchwork of fields and woods with streams and roads wandering all over the place, and cities present a spaghetti of roads and railways – an embarrassment of detail in which landmarks are often anything but obvious. Maintaining straight and level flight on course, while comparing map with landscape and keeping a written log of times, courses, landmarks, ETA's and fuel status, required mental alertness combined with the physical dexterity of a one-armed paper-hanger. One did not, in short, soar free as a bird.

As might be expected, our training was highly professional, and so we accepted the discipline (on the ground, anyway) and willingly kept nose to grindstone. But there was one gentleman on the station who needed the grindstone applied to his backside – and that was the cook in the airmen's mess. Given their means and the scale on which they had to operate, RAF cooks did reasonably well. That could not be said of Spitalgate. The food there was no doubt as good as that supplied elsewhere – until our man got his hands on it and converted it to swill. More than once I consigned his creation to the pigs and went off to the Naafi. To protect men from the criminally incompetent, authority provided a means of redress – an officer with a sergeant who bawled "Orderly Officer. Any complaints?" No one complained, of course. If anyone had, the orderly officer would have fainted. It was a charade.

In our case we complained with our feet. So many abandoned the mess for the Naafi that the administration was spurred into action. The first step was to close the Naafi at meal times. The next was to borrow an officer from the Central Catering Establishment. Improvement was immediate. "Good," I exclaimed, as I inspected the offering of the day, "Stuffed marrow!" "You're the first to know what it is," mourned the server as if his strenuous efforts had been wasted. When fresh eggs appeared at breakfast in place of the reconstituted variety, we began to suspect our cook to be not only incompetent but a fiddling rogue to boot. It was a suspicion soon confirmed. No sooner had our saviour returned whence he came than the fresh eggs vanished and the swill returned.

The proud boast that British officers see to their men's needs before attending to their own would have been more justified were the orderly officer and his sergeant to have eaten with the men. And the CO should have, too, for one randomly selected meal a week anyway. But perhaps that would breech military etiquette. As for us, we accepted the situation philosophically. At least we weren't starved or poisoned.

Weeks turned to months, and by the third week of September we had begun practising aerial combat and dive-bombing. Much more fun! But there was a shadow. One day on a cross-country, I had to confess to the instructor that I was lost. I had committed the elementary prunery of flying "course true" instead of "course magnetic". I was angry with myself. Knowing something was wrong, I had persisted in a vain search for landmarks instead of checking my course. I remembered my first winter climb, when I continued to descend although the lake I had expected to see wasn't there, and my Basil Fawlty reaction at Yorkton when my tank ran dry. This slow reaction to the unexpected bothered me. I now doubted I was sharp enough to fly fighters. Still, it was my wings I wanted. Which aircraft I flew was secondary. In the meantime, I was handling the Harvard well and enjoying life.

❦

"Good grief," exclaimed Tibbals, "my balls have turned blue!" It was September 24th. A few who had not yet gone to bed gathered to inspect the afflicted members with interest. "Why, so they have!" remarked one. "What have you been up to, you dirty sod?" And amid Tibbals' laughing protestations of innocence and general hilarity we turned in for the night. An hour later we were raided by a gang of half-drunken Dutchmen – the preceding course, returned from their graduation party. Their replacements, we knew, were to be drawn from Cranwell, which made us the last of the wartime intake. There was more good-natured foolery, and then the lights went off again.

Next morning, following a session on the Link, I reported to the flight. The flight commander saw me, "Condon, you're up for CFI's check. He's waiting in DogDog." Feeling suddenly sick, I grabbed my 'chute and helmet and walked out. This was no progress check but a scrub check, and I had been half expecting it. A few days earlier I had again, as at Yorkton, forgotten my vital actions, only this time my instructor had been in the back – and he had pounced.

Climbing into the CFI's silvery special, I fastened my harness, plugged in my helmet and began my checks. Unfortunately, I was a little nervous, and when nervous I tend to chat. "Let's see," I said as I was finishing my vital actions. "Ah yes. Oil gills open," adding airily, "Always forgetting that." *Now why should I say such a thing, when it isn't even true? Clot!* Then I took off for what I expected to be my last flight. It was a good one on the whole. There was one tense moment. Directed to do a runway landing at another airfield – ours was a rather bumpy grass field – I rounded out, blipped the throttle and waited for touchdown. Nothing! For one awful moment I thought the undercart was still up. Then I noticed a slight vibration. We were rolling down the runway. It had been a perfect three-pointer.

It made no difference. When I presented myself at his office later, the CFI was reading my records and frowning thoughtfully. At last he looked up. "I've decided to take you off flying," he said flatly. "I'm afraid you're too forgetful." He perused my documents again, "Do you wish to remuster as navigator?"

I had agreed to extended service only to win my wings. With my education there was no future for me in the RAF. "No, Sir. I'll take my discharge." He nodded, scribbled something down – and that was the end of the matter.

On my way to the mess, I bumped into Tibbals. "Hi," he said, "how'd your check go?"

"I got the chop."

He laughed, "Yeah. You wouldn't be grinning like that if you had."

"I don't feel much like grinning," I said. Then I went in for dinner.

☙

Remustered to AC2 with reduced pay, I was posted to a holding unit in London and about a month later found myself on a train to the demob centre. On the way north, I broke my journey at Grantham to drop in on the flight's graduation party. Cries of welcome greeted my appearance and someone thrust a pint into my hand. Then I was approached by Tony, a fair, aristocratic cadet whose slender frame matched my own. "What are you doing now, Phil?" he asked.

"Off to pick up my civvies, Tony."

"Well, I'll soon be joining you."

"What happened?"

"I'd passed my final flying test and all the ground exams, but still had some flying to do. Then I landed with my undercart up!"

"Bloody hell! That must have shaken you."

"Yes. And for failing to give me a red light the bod in the control tower received a reprimand, but I got the chop."

"I know how you feel. Well…perhaps it's all for the best, Tony. Good Luck."

I raised my glass. "Good luck, everyone."

Then I drained it and left.

☙

Of those who celebrated that night, three were dead within a year. Jim and Jock went on to a Heavy Conversion Unit and were killed in a flying accident, and Dave died in his Spitfire, shot down by the Israelis. A fourth, Steve, who had been chopped before me, managed to kill himself on a motorcycle.

Along with many ex-servicemen, I was to miss the comradeship and the sense of belonging to a greater whole. The young men I served with, many of whose names and faces now escape me, were as good as one could find anywhere. I feel privileged to have been one of their company.

PART FOUR

Phoenix Rising

1947 – 1956

Chapter 15 Return to Plumstead II   291

Chapter 16 Hunker Creek   305

Chapter 17 Vancouver   341

CHAPTER FIFTEEN

Return to Plumstead II

1
Doughmaker

London in November, 1947, was depressing. If the terror and rubble of the blitz had long gone, so had the wartime unity of purpose and the euphoria of victory. The nation was bankrupt and London looked it. The lights were on again, but in the usual fog and rain everything appeared more than usually shabby and run-down, including the people. Little was being built, rationing remained in full force and one queued for everything. The present was cheerless and the prospects bleak.

So it seemed to me at the time. Cast down in more ways than one, I had plunged to earth with no idea of what to do with myself. I could see that the CFI had really done me a service. Absent-minded pilots are a menace and I might have gone on to kill myself or, worse, an entire crew. Still, I felt stung by a sense of failure. Meanwhile, save for my demob pay, I had no money, and my goods would have fitted into a suitcase. I needed a job, anything, until I sorted myself out.

Things had changed at home since my last leave. George had

moved in as Mum's common-law husband, and Pauline had left to work as a lady's maid in Henley. Years later she told me that she had been sped on her way by Grandpa. One day he had told her that he hated my father, that he hated her, and that the sooner she cleared off the better – a sentiment not surprising in view of the way he had treated Mum after the first War, and another example of life putting in the boot at the tenderest spot. As for Dad, he had recovered from his brush with death and was still living with his sister Hetty and working as a carpenter. Whether or not he knew about George, I didn't dare ask.

It was George who solved my immediate problem. A few days after I moved in he said, "You'll be needing a job, won't you, Phil? Why not work at the bakery with me? Right now they need a doughmaker."

"Where is it?"

"Alderton's. It's around the corner. Just off Fletcher Road."

No queueing for buses? That was convenient. Done! So the battledress I had worn with pride became my workclothes and grew dusty with flour. Sackcloth and ashes, I thought in self-mockery.

As I stood peering ruminatively into the mixer, waiting for my last third of a ton of dough to clean the bowl and assume the smooth, satiny texture that indicated it was ready, a small piece of dough flew past my nose. I looked up, grinning. Then I flipped a piece back. I knew who the culprit was – the foreman, Jack Moxham. It was a little harmless horseplay that took place only between us and was an indication of mutual respect. At least, I respected him. I have worked in many places with men ranging from slender five-footers to 300 pound behemoths, but Jack was the best worker I have come across. A foot shorter than I, slighter and sallow of complexion, he worked quickly and efficiently. While he was foreman, the work of the bakery proceeded smoothly.

I had soon learnt the routine. As the doughmaker's hours were awkward – six in the evening to two in the morning, six nights a week – the job was shared with the under-foreman, week and week about, an arrangement intended to give the doughmaker time with his family. The work was easy, even for an absent-minded introvert. I began my shift by climbing a vertical iron ladder to the loft – rather like the miller in my childhood toy – and emptying four 140 pound sacks of "national flour" into the heavy bowl I had placed beneath the hopper. The only vital action was to tuck the cloth chute into the bowl first so the flour ended up there and not on the floor. Then I wheeled the bowl onto the mixer, added the other ingredients – water, salt, yeast, and one or two others according to conditions – and started it up. While that was mixing, I loaded the next bowl with flour; and when each mix was finished, I covered it and wheeled the bowl to the moulding machine. By the time the regular crew came in at nine, the sixth and last mix was being completed and the first had risen ready for them.

For the remainder of my shift I cut dough and helped on the oven plates. One began the first by cutting a swathe of dough from the bowl and heaving it onto the worktable. This had to be done with one swift, smooth movement, thus catching the dough by surprise before it could drape itself all over you. Then one had to cut the amorphous mass into two-pound pieces. On my first night, sawing frantically, I developed blisters. But the knack soon came. With one easy pass of the knife, cutting forwards then backwards, I was soon tossing pieces to Jack as fast as he could weigh them. With a "clack" of the scales if the weight was right, or a rhythmic "clack-clack" if he had to add or tear off some, Jack could toss a piece into the moulding machine every two seconds, a rate that kept George on the run at the other end. He had the boring task of placing the molded dough onto metal trays, loading the trays onto racks and then wheeling the filled racks into the proofer.

When not cutting dough, I helped load and unload the oven plates. There were four of these, each about seven feet by ten, arranged in pairs, one above the other. Mounted on wheels, they were simply pushed into the gas-fired oven like shallow steel drawers. Responsible for keeping track of the baking time for each plate of bread was the plateman, a deaf mute inevitably called "Dummy". Unloading the baked bread from the plates was warm work, especially for the man in the middle when all four plates were withdrawn at once, but one became used to it. The baked loaves were then loaded onto racks of wooden shelves and wheeled into the next room to await the deliverymen in the morning.

The rest of the crew, consisting of the under-foreman and two helpers, were responsible for rolls, small loaves and specialty breads such as Hovis. I started them off with a mix, but as their small mixer had only one bowl, if they needed another they did their own. Lacking a machine, they had to mould, or knead, the dough by hand, a process that soon makes unaccustomed muscles complain, as I discovered for myself when our moulder broke down one night. They also had to use an old-fashioned peel oven, so-called because the trays of bread were fished out with a peel, a long wooden paddle resembling a flat-bladed oar. And as this oven was situated to the side and above the plates, the fishing had to be done shoulder high. Their output was smaller than ours, but they had to work harder.

Jack had more to do than merely weigh pieces of dough, of course. While he was there, no bread was over-proofed, no plates left idle, no bread over-baked and, except for the night the moulder broke down, no emergency had arisen. I took this smooth running for granted. But of course it was largely Jack's doing. After about a year he left, and we had a new foreman. There was no emergency under him either, but we seemed always on the verge of one. If he worked harder than Jack, it was because he was inefficient. Too clumsy to do the weighing, he switched places with George. And when I was needed on the plates, he sometimes cut dough himself – and made as hard work of it as I had on my first night. As for keeping track of the proofing and baking, he clucked about the place like a flustered hen and made the rest of us nervous. By the end of a shift he must have been exhausted. I was sorry Jack Moxham left. He had been a fine worker. Just how fine I didn't realize until after he had gone.

Of course, there is more to the baking of bread than has been shown here. Waiting for my pay packet in the office one day, I gravitated towards a shelf of books and selected one on bread. It proved to be a densely packed tome of nearly five hundred pages on breads, flours, yeasts and a hundred other considerations in the baking of bread. I was impressed. So much on one simple human activity! It was not the first time, nor would it be the last, that I should be reminded of how little I knew. The sum of human skill and knowledge is vast and increases at a compound rate. Some skills need a lifetime to master, and the growing body of knowledge is such that even a specialist struggles to keep up in his field. The universe provides the most able and ambitious of minds scope and challenge enough and to spare. Nothing is simple, except perhaps mindedness.

ॐ

2

A Problem

With the immediate problem of employment solved, after a week or so my spirits had begun to lift and the mood of self-mockery had vanished. It was good to be home again. Now I appreciated my mother – and her cooking – more than ever. And though I was saddened by her separation from Dad, I considered it their business and accepted the situation. For this reason I never resented George, and we got along well. Grandpa had accepted my appearance without comment. In fact he had little to say to any of us. No doubt glad to have seen the back of my father, he paid the thirteen shillings rent, bought himself two ounces of cigarette tobacco and donated the rest of his pension to the bookies. Saturday evening I usually spent with Dad. We'd have a pint or two at his local pub, egg and chips at a tiny nearby cafe – created, like Cook's grocery, from the parlour and hallway of a terrace house – and then go on to the pictures if there was anything worth seeing. Before long I had fallen into a comfortable routine.

Yet the central problem remained. What was I to do with my life? Work at the bakery was almost a pleasure, but I had no wish to make a career of it. Eight years had elapsed since I had last lived in Plumstead. The terror and suffering of the War had passed me by and I had enjoyed one of the happiest periods of my life. Now I was back – twenty-one, whole, exceedingly fortunate – but little further ahead. I had to *do* something. But what? What experience did I have? Office boy and trainee pilot (failed). What education? Save for what I had gleaned from the RAF and the public library, little more than a school-leaver of fourteen. Professions were out, as was the civil service. The world of business? I had the business sense of the average dog. A trade, then? The government provided training courses for ex-servicemen. In fact, Dad had taken advantage of one. Not interested. A gentleman of leisure? Now that was more like it! Fortunately, I had neither the upbringing nor the means.

Rats! Even in their teens, others seemed to know what they wanted to do. Apart from enlisting in the wartime RAF, I had never had the slightest idea. Some simply got a job, married, produced children and even enjoyed contented lives. Why not I? A distant cousin had begun producing offspring at the age of seventeen, for goodness' sake. But I was not interested in women, nor in offspring. In any case, there was surely more to life than merely producing another generation. It seemed pointless. There *must* be a higher purpose. But what? Like the universe, life seemed a total mystery. And so I mulled the problem over, becoming more and more baffled and frustrated.

❦

3
Literary Influences

In the meantime, my mind was starving. Save for RAF notes and a few paperbacks, I had read nothing for years. And so, smiling as I passed by the house of the lilywhite girl who had set my boyhood heart aflutter, I directed my steps to the Plumstead public library. Who knows? I might even get some ideas there.

It was not information on occupations and careers that I sought. I had done that once, at Conway, and instead Pauline had brought me Smythe's *Spirit of the Hills*. Things had seemed most clear to me on the hills then, so it was to them that I turned now – or rather, as there *were* no hilltops in Plumstead for me to sit on and ponder, to books about them. The first to catch my eye was Seton Gordon's

Highways and Byways in the Central Highlands. Selecting that and one or two others, I bore my prizes off. Written in the style of H.V.Morton, Gordon's book proved to be a travel guide rich in historical anecdotes. As I had expected, it covered the general area of my climbs with the Mountain Rescue, but it was with the history that I became fascinated. Two men, Bonnie Prince Charlie and Montrose, between them seemed to have covered the entire Highlands. Appetite whetted, I sought more. Beginning with Charlie (at least I had heard of him), I went on a romp through things Highland: a history of the '45, a book on clans and tartans, and a few novels set in the period. It was all very fine and romantic – though it had not been so, I fancy, for the clansmen at Culloden or the Highland people in its aftermath.

Then I turned to Montrose. James Graham, first Marquis of Montrose, was a nobler man by far. Loyal to the cause of Charles I, he raised an army of clansmen and Irish MacDonalds and in one *annus mirabilis* conquered the whole of Scotland – only to lose everything in one disastrous battle. Afterwards, betrayed by a fellow Highlander, he was captured and shamefully executed. Following this story in John Buchan's biographies of Montrose and Cromwell and the fine historical novels of Margaret Irwin plunged me first into the Civil War period and later into that of the first Elizabeth – the kind of submersion that provides a flavour of the times and an appreciation of the people involved. I had become hooked on history.

Two other books influenced me greatly at this time. The first, *Other Men's Flowers*, by Archibald Wavell, is an anthology of poetry that he had enjoyed and memorized. Impressed that a soldier should like poetry, I read the lot and memorized some myself, including Browning's "Childe Roland to the Dark Tower Came". Memory not being my strong point, this last, at the rate of a stanza a night, took me five weeks. Why so much effort over this particular poem? I'm not sure. Perhaps it was because of a BBC dramatization I had heard a few years earlier, or perhaps because it is about a quest. It is a strange tale, woven by Browning out of one enigmatic line in *King Lear*. Childe Roland is one of a brotherhood of knights dedicated to a quest for the Dark Tower. Of them all, only he succeeds, and the poem ends with his raising a slughorn to his lips and blowing his challenge. What was in the tower and what happens next we never learn. I know now why Browning doesn't tell us. The challenge is the whole point and is intended to illustrate his belief that "'Tis not what a man Does which exalts him but what man Would do". The result of our endeavours is seldom in our hands. The attempt is all. Perhaps I sensed this then. Perhaps not. In any case, I was now hooked on poetry as well.

Why the next book should have caught my attention will at once be apparent from its title – *A Hermit in the Himalayas*, by Paul Brunton. As it happens, the book has little to do with the Himalayas and much to do with Brunton's experience of the Hindu religion. The details of the book and of companion volumes, *The Hidden Teaching Beyond Yoga* and *The Wisdom of the Overself,* escape me now – and I have no intention of re-reading them to refresh my memory – but their effect on me was profound. I found the concepts of karma and reincarnation compelling. If the physical universe is governed by physical laws, why should there not be laws for the moral and spiritual spheres too? Karmic law seemed logical. As for reincarnation – I have never been comfortable with the orthodox Christian view that we live but once and then are consigned to heaven (via purgatory), limbo or hell. Moreover, the idea that God should consign anyone to hell, a place of eternal torment of the kind depicted in *Paradise Lost* or *The Divine Comedy,* to me is repellent. So disproportionate a punishment could be inflicted only by a psychopath. There's no such place, though there are temporary hells aplenty. At least reincarnation gives sinners a second chance, or as many as they need. Like students, we sinners do not all learn at the same rate.

However, the essential point that I grasped from Brunton was that God is not only transcendent but also immanent, that He is not only beyond and far greater than the created universe but is also present within it, that He is in fact present within each of us, and that the higher self within each of us is one with God. It was a revelation. Already familiar with the idea of higher levels of consciousness from my reading of Gurdieff, I found it no great step to accept the idea of a higher, spiritual self and immediately took the further leap of linking God not only with the unseen magnificence I had sensed on the Welsh hills but also with the joy I had experienced there. Since my encounter with the Church in 1939 I had thought little about God, tending to associate Him instead with church, religions and all the accompanying baggage. At a stroke, I was now freed. God was a living spirit and was not to be bottled up in philosophies or religions, no matter which, nor in books, no matter how "holy".

I did not of course dismiss religions or that vast body of scriptures and other religious works of which I was almost totally ignorant (Some "baggage"!). That would have been ludicrous. But I felt that I did not have to accept things on authority. Rightly or wrongly, I believed that my awareness of a spiritual dimension and my experience of love and joy equipped me to judge the truth of things for myself – or at least to judge what I needed to know. Theologians may think this dangerous nonsense and in another age might have considered me a strong candidate for the heretic's bonfire. Perhaps. But from this time I felt that I had a silent inner guide and companion, one in whom I could trust. Does that mean I became aware of the presence of God? No. I have never to my knowledge had a "religious experience" nor have I expected one. And yet I felt close to Him. Then did I pray frequently? Hardly ever. Prayer for myself or for others seemed almost importunate. God knew my heart and knew what was needed. If prayer there was, it was a wordless reaching toward Him. For the rest, I trusted Him to direct my course and to administer the occasional kick if I went astray.

As if in confirmation of my new-found belief, joy entered my life once more. In that magical moonlit hour on Conway Mountain, for a moment I had felt the world to be pregnant with some hidden glory. Now I was to feel it again, this time in London. I had attended a late showing at the Woolwich Odeon and was returning home. The pubs were closed, the revellers long gone, and by the time I reached General Gordon Square the only people to be seen were a few queueing for a late bus. It was a fine summer night and on impulse I decided to walk home – not along the main roads, but up through the back streets as the spirit took me. Beginning at the station, I stepped lightly through that rather dingy area as if setting out for Lyonnesse, and as I did so my heart began to sing. With the terrace houses darkened and the deserted streets lit only by a few gaslamps and the stars, I felt as if I were walking through a sleeping suburb of a city built in Eden.

The glory remained hidden, of course – as did the solution to the problem of what to do with myself. Only I no longer felt baffled and frustrated. It would sort itself out.

Though I did not realize it then, the course of my life had to some extent been determined already. The impulse, as I said earlier, had long before been given – on the night when a young boy had bared his being to the thunderstorm. And it had since been confirmed by the wildflowers of Banstead, by the joy I had felt at Linton and on the hills, and by books that had come into my hands at the right time. But there was something else, something I had forgotten, and it lay silent like a time bomb, awaiting only the right time to explode and do its work.

☙

4

Decision

Of one thing I was sure. I would not tie myself down in London. I needed open spaces, and a week or two each year on the hills would not do. Early in 1948 I had thought of the sea and crossed the Thames to wander around dockland, noting the acres cleared of rubble where once had stood houses. For a while I had watched a seaman at work scaling rust from the side of a ship. No, that wasn't the way. Poor living and working conditions, poor pay, with no prospect of promotion – life at sea was a dead end.

Now, as the weeks passed, I found myself thinking more and more of Canada. I had felt at home in that great country. If one wanted open spaces, Canada had them. A man could breathe there. More books, this time about the lives of trappers, prospectors, settlers, and some novels – *White Fang, The Call of the Wild, The Trail of '98.* Even poetry (Robert Service) and a few pictures contributed their siren song – *The Gold Rush, 49th Parallel* and *Scott of the Antarctic.*

The call of the wild was strong. Yet I hesitated. Emigration was a serious step and would cut me off from my family. There was an alternative, though. I remembered Joe at Plas Curig. Of course, the Forestry Commission! That would give me open spaces and a healthy outdoor life. I therefore applied for an interview but first made a mental reservation. If, like Joe, I could be sent to Bettws y Coed, I would go. Otherwise not. I resolved to leave it to fate, or my inner guide, to determine which it should be. The interviewing board were pleasant. "From the ridiculous to the sublime, eh?" laughed one on hearing I wished to abandon the city for the outdoor life. Yes, there were positions open, and in a few years I could be a foreman earning as much as ten pounds a week. But, no, there were no vacancies at Bettws y Coed.

So it was beginning to look as though it would be Canada. My decision crystalized in the course of a flying visit to Idwal over the August bank holiday. When I had climbed there earlier with my cousin Peter, we had stayed at Idwal Cottage. This time, equipping myself from war surplus, I decided to camp out and Saturday evening found me pitching my tent on a hillside in Cwm Tryfan.

I was awakened next morning by the sound of coughing. "Is anyone there?" a voice asked.

Poking my head out the tent flap, I saw a Welsh hill farmer. "What is it?"

"That'll be a shilling, please," he replied. Receiving a blank stare, he pointed to my tent, "It's for the rent."

Wordlessly, I handed him his shilling. And then, though I didn't begrudge the money, I began to burn. Hitherto I had walked the earth freely. Now I was reminded that virtually everything was owned by someone else – even what I considered wilderness, and I was allowed there only on sufferance. I remembered the gillie's "This is private property. Ye must get oot." Had it been later in the year, we might well have been ordered off a mountain in case we disturbed the owner's grouse shooting or stag hunting. Where did I have a perfect right to be? The commons? I had outgrown those patches as a boy. The beaches? Some were private, the public ones were usually crowded and the shoreline between high and low tide was owned by the crown. Public footpaths? The right of way was often contested by landowners. The highway? Yes, but even that was called the "King's highway"; and if you were one of the great unwashed, like Jo the crossing-sweeper, you could be ordered to move on. "Our" house? It was Grandpa's, and he only rented it. I was not then aware of the evictions in Ireland, of the Highland Clearances, of the landowners' theft of much of the ancient common lands of England by means of Private Member's Bills, but in a small way I was beginning to feel something of the victims' outrage.

Aggravating this sudden feeling of being a trespasser in my own land were the crowds. August bank holiday weekend is not a good time to travel. The trains had been packed, and the number of people in Bettws y Coed had taken me by surprise. The tourists were back. Even Idwal seemed swarming with climbers. Now I was glad that I hadn't joined the Forestry Commission. The Snowdonia of my youth had been an aberration of the War and would never be the same again.[15]

By the time I returned to London I had made up my mind. Canada it would be. Immediately, I felt a sense of freedom and believed the decision to be right. Moreover, I knew where I intended to go – to the Yukon, as far from the madding crowd as I could get. Naive and romantic I may have been, but not so naive as to consider becoming a trapper, prospector or settler. I knew myself to be no handyman. I also knew the move would not solve the basic problem of what to do with my life. But I was prepared to work in the bush. The pay would be good and I might even make a man of myself. In the meantime I would keep my options open and could never become so comfortable as to allow myself to drift. Now, when to leave? Early May, I decided. Except underground, work in the bush is seasonal and doesn't open up until the spring thaw.

Though my parents must have been dismayed by my decision, typically neither questioned it. Pauline, too, had made a decision. Tired of being personal maid to a lady who proved to be a

---

[15]   It occurs to me now that there may have been a deeper reason for my anger. Considering what the hills of Wales had meant to me, paying "rent" for pitching a tent on an open hillside was akin to paying a fee for entry into Eden – or finding a moneychanger in the Temple.

wealthy man's mistress with little to do but paint her toenails, she applied to join the Land Army. The examining doctor noted her slight frame and shook his head doubtfully. "Work on the land is hard, you know," he warned. "I really don't think you are strong enough." When she insisted, he acquiesced, muttering, "Ah well, kill or cure." He didn't know my sister. Perhaps the young doctor who thumped my ribs at British Columbia House thought much the same of me. At least four inches taller and four stone heavier than I, he made me feel a mere stripling. Idly, I wondered how many men in British Columbia were as big as he. However, he kept his counsel. It was my old friend PN who voiced the doubts. Recently demobbed from the Royal Engineers, he was back home in Conway; and in March, 1949, I dropped in on him at the *Bluebell*. When I told him of my plans, he looked serious. "Are you sure?" he asked. "You're not strong, you know." I smiled, "Yes, I know – but I can't let that stop me, can I?" Then I left for a week or so in the hills. At least I would be fit.

Decision is one thing, the deed another. And as I lay in bed on the night of May 6, the same hand that had gripped my vitals when I received my call-up was at work again. This was my last night at home. All was in order. I had my passage ticket, passport, signed release from the RAFVR and a hundred pounds in the bank. Alderton's had served me well. As for the packing, it was done: my army rucksack, containing balaclava, spare clothes, toiletry and books – The Book of Common Prayer (a surprise gift from Dad), a New Testament, and an Oxford Shakespeare. The only outer clothing would be on my back – a US Army combat uniform. I intended traveling rough and that meant traveling light. Upon bidding me goodbye earlier that day, Dad had offered me two pieces of advice. "Now you're going to Canada, become a Canadian." That was sensible. But the second, "Don't get so close to another man that he can't go for a shit without you going along", had taken me aback. He didn't know me at all. Had he fifty sons, he couldn't have found one who needed such advice less. Now, in the morning I would have to face the parting from Mum, and I dreaded it. Our family seemed fated constantly to be split up, but the partings never became easier.

Some fifteen hours later I was aboard the *Aquitania*, watching the Isle of Wight fade into the distance. Mum and George had insisted on seeing me off from Waterloo. We had been dry-eyed, seemingly cheerful, but the pain had been palpable. At Southampton I'd had a surprise. As I leant upon the ship's rail watching the preparations for cast-off, Dad had come walking along the quay. Hearing my shout, he had spotted me, waved briefly and then turned to go. Like me, he disliked protracted farewells. I had watched him as he left – the military bearing, the familiar tilt of the head and never a look back. Bless him! He had come all the way from London just on the chance of seeing me off.

Now, as the coast of England slipped by on our starboard beam, I thought of my country. Oddly, although I was leaving behind so much that I loved, my only real regret was that I hadn't seen more of the Scottish Highlands. Scotland – I recalled some lines of Montrose that had struck me:

> *He either fears his fate too much*
> *Or his deserts are small*
> *Who dares not put it to the touch*
> *To win or lose it all.*

Well, I had dared – and the adventure had begun. I knew nothing of my deserts, but I had complete trust in my inner guide and did not fear my fate. And so this fuzz-cheeked innocent was casting himself on the wave to swim or sink, fully confident he would swim. What did not strike him at the time was that Montrose had eventually lost it all.

CHAPTER SIXTEEN

Hunker Creek

1
Rule of Thumb

The crossing took five full days. As befitting her age, the *Aquitania* had rattled her way across an unusually placid Atlantic at a sedate pace. Built in 1914 as a luxury liner, she had become a carrier of migrants, an old lady in her final year of service and with her glory days a distant memory. Night had fallen by the time we entered Halifax harbour, but the constellation of twinkling lights that greeted us brought me little cheer. Families lived there, surrounded by friends, and in all that great city I knew no one and none knew me! But this sudden sense of isolation was but a thing of the moment. In fact I was not alone. During the crossing I had become acquainted with an amiable Scot, one Jock (Yes, another one), and when he learned that I intended to thumb my way to Edmonton and seek work in the Yukon he had asked if he might come along. I had agreed readily. It might make rides harder to come by, but I welcomed the company.

Most of next day, May 13, was spent waiting in line to satisfy the concerns of immigration officials. As a result, it was well past eleven before Jock and I disembarked, nearer midnight by the time we cleared customs. It was hardly the most convenient time for immigrants to be landed, but volunteers were still waiting to extend a helping hand. The Canadian Red Cross treated us to a coffee and a padre from Church Services drove us to a B & B. It was a welcome we had not looked for but one we appreciated.

Next morning, after checking with our banks, we set forth on our grand journey. We did not get far. Though traffic had been heavy, few drivers had wanted to stop, and by evening we had only reached Truro, fifty miles north. Still, it was a start. We had supper at a café and then hiked out of town to spend our first night sleeping rough – on the luggage rack of a gutted bus. But without pads and sleeping bags, and with rain beating on the metal roof half the night, we had a miserably cold and uncomfortable time and were only too glad to hit the road at first light. At least the rain had stopped.

Sunrise brought some warmth and an encounter with a fellow wayfarer. Stopping to chat, I asked about the work situation. "Lousy," he replied, gloomily shaking his head. "I'm on my way back to England." This was not exactly what I wanted to hear. Still, war veterans may have flooded the labour market, but I doubted if many had rushed to the Yukon. Shortly afterwards, we were picked up by a van and taken to Moncton; but as we expressed our thanks and prepared to leave, the driver suddenly said, "By the way, I'm only stopping for something to eat. Then I'm going on to Montreal. You boys can stay on, if you want." Two days later, we were there. Despite the slow start, we had covered 800 miles in three days.

On the way, I'd noticed that some main roads were badly potholed and many of the little towns we passed through appeared rundown, although those in Quebec had fine churches. It was a reminder that the Depression had hit Canada hard – and made her fine war effort seem all the more remarkable.

As Jock's money hadn't come through, we stayed in Montreal for two nights as guests of the Salvation Army, sleeping on the floor of a cavernous hall with hundreds of other men, most of them locals but some transients like ourselves. One of the latter, an

English lad who'd worked his passage across and was hitchhiking to Vancouver, had all his kit stolen. Fortunately, his money was safe. I had used my pack as a pillow, as did Jock.

The next stage of our journey, from Montreal to Winnipeg by way of northern Ontario, proved to be a marathon that lasted ten days. How I felt at the time may be judged from this entry in my journal:

> YMCA, Winnipeg, May 28th: On this trip so far I have put all my
> trust in God, and it really is amazing how well things work out.
> Nothing so far has worried me at all.

I looked forward to each day with confidence, expecting all things to work together for good and interested to see how they would. That trust, though perhaps naive, proved not misplaced.

From Montreal, we headed west along the Ottawa Valley and by the 21st had reached North Bay, a bright little town on Lake Nipissing. Here we booked into a cheap hotel. Having spent the previous night in a barn, burrowing in the hay, and much of the afternoon hiking under a blazing sun in company with mosquitos and blackfly, we felt we had earned it. Besides, in the morning we would be heading into the wilds north of Lake Superior. There was no telling what we might encounter there.

It was as well we had a good sleep, for the next day passed without a ride and we had to hike until dark, stopping only to shelter from a rain squall and to eat at a roadside café. That night was spent on the floor of an uncompleted cabin, one with no doors or windows and, as we discovered in the morning, with no roof either. Before leaving, we lit a fire to warm up and enjoy a breakfast of canned beans – our usual fare on the road, together with canned peaches and potatoes scrounged from farmers.

With the sun the bugs returned. Mid-morning brought temporary relief in the form af a truck, but that took us only as far as Temagami National Park and further hours of torment under a baking sun. Eventually we were picked up by a cabbie who bore us over the gravel road at suicidal speed and dropped us at the next settlement. A long ride then took us beyond Matheson, bringing the day's run to a respectable 180 miles. While bumming potatoes from a farmer, we learnt we could sleep in the local flag station, a small cabin to shelter travellers while they waited to flag

down a train. Provided at whistle stops, towns too small to merit
a station, each contained an oil-drum stove and firewood but was
otherwise unfurnished. Though it meant sleeping on bare boards
again, at least we were warm.

During the night a wind blew up, and by morning the rain
that had occasionally pattered on the roof had turned to heavy
showers of sleet. Brewing up some cocoa, all we had left, we chatted
with two farm boys who had seen our smoke and dropped by to
warm up. Shortly afterwards a railroad gang burst in, soaked and
half frozen from having pumped their way up on a hand trolley.
Ignoring us, they shut the door, flipped the draft of the stove wide
open and then settled down to roll cigarettes and dry out. Before
long, the stove had turned cherry-red and began to convert the
crowded cabin into a sauna. Flattened against the wall by the heat
and feeling claustrophobic, I stood it for as long as I could but
then signalled Jock to leave. By now it was snowing, great wet
flakes, but I preferred to face the elements than be broiled.

That day, May 24, we got only as far as Cochrane, forty miles on.
In the morning we had hiked about five miles, sheltering from the
heavier showers at farmhouses and halting at another flag station
to bake some spuds we had bummed. Consisting of a few acres
hacked from the bush, most farms there probably provided little
more than subsistence, but the farmers were usually helpful.

In the afternoon, following a bitterly cold ride on the back of an
open truck, we had been picked up and taken the rest of the way
by an off-duty policeman. He'd been friendly, chatty, strangely
fond of his gun. "I always travel with this," reaching inside his
coat to produce a large revolver, which he proceeded to flourish.
"Sometimes I stop on the way for some target practice – pot a few
crows." Then, just as I'd begun to expect a demonstration, he'd
continued, "One day I picked up a guy, a big guy. After a bit he
turned to me and said, 'You know, I could take this car from you
and there's not a damned thing you could do about it.' 'That's
what you think,' I said, pulling this out. 'Now, you just get your
butt outta here and take a hike'."

Cochrane boasted a small cinema, and after supper we
patronised it. There was a heavy frost that night, but neither of us
gave a hoot. Thanks to our friendly cop, we were warm and snug

– in the local jail. Perhaps it was his way of thanking us for being harmless wayfarers and not desperados. All that bluster and gun-waving had been for our benefit, of course. It had not occurred to me that we might be thought menacing. And yet, taking another look at Jock – his stocky build, closely cropped head, a collarless shirt beneath a rough tweed jacket – I could see he might easily be taken for an escaped convict. As for me, well, crazed baby-faced killers were not unknown even then. Later on, one of our drivers confessed, "When I saw your uniform, I thought at first you were a couple of deserters." The wonder is not that we might inspire fear but that people stopped for us so readily.

By next evening, after stopping for a meal at Kapuskasing, we were at Hearst, roughly the midway point of our journey. We had been on the road for twelve days. The police there being less accommodating, we splurged on a hotel room – for $1 a head. After supper, I had a hot bath and turned in early. It had been a trying day. We had covered 140 miles, but two rides had been on open trucks and we had spent hours hiking against a blustery wind and showers of sleet and snow. Sensing I was developing a cold, I hoped the weather would improve soon. And so it did – but not before winter gave one last flick of its tail. A blizzard of wet snow blew up overnight and persisted until noon. Then the front passed, the wind shifted and the sun returned at last.

We had walked no more than a mile from Hearst before a car drew up and the driver greeted us with a cheerful "Where are you crazy buggers going?" A fair question. Behind were hundreds of miles of gravel road in a sea of conifers, and before us were more of the same. What I didn't know was that settlements there had grown along the railroad, which had been built before the highway, and that the two parted company at Hearst. The next inhabited place was 125 miles away! Although the highway there is only at the latitude of Land's End, this is nonetheless north country, capable in May of delivering 80°F one day and a blizzard the next. James Bay, 150 miles farther north, is at the latitude of Ireland. While its eastern shore is partly forested, to the west are muskeg and tundra. Polar bears roam there. Far from moderating the climate, the vast expanse of Hudson Bay seems to act like a sink, drawing Arctic air southward and the tundra with it.

Deposited at Geraldton, Jock and I stopped at a gas station for a coke and had a leisurely chat with the attendant. A war vet with more time on his hands than business, he seemed only too glad of the company. Soon afterwards, we got a ride to Beardmore and then another right through to the lakehead at Fort William, a town which once had been a major staging post for Nor'Wester canoe brigades. That night we slept at the Sally Ann, well content. We had not left Hearst until past noon and yet had covered over 300 miles, no more than two of them on foot. It had been a good day's run.

Next day brought our only sour experience, sandwiched between two of the best. Our third ride out of Fort William was provided by a cheerful logging contractor who insisted on bearing us off to his camp, where he instructed the cook to "fry the boys up some bacon and eggs." As we waited, chatting on the cookhouse steps, I looked around. Apart from us three and the cook, the camp was silent, apparently deserted. I assumed the men were working in the woods somewhere. If so, I didn't envy them. There wasn't a breath of wind; and the sun, blazing from a clear sky, made the previous day's snowstorm seem like a dream. Shimmering in the heat, the surrounding trees crowded in upon us, filling the air with their resin. I found it oppressive, stifling. Work in such conditions, with the added torment of mosquitos, did not appeal at all. Logging, I decided, wasn't for me. After the meal, our generous host drove us back to the highway.

Towards evening we came upon a fire look-out and climbed up, hoping to bed down under its roof. Finding a glassed-in office there, however, we immediately descended and walked on. We had gone no more than fifty yards before we heard a shout and saw a man running through the trees towards us. Stopping at a safe distance, he shook his fist, "You guys get the hell outta here. Go on, beat it." Upset because we had climbed the tower, I supposed. Surprised by his outburst, for we were clearly leaving anyway, I asked mildly, "Why are you so angry? We were only looking for a place to sleep." "Just beat it," he shouted. "We don't want your kind around here." He was pale and shaking, more from fear than anger. Seeing it useless trying to mollify him, we walked away.

With the onset of night we had a fireside supper of beans and peaches and then resigned ourselves to sitting hunched over the fire until dawn. We were near Upsala, a hundred miles north of Fort William. Suddenly, I heard a crunch of footsteps on gravel and a man entered the light of our campfire. "I saw the flames and figured it was a bush fire," he said. "What are you guys doing here, anyway?" His voice had a burr to it that Jock would recognize instantly. "Hell," he said when I explained, "you can't stay here all night. You'd better come to the farmhouse with me." Needing no further urging, we followed him back and there met his wife, also a Scot. They then went upstairs, leaving us bedded down on sofas.

After a breakfast of porridge, we offered to lend our Samaritan a hand for a few hours. And so it was off to the field, where we took turns riding behind the tractor on a potato-planter, a spindly, springy contraption which required seed potatoes to be hand-fed one at a time onto a rotating disc before it delivered them into the furrow below. Feeding the beast was like trying to roll a cigarette while trotting a horse. Meanwhile, the other had to gallop to and fro bringing up fresh trays of potatoes. Two machines, yet still labour-intensive! We found it a giggle.

Rewarded with a substantial lunch, we thanked our hosts and returned to the road, where we leant upon the farm gate exchanging memories of Scotland with his wife while awaiting our first ride. This turned out to be another policeman, uniformed this time, and soon there was more reminiscing, as he proved to be a former Spitfire pilot and flying instructor. "Bags of nostalgia," I wrote. "By the way," he said while dropping us off at Kenora, "there's a yellow school bus somewhere behind. Watch out for it. The driver is ferrying it to Calgary." There followed a short ride on a truck, and then we were picked up by another former flying instructor and delivered to the Winnipeg YMCA. We had covered over three hundred miles in about seven hours.

The next day being Sunday, we booked for two nights and spent a lazy day writing letters, washing smalls and lounging around. On Monday, after visiting the banks, we were on the highway by 10.30 and were picked up and taken to Portage La Prairie, where the driver insisted we have a beer with him. Afterwards we hiked a few miles from town and then sat on our packs, enjoying the sun and the open countryside. It was a relief to be free from the endless conifers of northern Ontario. As on much of our journey, away from cities the traffic was light and hardly anything passed for the next hour. But then, in the distance appeared a yellow bus. Surely, it couldn't be. Could it? There must be school buses all over the country. The bus slowed to a stop. Apart from the driver, it was empty. "Where to, boys?" "Edmonton," I replied. The driver nodded, "OK, climb aboard." As we settled ourselves, I grinned at him, "We've been waiting for you, you know." He looked at me sharply, "What do you mean?" I told him about our policeman's advice. "Well," he said, beginning to smile, "he almost got it right. But I'm going to Edmonton not Calgary."

He proved to be yet another ex-pilot. The country seemed filled with them! I had more in common with this one, though, for he had got as far as operational training (OTU) only to be chopped along with half his intake. The following morning, after sharing a motel in Dauphin at his firm's expense, we started out early. Crossing into Saskatchewan and stopping only for a late breakfast at Yorkton, we drove on through Saskatoon to Biggar for the best day's run of the trip, well over 400 miles. That night we shared a tourist cabin, a shack with an outdoor toilet "like the pit gardrobes of yore." Rolling grassland extended on all sides, and the sky, ablaze with stars, seemed enormous.

The next evening we reached Edmonton and were delivered, as at Winnipeg, to the door of the YMCA. The first half of our journey had taken twelve days, the second only seven; and in all that time, save for the guardian of the tower, we had encountered only friendliness and generosity.

2
North to the Klondike

"Do you have any mining jobs up north?" It was the next morning. Right after breakfast we'd called in at the unemployment office. The clerk scanned a sheaf of papers, "Well, there's not much doing right now. There's Yellowknife, of course, and they need a few men at Dawson City." He looked up inquiringly. "Dawson City," I said promptly. "It's placer mining," he went on. "Dollar an hour, seven days a week. Time and a half Sundays. We fly you up, but the company deducts the fare from your pay later." I nodded agreement. He hadn't asked about our experience and I had no wish to enlighten him. In a few minutes it was settled. We were to leave in the morning as part of a group of six replacements for men who had quit or gone sick. It seems I had miscalculated. The company we were to work for, the Yukon Consolidated Gold Corporation, or YCGC, had finished hiring even before I'd left England. Had we applied a day later we would have been too late.

The flight north, in a Canadian Pacific Airways DC3, was bumpy, and on the leg to Grande Prairie I felt distinctly queasy. It was the last leg, between Fort Nelson and Whitehorse, that caught my interest, for here we crossed the northern Rockies and the Cassiar Mountains. Though water on the lake ice showed the spring thaw to be under way, the entire region was still snowbound. Contemplating this bleak scene and wondering what I might have to face in a mining camp, I made a rare petitionary prayer – that, whatever happened, I be granted the courage to play the man. As for Jock, he showed little interest in the scenery. Like many on board, he was too intent on filling a paper bag.

At Whitehorse we took a cab to town and booked into the Regina Hotel. As our flight to Dawson would not be until the following evening, Jock and I spent most of next day playing tourist. Whitehorse appeared civilized and busy enough. Roads were unpaved and buildings mostly of wood, but there were a fair number of stores, cafés and hotels, even a cinema. Later, we wandered down to the river and peered up at the *Yukoner*, an old sternwheeler put up on blocks. Except on the hills there was no snow, and the Yukon was ice-free. We were accompanied by Dave, a young fellow who evidently preferred our company to that of the other men. A native of Winnipeg, he wore a serious expression and possessed a rather dry, self-deprecating sense of humour. He had signed on, he informed us, as a flunkey. "A what?" I exclaimed, hardly believing my ears. "A flunkey," he repeated. "I'll be working in the cookhouse." "'Struth," I laughed. "The last time I came across that word was in an old novel."

In the evening we boarded another DC3 and several hours later, after calling in at Mayo, landed on a dirt strip between hills. With a strong cross-wind blowing, the pilot had needed all his skill to set us down safely. Another, longer cab ride, and we were in Dawson. It was June 4th. "Ugly-looking place," I wrote.

> Seems like a ghost town. The hills are still snowcapped, and although I am writing this at 1.0 am it is twilight. Won't get darker until the end of August, apparently.... Seems unreal being up in Dawson City after reading about it. Still, it will be real enough later on, I suppose.

Rain had fallen overnight and it was grey and cold when we dropped by the company office in the morning. There we had a medical, filled in forms, and then were advised to visit the general store – the Northern Commercial Co., or "NC" – to buy on credit the necessary work clothes and sleeping bag. This left us time to look around. It was like stepping into the past. With its raised wooden sidewalks, false-fronted wooden buildings and unpaved roads, Dawson resembled a set for a western movie, but with cars and pickups instead of horses. That was the city centre. Elsewhere, some buildings seemed, and no doubt were, derelict. There were more hotels than stores, each with its own bar and each as ramshackle as the one we had stayed in, the Royal Alexandra. There the windows were unopenable and corridors rolled and pitched uncertainly – the result, I was told, not of builders the worse for drink but of thawing of the underlying permafrost. The Royal Alex also had a café and adjoined a small cinema.

Though travellers now could fly, with no road out Dawson was still isolated from the rest of the world, or the "Outside" as I learnt to call it. Save for mail and urgent supplies, all goods had to be transported between Whitehorse and Dawson by wood-burning sternwheeler, a 460 mile passage of the Yukon that took about a day and a half downriver and four or five days back up, depending on the current. And thanks to the climate, the river was navigable for little more than half the year. In consequence, the arrival of the first sternwheeler after break-up was still enough of an event to attract a small crowd of bystanders.

A few hours later I was on a dredge, shoveling muck from the lips of an unending chain of buckets. Of the six of us, one had been dropped off at Bear Creek and the rest driven on to Camp 11. It was Jock who was left behind. Save for a chance meeting near Squamish years later, we were not to see one another again. He had been a good companion. Although taciturn and blunt of speech, he had never complained even when the going had been uncomfortable.

ॐ

Dredge #11

The main gold-bearing area of the Klondike is a rough rectangle bounded on the west by the Yukon and on the north and south by two tributaries, the Klondike and the Indian River. Dawson City, at the confluence of the Klondike with the Yukon, marks the northwest corner. It is a region of low hills, wooded with conifers, poplar and aspen on the lower slopes and intersected by numerous creeks. The chief of these are Bonanza and Hunker, which flow north into the Klondike, and Quartz, Sulphur and Dominion, which flow south to the Indian River. The common source is a group of higher hills in the centre, and it is from their erosion that the gold no doubt came.

The ground had been well worked over in the fifty years or so since the Rush. Oldtimers had worked their claims with pickaxe, shovel and sluice box, laboriously thawing and digging down through permafrost to bedrock. After them had come the dredges of the Guggenheims and other companies, but these had largely confined their digging to the vicinity of the creek beds.

Now the YCGC was at work, turning over entire valley floors and leaving behind deserts of dune-like tailing piles. On small creeks independent miners could still be found, though, usually working with a bulldozer or hydraulic monitors.

The YCGC mining operation was carried out in three stages. The stripping crew led, removing scrub and washing away the topsoil with powerful hydraulic monitors. Behind them, the thawing crew laid down a grid of waterpipes. Vertical pipes, or "points", were driven down to permafrost and then connected to the grid with rubber hoses. As cold water thawed the permafrost, the tender of a line wrestled and pounded the points down to bedrock, a tiresome process. Trying to speed things up by pounding a point into permafrost did no harm to the permafrost and no good to the point. Frozen muck is tough stuff, and the water had to be allowed to do its job. The two flat crews worked at least a season apart and well ahead of the dredge. That had to operate 24 hours a day seven days a week and could not be allowed to lie idle. An idle dredge meant money lost.

YCGC's headquarters and workshops were at Bear Creek, about six miles from Dawson. The company's other camps were on the five main creeks and linked by a circuit of a hundred miles or so of dirt road that climbed over and around the summit hills. Altogether, YCGC had twelve dredges, three large ones with 16 cubic foot buckets and most of the rest with 7 cubic foot buckets, though each of the latter dredges displaced hundreds of tons. Not all were working in 1949, however. One had been lost to fire and two had worked out their ground. In fact, the machinery of one had been cannibalized to construct #11, the dredge I was to work on for the better part of four seasons.[16]

Camp 11 was then at the mouth of Hester Creek, sixteen miles from Dawson. Upon arrival, we were shown our bunks and after dinner sent to our respective jobs – Dave to the cookhouse, the others to the flat crews and I to the dredge, which was working Hunker Creek and was on the far side of the valley, digging towards us.

---

[16]   For a map and some details I am indebted to the Dawson City Museum and Historical Society.

And so I became a bow-decker, replacing a man who had been injured. It was rather like being on a ship, albeit a slow one.

To a greenhorn it also seemed at first an ugly and confusing one with a boxy superstructure and wire cables running everywhere. Inside was a confusion of noise – the hum of electric motors, rush of water, whine and clank of machinery, clatter of rocks, all punctuated by thuds as larger pieces of muck landed in the dump box. And yet, although it resembled a Rube Goldberg contraption with sound effects, the dredge was simple and functional.

In essence, it was a mechanical earthworm, endlessly ingesting the ground in front, extracting the gold in its gut and evacuating wastes at the rear – only it floated and carried its pond with it. The mouth was of course the bucketline. This chewed up the ground, mixed it with water and tipped the resulting muck into the dump box. From there, the muck slid into the gut, a large rotating cylindrical screen with sluice tables to each side. Powerful hydraulic monitors at the rear of the screen played upon the tumbling muck and washed the smaller particles through to the tables, where the gold was trapped by riffles. The residue from there was carried clear by twin tail sluices at the stern of the dredge, while tailings from the screen passed onto the stacker's conveyor belt to be dumped onto the tailing piles.

The hull of the dredge was flat-bottomed and rectangular, with an open bowdeck chamfered at the corners and bisected by the bucketline well, which extended partly into the superstructure. In front, a gantry of massive timbers supported both the bucketline boom and a gangplank for access to the dredge. Although a fifth the length of the hull, the bowdeck was thus constricted and in addition cluttered with cables, sheaves, spare buckets and bucket pins. There were no guard rails.

The superstructure resembled a pile of lego blocks. The largest, which enclosed two decks, had a small pump house at each side, and its roof formed the open upper deck. Here were two more blocks. A small one overlooking the starboard bow was the control centre, or winchroom. A large L-shaped one in the middle enclosed the dump box, screen and the main drive, an assemblage of shafts and gears rather like those that nearly mangled Chaplin in *Modern*

Times. At the stern another massive gantry supported the tail sluices, the stacker and the spud. This last was a kind of anchor, a heavy rectangular steel tube, pointed at the end. When dropped, it kept the dredge pinned in position as it pivoted on a cut.

Inside, the bottom deck was relatively clear, with a long workbench and access to the pump houses. The only cluttered areas were on each side of the bucketline well, where there were banks of cable drums with control rods linking them to the winchroom above. Mounted above the drums to port was the large electric motor that powered the main drive. Beside those to starboard was a boiler whose smokestack penetrated the upper decks and towered clear of the superstructure.

To the rear of the bottom deck, twin flights of stairs, port and starboard, led to the sterndecker's position, situated where the screen disgorged tailings onto the stacker belt. This second deck thus contained the gut, and from his position the sterndecker could observe the entire process. However, the sluice tables were screened off with heavy wire netting and the access door kept padlocked. No point in submitting the crew to temptation! Twin flights of stairs then led to the upper deck, with access to the winchroom and the crew mess.

A shift consisted of a crew of four – bowdecker, sterndecker, oiler and the winchman, or operator. The winchman on my shift was Cliff Weeks. Six feet two and 190 pounds of young manhood, he knew his job and was alert to shout a warning if he saw a greenhorn about to injure himself. He eventually went on to pursue a career with the Vancouver police. The oiler was Bob Ford, a bushy-bearded fellow with clear eyes and a ready smile. About thirty, I thought, until he shaved and transformed himself into a fresh-faced youth no older than I. The sterndecker I don't recall, as deckers changed so often.

As we were relieved by the evening shift at 3.30, my first day was short and I thought my work light and monotonous – an impression that proved less than accurate. In fact my work was varied. In addition to scraping bucket lips, needed only while we were in bedrock, I helped grease the bucketline rollers, kept the pump screens free from flotsam and occasionally rowed the skiff across the pond to move the power cable. I also had to spell the sterndecker so he could go for his meal. His was the monotonous job, for otherwise he had to remain at his post, the noisiest place on the dredge. His work was vital – to see that nothing in the gut plugged up, or the dredge would quickly fill itself. Consequently, he controlled the screen and the stacker belt and, like the winchman, could sound the hooter – a long blast for "stop" and two for "start". Four blasts from the winchman signified that a large chunk was on its way and warned the sterndecker to slow the screen and stacker belt. If the chunk was a rounded rock, he would have to escort it up the stacker in case it should roll back down and become a projectile.

My work was not always light, either. Now and again we dug up a glutinous blue bedrock that stuck to the buckets like toffee. Then I would have to exchange my shovel for a six-foot bar. And sometimes, when we were digging through pockets of old swamp, keeping the pump screens free from flotsam could keep me on the run. But such events were infrequent. Especially on evening or graveyard shift, there were times when I was free for as much as half the shift and could wander up to the winchroom, roll a cigarette and bullshit with Cliff.

Day shifts were busier, for then the dredge would be shut down occasionally – to effect repairs, change worn bucket pins, clean up the sluice tables or move the shore lines to new land anchors. Clean-ups were done once or twice during the two-week shift, when a crew from Bear Creek came to collect the gold. We would then lift the riffles on the sluice tables and pack the muck in buckets to a small sluice box for the men to sluice again. The usual payoff for a week's dredging came to about half a small bucketful, most of it a heavy black sand.

Changing land anchors became necessary when the dredge had moved forward a certain distance or had to make a turn. Moving the dredge forward, or across the pond from one cut to another, was done by the two stern lines. Pivoting the dredge in a cut was done by the bow lines, which passed through a massive block on each shore. Both the stern lines and the shore block lines were clamped to "dead men", so-called as the anchor was a section of log at the bottom of a grave-like pit. A regular two-man shore crew prepared these ahead of time and moved the lines with the help of the catskinner, or bulldozer operator, although sometimes we had to go ashore to help manhandle the heavy rubber-coated power cable over the tailing piles.

The shore crew consisted of the bull-boss, Smokey, and his helper, Mike. Well over two hundred pounds of bone and hard muscle, Smokey claimed to have been a professional wrestler. Having seen the way he could handle a sixteen pound sledge-hammer, I believed it. Mike, on the other hand, appeared in need of a helper himself. Bent and spare of frame and indeterminate of age and origin, he resembled Millet's *Man with a Hoe.* At first I thought him a mute, as I never once heard him speak. When I asked about it, however, one of his bunk-mates said, "Oh he can talk, all right. He talks in his sleep all the time, and he groans a lot, too. None of us can figure out the language, though." Nonetheless, whatever the nightmares that bedevilled him, Mike could dig a fine dead man. Curious, I walked over and inspected one. It seemed like the work of a professional gravedigger.

The catskinner, Frank, helped us only to move lines. Most of his time was spent building roads or moving equipment for the flat crews. Always present on day shifts, though, was the man responsible for operating the dredge profitably – the dredgemaster, Olaf Odegard. Like many of the older, more experienced men, he was Norwegian. About sixty and slightly built, he lived with his wife in a small wooden house on the far side of Hunker. His was a breed I came to respect greatly.

The only task to defeat me involved changing the bucket pins. Used to connect the buckets, they were L-shaped, the short arm being a flat flange that keyed into the bucket. Lifting them off the deck was a bit of a grunt, as each weighed about 150 pounds and was hard to grasp. Still, the problem for me lay in removing the worn ones. Though some could be poked out with a dolly bar, others had to be pounded out with a sixteen-pound sledge, a task that usually fell to Smokey. However, on one occasion he was busy elsewhere and only two of us were with Olaf. Squatting, the other man held the bar against the stubborn pin. When I didn't move, Olaf turned, looked around for the hammer and then at me. "You don't really expect me to swing that thing, do you," I complained. "I'd kill him. I can't swing a ballpeen hammer without missing the nail half the time." Then I stepped forward, "I'll hold the bar." On the other hand, I didn't mind climbing onto the bucket line to hammer away at an overlarge rock or piece of muck. Anything too big for the dump box presented a target even I couldn't miss.

ॐ

4

Camp Life

I don't know exactly what I expected of a mining camp – to be like those in westerns, perhaps, or a Brett Harte story, with drinking, gambling and fighting – everything but the gunplay. In fact Camp 11 was nothing of the kind. Sure, there was drinking, one fight, even gunplay – at the expense of bears sniffing around the camp – but rarely a disturbance. Men working seven days a week didn't need it. For the same reason radios were permitted only if the owner used headphones. Discipline was tight, and anyone making a nuisance of himself was fired. It was an effective sanction. The season was short, little over four months for flat crews, and the cost of flying up and out ate up most of a month's wages. Work was not easy to find then, and the Depression still haunted men's minds. When a few at my table began to chat during dinner one day, a voice suddenly snapped, "You're here to eat, not talk!" Meekly, the culprits ducked their heads and silence resumed, broken only by the scraping of plates. The owner of the voice had been the flats boss, a large Yorkshireman by the name of Harry Pogson. Balding, with bolting blue eyes, he had a matter-of-fact manner and tolerated no nonsense.

On my first evening in camp, I turned out to watch the ball team practice. Almost immediately, I was invited to take the bat – a new man, English, a good cricketer maybe. Sure. Three pitches, three wild swings – and like the famous Casey I struck out. Thereupon the team lost interest in me. It was just as well. All were young and some tended to burn the proverbial candle.

Returning to camp after a drinking spree some weeks later, one carload managed to overturn their Model A Ford. One of the injured was Louis, the man I had replaced. No sooner out of hospital than back in again! He must have been accident prone.

That same evening I came across more congenial company. Visiting Dave in his bunkhouse and observing a group playing hearts, I asked if we might join in. Before long, hearts and then bridge became our regular entertainment. And as most of the group turned out to be university students, bridge soon alternated with discussions on movies, books, music and a dozen other topics. So elevated an atmosphere I had not expected of a mining camp! It was not to be repeated in succeeding seasons, but by then I had other things to occupy my mind.

Nor did I lack for books – Cherry-Garrard's *Worst Journey* and Boccaccio's *Decameron* from the NC, and five hardbacks from the Dawson library, which happened to be moving house and was disposing of unwanted stock. These included Hugh Rutledge's *Everest 1933* and an anthology of Conrad's sea stories. How fine a writer Conrad is! His *Nigger of the "Narcissus"* is worth reading for the final sentence alone, although the title would no doubt have to be changed today.

In spite of agreeable working conditions and stimulating company, within a week I nonetheless began feeling depressed. I knew the reason only too well and in my journal bewailed "this ghastly, aimless drifting." I had accomplished the first part of my plan and found work in the Yukon, but now the problem of what to do with my life had reared its head once more. I had already decided that seeking the truth should be my main aim (The young must be permitted some optimism!), but that hardly constituted a career. What to do? I had held my own in discussions with university students. Why not try for university myself? I could qualify by taking courses by mail. I had little else to do. As for a career, it had to be something that would make a positive contribution to society. I decided on teaching. With history and English literature as my chief interests, I felt I had little choice. As a teacher, I believed I could share those interests and be a good influence on the young. The ensuing correspondence – with the University of B.C.,

I.C.S. (too expensive) and the Dept. of Education in Victoria – consumed weeks; but in October there arrived papers for my first two courses, English and Math. At the age of twenty-three, I thus began Grade 8, the first step in another, longer journey.

Whooping it up

Shortly before beginning my studies, I decided to go into Dawson with what remained of the ball team. I needed supplies. Assured I would have the time, after coffee in the café I took in a movie. (*The Snake Pit,* I believe. Quite moving.) Then I went looking for my transport, the Model A Ford. At last I found it – parked outside Liberty's, the local whorehouse.[17] Damn!

I had had an encounter with one of the girls already. While I was staying in the Royal Alex during a long change of shift, one of the men beckoned me into his room. Upon entering, I found several others there, chatting with a scantily-clad girl. Sprawled in bed, naked and looking pleased with himself, was another man. No sooner did the girl spot me than she came up and draped her arms lovingly around my neck. "Phil," she cooed,"you're just the one I've been looking for. I've always wanted to know how an Englishman makes love." *Bloody hell! Well, you're not going to learn from me, sweetheart. Besides, I haven't the faintest idea how... Wait a minute. Phil? How did she know my name...? Rats, I've been set up!* Gently removing her arms from my neck, I picked her up – she was nothing but skin and bone – and sat her on the bed. Now, how was I to make my escape without appearing a complete idiot? At this critical juncture, rescue arrived in the form of two burly Mounties who demanded to know what was going on. At that, we drifted off, all save the girl – and the man trapped in the bed, now looking as foolish as I felt.

I needed no repeat of that. Listening carefully, however, I could detect no sound of revelry within Liberty's. The season was late, I reasoned. Most of the flat crews had gone Outside and someone had told me that the girls had, too. Hoping my

---

[17]   Strictly illegal then, as now. But with Dawson residents outnumbered by miners and the women mostly married or young girls, authority wisely looked the other way.

informant was correct, I entered and to my relief found only Liberty and one man. "Where're the other guys?" I asked him, giving her a friendly nod. "Upstairs, playing poker," he grunted. There was nothing for it but to wait. Well, you can't sit socializing with a madam without buying drinks; and as the drinks were not the kind you could linger over, each being a shot of neat rye, I had several. In the event, it was Liberty who did most of the talking – about her dreams of retiring and of one day getting married.

By the time we rolled into camp, fortunately without rolling into a ditch first, the lights in my bunkhouse were out. In all the rooms but one, that is. And upon my entry a head popped out of it. Smokey. Clutching a half-empty bottle of overproof Lemon Hart, he beckoned me in and poured me two fingers. He wanted a drinking partner. Rats, it was gone three, and I had to be on the dredge by seven-thirty.

"What happened to you?" asked one, as I staggered into the washroom a few hours later.

"Nothing. Why?" Then I looked in the mirror. My face seemed to have been pushed into a fan. After leaving Smokey, I'd stepped outside the hut for some air but had immediately passed out and gashed my chin open. During my drunken sleep afterwards the blood had run all over my face. It was a long day. Now on the stern with little to do but watch the screen vomiting tailings, I spent much of the shift running up and down stairs in order to remain awake. Never again, I swore. And the only reason I had gone to town had been to get a can of tobacco and some air letters.

It was at night a week or so later that the fight took place. Ture, a big Finn with more gold in his teeth than ever I saw on the dredge, was drunk. So was Smokey. Having sunk a bottle of overproof rum between them, they had invaded the cookhouse, where Ture was treating himself to the cook's lemon extract. Dave and I were there, too, but sober. I'm not sure how the fight started, but the idea was certainly Smokey's. Maybe it was because Ture just happened to be the biggest man in camp. Seeing a fight imminent, Dave and I backed away hastily. They would wreck the place! Ture alone weighed more than the two of us put together.

And yet I feared for him. Although he outweighed Smokey by well over eighty pounds, he was older and lame. Smokey would butcher him!

But I was in for a surprise. As if by prior agreement, the two rushed together like ardent lovers too long parted and clasped one another in close embrace. For a while they grappled together, swaying and groaning in an ecstasy of passion. Then Smokey hooked a leg behind Ture – and over a quarter of a ton of meat and bone hit the floor with a crash that rattled the cutlery. There was more panting and moaning – it was almost obscene – until Ture suddenly yelped, "You gouge my eye." Climbing laboriously to his feet, he began wiping it with his handkerchief. There was no obvious damage. "That's not fair. You fight dirty, Smokey," he accused in a curiously high, whining voice. I found this schoolboy appeal to fairplay rather touching, but it had no effect on Smokey. Clearly pleased with himself, he was dancing around shadow-boxing. The fight was over.

Ture was again drunk the following night, and when the booze ran out he downed his room-mate's aftershave. Smokey had vanished. He had gone into Dawson to see why one of his cheques had bounced – and he never returned.

⚯

5

Phenomena

On July 4th, while I was still a bowdecker, Mitty Dubois, the dredge superintendent, came aboard with some visitors. When I dropped by the winchroom, they were chatting with Olaf. One of the visitors, a dapper little gentleman slighter even than Olaf, looked strangely familiar. With a start I realized that it was Field Marshal Alexander in mufti. Once Montgomery's superior, he was now Governor-General of Canada. Just as medieval artists had portrayed kings as being physically larger and more imposing than lesser folk, I had imagined him taller.

A week or so following this surprise we found ourselves digging through pockets of what Cliff called rotten moss. "Watch

325

out for mastodon ivory," he told me. "We can get up to fifty cents a pound for it." Mastodon ivory? Fancy that! Temporarily on the stern and thinking of gleaming white tusks, I kept a mercenary eye open. I soon understood why it was called "rotten" moss. Every so often I would hear a splash and then, together with an overpowering, sickly sweet smell, a great slop of moss and goodness-knows-what would come rushing down the screen. But, alas, no gleaming tusks. In the event, over a period of days I picked up a number of curved chunks of what appeared to be rotten wood, only it was very heavy. About fifty dollars' worth, I guessed. The jeweller gave us fifteen. Oh well, so others had made fortunes out of ivory and untold thousands had seen Field Marshal Alexander – but how many can claim to have had a whiff of decomposing mastodon?[18]

Discovery Day, August 17th, came and went uncelebrated. I was on evening shift and so couldn't get to town. Perhaps it was just as well. And as August declined with the sun, the night returned, bringing fine sunsets and then the stars, which reappeared like old friends. It also brought frosts, and soon the aspens and poplars were showering the forest floor with gold and splashes of scarlet. Before September was half gone the woods were dark. Now, even by day, temperatures never climbed above freezing, the ground remained hard as rock and sometimes the sky became canopied with immensely high iron-grey clouds – all warnings that the long winter night was approaching. Then, with October, came snow. Sifting down in the smallest of flakes, sometimes in single crystals that glittered in the camp lights, it would mantle the earth for seven long months.

Along with night and the colours of fall came something I had been eagerly anticipating – the Northern Lights:

---

[18] About this time a dredge in Alaska dug up a complete baby mastodon. A photograph showed it lying on the bucket line, almost cut in two by a bucket lip.

Graveyard Shift
Hunker Creek, 1949

The vibrant hum of electric motors,
the whine of pumps and the rush of water,
the insistent rumble of the main drive,
the thud of falling muck in the dump box,
the clatter of rock tumbling in the screen
as it revolved, ringing on its bearings,
- all the discordant, multitudinous
harmony of a working dredge, mere noise
save to the accustomed ear, grew muted
as I stepped outside to the upper deck
and inhaled the air of a Yukon night.

In the glare of powerful lamps the dredge
slowly swung its bow in ponderous arcs,
swaying, sometimes kicking, against the spud
as manganese steel ripped into bedrock,
and from the roiling water buckets climbed,
clanking, complaining, in an endless line;
flickering smudge pots, slung beneath the sheaves,
jigged awry in jazztime, while everywhere,
from bow to stacker to the gantry top,
a thin rime winked and flared with icy fire.

Beyond the pool of light in which we worked,
a frozen wilderness on every side
stretched still and dark, lit only by the lights
that marked the sleeping camp and by the stars,
which stared from an immensity of space
with cold, unwinking gaze. So far were we
from cities and the world of men, we seemed,
I thought, like exiles, doomed to grub for gold
near the sunless edge of the world.

But then
a pale green fire slowly dimmed the stars,
grew flushed with rose and, undulating, flamed
athwart the night – like God's bright skirts, perhaps,
or fringe of some vast, cosmic tapestry;
and bursting from the zenith's height, white beams
blazed into being and with instant speed
struck there! and there! on all sides lancing bright.

And now the dredge seemed but a toy – and we,
mere children playing in a muddy pond,
while all around, in silent majesty,
with endless care and surest aim profound,
the journeywork of heaven was performed.

1949 must have been an unusually good year for the aurora, for from late August through November there were many such displays. All told, I spent four seasons and one winter in the Yukon but rarely saw them again, and never so brilliant.

Soon I had more cause for wonder. One day the air filled with a light mist composed, not of water droplets, but of fine ice crystals. Hanging low in the sky, the sun had become a fuzzy yet still brilliant ball at the centre of a pearly halo. On the same plane as the sun, a second pearly ring encircled the horizon and intersected the halo, so that the two together resembled an immense signet ring with the sun as the central adornment. Where the horizontal ring, or parhelic circle, met the halo sat brilliant sundogs with two more to each side, for a total of six, evenly spaced though of diminishing brilliance. And crowning this astonishing vision, perched atop the halo like the horns on the symbol for Mercury was a short section of inverted rainbow.

The apparent size of the phenomenon, as with the rainbow, was no doubt an optical illusion. Still, it was the sight of a lifetime. Thinking about it later, I recalled some lines of Henry Vaughan:

I saw Eternity the other night
Like a great *Ring* of pure and endless light,
All calm, as it was bright...
This Ring the Bride-groome did for none provide
But for his bride.

❧

6

Shutdown

About the middle of October, I found myself with another crew. My new winchman was Hans Oiom, a Norwegian. Apparently he and Ture could not get along, and so Ture and I switched places. My oiler now was my room-mate, Otto, also a Norwegian. He snored abominably, but he was friendly and we got along well. Though in his late fifties and rather vague of eye and speech, he could be disconcerting, for he was given to making sudden unexpected movements. Early in our acquaintance, as we sat on our beds chatting, he had shot out a claw-like hand and snatched for my nose. "There," he chortled, "If anyone gives you trouble, just stick two fingers up his nose and twist." And so when he suddenly shot out his hand one day on our way to the dredge, I recoiled nervously, thinking he was after my nose again. But no, he was pointing over my shoulder. "Look," he cried, "wieners!" Wieners? What was he on about? Looking behind me, I couldn't see any sausages or dachshunds about. Shooting out that hand once more, he shook my shoulder impatiently. "No, look – wieners in the sky." Oh dear, I thought, the poor old bugger is losing his marbles. But obediently I turned again and looked up – and there, shining brightly, was Wieners, the evening star!

Towards the end of November our long change came up again. Our "week-end" in Dawson proving a quiet one, we decided to leave town early and drop in at the Arlington Roadhouse before going on graveyard shift. Doubtless gladdened by such unexpected company, the elderly proprietor (Nels, I believe his name was) produced not only a few bottles of beer but an orchestra as well – a portable phonograph and a few old records. And there, in our clumsy shoepacks, we danced – with each other, in the absence of ladies. My partner was old Otto. Rheumy-eyed and given to talking to himself he may have been, but he was surprisingly spry for his age. My dancing partners since may have been prettier, but they could hardly have been more enthusiastic.

On November 27th, after hovering between 10°F and -10°F for weeks, the temperature suddenly plunged to -22°F and shut the dredge down. There were two days for repairs and maintenance, and then the season ended.

❧

7
Exercise Sweetbriar

The work had been less remunerative than I'd hoped. Although I had earned about $1500, modest expenses and the deductions (including tax, $2.25 a day for board, and the cost of my air fare) had swallowed up $700 of it. I had decided to remain in the Yukon – I really had to spend one winter there at least – but another job was essential or my bank account would be drained. Not wishing to work underground, I skipped Mayo and flew to Whitehorse. With me was someone else with the same idea – Bob, a decker from another shift. "The only thing we have is a call for a couple of heavy lifters," said the clerk at the unemployment office. Bob and I looked at one another. Shorter than I, he was stronger, perhaps, but not by much. "Who would we be working for?" I asked. "The RCAF," replied the clerk. "We'll take it," I laughed. "It's all right, Bob," I explained as we left. "No one ever kills himself with work for the government."

In the event, the heavy lifting took only hours, but the job itself lasted three months. For that we had to thank "Exercise Sweetbriar," an arctic exercise involving combined Canadian and American air and ground forces. On first coming to Whitehorse, I had been surprised by the size of the airfield. With long paved runways it was clearly far larger than was needed for the civil air traffic of the time. It had in fact been built as a military air base, part of the Alcan Highway project of 1942/3. Now in December it was abuzz with the coming and going of C54 and C47 transports, F80 and Vampire jet fighters, P51 Mustangs and helicopters. The Canadian army contingent included a battalion of the Princess Patricia's Canadian Light Infantry. Which American units were involved I don't know. Idly I wondered why they thought they might have to fight in the arctic. Against a Russian invasion? That didn't seem likely. What none could have foreseen, of course, was that before 1950 was out some of the men who took part in that exercise would be fighting for their lives in just such weather conditions – but against the Chinese in North Korea.

The winter was cold, with long nights, endless grey skies and yet relatively little snowfall. Engaged for the most part in unloading trucks and stacking supplies in warehouses, I seldom had to work outside for long, though. It was like being on detachment at Skellingthorpe again, only our quarters, well-heated H-blocks, were more comfortable. Over Christmas the temperature fell to -58°F, a low not uncommon then.[19] Fifteen minutes outside in that left me feeling as if I were clad in pyjamas! Thereafter, the temperature ranged from 0°F to -35°F. How much the troops enjoyed their romp in the snow I have no idea. I saw only the aircraft. With the coming of spring, however, the sun often appeared and working outside, even at -20°F, was a pleasure.

"Sweetbriar" over, in mid-March I was laid off. Working a forty-hour week at a dollar an hour had done little to fatten my bank balance, but at least it had covered the winter's expenses. Now, with two weeks to go before returning to Dawson, I decided to hitchhike to Fairbanks. After barely an hour's wait on the highway, I was picked up by Al, an Afro-American driving up to look for work, and in two days we were there. On the way, I'd savoured a magnificent sunrise over Kluane Lake and a view of the St. Elias range from the Donjek River. The country along that section of the Alcan is majestic. It had seemed a pity to hurry through it in a car. As for Fairbanks. it saw me only

---

[19]   The official low for Canada, recorded in 1947 at Snag, near the Yukon-Alaska border, is -81°F.

long enough to shock me with its prices. After a meal I was on my way back.

The return, in contrast, provided more time for admiring the scenery than I would have wished – six days, in fact, including one with no traffic at all. Still, the journey was not without incident. The third day back began with a short ride to Kelly's Roadhouse, near the Yukon border; but when nothing else came by, at nightfall I gave up and went inside. Though I was the only customer and had been parading outside for hours, the proprietor proved singularly uncommunicative, for after pouring me coffee without comment he ignored me. Finishing in silence, I stubbed out my cigarette and then asked for a meal and a bed for the night, only to be told that neither could be had, despite a large sign outside to the contrary. But the proprietor (an American cousin of the Gorphwysfa Nose, no doubt) was most helpful. "Five miles down the highway you'll see a road coming from the right. Go up that and after a bit you'll come to a motel. You'll get a bed there." Surprised at being turned out into the sub-zero wilderness, I nevertheless thanked him and crunched off under the stars, pondering the while on wolves and their ways and having mental images of green eyes and gleaming fangs.

The "motel" proved to be a log building set in a roughly fenced clearing some hundred yards off the side road. Unfortunately, no lights were showing, and when I opened the driveway gate a furious barking went up. Dogs, at least two, and big ones! Hastily, I slammed the gate shut. Wolves have never been known to attack people in North America, but guard dogs are another matter. There was nothing for it but to go back to the highway and a long night of walking up and down. Damn! I'd had more than enough of that already.

Before I had gone more than fifty yards, however, I heard the sound of an engine behind me. Turning, I saw a jeep approaching with two figures muffled up in parkas. As it drew abreast there was a loudly exclaimed "What the...?" and the jeep skidded to a halt in a cloud of frost smoke. Climbing down, the driver approached me. "What the heck are you doing here at this time of night?" he demanded. I suppose his astonishment was understandable. Wearing a cotton windbreaker, a balaclava, pants tucked into flight boots and a moustache adorned with ice, I probably resembled an errant member of Scott's expedition. "At the roadhouse they told me there was a motel here," I explained, "but there's no one around except for some large unsympathetic dogs." For a while the hooded figure remained silent, and then he motioned to the jeep, "You'd better come with me."

It appeared I had stumbled across Northway, which had acted as the "enemy" air base for *Exercise Sweebriar*, and my driver happened to be sergeant of the guard on one of his rounds. Taken into a barrack block, I was shown to a bed and there, while curious GI's looked on, I was subjected to a friendly inquisition over a can of beer. Satisfied at last that I was what I said I was and not a Russian spy, the sergeant bore me off to the mess, had the cook fix me bacon and eggs and then, when I'd finished, invited me to join him on his interrupted round. All of which explains how I came to inspect the guard at an American air base. And as if that were not enough, after breakfast next morning he drove me back to the highway. I doubt whether any other army would have been quite so hospitable.

Two weeks later I was back at Hunker Creek, cutting the dredge free of its winter shackles. The ice in the pond was over five feet thick.

❦

8
Postscripts

None of my other seasons was as eventful as the first, but my courses kept me occupied. For much of 1950 I remained with Hans Oiom, first as sterndecker and then as oiler. I liked Hans a great deal. He had iron grey hair and a pair of clouded grey eyes that seemed often to focus on the horizon as if he were meditating. There was a guilelessness about him, even innocence, that I found attractive. Like most winchmen on #11, he was married and commuted from Dawson.

That winter the camp was moved nearer to Dawson, opposite Last Chance Creek, a name that I hoped was not a portent, and in the 1951 season I became oiler for Roy Butterworth. Tall, lean and as alert as a hawk, Roy also had received some training as a pilot, and it was he who took me on my first moose hunt, along with Rory our bowdecker. As a reward for our success his wife fed us a magnificent wild duck pie. Roy and I got on well together and I remained with him until I was made winchman. As for my courses, working on them was easier in my last three seasons as I had a room to myself and a table where I could rattle off essays on a portable typewriter. For the tests, I would go to Olaf's house, where he acted as invigilator.

At the end of the 1951 season, together with Peter, a Polish lad, for a while I worked on a hydro-electric construction project in Mayo. We went by road, if one could call it that, as the leg as far as Stewart Landing was merely a pair of ruts meandering through the woods. Then, following a night in a hotel crammed with carousing hard-rock miners, we had been taken on. Contruction camps tend to be boisterous. But not this one. Apart from the clatter of diesel engines, kept running day and night because of the cold, it was almost as quiet as a monastery. The reason was simple – no one had time or energy enough to be boisterous. Transported to and from the worksite on open trucks, for seven days a week we began work in the dark and finished in the dark twelve hours later, with half an hour for lunch. By the time we had cleaned up and eaten a mountainous supper, we were fit for nothing but sleep.

On my first day, as I stood with other shadowy figures on the back of the truck and felt my breath congealing into ice on my moustache, I wondered what I had got myself into and for the first time felt a pang of homesickness. To adapt some lines from Robert Louis Stevenson,

And all that I could think of, in the darkness and the cold,
Was that I was far from home and my folks were growing old.

Then I glanced at Peter. In the wan light of the stars he looked about as cheerful as a constipated dog straining to pass peach stones. Immediately feeling better, I grinned at him.

For two weeks I worked mainly inside the tunnel, which suited me fine as the outside temperature ranged between -35°F and -42°F, and then after a final pour of grout I was made a bull cook. Normally he is responsible for camp maintenance and cleaning; but my task, and that of the night man, was simpler – to haul sledgeloads of wood around the camp and keep the fires going. The ones we had to visit most often were those in the outside toilets. Not relishing sitting their bare backsides on a plank at forty below, the men would open the drafts wide and let the fires roar away.

After a week of this I quit. The job was winding down and I'd no desire to spend Christmas in a hotel full of drunken miners. On finding all flights out already booked, four of us persuaded a cabbie to drive us to Whitehorse for $50 a head. It was a risky business and we nearly came to grief at the start. The all-weather road between Mayo and Whitehorse had been completed the year before, but there was as yet no bridge over the Stewart. This meant we had to descend to the river and cross over on an ice bridge. However, we got stuck in deep snow at the foot of the bank. Piling out, with much heaving and cursing we managed to get the cab moving – only to see it take off like a scalded cat and not stop until it reached the top of the far bank. It was then only twenty below, but a brisk wind gave all of us frostbite before we could rejoin the cab. There were no further misadventures, fortunately, for I can't recall seeing one other vehicle during the entire two hundred and forty-odd miles. I didn't envy the cabbie his lonely trip back. He earned his money.

At the end of October, 1952, to make way for a married man, I was transferred over the hill to Sulphur Creek. The season ended while I was on graveyard shift. And it ended with perhaps an omen – for at the edge of camp, perched silently on the same tree every night, a pair of ravens regarded us with unblinking jet eyes as we crunched by on the trail to the dredge. Had one croaked, "Nevermore", it would have been surprising but apt, for this was to be my last season in the Yukon. Just before leaving Hunker Creek I had completed my courses and next year would begin university.

Hunker Creek had provided precisely the conditions I needed. I had been lucky. Had I arrived in Edmonton one day later, I would not have got to Dawson that year. Of the six replacements, I was the only one to go on a dredge, which gave me two needed advantages – a long season, April to November, and eventually a single room. And at Hunker I remained while others were transferred over the hill. By the time I followed, I had already completed my courses. I have worked at eight other camps, six on construction, and I doubt very much that I could have completed my courses in any of them, certainly not in communal bunkhouses. As for working in town, I doubt whether I could have earned money enough to put myself through university.

Hunker Creek was my retreat, providing work for body and mind. And routine physical labour, provided it is not onerous, brings its own blessing – it leaves the mind free. There for four years I was happy, especially at Last Chance. At times I felt close to God and for the last time experienced brief periods of joy. Ironically, it was at Last Chance that I received a real portent of what was to come. For it was there I had my second recurrent dream, the one in which the Face swam up from out the darkness of the pit and reduced me to terror. But I did not understand its meaning then.

⊙⦙⊙

My friend Dave, the flunkey, did not return in 1950, but we exchanged Christmas cards for a few years. Cliff Weeks tracked me down during the gold craze of the 'Eighties. He had the idea of working a dredge as a living museum and wanted me as PR man. I declined, though. At the time, teaching was about the only thing that justified my life. Why the idea was thought not practical became clear the following summer. I had flown to Whitehorse with John Misurelli, a colleague who had once taught there, and we drove up to Dawson for a day. It was seething with tourists, the campground was filled, and claims were being worked everywhere. But dredging had ended in 1966 and the dredges were now forlorn wrecks. To get one running again in ground that had been virtually worked out would have been far too costly.

Still, #4 at Bonanza was open to tourists; and on learning the guide was none other than Roy Butterworth, we went aboard. We found him in the winchroom, explaining the workings to a small group. Standing at the back, I listened until he called for questions then raised my hand, "Where do you keep the spring, then?" "The spring?" he repeated, puzzled. "You know," I added, demonstrating, "the thing you wind up to make it all go." He frowned, and during the pregnant silence that ensued I could almost read his thoughts, *Who's this smartass?* But then recognition dawned. "Well, Jesus Christ," he burst out, "it's my old oiler!" Laughing, he explained to the gaping tourists, "Folks, it must be thirty years since we worked together." Afterwards, we retired to his trailer and reminisced over a beer. It was good seeing him again. We had long been exchanging letters at Christmas and would continue to do so until his death a few years later.

The only other workmates I ever saw again were Hans Oiom and old John. The latter was lame and had ended his working life taking test pans from the bucketline. Upon retiring, he had gone to Vancouver and spent many of his final years in the Ambassador Hotel. Sometimes, while waiting for a bus, I would see him there, sitting by the lobby window. I had never felt comfortable with John. He had a face of stone and a way of staring at me with his faded grey eyes that I found oddly disconcerting. In our years on the dredge we had barely exchanged a word. Still, it is one of my many regrets now that I never went in to speak to him. He reminds me of the rows of silent men I had seen sitting in the Regina railroad station in 1945. They, too, had stared with expressionless faces. Canada has many such men – men who spend their working lives in the camps and then, whether through loss of family or failure to marry at all, find themselves facing old age alone.

As for Hans, we met by chance on Granville Street in the late Fifties and dropped into a café for a chat over coffee. His hair now a snowy thatch, he told me he had just flown in from Norway, where he had attended a sister's funeral. "Then you're living in Vancouver now, Hans?" I asked. He looked at me with some surprise and then snorted, "Hell, no. I'm on my way back to Dawson tomorrow. They're all crazy out here."

Dear Hans, no doubt you are long dead. Perhaps it's just as well you are not here to see things as they are today. The "Outside" is no saner – and now it is everywhere, even in Dawson.

#11 at Hunker Creek, May-1950

Harry Pogson on a monitor, 1950

Bow-decking

Hans Oiom on #3, 1938
(Courtesy Yukon Archives, Tidd Coll.)

Author,
Last Chance, 1951

Roy Butterworth on #11,
1951

Jan, 1952

Author, above Kildala Pass, 1953

Kathy and Les Fisher, 1970

CHAPTER SEVENTEEN

Vancouver

1
A Time for Friends

A sudden plunge to -35°F brought the 1950 dredging season to an early end, and after five cold days on repairs I flew out to Whitehorse. Much as I had appreciated my time with the RCAF earlier, one winter seven months long had been enough. It was time to go outside. And so on November 16 I boarded a train for Skagway. Built in the hope of reaping a bonanza from transporting hopefuls to the Klondike, the White Pass and Yukon Railway is a narrow-guage line that follows the gold-rush trail between Skagway and Whitehorse. Its construction involved the labour of thousands in an epic two-year effort. Unfortunately, by the time the railway opened in the summer of 1900, the rush was over. Today it operates summer tourist excursions only, from Skagway to the summit, but in 1950 it was still a working railway with steam locomotives. Revenue probably came mainly from freight, as on the one passenger coach on my train there were only four or five of us. It was heated by a small coal stove, which we stoked ourselves.

After stopping for lunch at Lake Bennett, where parts of the lake were still open though obscured by drifting frost smoke, we continued to the summit. Of the sensational descent I saw nothing, however, as the sky was overcast and night had fallen. As for Skagway, though no doubt more law-abiding than in the days of Soapy Smith, like Dawson it seemed lost in a time warp. The following evening found me aboard the SS *Princess Louise*, enjoying a fine three-course dinner, complete with linen napery – and no one, not even the steward, sniffed at my work clothes, which were all I had. We sailed just before midnight; and a few days later, well-fed and relaxed, I checked into the Ambassador Hotel in Vancouver. I could not know it, but during the next few weeks I was to make lifelong friends and meet my future wife.

Eileen

Resplendent in new clothes from the skin out, I watched the dancers at a social evening of the Anglo-Canadian Fellowship. After a week at the hotel I had moved into a boarding house in Vancouver's West End and there had decided to make an effort to meet people. But I was not to play wallflower long, for a slender, dark-haired girl came up and with a sweet smile began straightening my tie. Brave girl! Naturally, I asked for a dance. I didn't know one from the other, but I could keep time with the music and to my surprise found we moved as one. No matter how I improvised, this amazing girl followed so easily that I felt almost like Fred Astaire.

Eileen and I dated regularly after that, meeting at a restaurant and then going on to the Embassy, a dancehall on Davie Street. Usually we went early and left when it became crowded. Learning she liked horses, I decided to take her riding. But there was a small matter to attend to first – I had to learn how to ride. So one fine day I presented myself at a livery stable near Denman Street and asked to rent a horse. "Sure," said the liveryman, bringing one out. "This is Peter. What kind of saddle do you want?" "What kinds do you have?" I asked cautiously, staring up at Peter, a large piebald with a rather stupid face. "English, western and military," he replied. Well, English saddles were out – nothing to hold onto. And western saddles had that great horn in front. Could be damaging. "I prefer the military saddle," I said. With Peter saddled, I climbed aboard. Now, how to steer it? Lay the reins across the neck in the manner of movie cowboys or tug on the reins? I didn't dare ask. Fortunately, Peter was facing in the right direction and so I tapped him with my heels and he obediently started forward. So far so good. At Denman Street I reined him in, checked for traffic and started him up again. At a stately plod, we thus reached Stanley Park. I never even had to turn him. He knew the way and had considerately turned of his own accord. Well, this was easy!

Sure. No sooner had we entered the park than Peter broke into a trot and headed for the nearest tree, one plentifully supplied with low branches. I laid the reins across his neck. No result. Tugged sharply on a rein. Nothing. Tried reining him back – and then had to duck to avoid being swept off. There was no doubt about it. Peter knew he had an idiot aboard and wished to be rid of him. "You mustn't let him do that," cried a woman who had been observing us with interest. *No, really?* Meanwhile, foiled in his first attempt, the brute had wheeled and was trotting smartly towards a thicket. Well, if he couldn't take a hint…. Setting my feet firmly in the stirrups, I grasped the left rein with both hands and heaved. That caught his attention and I managed to get him back to the trail. He then tried another ploy. What's that, a duck? He shied violently. A piece of paper? Another shy. This continued until I tired of it and gave him a sharp kick in the ribs, whereupon he broke into a trot. Another kick sent him cantering. It was rather like riding a carthorse. I never managed to make him gallop, no doubt for the same reason he hadn't tried bucking me off – he was too lazy. We had reached an understanding, though, and so completed our circuit of the park without further incident.

Before risking Eileen, I tried two other horses. The first one, a melancholic beast resembling an undernourished mule, gave no trouble but no joy either, for it lacked shock absorbers and rattled my teeth. But the next, a chestnut mare, proved a delight. Willing, eager even, she needed little prompting to gallop, and soon I felt a veritable Tom Mix. But pride goeth, etc. From a side trail suddenly emerges a woman with a small white dog. Dog sees horse and charges, yapping furiously; horse applies all four brakes at once; while I, faithful to the laws of motion, describe a graceful parabola and come to earth with a sickening thud. Damn the woman! Not daring to look at her lest I snarl or be even ruder, I remounted – and the mare was off even before I was properly seated. A fine, spirited horse! Eileen and I enjoyed a most pleasant ride. I had Peter again, and we both behaved like gentlemen. But I had learned one thing – the park was no place for galloping full tilt.

Eventually, I invested in a formal lesson. But riding in circles being shouted at by a butch female soon cured me of any urge to become a rider and I have ridden little since. One needs to learn young, so that riding becomes second nature. Besides, I believe horses, like women, sense absentmindedness and sometimes resent it.

Though I enjoyed Eileen's company, it often left me tense, as if I were resonating to an undercurrent. I learned later that she had broken with a previous boyfriend while in his car, and in a mindless pique he had tried to kill them both by deliberately wrecking it. She had escaped serious injury, fortunately, but had been badly shaken. In any case, as with Jean at Bentley Priory, I had no intentions and after a while felt it fair to warn her not to take our relationship seriously. She said nothing at the time, but evidently she determined that if she couldn't have me then her best friend should, for she made every effort to throw us together. The following week she suggested we spend an evening at the Peter Pan Club. She would be bringing a friend, she said, and would pick me up in a cab. The friend was Jan. Before going on to the club, we called at Jan's house for records and I accompanied her to the door. And it was there, as she searched her handbag for the key, that I had the clear intimation she was to be my wife. It gave me a sense of certainty that never left. Afterwards, when Eileen told me Jan was glum because I had shown her so little interest, I had all the push I needed to begin dating her. Some weeks later Jan and I were invited to a going-away party. Eileen had become engaged and was leaving with her fiancé for England, there to marry and settle down. She'd had a second string to her fiddle all along.

I never saw Eileen again, but as her parents – both Irish, which perhaps explains their mercurial temperaments – were friends of Jan's parents I would see them from time to time. Years later I had occasion to drive to Squamish with the father. A self-employed builder, Jack was short and stocky, and liked large, powerful cars. I soon regretted going with him, as being behind the wheel transformed this normally amiable man into a maniac. Hurtling along the winding road at well over the speed limit, he braked for bends at the last moment, tailgated slower cars mercilessly and then glared at their drivers as he roared by. He was letting off steam, of course, and well I knew the source of it. To put it bluntly, he was afraid of his wife. Mona was a slim redhead with green eyes and a sweet smile – but the smile masked a dragon that could belch fire in an instant. She dominated her husband by the highly effective practice of public uproar, the more witnesses the merrier; and more than once I found myself squirming as she directed her blowtorch onto the unhappy Jack in front of friends. I wonder if Eileen's husband realized how fortunate he was in having placed a continent and an ocean between himself and his mother-in-law.

❦

The Manor

While still dating Eileen I fell in with three fellow expatriates and at their invitation moved into Barclay Manor, their grandly named boarding house in the West End. During that and succeeding winters until I began university, we were almost inseparable. Though we eventually went our separate ways and at times lost touch, we have remained friends for life. The eldest, Jack Rogan, is a warm, even-tempered Geordie who had served first with the Auxiliary Fire Service in the London blitz and later with the RAF. The stresses of war and migration seem to have given him the desire for a quiet life, however, for upon arriving in Vancouver he found work in a BC Government liquor store and there remained until retirement, following the even tenor of his way serenely – apart from a sudden flurry in his late forties when he surprised us all by marrying. After retiring, he and his wife divided their time between an apartment in the West End and a holiday home on the Sunshine Coast. In his eighties he kept fit by swimming miles every week and now well over ninety plans to visit family in England. "I believe he means to outlive us all," fondly exclaimed Dick, the next senior in the group.[20]

Dick Truman, a native of Reigate and a nephew of the actor Ralph Truman, had served in the Army. A sturdy six-footer, he is a practical extrovert and, in effect, has been our social convener, doing his best to maintain contact with us and other Manor regulars and in recent years holding annual dinner reunions at his home. After several seasons working on the Kitimat project he bought a truck in an attempt to start his own business. When this failed – his timing was bad, with contracts hard to come by and competition cutthroat – he became a sales rep for John Deere. In the 'Sixties he took his family to England but soon returned, put off by the casual attitude to business he found there. Eventually he became a successful real estate agent and, now retired, lives in Delta with his second wife, Brenda. His only child, Susan, is one of my three godchildren.

The youngest of us, Gerry Richardson, was a product of a Croydon grammar school. Lightly built and prematurely balding, he had a sunny smile and a slight stammer. Unlikely as it might seem, he began life in Canada as a warder in a penitentiary. Unsurprisingly, though his genial nature masked a will of steel, he did not remain one for long. It was not the hostility of inmates that decided him to quit, however, but having to witness an inmate being flogged until he lost control of his bowels. The crude expression "Having the shit kicked out of you", it seems, is founded upon fact.

Before moving to the Manor, Gerry had put up at the YMCA. It was there, during his first Christmas in Canada, that he and other residents conceived the idea of providing a free turkey dinner for down-and-outs. Granted permission to use the kitchen, they raised the cash – largely from among themselves – and set to work. "We had circulated posters and handbills," he wrote,

---

[20]   He didn't make it. Only days after returning from his visit to England he died in his shower of a heart attack. "Good timing," said Dick, "That's the way to go!"

"but as I sweated away basting the turkeys, I belatedly began to wonder what we'd do with them if no one showed. I needn't have worried, though. So many came that they ate the lot, and for our Christmas dinner we had to go to the White Spot!"

But all this I learnt later. For the first month or so I often found Gerry subdued, even wistful. It transpired that the stammer barely noticeable to us loomed so large to him that he had been seeing a speech therapist. Apparently the cause had been a minor childhood trauma. Whatever the treatment, it proved successful. For after wrestling the stammer to mere hesitation, he began sporting colourful ties, laughing heartily and, in short, to being so ebullient that Dick and I sometimes had to sit on him. "Having a second adolescence!" muttered Dick drily. Eventually, a new Gerry emerged, confident, at ease with himself and more genial than ever.

In some ways, he and I were much alike. We both tended to agonize over relations with girl friends, in contrast to the practical Dick, who kept his own counsel, and the imperturbable Jack, who seemed to lack interest in women altogether; we both were moved by ideas, music and literature; and we both were highly introspective. In fact, he was more introverted even than I, often becoming so rapt in thought that he grew oblivious to his surroundings. When he decided to buy his first car, I toured the used-car lots with him. ("Aw, why don't you quit fucking around and buy a car," snarled a gravel-voiced salesman after we had inspected his lot for all of five minutes!) Eventually Gerry settled on a Chevy sedan (from another lot) and we spent next morning washing, waxing and polishing it. Then we went for a drive. We got as far as Burrard Street, about four blocks, where he signalled a left turn. Naturally expecting him to use the nearest lane, I didn't warn of the car coming from the right. Wrong decision! Gerry hit him dead centre.

Like Dick, Gerry spent several seasons working at Kitimat; but in the 'Sixties he returned to England, where he married and settled down to life as a teacher. I visited him there after the birth of Philip, his first son. It was some twenty years before we met again, when he flew over for one of Dick's reunions. Although we had long been exchanging letters at Christmas, we then began a more frequent correspondence that lasted until his death in 2001.

Three other expats joined the group from time to time. John Kinvig, also ex-RAF, obtained a business degree by correspondence while still working full time and then pursued a successful career with a major business machine company. We still meet at Dick's reunions. A rarer visitor, Ray Baglee, struck me as a likeable rogue. Well built, with dark hair and a husky voice, he had the kind of smouldering good looks that must have devastated the ladies. Like us, in his early years in Canada he tried many jobs, including reporting (until the paper checked his background), fishing and mining. It was while employed at the Britannia Beach mine that he first married. "And when the happy couple returned from the ceremony," Dick told me, "the police were waiting." A close acquaintance had apparently absconded with the company payroll and they thought Ray might know something about it. In this case he didn't.

I last saw him at one of Dick's reunions. He was then in his late fifties but looked younger. Apparently, he had done well for himself, for he claimed membership in the prestigious Point Grey Golf and Country Club. It proved true, too. But the source of his prosperity came as an even greater surprise. After a long investigation by the RCMP and the US Secret Service, he and five others were soon afterwards arrested and convicted as leaders of a successful (temporarily) counterfeiting ring, one of the biggest in North America. Their specialty had been top quality US $20 bills, sold in wholesale lots over the border. And so, at the age of 59, Ray found himself headed for prison. It is reported that when asked whether he had anything to say before being sentenced, he had replied, "Well, Your Honour, the fellow who sold me the printer told me I could do nothing but make money with it." If true, it would be in keeping with his somewhat mordant sense of humour.

We were not alone, it appeared, in knowing him less well than we thought. After he was felled by a heart attack at age 70, an obituary in the Vancouver press described him as the local mystery man, one who – though known to the press, to many of the elite, the underworld and the security services – carried "many secrets to the grave, including the matter of who he actually was."

Then there was Gavin. Born in Cheltenham and unlike the rest of us emphatically upper middle class, Gavin Walker had worked for the Raj as an inspector in the Indian Police and was a fine example of the many enlightened and dedicated public servants that Britain sent out to the Empire in its final decades. During the War, however, he had given up his career to join the RAF. Taller than I and with a strong, angular build that made him seem, when seated, all elbows and knees, he had a warm and generous nature. At times, though, his face clouded with melancholy. Why, I cannot say. Perhaps it was because he never married, or because he found himself in a time and place to which he did not belong. If the latter, that may partly explain the bond between us, for I was feeling at odds with the times myself.

How he spent his early days in Canada, I'm not sure. I'm told he tried logging and presented himself at his first camp complete with bowler hat and umbrella – but the latter must be a canard. Eventually, he decided on teaching. Not having a degree, he had to attend Normal School, along with fellow aspirants a decade or so younger. A more trying ordeal for him would be hard to imagine. For in their proper anxiety to shield the young from undesirables, Normal Schools tend to be overly suspicious of those who question the received wisdom. His impatience with jargon and unwillingness to toe the party line in silence thus brought upon him the inevitable – rejection for not showing the Proper Attitude. And so he returned to England, where eccentrics are less remarked upon, and took up teaching there.

By chance, we met again in Oxford in the early 'Seventies. It was a rather sad reunion. Apparently Gavin had just been fired from his school for engaging in fisticuffs in the staffroom! He offered no details, no explanation for this untypical behaviour, but he was so unusually talkative that I thought him clearly close to a breakdown. As for me, I was unusually quiet, for I was in much the same state myself. Perhaps that explains why neither of us thought to exchange addresses. As a result, to my lasting regret we have since lost touch.

❦

Time rested lightly upon me in those winters at the Manor. I continued work on my courses, but only enough to hold conscience at bay. With a girl and new friends, I had other things to do. As temporary gentlemen of leisure, Gerry, Dick and I spent hours chatting (Gerry in particular had wide interests and an inquiring mind) or playing tennis (badly) in the park and darts in the Manor (Gerry was hopeless). A few times I tried skiing – Grouse Mountain alone, Manning Park with a young dentist more interested in girls than in the slopes, and Diamond Head with Jan (We were sole guests at the lodge and had Garibaldi Park to ourselves!) – but I could not summon interest enough to take lessons.

Once again, music entered my life. The occasional café juke box aside, in my eighteen months up north I'd had to rely upon memory. Now I found myself with others who liked classical music and we freely shared LP's and a portable phonograph. Until then, as far as classical music is concerned, I had liked mainly Romantic composers, especially Beethoven and the Russians, but now I began to appreciate Bach. Gerry and Jack were responsible. When they burst into song one day, I was immediately drawn. "What's that you're singing?" "St. Matthew's Passion," replied Gerry. "Jack and I are in the Bach Choir. We'll be giving our performance soon. You should come." I did; and not surprisingly, given my love for choral singing as a boy, I was much moved. At the time, I was exploring Brahms' major works and liked them immensely. Now I became drawn to sacred choral music as well.

I have said elsewhere that music has been an important part of my life. And it has. However, as with climbing, my experience of it has been limited. I know nothing of musicology, cannot read a note and to my regret can play no instrument. As for concerts, in a lifetime I have attended twelve – three operas, three musicals and six performances of choral works. Other music I prefer listening to alone, away from the distractions of a public perfomance. Nonetheless, music is with me every day – from radio, recordings and my mental tapes.

"You're a bit of a snob about music, aren't you?" a colleague said one day as we sat smoking together in the staffroom.

"Why? Because I like Brahms, Bach and so on?"

"Yes."

"Well, that doesn't make me a snob. I like many kinds of music – folk songs, pop, even some rock and jazz. I see them as flowers, some very beautiful. But at times I need mountains and the swing of the sea."

"Music," a friend remarked recently, "is a mystery." It is certainly a language, one that speaks to us on many levels – physical, emotional, intellectual and spiritual. It can set feet dancing, arouse martial ardour or bring tears to the eye. It can be schmaltz, in-your-face offensive, or send the spirit soaring. And it can conjure up other places, other times, and evoke feelings for which no words exist. Some music I have found magical, like *The Oak and the Ash*, the folk song that transported a London schoolboy to a time and place he had never known. A recent example is a tune that was played in a dancehall scene in an otherwise forgettable movie and instantly attracted me. It seemed redolent of the Highlands and a way of life gone forever. I had never heard it before and a year or so passed before I heard it again. This time it was sung – and in Gaelic. I'd been right. It was a traditional Highland song, *Chi Mi Na Mórbheanna*. How I had known I cannot say. Vaughan Williams' *Fantasia on a Theme by Thomas Tallis* also seems a lament for what has been lost (or for what can never be), but is quintessentially English. For some reason I find myself drawn to pieces in a minor key. Perhaps it is the Celt in me.

Unlike art, sculpture and architecture, which extend into space, music extends primarily into time. Yet it exists in space, too, for it expresses itself through physical sound waves. If proponents of string theory are correct, music is fundamental to the universe and the whole of Creation like a vast, cosmic symphony. The Bushman's claim that the stars have voices and the ancients' talk of the Music of the Spheres might therefore not be too far adrift. Music a mystery? Yes, and it will perhaps remain so.

Access once more to a public library enabled me to catch up on some reading as well. Since reading Paul Brunton, and partly because of it, I had become aware of mysticism. Deciding to explore, I began with William James's *The Varieties of Religious Experience*. The anecdotal material I thought especially fascinating. This was not the reasoning of philosophy or the expounding of scriptures but accounts of living experience – of an ineffable, ecstatic inner experience.

Such accounts should be treated with caution, of course. As in the case of witnesses to crime, the subject may simply be mistaken, even deluded. And the experience itself, as behaviourists claim of near-death experiences, may be a result of changes in brain chemistry like those brought about by LSD. Perhaps. But I find many accounts compelling in that the experiences were life-transforming. That some are reported as being accompanied by voices, visions, stigmata, even levitation – the sort of things that cause some to wonder and others to scoff – gave me pause. However, some advanced contemplatives[21] warn that such phenomena should be ignored as being of little importance. In fact they point out that the ecstatic experience itself, which they sometimes term a "comfort," is not the aim of contemplation. Union with God is. By God's grace, they claim, this may be achieved – but only with love, self-abnegation and contemplative prayer, an arduous course that is often accompanied by much trial and suffering.

One effect of this reading is that I felt as if in climbing Conway Mountain for the first time I had found myself facing not the Carnedds but the icy Himalayas! The prospect was daunting. I could see now that my aim of seeking "the truth" was overambitious, to put it mildly. Very well, but I could still seek that which was true and good and, along with millions of others, still feel drawn to God. But I knew I had neither the vocation nor the ardour to be a contemplative. As for a religious experience, comfort or not, on the whole I preferred not to have one. What if God should require of me something I felt beyond my capacity? The thought alone was enough to make this timid soul sweat. It was the beginning of a healthy fear of God, a fear not of punishment but of being weighed in the balance and found wanting. In the darkness of its own little ego, the candle may believe it is casting a fine light. But cometh the sun – and the candle is mortified to find itself a mere taper, and one producing smoke more than anything else. So, rightly, I felt humbled. But I

---

[21] Unfortunately, the terms "mystic" and "mysticism," are too often confused with esoteric mysteries, psychic phenomena, occultism, even charlatanry. But I suppose we are stuck with them.

was young, full of juice, perhaps not humbled enough. Life was shortly to remedy that – and with a vengeance.

ᎾᏉᏸ

2

Jan

When first we met, early 1951, Jan was eighteen and I, twenty-five. Though I felt little more than a youth myself, the age difference weighed upon me. When we went out together, Jan dressed to appear older, more sophisticated, but she was nonetheless a young girl and vulnerable. Not for the world would I take advantage of her or hurt her in any way. Though I was powerfully attracted to her to a degree I had never experienced before, nor have since, the elder brother in me was strong. One could say that I loved her from the beginning. But at the time I was anything but sure of that, despite my certainty that we were destined to become man and wife.

Jan was the only child of Leslie and Kathy Fisher, owners of an antique shop in Walton-on-Thames. After the dismal conditions in post-war Britain had decided her parents to sell up and come to Vancouver, she had finished her education at the Vancouver School of Art. There, among other things, she'd had experience in dramatics and had taken part in a production of *Brigadoon*. Whether she could sing or not I don't know, but she had a fine speaking voice – clear, unaccented, musical. That first winter I saw her take the lead in *Shadow on the Nile*, a play set in ancient Egypt. What it was about I have little idea, as I had eyes only for her. In makeup and costume as Nititis, Princess of the Nile, she made Nefertiti by comparison seem as attractive as Wallace Simpson.

Jan had hazel eyes, black hair – slightly shot with red, for her mother was a redhead – skin like fresh cream, and the figure of a young gazelle. As for her features, they were mobile and expressive. Like me, she enjoyed reading and classical music. She also shared with me a keen sense of the ridiculous, and her lips had a delicious way of trembling with suppressed laughter. And I, needless to say, was often the occasion of it – as on the day when I solemnly assured her that "what is soose for the gauce is gauce for the sander," an example of the spoonerism that would later amuse my senior literature students ("We now come to those well-known Romantics – Sheats and Kelley."). Moreover, before long I found her nature to be as lovely as her person. Were I to liken Jan to any other woman, it would be to Prospero's Miranda. Though not naive like her, she had her openness of nature, and by the next winter made no secret of the fact that she wanted me for her husband.

In the event we were not to marry until the fall of 1956, over five years from the time we first met. As a result our relationship became an increasing strain on both of us, especially after we became engaged, for by then Jan had blossomed into womanhood. The fault was entirely mine. The fact is I would not a husband be – not yet, anyway – nor a lover, even had she wanted me to be. That, I felt, we would both regret. My seeming irresolution, I'm sure, was exasperating. At times she must have felt like strangling me and, had she done so, it could have been considered justifiable homicide. In fact she remained remarkably patient and forbearing.

Jan may have been my Miranda, but I was no Ferdinand. When first we met, I still had my courses to complete and five years at university before I could even begin my career. There was something else, something I never told her. Before leaving England, I had promised my mother not to marry without first coming back to visit her. It was a promise she had asked for and which I had given readily. I knew she feared that otherwise she would never see me again, or at best not for many years. University, a visit home, marriage – with my slender resources I seemed faced with an insurmountable mountain.

At first, though, the mountain remained a distant prospect. We were, after all, still in the process of getting to know one another. We seldom went dancing. I'd had enough of the Embassy and its stagline. Instead, we would usually take in a movie and for dancing contented ourselves with attending the Beaux Arts Ball with some of her friends from the Vancouver School of Art. Sometimes Jan came to Barclay Manor – but not often, as the temptation of being alone in my room together was a bit much for both of us. More often I was a guest in her home, where her parents made me welcome. After supper, we usually watched television and sometimes made a four at canasta.

Before long it became evident to me that her parents were not particularly happy together. I was to remain close to Kathy and Les for the rest of their lives and became fond of them both. Kathy was cheerful and vivacious, with a rather wicked sense of humour. Of the two of them, she was the stronger. She had to be, for Les was an alcoholic. Normally, he kept his drinking within bounds, about a bottle of whiskey a day; but if they were separated – as once when Kathy was in hospital for a week or so, or when he visited his half-sister in England alone – he tended to fall apart and drink himself into a stupor.

Sometime after his death, Kathy revealed to me that she did not have a high opinion of her husband. It was understandable, perhaps. She knew how much he had depended on her and they had not had physical relations for decades. Moreover, on coming to Canada she had wanted to go into business again, but Les had always refused. She found this frustrating, as she had good business sense and they would likely have made a success of it. Instead he continued working as credit manager for a local roofing company. The pay was miserable but he no doubt counted on a pension. If so, he was to be disappointed. When he was close to retirement, his company was taken over by an American corporation which promptly moved in its own management – and Les found himself out, pensionless.

I have a better opinion of him. It is true that in some ways he was a limited man. There was his alcoholism and his need for his wife to help control it. His taste in music ran to Mitch Miller and Lawrence Welk, he never to my knowledge read a book, and he had only two close friends. What demons drove him I don't know, but the fact that he had a half-sister suggests a childhood background of a broken family. For all that, I found him to be an intelligent man and one who could be relied upon in an emergency.

That he was far from a fool he had demonstrated by besting a firm of lawyers. Upon leaving England he had rented out his house. The reason was simple: because of currency restrictions then in force, had he sold it he would not have been able to take the money out of the country. The only way to recover his equity would be to sell the house in Canada to someone who intended to return to England. This he did, taking care to warn the buyer of the problem he would face should he change his mind and wish to return. Inevitably the buyer did change his mind and on his return to Canada sued Les, claiming the deal had been fraudulent. "Not a thing to worry about," the lawyer assured Les. "There was no fraud, nothing illegal, and so he hasn't a leg to stand on." He then proceeded to lose the case for him! Having had some legal training, Les launched an immediate appeal; and when the time for the hearing came up, Kathy, Jan and I accompanied him to Victoria to lend moral support as he argued his own case before three appelate judges.

In the meantime, the law firm had presented Les with a large bill, which he refused to pay. Unable to sequester his car or his house – he had forestalled them by having both made out in Kathy's name – the firm garnisheed his wages. Les could do nothing about that. However, when the appeal court handed down a unanimous decision in his favour, he immediately filed suit against the firm, alleging they had mishandled his case through laxity and incompetence. Then he called at the Victoria office of the firm's senior lawyer and served him the subpoena personally. "Christ!" exlaimed the great man as soon as he grasped its import, "you can't do this. I'm the Attorney-General!" The deal was immediate. Suit and countersuit were dropped – and the firm never received a penny.

A few years following his dismissal from the roofing company Les obtained a licence to sell real estate and he and Kathy moved to Victoria, where they enjoyed a comfortable living. When, at the age of seventy, he was diagnosed with lung cancer, he immediately stopped both smoking and drinking – and for the remaining months of his life I never heard a word of complaint from him. Kathy survived him for some years.

⊙⥊⊙

April, 1952: Jan and I were sitting on the living-room sofa. We were alone in the house. Our second winter together had ended, and I was due to fly back to Dawson next day. But the mountain

356

had been looming ever larger in my mind. The situation seemed hopeless. Besides, it was not fair to her. As a result I had just told her I thought it best we break up and not see each other any more. Then I began to walk out. Suddenly, I was brought up short. My work gear was stored in her basement! I couldn't leave without it. And so I turned. Jan had risen to her feet and was standing in silence, two great tears rolling down her cheeks…. It was no use. I couldn't leave her – and in a moment I was holding her in my arms, kissing away the salt tears and telling her so. "A woman's strongest weapon is her tears," my mother had once told me. Jan's tears, neither feigned nor intended as a weapon, had just prevented me from making the biggest mistake of my life.

❧

3

Engagement

While in the Yukon, from time to time I heard reports of a construction project that had started up at Kitimat, on the northern B.C. coast near the Alaska Panhandle. Apparently an aluminum smelter was being built there. In fact the project was a huge one and consisted of three stages: a large dam on the Nechako River to create a reservoir; miles of tunneling through rock to convey water to the powerhouse, followed by over fifty miles of powerline; and finally the smelter itself – plus a whole new town! This project, involving the investment of $500 million (about $5 billion in today's funny money), provided work for thousands and catapulted the B.C. economy out of its post-War doldrums.

Thanks to my dredging experience, in April, 1953, I joined the Union of Operating Engineers and was offered work as oiler on a power shovel at Kemano. I would be working for Morrison-Knudsen. The job does not exist today and perhaps never did before, as the oiler had little to do. The union justified it as an apprenticeship for would-be operators, but really it was only a way to put an extra man to work. In the event, no operator I worked with offered to teach me a thing. (Why train future competition?) The contractors did not quibble, as they were paid on a cost-plus basis. As for me, while not relishing standing around while others worked, I didn't quibble either. I was being paid more than I had earned as a winchman on a dredge.

Kemano, a large encampment at the foot of Mt. Dubose, was the main construction site for the middle stage of the project – the tunnels, powerhouse and powerline which together would supply electricity to the smelter and townsite at Kitimat. At the time I arrived, the dam on the Nechako River had been completed and the reservoir was filling, but much remained to be done on the second stage. When this was complete, water from the reservoir would flow to the 2,400-foot level inside Mt. Dubose and then plunge down penstocks to the powerhouse 2000 feet below. The power generated by such a fall could be imagined.

After a few days in the workshop I was assigned to a power shovel at work in the powerhouse. Blasted out of the bowels of the mountain, it was nowhere near complete, being merely a cavity in the naked rock; but it could have held the main body of Notre Dame Cathedral with room to spare! Given that much space, I can scarcely claim to have experienced claustrophobia; but when I contemplated the mass of rock hanging 130 feet or more above my head, I found myself hoping most earnestly that the scalers had done their job.

Surrounded by mountains, I of course had to climb one. Sunday provided the opportunity. All nearby mountains were steep and thickly wooded, and exposed rock consisted of smooth boiler-plate slabs. Not exactly attractive. And so I hiked up a valley to a more welcoming peak and a few hours later sat at the snowline admiring the view. It was not smart climbing there alone, but I'd been unable to persuade anyone to join me. Two former British soldiers I had approached had greeted my invitation with silence, during which both stared at me as if I were from Mars. "No thanks," one grunted at last. "We had enough of rotten mountains in Italy."

A few days later I found myself boarding a De Haviland Beaver float plane at Kemano Landing. Together with several other men I was then flown over the hump to Kildala, some 25 miles north, and from there driven several thousand feet up a mountain to the tented encampment of Dala Heights. There, well away from the heat, mosquitos and deer flies of the lower levels, I remained until it was time to leave for university. For much of the time I was alone with my operator, digging footings for pylons. It was rather like a holiday with pay.

One Sunday I managed to climb one of the local peaks. I had hitched a ride along the powerline road to Kitimat in order to look up Dick and Gerry and spend a few hours with them. On the return trip, discovering my driver to be Swiss, I suggested we climb the peak above Kildala Pass. He agreed readily – it was only about a thousand feet higher – and we were rewarded with a superb view of the surrounding mountains.

☙❧

The University of British Columbia is on Point Grey, at the western edge of Vancouver and largely separated from it by a swathe of wooded parkland. A hundred feet or so above the sea, it commands fine views – of English Bay, with merchantmen at anchor and white sails leaning on the wind; of Lionsgate Bridge, Stanley Park and downtown Vancouver; of the busy harbour approaches, the North Shore mountains and the distant Tantalus Range; and of the Gulf Islands across the Strait of Georgia. It is a setting second to none.

UBC had nearly six thousand students when I arrived in 1953, and for the first days an air of general excitement pervaded the campus. Freshmen rushed about joining, or endeavouring to join, Greek-letter societies; while bands of other students, uniformed in red cardigans, trooped around chanting "We are, we are, we are the engineers." Most curious behaviour! I was not excited, though. I was twenty-seven, for one thing, almost a decade older than fellow freshmen. And for another, paying my own way and intent on getting my money's worth, I had enrolled in six courses rather than the required five. I expected to have to work hard and was thus interested neither in the social whirl nor in joining anything. In fact I was thankful to learn that as a veteran I was exempt from required "physical activities". I'd had enough of games and physical jerks in the air force.

359

Having also had enough of communal living, rather than live on campus I rented a room near the university gates. My meals I usually took at the University cafeteria, although on occasion I treated myself to a supper at Deans, a nearby café popular with students. The owner of the house, Mrs. Bennet, was a most pleasant lady – and a widow, I believe, as I never saw sign of husband or children. Another lodger occupied a suite in the basement – a priest, Mrs. Bennet confided, and one sadly given to tippling. She would sometimes hear him stumbling about downstairs at night, and the empty tins she found there suggested that he had been consoling himself with the communion wine. Required to be celibate, besieged by the cares of his flock, his prayers met with silence, he must have been desperately lonely. Or so I imagined.

I soon fell into a routine. Saturdays I spent with Jan. For the rest of the week I attended lectures, read, or pecked away at essays on my Royal portable. Blessed with a memory not notably retentive or reliable, I prepared for tests by organizing and rewriting my notes. Visitors to my room were rare – Jan once, in tears because Les had been beastly (Kathy was in hospital and he'd been drinking heavily), and a young freshman seeking ideas for a short story. And so my evenings were quiet. I had no radio, no phonograph, and I heard Mrs. Bennet only if she wished to speak to me. Otherwise, nothing broke the silence save the clatter of my typewriter keys or, on foggy nights, the repeated mournful warning of the Point Atkinson foghorn. Sometimes, if the wind was in the right quarter, the distant boom of the nine o'clock gun would remind me it was time for a coffee break at Deans. Save for the days with Jan, it was a monkish sort of life – rather like that at Hunker Creek, but without the benefit of physical labour.

As for my courses, I was not disappointed. However, I found UBC too much like high school. I had expected seminars and consultations with tutors but had none, perhaps because there were too few staff for the number of students. Moreover, no matter how good the professors, listening to lectures was not my preferred learning style. I was accustomed to working alone and at my own pace. I encountered nothing too difficult, though I had to work hard at math, but at times I felt that, like a French goose, I was being fed more than I had time to digest.

Christmas came as a welcome break. To earn extra cash I stacked cases of beer and filled shelves in a government liquor store, but that still left me plenty of time with Jan. Treated as one of the family, I found Christmas week an especially happy time, and we rounded it off by celebrating New Year in the main ballroom of the Vancouver Hotel.

Late one evening in May, 1954, alone with Jan in the living-room – her parents had discreetly disappeared – I asked her to marry me. Excited, she ran into the kitchen to tell her mother, and I followed. "Has he, dear," said Kathy, betraying no surprise whatever. "That's nice." Addressing me, she added, "You had better tell her father. He's in the front room." This was their bedroom; and when I went in with the glad tidings, I found Les sitting on the bed in the dark, smoking a cigarette. He betrayed no surprise either. "Ah," he rasped bitterly, "now you've knocked a nail into your coffin, haven't you." Evidently he was in the doghouse again.

In the morning Jan and I took a bus downtown and we dropped into the Persian Curio shop to choose the ring. No diamonds – just a slender, inexpensive ring of braided gold – but she was content. There had been no discussion about a wedding date, either, and she was content with that, too, for the time being. As for me –

That day,
The day we bought the ring together,
That day I prayed, my love, to Love
That I might love with all my heart
Both Love and you together,
Ever.

It was a prayer that would be largely answered – but not quite in the way I had expected.

Next Day I flew north, this time to Kitimat.

361

Decisions

Kitimat townsite was a vast, empty expanse in the forest. Cleared of trees and underbrush, it was busy with belly-dumps, cats and power shovels, but as yet lacked roads and drainage. For me the only thing of interest was the lunch break. Some men had begun sharing lunch with any bear that chanced by. Bad idea! For other men followed suit until nearly all were bringing extra sandwiches. The result was inevitable. The bush telegraph hummed – and before long, troops of bears regularly lumbered out of the forest at lunchtime expecting to be fed. Needless to say, when all your sandwiches were gone, the next bear would assume you were holding out and become understandably upset. One such disgruntled bear made me seek sanctuary in the shovel and even climbed on after me. Fortunately, there was a passage around the engine into which the operator and I could squeeze but the bear couldn't. On another occasion, one man offered a bear a sandwich as if to a large dog that would sit up and beg. The bear had more sense than he did. Ignoring the sandwich, with a sudden swipe of its paw it snatched the lunchbag from the other hand. It's a wonder it didn't take the arm too.

That summer, as I watched the shovel operator earning our pay, I gave some thought to the subject of love. What was it? It was certainly not sexual attraction, desirable though that might be between husband and wife. I loved my parents and there was nothing sexual there – despite what Freud might say. And it was not an intense form of liking. As a small boy I had loved my father but had not particularly liked him. Nor was it simply *feeling*. Feelings change. One may be happy one day, miserable the next. Love endures, or should. Certainly it is usually accompanied by feeling. At one extreme it may be anguish, as when I wept for my mother in the bar of our pub. And at the other, it may verge on the ecstatic. In physical proximity to Jan I often felt an attraction that was not sexual alone but something other – and far better. It was as if we were resonating in harmony. Such a feeling comes, perhaps, only when the love is mutual.

No, feelings happen or are given. Love must contain an element of choice, commitment or, at the very least, of consent – of choosing to open one's heart to it, as it were. Moreover, although one could not *will* oneself to love, one could choose to act *as if* one did. That, too, is love – a disinterested love, one that springs from compassion or concern for the other and seeks nothing in return. It is not the kind on which to base a marriage, of course. Different kinds of love, then.

So I turned the matter over in my mind, all of it obvious enough, I suppose, but I had to get things straight. I was satisfied of one thing, though – that I loved Jan. But was I "in love" with her? Not knowing what that meant, I assumed I was not. As to what love was – that, like the universe and life itself, remained a mystery.

There was something else I did that summer. From the beginning I had written regularly to my family but had not breathed a word about university and the years of courses that had gone before. Now, having successfully completed one year at UBC, I told them what I had been up to. I should imagine they were somewhat taken aback.

That winter I again took six courses, including a third-year course in medieval history. This time, however, I stayed at Acadia Camp. Like Fort Camp, also on campus, it consisted of wooden huts built after the War to accommodate the influx of veterans. There I shared a room with two others – Doug Howie, a South African, and "Andy" Anderson, an expat from Bromley. About my own age, they were congenial company, and so I felt less isolated than I had in my first year.

As usual, I worked in the liquor store during the Christmas break, but this time Jan and I celebrated New Year at The Roof in the Vancouver Hotel. Dressed in a formal gown, white with red candy striping, she looked ravishing. During the following months, however, the mountain loomed ever higher. Engagement had bought me time but had not solved the problem. I still could not reconcile marriage and a visit home with three years more university to go. We had known one another now for four years and Jan was nearly 23. Her biological clock had to be in overdrive.

One day, sensing that something was worrying me, Jan said, quite calmly, "I've decided to release you from your promise. I feel you're not happy with the engagement." Her generosity and courage staggered me – but I didn't wish to be released. I had made a promise and meant to keep it. Reassured, she and her mother later came up with a solution to the problem of money. We could marry. With my summer earnings we could furnish a small rented apartment and pay for university, and then we could live on Jan's salary. I was not expected to do everything myself. Solved! I should of course have told them about the promise to my mother, but like a fool I didn't. Instead I appeared to vacillate. I rather think Jan gave up on me after that, for by the time I finished my second year at UBC she had gone. Possibly at the suggestion of her mother, she had found employment at the University of Montreal and put two thousand miles between us.

But I *had* made a decision. I would take a year off from UBC and spend the winter at home. This time I found work in Vancouver – as decker on a suction dredge. That summer I rented a room in the Manor, a small, L-shaped one behind the washing machines in the annexe basement. It had a camp bed in each arm and was illuminated by one naked light bulb and a small window that afforded a bug's-eye view of the lawn. This I shared with the spiders and another man. It was merely a place for us to doss in, and I doubt whether we exchanged more than a dozen words the whole time I was there. As the company crew truck came too early for me to breakfast at the Manor, I had to eat downtown at the White Spot and then bus back to the pick-up point at the entrance to Stanley Park.

The dredge was at work in First Narrows, deepening the harbour to accommodate larger ships and piping the spoil onto the north shore to serve as a foundation for future industrial development. Later it moved to Second Narrows. Like the gold dredges it swung on a spud, but in this case the bow lines were secured to ship's anchors. A tugboat stood by to move anchors and other equipment and to serve as a safeguard should the dredge drag anchor, for tides in the Narrows ran at seven knots.

Though not hard, the work at times called for both muscle and weight, with neither of which was I well endowed. As the regular day shift, we had to replace wearing plates in the pump. Done on average once a week, this required a heavy-duty chainblock, sixteen-pound sledgehammers, rat-tailed wrenches with five feet of piping, and nearly eight hours of effort by the crew. Another task involved the replacement of worn sections of pipe, each of which was mounted on its own float and connected to the next by a steel collar. To allow free play at the joint, each end of the pipe belled into a hemisphere. Removing a section was easy enough, unless the nuts were rusted on, but replacing one wasn't. Then the collar had to be manhandled up the belled end, a task that required the co-ordinated efforts of three men – one sitting astride the pipe with a pinch bar and two heaving up on the collar while bobbing about on a small float. As each collar weighed well over 400 pounds, the task invited a hernia. As for safety precautions, there were none. Hard hats, steel-toed boots and life-jackets were neither provided nor required. One could buy them downtown, of course, but I don't think any of us thought of it. Nor were there guard rails on the dredge. A modern safety man would have had a fit.

Save for a week off to enjoy an attack of shingles, I endured this regime for two months or so. And then in August I quit. Forty hours a week at a dollar an hour had brought in nowhere near enough. I had to leave town after all.

Where is it now, the glory and the dream?
                                              - Wordsworth

Up to the end of November I worked in Squamish as an oiler for Emil Anderson. Situated at the head of Howe Sound, about thirty miles north of Horseshoe Bay, Squamish today is linked to Vancouver by BC Rail and by a highway that continues to the Whistler ski resort and beyond. But it was then only a small logging town and the terminus of the Pacific Great Eastern Railway. To reach it from Vancouver, one had to go by coastal steamship, as the only road south from Squamish was a rough track to the small mining community of Britannia Beach. Beyond that, the mountains plunge straight to the sea.

Now Emil Anderson was extending the railway to Vancouver, a costly undertaking that involved much drilling, blasting and filling.

After the dredge and my dismal subterranean cell, I felt liberated. Even the bunkhouse was a luxury, despite bunkmates, diamond-drillers mostly, who spent Saturday evening in town and then all night in the bunkhouse pickling their brains in alcohol. Still, most of them were good men at heart – the sort, as the cliche´ has it, that would give you the shirt off their backs. And maybe that's all some of them ended up with. I asked one of them what he intended to do when the job ended. "Will you go to Vancouver?" "Yes," he said, "I'll get a room on Cordova Street." "Skid Row!" I exclaimed. "Why would you want to stay in a place like that?" He replied simply, "That's where all my mates are."

Then there were the mountains – the steep, thickly timbered peaks that lined the sound; the Stawamus Chieftain, two thousand feet of almost vertical boilerplate slabs that loomed over our camp; and Mount Garibaldi, a magnificent 8,739 foot glaciated peak a few miles to the north. I was in my element once more.

One Sunday I set out to climb the Chief – from the rear, of course. It proved a mere scramble. And upon reaching the top I sat on the edge, looking seaward and dangling my feet over the gulf as once I had done from Conway Mountain. Not a sigh of wind! The trees motionless, the sound calm, the only sign of human activity a slender column of smoke from the Woodfibre mill – otherwise nothing but mountains, sea and sky. And beyond Squamish, Mt. Garibaldi, wearing a bright mantle of fresh snow! All was peaceful, so beautiful…. And it was then, with a sinking heart, that I *knew* – that the magic I had felt as a boy, and for long afterwards, was gone. There was something else, something that had happened so gently that I had barely been aware of it – I no longer felt close to God.

Homecoming

In early December, I packed a few things and left for the bus depot. I'd rejected the idea of flying home and instead had booked passage on the *Queen Mary*. To arrive at my mother's door in mere hours after so long an absence would have been disorienting. Besides, with all winter at my disposal I might as well enjoy the journey. Traveling to New York by train proved too expensive, and so Greyhound bus it was – via Seattle, Salt Lake City and Chicago.

Even with a night off in a Salt Lake City hotel, I found five days and nights on a bus a bit of a marathon. Still, I was much impressed with Greyhound. Despite the unpredictability of road travel, their buses had run on time, and I had two full days in New York to do the usual rubbernecking. And there I saw an unexpectedly familiar face in the crowd, for standing on a kerb hailing a cab was Mr. Jaggers himself, or rather Francis L. Sullivan's version of him.

It was night when I disembarked in Southampton, little richer than when I had set out and with the same rucksack on my back. But at least I was wearing a suit now instead of a war-surplus GI uniform. For a while I stood chatting with a young couple I had befriended on board. Then I glanced at the crowd waiting to greet us. Almost immediately I saw my father. He was at the back, standing at a higher level and looking down at me with tears running down his cheeks. Pretending I hadn't noticed, I grinned and waved briefly. Then I bid the couple farewell and joined him. What we talked about on the train to Waterloo I cannot remember. I recall only that London Bridge Station appeared inexpressibly gloomy and Woolwich even more so. And there, after a brief ride on a 53A bus, we parted again. Dad dropped off at his usual stop, while I went on to *The Woodman*. Only few steps now and I was at my mother's door. I gave my usual rat-tat-tat with the knocker and heard familiar footsteps in the passage. She was almost running.

Later, as I lay between the well-remembered icy sheets, the little bedroom lit dimly by the solitary gas streetlamp outside,

367

I felt a wave of sadness. In contrast to the lights and bustling prosperity of New York, London appeared as shabby and depressing as it had in 1947. True, rationing had ended (ten years after the War!), but otherwise little seemed changed. My parents had changed, though. They were older, appreciably so. And then it was my turn to shed tears.

I awoke in a lighter mood. There had been another change. Grandpa was no longer there. He had developed dementia after I left, and Mum and George had had a terrible time with him before he died. Now, all was well, and I was glad to be home. A few days later, Pauline arrived with her husband and child. They had come to stay over Christmas. We were all together again at last – except for Dad, of course.

That winter I spent more time with Dad than ever I'd had the chance to before. Saturdays we usually went up to London, visiting museums, art galleries, St. Paul's, the Abbey, the Tower – in short, seeing more of London than the ordinary Londoner would perhaps bother to. For refreshment, liquid and otherwise, we favoured a "Chef and Brewer" pub on Charing Cross Road. *Kismet* was playing then, at the Stoll, I believe, and I attended two performances – one with Dad and then, as we had enjoyed it so much, another with Mum.

I haunted London on my own as well, to take in a movie or a choral concert or merely to explore. Of three choral concerts I attended, one I found particularly affecting was a performance of Bach's B Minor mass in Westminster Hall. Altogether, nearly half my lifetime's concert-going was done that winter. But the most memorable experience was a visit Dad and I made to St. Paul's. It was late afternoon on a cheerless winter day; and as we walked about in the silence, looking at the statuary, dusk was gathering. Suddenly, lights were switched on and a procession of white-surpliced figures filed quietly in. Candles were lit and then a service was begun. It was evensong. And in all that great, dimly-lit cathedral there were no other visitors, no congregation – only the celebrants and we two. I felt almost sorry for God.

With the coming of spring I went to Woodstock to stay awhile with Pauline and her family; and I seized the opportunity to visit the Ashmolean Museum and Oxford colleges. In marked contrast to today, Oxford then was quiet, with no tourists, little traffic and a bus service that was good – even if the buses were unheated rattletraps. Pauline took me on a tour of Blenheim Palace, the vast edifice built for John Churchill, first Duke of Marlborough, and with her husband Reg I made several circumnavigations of its extensive park. A native of Woodstock, Reg was something of a local hero, as he played football for Oxford United and captained the local cricket team. He was not paid for this, of course, but earned his living as a glover. When I knew him better, I found he combined his athletic build with a gentle nature. In over fifty years of marriage he has never raised a hand to my sister. I suspect, however, that she has clouted him a few times.

Then it was time to return to Vancouver. Seven years more were to pass before I saw my family again, more than fifteen years before we could again spend Christmas together – and by then Dad was dead.

ᕹ

The best-laid schemes…   – Robert Burns

The return voyage in the *Queen Elizabeth* was as uneventful as the one over, but the bus journey proved even more of a marathon. The reason was simple enough – I had run short of money. After paying my fare I hadn't enough for food, let alone a hotel, and for the last two days had to subsist on coffee alone. As a result I arrived in Vancouver ravenous and without money enough for a bus fare. I had to walk to the Manor.

Crunch time! Jan was home and I had to see her. But how would I feel about her? How would she feel? One thing was certain – the matter between us had to be settled. There could be no more dithering on my part. Yet like a coward I did dither – for three days. Finally, I plucked up courage to phone her, and she agreed to meet me at our favourite rendezvous, the cocktail lounge of the Vancouver Hotel.

The popular cocktail lounge then was in the Georgia Hotel. Bright, cosy and noisy, it was always jammed with chattering patrons sitting cheek by jowl, or cheek by ham, rather. Which is why Jan and I avoided the place. By contrast, the one in the Vancouver Hotel was discreetly lit and cavernous, with tables well apart and mostly empty. One could hold a conversation without having to shout.

It was evening when we met. She was wearing a little Juliet cap fashioned from blue feathers and looked extremely fetching. I cannot recall our conversation. I know only that I was delighted to see her again. And as she sat in the subdued lighting, smiling at me across the table, the conviction that I'd had when first we met, and which had never really left, returned with redoubled force. We were meant to be husband and wife. I *knew* it. I had kept the promise to my mother and now, like spring snow in a chinook, all doubts had vanished as if they had never been. And I felt enveloped by love.

Before we parted, the decision was made. We would get married in September and then live according to the plan suggested earlier.

Within a week Jan was showing me the place she and her mother had found, a basement room in Kerrisdale, one that was small and windowless. The alcove that served as a kitchen contained a stove, a sink and a small cupboard down one side and room only for the cook on the other. Across the basement, the bathroom was fitted with a toilet, a washbasin and a shower with plastic curtains. Clearly the owner, a retired doctor, had spared no expense. I looked at it doubtfully. I was accustomed to living rough. But Jan?

"I know it's small," she said brightly, "but it will be all right when it's decorated and furnished."

"Are you sure?" I asked.

"Well, it's not as if we'll be in all the time," she replied. "We'll be out during the day. Besides," she added, "it has advantages. It's in a quiet area close to our bus routes – and it's cheap."

I looked the room over again. A ten-inch shelf ran around three sides. A place for my books. "OK," I nodded.

In the meantime, I had registered for my third year at UBC and found work. I would be going to Kitimat again. At the airport I gave Jan a cheque for $400, which left only enough in my bank account to keep it open. "I'll send more when I get paid," I promised. As we embraced, I asked, "If you meet me here when I return, would you wear that little Juliet cap again?" Then I left.

Our course was set and the way ahead seemed clear. It would be a struggle, but together we should be able to cope. So I thought.

PART FIVE

Ashes

1956 – 2006

Chapter 18 Marriage   375

Chapter 19 Teacher   395

Chapter 20 Epilogue   422

CHAPTER EIGHTEEN

Marriage

1
"...the Punishment of the Damned"

When I was last there, Kitimat townsite had been cleared and graded virtually flat. Now, in 1956, it resembled a scene from *All Quiet on the Western Front,* with great heaps of earth, gargantuan trenches and mud everywhere. The storm sewers were being installed. For a month or so I worked there as oiler on a power shovel, with little to do except hook up a sling when the operator wanted to move the wooden pads on which the shovel rested. Then I was sent to the workshop and employed as a general dogsbody – sometimes at the end of a shovel, digging in a ditch. Later I was placed with a power shovel near the smelter. I didn't really care what I had to do. With overtime, I was making more than twice as much as I had on the suction dredge the previous year.

August neared its end, and soon I would be with Jan again. In a little over three weeks we would be married. I was looking forward to our life together and had every reason to be happy. Yet I was not. For some days now I had been feeling vaguely oppressed – as if I were suspended in the stillness before a storm.

It is dark. In our bunkhouse we have turned in and the lights are out. But it is not peaceful. There is a racket going on outside, and one of the men goes to the door and shouts for quiet. The noise abruptly stops and he returns to bed. A moment later a shadowy figure enters and clumps over to the bed opposite me. He leans over and growls something – and is promptly told to "fuck off". I cannot lie there doing nothing, and so I turn on my light. "I agree with those sentiments," I say. At this the intruder straightens up and looks at me. He has clearly been drinking. Then he begins walking towards me.... Shockingly, with no warning at all, I am flooded with terror, overwhelmed by it, and when he reaches me I find myself cowering against the wall. "Leave me alone," I plead. "Just leave me be." And as he stands over me, swaying a little and looking down, a part of my mind seems to have drawn aside and become a powerless observer. "You're a prick!" he sneers, and then leaves.

The light is suddenly intolerable; and with something between a sob and a laugh, I switch it off. I feel disoriented. I know only too well what has happened. But why? I am aghast. My worst fears realized! A coward after all, and my life trashed in an instant! What would Dad think? The son of a soldier turned into a cringing poltroon, not by shot and shell, but by a drunk – and not even a big drunk! The men of the Somme, a time when courage and life were cheap? What would they think of you, boyo? "These men are worth your tears. You are not worth their merriment." No, not even their notice. And there are hundreds of men in camp, many of them veterans – and from both sides in the War! Oh, God I have not only disgraced myself but let my country down as well. Soon the whole damned camp will know.

As my mind raves on, conducting a fevered dialogue with itself, I become aware that I am groaning aloud but am powerless to stop it. I wasn't a coward as a boy. I punched that boy in the mouth for pulling my sister's hair. Drew blood, too. And I was only eleven, still in short trousers. He was older, bigger than me, a third-former, and the only reason I could reach him was that we were seated in a bus. Then why now? I hadn't feared the intruder, and yet terror had taken possession of me as if at the flip of a switch. I feel betrayed – and by my inmost self. Men so disgraced have been known to blow their brains out. Yes, well to hell with that. That is to run away. And if there is life after death, I'd merely be taking my disgrace with me. I can't escape from myself. It's the punishment of the damned. Challenge all comers to a fight, then? Sure, I would succeed only in becoming ridiculous as well as contemptible. The situation seems irremediable. And so, like Faustus awaiting the coming of Mephistopheles, I sweat away the night and dread the dawn.

Yet I did make a decision that night. If I couldn't make up my mind *what* to do, I at least knew what I would *not* do. I would not run away and hide, and I would not slink around the camp like a cur with its tail between its legs. Instead, I would work out my time and walk like a man – even if I didn't feel like one.

It was a difficult two weeks. In the morning the men in my bunkhouse ignored me and said nothing. In the evening the intruder had the gall to come back, sober this time. Instantly I jumped to my feet and faced him. "You're not wanted in here," I snapped. "We won't put up with it." He looked at me, at the men gathering around, and then shrugged. "I don't give a shit," he said and walked out. I returned to my bed and sat down. I felt empty. *We* won't put up with it? "I", I should have said. But I no longer knew who or what "I" was.

Late that night, two newcomers arrived and took the beds next to mine. They were drunk, but I dropped off despite the racket. Having had a stressful day and no sleep the previous night, I was exhausted. In the morning I awoke to find them gone. But they had left a memento of their stay – during the night one had been unable to make it to the latrine and had shit on the floor. An apt comment on my own behaviour, I thought. Needless to say, the pair had taken their kit with them and never returned.

Before long, eyes were regarding me speculatively. The news had spread and I readied myself for trouble. I well knew that vulnerability tends to attract jackals. But as yet no one had tried anything. To make things easier for anyone who might want to, I went to the beer parlour, sat up at the bar and had a drink. And there, like the Ancient Mariner, I overheard the following conversation, the voices carefully pitched to be loud enough for me to hear but not enough to be taken as a challenge:

"Is that the guy?"

"Yes."

"But wasn't he in the air force?"

"What's that got to do with it?"

Nothing about penance, though. And how did they know I'd been in the air force? It wasn't something I had advertised.

Only two men spoke to me in the time I had left – one to remark that I looked "grim", the other to ask if it had been the intruder's beer bottle that had been the problem. "No," I said. "Then why were you so afraid of him?" He was genuinely puzzled. Well, that made two of us. "I don't know," I replied.

Perhaps my subsequent behaviour had not quite conformed to what is expected of your run-of-the-mill coward.

꧁

2

Honeymoon

Jan and Kathy were waiting at the airport to meet me. Jan had on the little Juliet cap and looked charming as ever. I kissed her and asked if she was not feeling well. Surprised, she replied, "No, I'm fine. Why?" "You seem a little pale," I said. It appears I had seen something that neither she nor anyone else had noticed. The significance of that would emerge later. After a meal at their home, I went on to Dick's place, where I was to stay until the wedding. Before leaving, I had arranged to meet Jan again that evening.

It was no use putting it off. I had to tell her. It would be dishonest and unfair not to let her know what kind of man I was. Damn my rotten fate! All movies seem to end with the hero performing deeds of daring before the admiring eyes of his girl. I had to confess to mine that I was a miserable coward.

As usual, the cocktail bar in the Vancouver Hotel was virtually empty. I ordered our drinks – and then braced myself. "Jan," I said, "There is something I have to tell you. When you hear what it is, you may wish to call the wedding off."

She looked most alarmed.

Haltingly, I told her what had happened at Kitimat.

As I did so, her face cleared. "Is that all?" she laughed. "I thought you were going to tell me you had met another woman."

The next day Kathy drove us to Kerrisdale for me to see the result of their work. The room had been painted a tasteful pink, brighter and far warmer than the original washed-out yellow. The furniture, a leafed table, chairs and small sideboard, was in the modern style. For a bed we had a bed-sofa, with the sofa forming one side of the bed and not the head. There was barely room enough for the latter kind. For the same reason, the leaf had been left out of the table. Our future home appeared cosy and attractive. I was impressed. Then we drove back to the house for lunch.

While we were at table, the telephone rang. Jan answered it and a moment later returned to the kitchen, her face red. "Do you know who that was?" Without waiting for an answer, she went on, "The landlord. He has just raised the rent. How could he find the nerve to do such a thing? We haven't even moved in yet." I was amused. It seems the good doctor had also been impressed by their efforts. "Never mind," I said soothingly, "You look most attractive when you're angry."

Before the wedding Jan had a medical, but I didn't bother. I knew I was fit and well. I did, however, visit a dentist to have my teeth seen to.

"Only one filling needed," he said, readying his needle.

"Never mind that," I said. "Just go ahead and drill."

"What? Are you sure?" he asked, surprised.

"Go ahead"

"Most unusual – especially as it's a front tooth. They're the most sensitive as a rule." He was curious, fishing.

Let him fish. As it happens, I was almost as surprised as he, for my decision had been made on the spur of the moment. Why should I do such a thing? To prove to myself I was not afraid of pain? To punish myself out of a sense of self disgust? Or was it in the hope that one pain would drive out another? I don't know – maybe all three. In the event, it didn't hurt all that much, and it did no good whatever. Apart from fixing the tooth, that is.

On September 22, my father's birthday, Jan and I were married in St. Anselm's, the little Anglican church inside the university gates. Gerry was best man and Jan's friend Bernice was maid of honour. ("Bare knees and brown," Jan called her.) The guests were requested to sit anywhere, as the usual arrangement would have looked a trifle odd with fifty or more on the bride's side and only four on the groom's – Dick, his wife Marjorie, Jack, and Gerry's girl friend. In her simple white bridal gown Jan looked lovely. I wore my tailored suit of grey worsted. And my knees were trembling.

I remember little of the reception. I know we were driven there in a large sedan owned by the more prosperous of Les's two friends, and I remember our cutting the cake. It was about then that Jan nudged me in the ribs and said, "You're supposed to make a speech now, thanking Daddy for all the work he has done." *Bloody hell, why doesn't anyone tell me about these things?* Needless to say, I rambled. At one point I "commiserated" with her father "for not losing a daughter but gaining a son". Somehow, that didn't sound right. Mercifully, soon afterwards we were whisked off to her parents' house, where Jan changed into her going-away outfit – a tasteful black dress and coat, topped off with a preposterous white hat that perched on her head like the extended wing of a snow goose. Then we were driven downtown to the ferry terminal. We were off to Vancouver Island for our honeymoon.

"You were lucky," said Pauline ruefully when I described all this to her; "I had no honeymoon at all – just a few days at Mum's house. Our wedding was at the register office. We had a hired car and all of us jammed into it – Reg, me, Mum, George and Lyly, Mum's neighbour. You should have seen Mum. She had put on weight and looked a frump. I'd never seen her dressed so badly. And when we got to the town hall, waiting outside were three little Condon aunts, Hetty, Mary and Esther, all dressed in black and all wearing their shovel hats…"

"Like the three weird sisters," I said.

"Eh? Yes. Well, they all had wedding presents. From Hetty I got a little flowered bowl, from Mary a pair of stockings and from Esther a half pound box of chocolates.

"As soon as the ceremony was over, Reg stuck his hands in his pockets and walked out. He had to be called back to sign the register and pay the fee. The reception was held in Mum's front room, with a little ham salad, cake and some sherry. Afterwards, Lyly sang, while her brother played the piano. Old songs, 'Only a Rose' – you know the sort of thing. She had a terrible voice. While we were there, John Green dropped by from work and gave me his wedding present – a set of dessert dishes, all still covered with sawdust and wrapped in newspaper."

"Hot from the market in the square," I said, laughing.

"That's right. And in the evening, as we waited to go to bed, all Reg could do was sit by the fire reading the sports section in the papers. Talk about romantic!"

Jan and I spent our honeymoon at Yellow Point Lodge, which is on the coast just north of Ladysmith. Having once worked there, she knew it well. There could not have been a better choice. Its casual, friendly atmosphere reminded me of Idwal Cottage as it was during the War, only it was much larger, you had a room to yourself and you were not expected to share the chores. It was the dream child of a remarkable man, Gerry Hill. While serving in France during World War I, he had planned a resort that would attract those who appreciated a quiet holiday in unspoilt natural surroundings. The result is such that there is little need to advertise. Word of mouth and loyal guests who return year after year have been enough.

The lodge is a log structure built around a tall arbutus tree, with extra accommodation in log cabins scattered among the trees. Jan and I shared the honeymoon suite, which had its own bathroom and a veranda facing the sea. In fact we could step off the veranda onto bare rock – and were on the beach! There was no radio or TV. The idea was to forget the outside world. But with 165 acres of woodland there was plenty to do – swim, fish, mess about in boats, play tennis, hike or cycle. Or one could simply relax on the beach or in the lounge, which had sinfully comfortable sofas, a rock fireplace big enough for six-foot logs, and the arbutus tree poking through the roof. We took our meals at table with the other guests. As the season was over, there were no more than a dozen, including another honeymoon couple. In fact even in season there was room for only about sixty. Gerry Hill had designed it that way. He was not interested in making as much money as possible, and too many guests at once would have defeated his purpose.

Our week's honeymoon flew by. On the last day, Jan called me over to introduce me to Gerry Hill. Then she said, "Mr. Hill has just given us a wedding present – another week at the Lodge!" He would never know just how much that act of generosity meant to us.

At UBC I had as usual enrolled in six courses; but having started more than a week late, I found my first maths lecture incomprehensible and so dropped the subject. I had done well in it thus far – but at the cost of too much time and effort. Somehow I didn't think Jan would appreciate my burning any midnight oil.

From the beginning she made it clear that chores should be shared. Though I detected her mother's hand in this and hoped they were not ganging up on me, I was amenable – as long as I didn't have to do the cooking. I was used to caring for myself and didn't expect to be waited on hand and foot. In fact, after spending so much time in camps I found married life an unbelievable luxury. And I was no longer alone. In Jan I had found not only a wife, but a partner and companion as well – a lovely, intelligent and entertaining one.

We soon settled into a routine. We had no TV, but we had a radio and listened to the CBC morning news as we breakfasted. It was always preceded by a joyful and triumphant little trumpet piece by Bach. I have since heard it only once but still associate it with that happy time. Then we would leave together, walk one block to 41st Avenue and wait on opposite sides for our buses – mine to UBC, hers to downtown, where she worked for the Thomas Cook travel agency. After supper, while I got down to my studies, Jan would take a nap on the sofa. At the time I thought it a little odd. She was only twenty four, after all, and her work could not have been that hard. The reason would become apparent soon enough. As for me, for a change

I had a light load – four courses. The fifth required no study. Thinking I would have six courses, I had enrolled in Harry Adaskin's music appreciation course as a treat. The light load was to prove fortunate.

November, 1956. We had been married for not quite two months. While researching for an essay, I had just read an item about the physiologist Pavlov. The Neva had overflowed its banks, flooding St. Petersburg, and Pavlov had rushed to save the dogs in his basement laboratory. He arrived to find that it was already flooded and that some of the dogs had only inches of air space left in their cages and were hysterical with terror. Later, quite by chance, he made a discovery that interested him greatly. *He had only to trickle a little water under the door for some dogs to be instantly reduced to terror again.* On reading this, I became interested as well. How ridiculous for a dog to be terrified of a mere trickle of water! *Or for me to be terrified of a little drunk!* I was stunned. Surely people would not be affected in the same way as dogs. No? Any British child would know the truth of the conditioned response: sweets come in paper bags, and the mere rustle of a paper bag instantly causes one's mouth to water. And so I became aware of dissociation, a condition in which one part of the brain takes control while the rest is frozen helpless. Usually it is caused by a trauma of some kind and in severe cases may result in dual or even multiple personality. The feeling I'd had in Kitimat, of being a helpless observer of myself, I had had before – as a terrified boy in the grasp of Blue Jowls! Had the intruder resembled him in some way? Or had the terrified boy been due to break out anyway and had been awaiting only the chance?

I can see, now, that there had been warning signs. A sudden attack of stage fright as I was beginning a brief assigned talk to a class in my second year at UBC! Dry mouth, uncontrollable shaking! It had come as a humiliating shock. After all, I had been ready and confident beforehand and had once faced a theatre audience of hundreds with no problem. Then there was the feeling of oppression before the event at Kitimat. There was nothing psychic about it. It was as if I had sensed at some level that Junior was on his way. I know this to be true, as I was to experience the feeling again, decades later. There had been one other warning, the clearest of all: my second recurrent dream, nightmare rather, the one which had come to me at Last Chance and made me fear to sleep. The disembodied face that had swum up from the darkness of the pit and hissed menacingly, "Rememberrr", a black face with white markings – it had been the negative image of Blue Jowls!

I had been right about the cadet at Brough, then. Someone *had* got to him as a child. And Riever on his bucket like a child on its potty. At the time, that was what he had become again. It takes no great leap of imagination to guess who was responsible for his original trauma. Now I was glad that I had not judged them. Had I done so, I would have condemned myself.

The revelation helped, but only a little. What had happened may have been beyond my control, but the humiliation remained – for I still *felt* like a coward. Believing that Junior could take over and humiliate me again at any time, I felt I could never trust myself again. I had been robbed not only of my pride but also of my peace of mind.

Cowards die many times before their deaths;
The valiant never taste of death but once.
Shakespeare's Caesar confuses valour with fearlessness. They are not the same. There was one thing more I had learned – why I tend to freeze when something unexpected happens. Blue Jowls had seized me before I had even seen him. It was the suddenness of the attack that had done the damage. For good reason I do not like surprises.

I told Jan nothing of this, for events were to drive it from my mind. As we lay in bed together a night or so later, I became aware that she was silently weeping. Alarmed, I asked, "What on earth is the matter, Sweetheart?" "There's a lump in my breast," she whispered.

ॐ

3
Cherry Blossom

Kathy picked us up in the morning and drove Jan to her doctor, dropping me at her house on the way. The lump was a large one. How could he have missed it? When they returned, Jan and I locked eyes – and then she ran and threw herself into my arms. There was no need for words. The tumour was malignant. Her pallor and her evening naps had been explained in the cruellest possible way. There was more, something I was not told until much later: with brutal directness, the doctor had told them that the cancer had spread, that metastasis had advanced so far that it was too late to save her.

The following days were nightmarish. Kathy immediately sought another doctor, one less defeatist, and on the advice of a friend engaged Dr. L. C. Steindel, a choice we never regretted. (Inevitably, Jan nicknamed him "Elsie".) Further examinations followed, and then Jan and I found ourselves waiting outside an office while Dr. Steindel and specialists discussed the course of treatment. We knew already what the choices were: radical mastectomy and radiation therapy, or radiation therapy alone. Neither of us voiced our fears as we sat holding hands, but to me the thought of her tender young body under the knife was unbearable. The decision, radiation therapy alone, thus came as an immense relief – although it meant, of course, that her condition was too far gone for surgery to be effective. And we both knew it. As for our lovemaking, warned that pregnancy would cause the cancer to explode, we had to take such extreme precautions that it resembled a clinical exercise.

Throughout, Jan continued to work and I to attend lectures as best we could; but I couldn't bring myself to study for the forthcoming term exams and had to ask the Dean to have my grades based on course work and the finals alone. Meanwhile, Les had a suite put in his basement, and we moved in just before Christmas. In addition to a washroom and a toilet we now had a bedsitter with its own window and a double bed in place of the sofa. We had no need for a kitchen as we ate with her parents. The festive season that year was not a happy one, but we hid our fears and were as cheerful as possible under the circumstances.

Another of Kathy's friends put us in touch with "The Infinite Way," a religious movement based upon the teaching of Joel Goldsmith. The local group was led by Jessie Porter, a bright, intelligent woman in her sixties, and Jan and I began to attend weekly meetings in her West End apartment. At this remove I cannot recall the teaching in detail, but it was akin to Christian Science. In essence, the movement held out the possibility of spiritual healing. While I knew healings inexplicable to science have taken place, like some reported at Lourdes, for instance, I also knew only too well that they were rare. Still, Jessie gave us hope, and for that I shall be forever grateful. We may have been clutching at straws but, illusory or not, that hope forced us to think positively and helped hold despair at bay. As a result, our remaining time together was happier than it otherwise could have been.

One fine day in March, following a session at the cancer clinic, Jan and I chose to walk home. It wasn't far – little more than a mile. A warm sun was shining, birds were singing, trees were in bud and the cherries in bloom. Spring had arrived in a rush – the time when nature explodes into life, the time of hope, of renewal, of the Resurrection. Coming across a small cherry ablaze with blossom, we paused, arm in arm, to gaze in wonder. "Oh," Jan murmured, "how proud it must be!" I looked at her. There was no pain as yet, the therapy was having no unpleasant side effects, and there were no outward signs of anything wrong. My wife looked lovely as ever. But the contrast between the life that was flourishing about us and what was growing within her struck me dumb.

April, 1957. After my finals, I was taken on at my regular liquor store and was soon made cashier. "Now you have a job you must get yourself a car," said Les one day and drove me to Terry's English Car Service. A little later, $100 poorer, I drove off in my first car, a used Ford Prefect. A khaki jalopy long overdue for the scrapyard, it died on us regularly for the first month. "Probably the points," said Terry, scratching his head. Removing the distributor cap, he filed them a little. "There. That oughta do it." "Could it be a loose wire?" I suggested when I returned the car again. "Dunno," Terry confessed, scratching his head. "Maybe it's the alternator. I've got a used one here. We'll try that." Eventually, I drove to a tune-up shop and explained the problem. The mechanic reached behind the dashboard and fiddled with something. "What was it?" I asked. "Loose wire," he replied.

To give the car its due, it never let us down again. Mind, I had to run a hose from the oil intake to the outside atmosphere to avoid our being overcome by fumes, and its speed was limited to 40 mph. If I attempted to drive faster, the car would shimmy and weave in a most alarming fashion. As a result our progress along a highway resembled a funeral cortège, with us in the lead and a long tail of frustrated drivers behind. Still, it enabled me to drive Jan to the clinic, to Jessie Porter, the beach – or anywhere we fancied. It even managed to get us to Mount Baker and back in one piece.

If the car did break down once more, this time it was the fault of the driver. We had driven to Jessie's place for our weekly session, but for some reason I didn't want to go in that day and I told Jan as much. "You go and I'll pick you up later," I promised. "Don't bother," she replied. "I'll take a cab." "Don't be silly. It's no bother. I'll pick you up." But no, she was adamant, obviously put out because I didn't want to come with her. At last I exploded, "Bloodywell take a cab, then." Slamming the car door, I threw the gear into first and then stamped on the accelerator. There was a loud bang, and the car refused to move. I had broken an axle. Neither of us saw Jessie that day. After towing me to a garage, Les drove us home. As we sat together in the back, Jan turned to me. "You see," she said demurely. "You see what happens when you get stroppy with me."

It was in the car that I made the discovery. As we sat on Burrard Bridge one day, stalled in a traffic jam, it seemed that once more I was enveloped in love, that it played about me like an invisible lambent flame. I knew that I loved Jan, had done from the beginning, but now I knew myself to be that most fortunate of men – one who has fallen in love with his wife.

"Oh, My Babies!"

The therapy seemed to be going well, but a day came when we were told that Jan's ovaries had to be removed. Her estrogen was feeding the cancer and had to be reduced. "Oh, my babies!" she murmured. Now we would never have children of our own. I could only look at her in helpless misery. Visiting her after the operation, I was dismayed to find her still unconscious and looking pale as death. "She's all right," the nurse hastened to reassure me. "It's the effect of the anaesthetic." There followed several days for observation, and then Jan was allowed home. While recuperating, she was to sleep in her old bedroom.

A week or so later, Kathy called me into Jan's room. "Feel," Jan said, pointing. Gently I probed her breast with my fingertips. "There's nothing there!" I exclaimed. "It's gone!" And again we locked eyes, this time with dawning hope.

It would prove to be a cruel, false dawn. A cancerous tumour well deserves to be called "malignant". With no warning pain, it stealthily establishes itself in the unsuspecting victim and then, if not found and treated in time, sends forth colonies to other parts of the victim's body, where they remain more or less dormant. If the original tumour is removed, however, these colonies spring to life. Then comes the pain. Doctors know this. But as yet we did not.

A doomed hope is still better than none, and during the following months we were happy together. There had been one small consolation for the operation: for the first time it freed us from fear of pregnancy and allowed us to make love as nature intended. I think Jan believed this to be rather naughty, for she later asked me never to tell anyone what we did. It was an unnecessary request. Unlike some boastful youths, men do not discuss such things with their friends. Besides, we married as virgins, were never more than children in the art of lovemaking, and what we did was informed by love. Meanwhile, at the age of twenty-five Jan had to undergo the hot flushes of menopause.

September arrived, along with fall and our first anniversary. We would have liked to celebrate it at Yellow Point, of course, but Jan was working again and neither of us was in a position to ask for time off. Instead, I gave her a small addition to our family – a dachshund puppy, which we named Simon. Her parents had a dog – Granny, a watery-eyed chihuahua of advanced age and uncertain temper. But Simon was ours. Now we were three.

"Farewell, Gentlemen"

Christmas, 1957, was happier than the previous one. Touring the shops with Kathy to find something for Jan, I saw a black knitted ensemble with an enormous white collar and pendant tassel. It was expensive, but Kathy liked it too and we bought it together. Jan wore it Christmas Day and looked ravishing. In return she and Kathy presented me with a telescope kit, consisting of a pyrex blank, glass tool, grinding and polishing powders, eyepiece and a diagonal flat – all the essentials for a six-inch reflector. Jan knew of my interest in astronomy and at some time or other I must have mentioned that I would like to build a telescope of my own one day. Now I had to put up or shut up. We rounded out Christmas week at a New Year's Eve party in a friend's house. Jan went as Nititis, Princess of the Nile. She was a woman now, no longer the sylph who had worn the costume in the play; but with Kathy's help and a few judicious safety pins, she just made it.

One advantage of the kit was that it gave me something else to think about. No instructions came with it, but I found a book of articles on mirror-grinding that had been published over the years in *Scientific American*. The earliest had been contributed by William Parsons, Earl of Ross, who had died in 1867. I began by filling a barrel with rocks and fastening the glass tool firmly to the top. This was my work bench. Next, I labeled some salt cellars to keep different grades of grinding powder separate, as mixing them could cost hours of extra work.

Then, with Simon eager to help and Jan recording our progress with little sketches – as she did throughout our marriage – I was ready for the grinding. Beginning with the coarsest powder, one does this by rubbing the mirror blank forward and back on the tool in short strokes. This grinds the middle of the blank more than the edges. Every few strokes, the blank must be rotated a little and a step taken round the barrel. Once the mirror has a deep enough concavity, it is ground with ever finer powders to a satiny finish. The result is a spherical mirror.

The next stage, polishing and figuring, is the tricky one. The tool is covered with beeswax, scored with cross-hatching, and then the mirror polished with cesium oxide (if I recall rightly). Every half hour or so, a foucault knife-edge test must be done. This calls for a light to be shone on the mirror and the edge of a knife placed at the focal point of the reflection. The pattern of the shadows this casts onto the mirror shows whether or not the mirror has the desired parabolic shape. If it hasn't, the beeswax tool must be reshaped and the figuring begun anew.

After bringing the mirror to the desired state, I mailed it off to be coated. It was then late February. But by the time it was returned I was no longer interested.

In late March, one year from the time we had stood entranced before the cherry tree, Jan took a week off from work and flew to Hawaii to see Joel Goldsmith, the hope being that this might add one more weapon to our spiritual armoury. On her return, she was wearing sandals, a black and white muu-muu, some fragrant leis – and looked radiant. I felt proud of her. She placed a lei around my neck and then we embraced. But she had little to say about her visit with Joel.

It was shortly after her return that the pains began. When Jan told me, I uttered a cry of anger and despair. Bitter reality was made manifest at last. The hope we had been clinging to was gone. We had been fooling ourselves. There was to be no healing, not spiritual or otherwise. She was going to die, was in fact dying. A little later, calmer than I, she quietly handed me two of her little sketches, one with the caption "i am glum tonite", and the other, "but I can still beetcha at ping pong." It was typical of her spirit that she should try to cheer me up!

Time began to play tricks, or so it seemed to me. It was as if the cancer, sure at last of its victim, had redoubled in virulence. Having invaded the pleural cavity, it began to make breathing difficult. One or two drives, a final visit to the beach – and soon Jan was forced to take to her own bed. There were visits by Dr. Steindel to drain her pleural cavity. Now no longer strong enough to walk, she left her bed only when we took her to the living-room for an hour of television in the evening. Throughout, all of us hid our feelings, not least Jan herself, and kept up the appearance of cheerfulness.

St. Anselm's, September 22, 1956   Final Visit to the Beach, April, 1958

Last Sketch

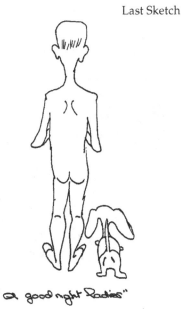 

"a good night Ladies"   "farewell gentlemen"

Author, Peace River, 1967   Author, Mt. Stephen, 1962

English 91 (Lit. 12), c. 1966

The Hales: John, Wendy, Monica,
Andrew and his bride, Yvonne, 2001

392

It was only when removed to the hospital that she broke down. She wanted to go back home. Looking up at me she cried, "What kind of man are you?" *No man at all*, I thought wretchedly. It had been the doctor's decision. She required constant care now and would soon need oxygen. There was nothing I or her parents could do about it. Yet I felt I should have torn down the walls of heaven for her. The next time we saw her, however, she was her usual cheerful self, and remained so to the end.

Discussing Jan's condition with Dr. Steindel, I remarked on the sudden spurt in the cancer's growth. "Yes," he said. "Removing the ovaries bought us time, but unfortunately the pituitary gland eventually takes over production of the estrogen." Pausing, he added tentatively, "Of course, we could always operate." *Subject my darling to brain surgery?* "No," I said. "It would only prolong her dying!" He nodded. And that, rightly or wrongly, was that.

We visited her every day. Being on evening shift, I would drop in again on my way home and sit with her a while. But by then she was asleep and unaware of me. Once placed in an oxygen tent, she gradually retreated within herself, absorbed in the intensely personal business of dying. For my part I felt like one of the living dead, outwardly normal – sleeping, eating, working – but inwardly held in a state of suspended animation.

May 25. "Philip!" I awoke with a start. It was Kathy, still in her night clothes. "They want you at the hospital." Climbing into my pants and throwing a coat over my pyjamas, I grabbed the car keys and rushed off. As it was early Sunday morning, I merely slowed for stop signs. But I was too late. Jan was dead, her face contorted in its final rictus. I stood looking down at her for a while, then I stooped and kissed her on the neck. She was warm.

As I left the ward, Kathy and Les came hurrying up, fully dressed. *How did they get here so fast?* I smiled at them. (*Smiled?*) "She's gone," I said. Moments later, or so it seemed, as I sat in my car, hunched over the wheel, Les shook my shoulder, "The doctor's here. He wants to see you." Dr. Steindel was in the corridor, talking with Kathy. He was shaven, fully dressed. "You mustn't feel bad, Doctor," I said. "You did all that you could do." There was a moment's silence, and then he said, "I have something to say to you, although you may not understand it now: Try to think of what you have been given and not of what you have lost." I looked at him dumbly – and then returned to the car.

So, it was over. I understood Dr. Steindel well enough. In the state I was then the words might have come from God himself. Translated as "Count your blessings and try not to feel sorry for yourself," they imply that the grief one feels is not for the other but for oneself. While I am sure the doctor meant no such thing, that is the implication – and I felt sick, for I saw an element of truth in it. We cannot feel another's pain. We feel only our own. The best we can do is empathize. Still, it wasn't a matter of thinking about my loss. After all, the loss was not mine alone. Jan had lost everything. It was a matter of my feeling it. About that I had no choice. Whatever the truth, grief is one measure of our love.

There was some consolation. Jan had not been marked externally. She was spared that. And although it had been a slow and cruel death, it had failed to overcome her spirit. Throughout, she had borne herself cheerfully, without complaint, and had died with courage and grace. There was something else. On one of our last occasions together she had whispered to me, "I feel surrounded by love." I felt then that all was well with her. She was in God's hands.

Jan died two months short of her twenty-sixth birthday. I could only imagine how Kathy and Les must have felt. As for me, the world had become an ashheap.

CHAPTER NINETEEN

Teacher

1
Duty

Following Jan's death, for our mutual support I continued living with her parents – but in her old room, as the suite was rented out. I finished building the telescope and then turned it on the heavens. More stars were visible, of course, but space seemed even vaster than before. Emptiness regarded the void and the void stared back. Then I took the telescope apart. I never used it again.

In May, 1960, as one in a long line of gowned figures, I had my hand shaken by Dean Gage and was awarded my degree. Then I rejoined my supporters, Kathy and Mrs. Steindel. The latter had every right to be there, for it was her husband's refusal to present a bill that made my early graduation possible. As I had taken a third-year course in my second year, I had needed only four more for my degree. Three I had completed in summer sessions, the fourth during teacher-training. Unfortunately, cramming in my final year in this fashion affected my grades and I had to be content with a Second.

I cannot say I enjoyed my year in the Faculty of Education. Apart from the philosophy of education, most of which I soon forgot, I found the courses boring and for the first weeks retired to my car between lectures and read the *Confessions* of St. Augustine. Later, however, I spent much of my free time in the cafeteria, drinking coffee and having bull sessions with a group of my fellows – all graduates and some from other professions. It was a relief from the stultifying atmosphere in the classes.

One of the group, Perry Darling, was to become a life-long friend. A fruit farmer from the Okanagan, he was shy and his appearance and mannerisms put me in mind of a middle-aged English country vicar. He was a gentleman, in other words, and one with a passion for Mozart. He had recently separated from his wife. Under what circumstances he did not say, but his somewhat hesitant manner of speech suggested that his self-confidence had been shaken and did not augur well for his future in the classroom. In the event, throughout his one-week fall practicum[22] his overstrained nervous system treated him to diarrhoea and wisely he dropped out. He was lucky to discover his unsuitability early. Having a science degree, he instead went on to pursue a less stressful career at a centre for tick research in Kamloops. But we were to keep in touch for the rest of his life.

My own practicum – at Vancouver Tech, a high school of some two thousand students – had gone well enough, though the principal had given me food for thought. He had challenged me in an empty corridor one day: "Who are you?"

"I'm a practice teacher."

"Teaching what?"

"English."

Already walking away, he tossed a parting shot over his shoulder, "Ah, 'Hail to thee, blithe spirit' and all that sort of rot, eh?"

My spring practicum, however, had been a disaster. In theory one was supposed to observe the sponsor teacher for a while, take over one or two of his classes, receive some helpful criticism and then by the third and last week of the practicum assume his full load. That is not what happened. Lucky Jim nervously enters

---

22   A period spent in a school to observe and practice teaching

a classroom in Squamish High School. The students, Grade 8's, are already at their desks. Their teacher, a middle-aged woman, eyes me up and down for a moment and then snaps, "Well, are you ready to take over?" Startled, I stammer, "I thought I might observe for a while first." "Hmph," she snorts. She teaches for that period, dismisses the class, and then, throwing up her hands with an air of finality, says, "There. It's all yours." Whereupon she leaves the room – for a holiday, apparently, for I see her no more.

If I recall virtually nothing of the next three weeks, it is perhaps not surprising. I had been given a copy of her timetable and a rough outline of where to go, but I had only two lessons ready – one each for English and Social Studies. Much desperate burning of the proverbial oil in my motel, conjuring up lessons mostly out of thin air. My experience having been a few periods of teaching English to Grade 11 boys, I was about a thousand feet above the heads of my unfortunate Grade 8's. Some had a break from me, however. One day, the English department head asked if I would like to teach her Grade 11's for a period. Yes, I would. Grade 11's! After Grade 8's they seem virtual adults, eyes bright with intelligence and a desire for knowledge. Not receiving an assigned topic, I decide upon a comparison and contrast between Browning's "Rabbi Ben Ezra" and "The Rubaiyat of Omar Khayyam." At the appointed hour, there follows a dissertation on this fascinating topic and a board full of notes. Then I pause and ask for questions. A long silence ensues. At last a hand creeps up and a voice asks timidly, "Are you going to teach at university, Sir?"

An intelligent question! My "lesson" was of course preposterous, doubly so since it is highly unlikely that anyone in the class had even heard of the selections let alone read them. In self-defence I can only plead that I was in a state of desperation bordering on lunacy.

But the best was yet to come:

After an aeon the yearned-for final period arrives – and with it cometh the Inspector-General, that is, an inspector from the Faculty of Education. Sixtyish and gaunt, he wears a pepper-and-salt suit and a jaundiced look. Afflicted with terminal dyspepsia, perhaps. Somehow, I get through the lesson and dismiss the class. Then, while most of the students are still in the room and making no effort to keep his voice down, he tears into me. Why did I do that? Can I explain why I failed to do this? Why did I not have a piece of string? *Etcetera*. Finally, he pronounces judgment, "You've no business being a teacher!" With that, he stalks out.

In a letter to Jan, written at Last Chance, I had announced somewhat dramatically, "Be of good cheer. I shall arise like the phoenix." And so I had – only to be shredded in mid-flight. Thus on graduation day, as I posed in my (rented) gown for Kathy to take my photograph, I felt no pride in my achievement, not even satisfaction. It might be said that I was discouraged.

In the full expectation that my first year as a teacher would prove yet another humiliating disaster, I selected Maple Ridge for my debut, it being as far as possible from where I lived yet still within reasonable commuting distance, one hour's drive. In the event, the disaster did not happen. But that first year, teaching Grade 10 English and history at Maple Ridge High School, with a class of Health and Personal Development thrown in, proved an unremitting treadmill. Mindful of my painful experience at Squamish, I left nothing to chance. My lessons were organized down to the last detail and my marking was conscientious. As the lessons had to be produced from scratch and the marking load was considerable, each class having thirty-five to forty students, I had relatively little sleep, five hours a night at most. I managed only by taking an hour's nap after supper. Drained by the day in the classroom, I felt unable to face hours of lesson-preparation without first seeking sanctuary in temporary oblivion.

I cannot say I was a good teacher that year, but I was learning my trade. The powers-that-be thought well enough of me, anyway, for at the end of June I was transferred to Garibaldi Junior High as a replacement for their senior English teacher, who had been made a principal. Garibaldi was slated to become a senior high, and I was to teach their first Grade 10's.

Having survived my first year, in the summer of 1961 I moved into a cottage in Maple Ridge. I was to remain there and teach at Garibaldi for the next nine years, in which time the school became a senior high and its enrolment almost doubled. It was a happy school on the whole. The staff got on well together, and to my pleased surprise I discovered that I liked my students. Generally, I found them fair-minded, even generous (if one did one's job!), and I remember many with affection. They were not angels, of course. One beginning teacher had a terrible time – day after day his classes in an uproar and a stream of students sent to the office for discipline. Apparently some had even thrown things at him in the classroom. For his students it was a wasted year; for him, a nightmare that probably tormented his sleep for decades.

June, 1964, saw our first graduating class, seventy-five or so young men and women. Over forty of them had elected to take En. 91 (later renamed En. Lit. 12.) with me. Chiefly poetry, *Beowulf* to the modern period, this excellent course also had two plays (*Macbeth*, Synge's *Riders to the Sea*) and a variety of essays and short stories. Like many such survey courses, though, it was overlong, and so finishing in time for the government exam was a bit of a scramble. Despite this, all had passed – a testament to their love of literature and their willingness to work. This pass rate was to be maintained over succeeding years, though from time to time a student might drop out because of the heavy workload. My part in all this was to fill in some background, to clarify difficulties, and to allow Chaucer, Shakespeare, *et al.*, to speak for themselves. Naturally, my own love of literature also helped.

A selection I had difficulty reading without emotion was Lamb's "Dream Children." For a different reason there was one I could not bring myself to read to the class at all – Dryden's "Alexander's Feast", in which as if to the clash of cymbals the chorus chants, "Happy, happy, happy pair! None but the brave, None but the brave, None but the brave deserves the fair." On the other hand, my sympathy for Macbeth, with his mind "full of scorpions," and for Milton's new-fallen Satan, tormented by the thought "of lost happiness and lasting pain," probably gave my reading of them added force.

In addition to fairness and kindness, good teaching calls for focus, consistency and firmness – or things soon fall apart. I owe my students more than they know, for having thus to focus my whole attention on the task at hand not only helped them but also had the further beneficial effect of preventing my mind from dwelling on itself. I was at peace in the classroom.

During the school year, then, I had work enough, together with the comfort of music and books, to keep my scorpions at bay. Long week-ends, Christmas and Easter, all spent with Kathy and Les, came as welcome breaks. The problem emerged in the summer holidays. Though these, too, were welcome; it was then that the emptiness of my life weighed heavily and sometimes set my mind to gnawing at itself like an injured dog. It was not only the loss of my wife and the canker of the Kitimat experience that stung. The fact is that I have an over-active superego, if there is such a thing. Conscience, anyway. This denies me credit for virtues, but lashes me mercilessly for my failings. It claims that praise of me is ill-merited, but that all criticism is fully deserved. In trying to make me feel guilty even for my grief, its interpretation of Dr. Steindel's well-meant advice is typical.

Still, despite this tyranny I lay no claim to being a terrible sinner of the kind seen in James Thomson's lines:

> Once in a saintly passion
>   I cried with desperate grief,
> "O Lord, my heart is black with guile,
>   Of sinners I am chief."
> Then stooped my guardian angel
>   And whispered from behind,
> "Vanity, my little man,
>   You're nothing of the kind."

No, nor am I. Nonetheless, I am inordinately sensitive to my failings. An inverted form of pride, perhaps? If so, I have been well paid for it.

Inevitably, depression and I often become fellows. Blaming myself for this, as I do, only depressess me further, as does the thought that untold millions have to endure real suffering. I take no comfort from the misery of others, quite the contrary. As for telling myself to snap out of it, that is little better. I endure in the hope that I have done my duty to the best of my ability, and by reminding myself that depression is a temporary state. Fortunately for me, it is.

❦

2

Summer Explorations

Given my social exposure as a teacher and my tendency to be a loner, not surprisingly I sought little social life during those years. Nearly all my friends were married, of course, and I became "uncle" to seven children, godfather to two and had two named after me. But a single, middle-aged man, like a maiden aunt, is a spare ha'penny and something of an embarrassment both to himself and perhaps to his friends. As for dating, unless I viewed the woman as a prospective wife, I saw little point. In 1964, however, I became strongly attracted to a waitress in a café I sometimes patronized. There was a wholesomeness about her that drew me. But when eventually I suggested a date, she smiled and said she had a boyfriend. Thinking "faint heart ne'er won a fair lady," as my mother had told me more than once, I phoned the café the next night. But I didn't know her name, of course, and so the person who answered, understanding the situation right away, exploded, "Listen, stop bothering the girl, or I'll call the police." It seems she had been subjected to unwelcome attention from others. Naturally, despite my wholly honourable intentions, I immediately felt like a seedy stalker and gave up. Perhaps it was just as well, as I was thirty-eight and she no more than twenty. Despondently tossing his climbing gear into his car, Faintheart then left for the Rockies. There has been no other woman since, although some have shown interest in me.

Perhaps because of this rejection, that summer I felt lonelier than usual; and after weeks of speaking to no one but gas station attendants ("Fill her up") and waitresses ("Sunny side up") in near desperation I took a climbing course in Banff. But if I had expected my loneliness to be assuaged, I was to be disappointed.

401

Our rock-climbing mentor, a pudgy little Englishman, made no secret of the fact that he detested me from the moment I opened my mouth; and my fellows, a generation younger than I, had little time for a quiet, rather melancholy middle-aged man and on the whole ignored me.

Nonetheless, despite being made to feel an utter outsider, I found the experience worthwhile, for the course finished with two climbs – an interesting rock climb on Castle Mountain (the summit ridge was reached through a hole at the top of a chimney) and an ascent of the north peak of Mt. Victoria. It was on the latter that at last I saw the climbing style of a professional guide demonstrated – in this case by our leader, Peter Fuhrmann. It was a lounging pace, slower than I had expected, and regardless of the slope the same rhythm was maintained right to the summit. Like an infinitely variable gear, only the length of stride changed. As a result, far from panting and sweating, I found the climb virtually effortless, all 5,500 or so feet of it. Apart from a brief pause on the glacier to strap on crampons and rope up, we rested only twice – to breakfast as sunrise reddened the summit high above us and to enjoy the view when we arrived there. Clouds gathered on our descent; and as we stepped off the glacier, thunder began to growl and grumble about the peaks. My one experience of true mountaineering had been perfect. Almost.

Except for one summer at UBC to pick up the extra credits needed for my permanent teaching certificate, all were spent visiting family in England or exploring B.C. and the Rockies. This exploration, alone and with friends, by car and on foot, has left me with many good memories. Of a solo hike to Berg Lake, for instance, where I climbed above the snowline to about 9,000 feet in order to obtain a better view of Mt. Robson. It is from such a viewpoint, high on a neighbouring peak, that a mountain's scale can best be appreciated. Viewed from its foot, it is foreshortened. And of a month spent climbing in the Rockies with Ralph Wass, the level-headed Yorkshireman who had been education officer at the B.C Pen. Linking up with a young couple at Radium Hot Springs, we hiked over Ferro Pass to Mt. Assiniboine and then camped by Cerulean Lake for a week. Although we had ice axes and ropes, we were not equipped for serious mountaineering; and so, gaze longingly though we might, Mt. Assiniboine was out. But we climbed where we could. On one mountain we were led by a mountain goat, which casually nibbled its way up faster than we could follow; and on another by the wife, who emulated the goat and left us men toiling in her wake. On reaching the top, we found her stretched out, pretending to be asleep. I don't know how the husband felt, but I had to resist an urge to give her a good kick.

On leaving Assiniboine we split up and Ralph and I went on to Yoho, where we climbed Mt. Stephen. Our route was a mere scramble; but the first 3000 feet or so, consisting largely of steep hardpan, had no level place even for the foot and in consequence was as tiresome to descend as to climb. Still, the view from the top was worth the effort. The drop-off is sensational, and the transcontinental train crawling along its track a vertical mile beneath our feet seemed little more than a silver millepede.

I have pleasant memories, too, of times spent with Ralph and his family. For a while, he and his wife Jenny taught in Maple Ridge, and I often spent Friday evenings at their home. Ralph made a point of welcoming me at the door with an opened bottle of beer, and as a result the children took to calling me "Uncle Beer." With the children abed, Jenny would go off for a nap and Ralph and I would blow off steam by playing table tennis according to a cunning handicap – the winner of a point had to take a swig of wine. After a while, Jenny would reappear and in ten minutes have a magnificent meal on the table. It was a pleasant way to unwind after a week's teaching.

The couple had a remarkable ability for finding interesting places. Years before the Hippies discovered Long Beach, on the west coast of Vancouver Island, we had camped there and had the whole beach to ourselves. It was then accessible by logging road and only on weekends. On another memorable weekend we had an entire park to ourselves – Sidney Spit, a marine park on the north end of Sidney Island. As we sat by the campfire, digesting our supper under the stars, Ralph decided to wade out to pull in a tethered raft floating offshore. Suddenly there was a shout, and in a cloud of spray he came galloping back like a high-stepping pacer under the lash. "Bloody great fish," he gasped. "Swam right up to me!" This brought precious little sympathy from his wife. "Men!" she scoffed witheringly. Hoisting her skirt, she thereupon waded out to pull it in herself. "It's all right for you," Ralph shouted after her. "You haven't as much to lose." He and I then spent over an hour on the raft with a flashlight, watching the fish large and small that, attracted by the light, swam out of the darkness – phantom fish, fish visible only as eerie outlines of phosphorescence. A hand plunged into the sea became similarly adorned, and a splash created a glittering shower. Magical!

Once they'd had enough of Maple Ridge, they decided to try teaching in one-room schools in the Chilcotin. I helped them to move there, Ralph driving his family and belongings in an old Woodward's van, and I their car, a twin of my old Ford Prefect. Leaving them at Riske Creek, I flew out from Bella Coola, where in 1793 Alexander Mackenzie had reached the Pacific "from Canada, by land". Getting there involved my taking a bus journey over 250 miles of dirt road through virtually unpopulated country – a mere handful of scattered ranches, fish camps, and small communities. (With so few passengers, the bus probably paid only because it also transported essential supplies, such as tobacco and booze.) It was on this trip that, outside of paintings, I saw my first highland cattle. And the fishing lodge where we stopped for lunch would have looked more at home in the Black Forest. Cats, dogs, goats, chickens, ducks and farmyard geese wandered freely; and the lodge, built out of varnished peeled logs, was spotless inside and out. The interior, austerely adorned with fine prints of David's neo-classical paintings, no doubt reflected the taste of the owner's wife, who put me in mind of a German hausfrau. I learned later that she was in fact German and had once been an opera singer. The final section of road, which we covered at night, involves a descent of about 5,000 feet – mostly by means of steep switchbacks on what is known locally as "The Hill." Considering a road there not feasible, or more likely too expensive, the B.C. government had declined to build one, and so the locals had rallied forces and built it themselves. B.C. is full of such surprises – and such people.

In the summer of 1967 a colleague, Walter du Temple, invited me to celebrate Canada's centenary with him by taking a canoe trip

from the watershed near Prince George to Peace River City, in
north Alberta, a river distance of some 450 miles. Our route, via
the Parsnip to Finlay Forks and thence down the Peace, would
partly retrace the voyages of Alexander Mackenzie, Simon Fraser
and a redoubtable Governor of the Hudson's Bay Company, Sir
George Simpson – only we would be going downstream all the
way. It was the chance of a lifetime. Drawing up a plan and lists
of supplies proved a pleasure in itself. For a canoe, we decided
on a traditional wooden design and bought a beautiful 18-foot
Chestnut, which we named "The Green Lady."

In the event, we didn't set off from the watershed. All the
launch sites at Summit Lake seemed to be private property, one
even sporting the sign "Launching Fee $1.00." Beginning our
wilderness adventure by launching from someone's backyard not
being to our taste, we instead had our transport drive us to the
public park on Mcleod Lake and we camped on the beach. The
next morning was spent sorting out our gear and tying it up in
plastic bags. After lunch, these were loaded into the canoe and
then secured under a canvas cover firmly lashed to the gunwales,
thus ensuring, we hoped, that the bags would remain aboard if
we overturned and keep us afloat if we were swamped. As a final
touch, we hung an ensign at the stern. Then, although delayed
until late afternoon by a headwind that kicked up sizable waves,
we set out on our voyage.

That evening, as we made camp on a sandbar near old Fort
Mcleod, two Indians came by and began setting fish nets. Their
canoe, I noted, had an outboard motor. Only romantics paddle
now. Crossing the lake in the face of the wind had been tiring
to unaccustomed muscles and our progress had been slow; but
next morning all suddenly changed upon our entering the little
Pack River. As if seized by a living thing, we were carried off, and
I now began to feel a part of nature instead of merely a tourist
observing it. It was exhilarating.

In the afternoon, having crossed Tudyah Lake amid rain
squalls and rainbows, we made ready for our first rapids. "Cross
Rapids," said Wally. "Nothing to worry about. It's the other two
we must watch out for – the Finlay and Ne Parle Pas rapids on
the Peace." Nothing to worry about? Good. But upon re-entering

the Pack, we were whisked around a bend and found ourselves facing shallows, white water, rocks everywhere. Where was the inverted "V" marking the main channel? Too late! Paddling frantically to avoid one rock, we hit another. There was an ominous crack – and then we were through. Pitching camp on a sandspit, we hauled out the canoe and checked the damage – paintwork scratched, a plank and a rib badly cracked, but the canvas was intact and the canoe leak free. We were still operational.

A little sobered and alert now to the danger, the next morning we entered the Parsnip, a fast-flowing river that slithered through the woods like an enormous olive-green snake. There were no rapids, but we had to keep a sharp lookout for sweepers and snags, either of which could overturn the canoe or, worse, wreck it. For me this proved to be the best part of the trip; but it was all too short, for by noon the next day we had reached Finlay Forks, where the Parsnip and the Finlay merge and turn east as the Peace River. We had covered 75 miles in little more than a day. Since leaving Mcleod Lake, we had seen only two men – a bearded hermit who waved from the porch of his log cabin as we swept by, and a fellow adventurer bivouacking under his upturned canoe in the manner of the voyageurs. At Finlay Forks, however, we tied up to a wooden jetty and found that it led to a small logging camp. Though it at first seemed deserted, we found the cook and persuaded him to sell us some steaks.

Before entering the Peace, Wally suggested we try going up the Finlay for a while. But after paddling hard for an hour, we turned back. Despite this effort, we had gained less than a mile – and a great deal more respect for the voyageurs. Still, even those hardy men were defeated by the swifter parts of a river and had to line up, or tow, their canoes.

Now for Finlay Rapids. The best way through is on the right, said Wally. This time his information was accurate and except for a dash or two of spray we got through without incident. That evening we camped on a sandbar, well clear of trees, and prepared our meal. So far, the weather had favoured us – cumulus clouds riding a fresh westerly, with the few rain squalls serving only to refresh us. However, as we began eating our steaks, the wind suddenly died and out of nowhere there emerged a dancing, whining, stinging cloud. Mosquitos! We had insect repellent but had not expected this onslaught: mosquitos probing everywhere, even perching on our cups, drowning in our tea, riding our hands and our steak as we tried to eat. It was frightening. Scrambling into our tent, we zipped it up, sprayed it with Raid and finished our meal in stifling discomfort. Then the wind returned with a vengeance, pouncing on our tent, shaking it violently and threatening to blow our gear away. Dashing out with shouts of relief, we pegged everything down and then brewed fresh tea. Fortunately, the mosquitos were never so bad again.

"The best line seems to be by that large rock," said Wally, "and then along the edge of the back eddy." Spotting the rapids in good time, we had beached the canoe by a small creek and walked along the bank to inspect them. Lighting our pipes, we sat and pondered, from time to time tossing in a stick to observe its progress. Finally, we made the decision – we'd go through with our gear on board. A little later and damper we were congratulating ourselves: "Well, the Ne Parle Pas wasn't so bad after all!" "No. Can't see what all the fuss is about."

Its surface as dark and smooth as obsidian, the river was running fast and deep. For some time now its course had been straight, and with the wind at our backs we had been making good time. But then, far ahead on the left bank, a structure appeared. As we drew nearer, it resolved into a signboard. Signboard? In the wilderness? Curious, we angled towards it. And then my heart leapt. Painted on it in rough red letters was this warning:

DANGER

APPROACHING NE PARLE PAS RAPIDS

WATCH FOR LOGS

Disbelievingly, we peered downriver. Where were they? The river was perfectly smooth for as far as we could see. Suddenly, I saw a flick of white, and then another and another. Spray! The rapids were lurking in ambush below our line of sight. Had it not been for the signboard we would have been into them before we knew it. As it was, we had time to inspect them at leisure and determine the best line. Anywhere else we would have been swamped.

Wally had again been misinformed – there were not three rapids to watch out for, but four.

"You're lucky. The last three canoes to go through were overturned." We were at a riverside gravel pit near Hudson Hope, where a dam blocked the way. In any case, the rapids there were too much even for the voyageurs, who had to portage round them. We wouldn't have to carry a thing, though, for the speaker had kindly offered to take us in his pickup. In the event, our portage proved more dangerous than the rapids, for he drove the dozen or so miles of dirt road at high speed, with the truck bouncing about and us hanging on desperately, each with one hand for the canoe, which threatened to carry away, and the other for our lives. "Thank you," I said, breathing more easily once we were safely at the launch site. Handing the maniac enough to buy himself a bottle or two of rye, I added, "This isn't a payment. Think of it as a thanksgiving offering." Somehow, I don't think he caught my meaning.

We had covered about 200 miles and still hadn't reached the midpoint of our voyage. Save for the men at the gravel pit, we had seen only the two Indians, the two on the Parsnip and the logging camp cook. Nor had we seen much game. It is not plentiful in that region; and as the rivers eventually drain into the Arctic Ocean, there are few salmon. There may well be plenty of other fish, but we caught few – all of them trash fish, which turn to bony mush when cooked. I can see why even the Indians there were occasionally half starved.

The rest of the voyage was uneventful. As we had portaged around Hudson Hope, the only town we passed was Fort St. John, where the Alaska Highway crosses the river. We were now in the Peace River country, a sparsely populated region of bush, large ranches and wheat farms. Not that we saw much of it, as the river runs between high bluffs most of the way. Nor did we see many people – a solitary cowboy riding the skyline, two or three in a motor launch fighting its way upstream, and the captain of a small ferry by the Alberta border. This last informed us that we had 60 miles to go, with the Dunvegan bridge first and Peace River City "around the corner." Some corner! It proved to be 50 miles long. But perhaps we had both misheard, for the distance from the border was in fact closer to 160 miles.

We were sitting in silence by the campfire, each of us alone with his thoughts. Tomorrow we would reach Peace River City and be back amid the din and rush of civilization. With the weather continuing fine and a wind freeing our camp from mosquitos, we had decided to dispense with the tent and spend our last night in the open. Slowly, daylight faded in the western sky and one by one the stars winked on until the Milky Way was revealed, shining beneath the outspread wings of Cygnus like a dash of phosphorescent spray. Tapping out our pipes, we slipped into our sleeping bags. Lightning was flickering fitfully about the northern horizon. Summer lightning – nothing to bother us. Then, with the wind blowing sand into my hair, I drifted into a dreamless sleep.

By the following summer, the dam had been completed and the diversion tunnels closed. Water backed up swiftly, eventually drowning our entire route from the Pack to the dam – and eighty miles of the Finlay as well. Deep beneath what has become the largest lake in B.C., the Ne Parle Pas Rapids have become truly silent at last.

3

Return to Plumstead III

Although the nine years at Garibaldi had been exceedingly generous to me, more and more I had a gnawing sense of life failure. By 1970 I was forty-four, rich in the love of family and friends and in the regard of my colleagues and students, but I had little to show for my years of effort. Not that I set much store by material possessions. But I cherish family, and I had no wife, no children of my own. It was then that, for reasons I thought good at the time, I resigned from my position at Garibaldi. My mother was now 70 and I wished to spend time with her before it was too late. Linda would soon be leaving home and I knew this would create a crisis for Pauline, who had built her life around her daughter. Also, I felt teaching in London would broaden my experience. Meanwhile, before leaving for England, I would take a few months off, do a little climbing and – who knows? – might even meet someone.

There may have been another reason, perhaps the real one. From the day I walked away from my school that June, I began to fall apart. It was as if I had thrown away the one thing holding me together. I believe now that the breakdown was due anyway, that subconsciously I sensed it and like a sick animal wanted to crawl off and hide.

What I did that summer I can't recall. In October I spent some time with Ralph and his family at Valemount, another interesting place they had found. From there I drove north to Chetwynd to visit a colleague, west to Terrace, then back east to the Banff-Jasper Parkway as far as Athabasca Falls, where aspens were shedding leaves of gold with no one to admire them but me. From Edith Cavell road, I hiked a dozen miles into the Tonquin Valley and bivouacked high on Mt. Clitheroe. I had little food, no tent, only a sleeping bag and a plastic sheet. As no one knew where I was, it was quite irresponsible. Back to Valemount, where I hunted moose with old Mike, one of the locals, and was in on a kill. Struggling to remove several hundred pounds of moose guts proved an interesting experience. It was cold by then, below zero at times, and the snow was deep. Thence to Victoria for Christmas with Kathy and Les. Finally, in April of 1971, after months of aimless wandering in a kind of mental limbo, I boarded the P&O cruise ship *Oronsay*, which was homeward bound at the end of a world cruise.

Ship of fools! Well, there was one fool, anyway, and my downward spiral continued. The voyage presents itself to memory now as a series of scenes. Of half-drunk ship's officers doing their duty on the dance floor (and perhaps elsewhere afterwards). Of the ship's searchlight combing the Pacific off Central America for a woman who had thrown herself overboard, and of her outspread body floating in the spotlight when it found her. Of myself, sitting alone late one night in a deserted passageway. Came a voice, "And what's your story?" It was the Staff Captain. Absorbed in thought, I hadn't heard his approach. Was my state that obvious? "I lost my wife," I replied. That was part of it, anyway. "Ah," he nodded, "I, too." "Things are not the same, are they?" I added idiotically. "No," he said.

Of a pimp who accosted me on a Kingston street to ask if I wanted a woman. He was sharply dressed – fedora, sportsjacket, purple shirt, yellow tie. "Hell, no," I laughed. "I'm trying to get away from bloody women." It was half true. I was being pursued on board by a female with blue-rinsed hair, and from port to port by letters from a friend's wife. My one sexual "adventure" had taken place with her only weeks earlier. She had persuaded herself that my affectionate farewell hug was evidence of overpowering passion and in no time at all had stripped to her knickers. I had played the part of a mesmerized rabbit. But it wasn't an affair she had been after. It was me. It had been a painful experience – not the cause of my breakdown, only a helpful boot on the way. Fortunately, I had already booked my passage home. The pimp and I had quite a chat. He told me he had been a merchant seaman at one time and knew Vancouver well.

The final scene is of elderly people feeling their way uncertainly along the ship's passageways following our docking in Southampton. I'd had no idea there were so many on board. In mid-Atlantic we had been overtaken by thirty-foot seas, kicked up by some monster of a storm to the south. Though the ship's motion had been relatively gentle, for the rollers were coming at us from directly astern, it had been enough to upset some passengers, especially the elderly. Many no doubt had dreamed of a world cruise for years – only to find themselves spending much of it in their cabins.

ೲ

If the sun and moon should doubt,
They'd immediately go out.

\- William Blake

Pauline and Reg were waiting to greet me at Southampton and drove me to Plumstead. Later, Pauline told me that Mum soon realized something was wrong with me and was frightened.

Not knowing what to do, she did the best thing she could have done – acted as if all were normal. Feeling as if my psyche had unravelled into a dust bunny, I was anything but normal. In fact I seem to have undergone some kind of psychological collapse. For two years I cultivated a small rockery in Mum's garden and made little things out of plastic. Unusually for me, I didn't haunt the public library but instead spent my evenings watching programs such as "Are You Being Served?" on the telly, that kind of safe, silly little world being about the only one I felt comfortable in. Although I had been driving for at least fifteen years, my state was such that I now took a driving course! A bit re-assured by this, I bought a wreck of a car for a hundred pounds and took Mum and George on day tours through Kent.

Twice, greatly daring, I drove them to Wales to revisit old haunts. It was there that we encountered Basil Fawlty, who was then the owner of an Aberystwyth guesthouse. As is common in such establishments, place settings for dinner were set so as to force guests to sit haunch to haunch. To give myself more elbow room, I moved to the end of our table. In a flash our host materialized at my side. "Your place is set there," he snapped, pointing a long, bony forefinger at it. He was tall, angular, and spoke with an upper middle-class English accent. "So I see," I observed mildly, "and I seem to be sitting here." For a long moment he stood glaring at me, with the unspoken question hovering between us – Which should be moved, the setting or me? The room, I noticed, had grown remarkably quiet. "Right," he exclaimed, having at last made up his mind. Suddenly seizing the setting with both hands, he slammed it down in front of me and then retreated to his post by the door. Standing with his arms folded, from there he fastened a basilisk stare on me throughout the meal, from time to time exclaiming, "Little boxes. People in little boxes. Little boxes on wheels." It seems I was not the only one having problems with his wits.

Returning to Wales alone, I climbed Snowdon, noting that almost every track had climbers and tourists, most of the latter inadequately clad, and that scavenging seagulls had supplanted the jackdaws. The thought of visiting Idwal was unbearable, and so I went on to Tal y Fan. On its summit, I thought of the time I had sat there in the snow so long ago. Where now was the confidence? the joy? the sense of oneness? Thirty years separated the man from the boy, years in which he had striven to better himself. Yet as he sat there now, musing forlornly, the man felt himself less than the boy he had once been.

While living with Mum and George I made no contribution towards my keep. I told myself that I was saving the money for them; and in fact before returning to Canada, I placed a fair sum in their postal savings accounts, splitting it so each would have "mad money". But why should I do such a thing? Was it a disguised cry for help?

Desperate, I eventually swallowed my pride and presented myself before a psychologist. I began by recounting what had happened to me at Kitimat. This proved a mistake, for he quickly cut me short. Visibly bored, he waved a hand dismissively, "Merely a case of panic. What do you expect *me* to do about it?" Glaring at him with what I hope was obvious dislike, I replied, "Give me some of your damned pills, I suppose." Oh yes, he could do that. Clearly relieved, he scribbled out a prescription and tossed it across the desk. He had given me no chance to come to the cause of the panic, to discuss dissociation, to ask why despite years of successful teaching I was having a breakdown now and what I should do about it. That I would have to work out for myself.

I should have told him to throw his physic to the dogs – and himself with it.

ʘ

Therapy

After two years flat on my face, I bestirred myself. A neighbour had asked me to tutor his teen-age grandson in English. I did so and, thus encouraged, decided it was time to resume teaching. After writing to the Inner London Education Authority, I was called to their local office and required to fill out a form detailing my life since the age of fifteen or so, which I did without of course mentioning what I had been up to, or rather brought down to, in the recent past. "With a background like this," commented the official upon reading it, "you should have the necessary inner resources." *So I should,* I thought bitterly, *only they seem to have evaporated.* Thus I became a support teacher – part time.

At my first school, a selective school for the technically minded, I was given one class of English and three of religious instruction. I soon discovered RI to be highly unpopular. Third formers tolerated it, fourth formers were sullen, and fifth formers mutinous. It was not too popular with me, either. There is a place in school for the study of comparative religion – but as an elective. Thrusting it upon the unwilling I believe to be counter-productive. As for my English class, rowdy fourth formers, they were half willing to be taught but not to work.

In addition I was asked to help a small group of sixth formers with their English. They could read a little, but knew next to no grammar and could barely write sentences. What I was expected to accomplish at that stage of their schooling I can't imagine. One teacher asked me to give extra English to her class during tutoring period. This I started to do, only to be asked by the department head to desist. There was evidently an undercurrent of dissatisfaction with the level of English in the school. One day another staff member directed my attention to a handwritten notice pinned to a board in the staffroom. Signed by the department head, it stated that he was leaving for a few days "to take a coarse [Stet] in Shakespeare." But to blame the state of English in the school upon a mildly dyslexic teacher would be grossly unjust. Possible causes are many. Only some may be systemic, perhaps dating back to beginning reading. For many of the boys, I imagine, reading would not rank high on their list of interests. And then there is the nature of the language itself. Although its structure is straightforward enough, the relationship between spelling and pronunciation can be baffling.[23]

Though I perceived the need in the school, for me to do anything about it would have required years of commitment. And before I could start, I would have to endure a year of RI. I was not prepared to do it.

The fact is I still had problems of my own. Although not in

---

[23]   Consider "ough" in the following limerick: A puff adder trying to slough / its skin in a trough by a slough / would not cause alarm / on an African farm / though it ought in the borough of Slough.

control, Junior was abroad and made me feel less than a man. I noticed I had a disturbing tendency to react to the older boys at their own level, for when faced with bad behavious or disobedience I felt a strong impulse toward violence. That is not an appropriate reaction for any man, let alone a professional teacher. Violence stems from weakness, and I'm sure the boys sensed it in me. The fact is that my mental state at the time was a terrible one. I felt as if I were standing in mid-air, clutching the shreds of my selfhood about me and with an abyss yawning beneath my feet. It is not a state I would care to experience again.

Feeling that for all the good I was doing I might just as well not be in the school at all, at the end of the term I quit.

My next school proved even more interesting. A comprehensive school of some fifteen hundred boys, it had been formed only that year by the amalgamation of a secondary modern school with a grammar school. My arrival co-incided with its second term. As might be expected, the school was having teething problems; but to me, given my state of mind, for a while it seemed more like a lunatic asylum.

I again had four classes, two of English and two of history. Two were in the new building, an edifice with two levels of classrooms on either side of a central concourse, rather like an American penitentiary without the bars. My first, an English class of upper band fourth formers, presented no discipline problem but showed little interest in anything. Teaching them was like trying to teach a wall. To condemn an entire class, of course, is to condemn the teacher. But I wasn't that bad, and it wasn't the entire class. The passive resistance stemmed from class leaders – bad apples. I identified two, but as they did nothing overtly wrong there was little I could do about them.

My second class consisted of remedial third formers, a group of about twenty boys, most of them non-white and probably there because of language difficulty. It was the small group of whites I felt sorry for, as they were virtually illiterate and at the bottom of the heap. I was supposed to teach medieval history. While it was easy enough to engage their interest with tales of knights, castles, medieval warfare and life on a feudal estate, I also had to get them actually to do something. Our textbook being simply written and well-illustrated, I prepared work-sheets for them, each with questions based on a specific paragraph – the sort of task an average student could do in five minutes. I soon discovered that unless I used the same words as those in the text, most of the boys couldn't complete them. In other words they were searching for the key words, not really reading. In an effort to encourage them I put their names on the wall and gave them a red dot for each sheet attempted and a gold star for each five. My mistake! Most collected a respectable number – one boy's collection ran half way around the room – but several whites didn't even reach their first star. They must have felt crushed. And I felt an incompetent idiot.

My other classes were held in the old grammar school, where my room was the kind with a lofty ceiling and large windows. Victorians were great believers in the benefit of fresh air. However, although equipped with a long pole for opening the windows, it had no blackboard. The schoolkeeper had to dig up one for me – the kind that goes with an easel. Pushing my desk against the wall, I propped up the board on that.

My history class there, thirty or so second formers, squirmed a lot but proved otherwise reasonably well behaved. That was promising. The blow fell when I asked them to hand in their first homework. Only three or four boys had done it; at least half hadn't bothered to bring the textbooks back, and some not even their notebooks! Thenceforth, only those boys who wished to do homework were allowed to take books home. On collecting notebooks for marking, I received another blow. Most were a scribbled mess and totally useless. Only one boy was following my directions, with his work neatly written, well spaced and with all the headings underlined with a ruler. As a reward, just before Christmas I gave him a prize, a copy of *The Hobbit*. How would the others react to that? To my surprise all spontaneously applauded. I could have wept. They were not bad boys. But most had work habits that ranged from none to poor. They were wasting their time in school.

How many boys were in my last class I don't know. They

were remedial fourth formers and at any one time only about half bothered to attend. I can't really blame them. I had them twice a week, the second time being a double period last thing in the afternoon. As far as I can recall, I had no textbooks and they had no notebooks – or if they had, they didn't bring them. What was I to do with them? Having spent at least three years doing remedial English already, they would have used all the available materials in the school. I was used to teaching senior English, for goodness sake. I had had no training in remedial work. What I did with them I have no idea. I know I felt totally incompetent and still have nightmares about it. Moreover, the behaviour of some was intolerable, at least to begin with. During my first double period with them one boy ran around the room with a felt pen, scribbling "Fuck you" on the walls. It seems he could spell. After ignoring repeated orders to desist, he at last turned and faced me defiantly, pen poised and grinning like a lunatic. He was no small boy, either, but as tall as I. Unable to stomach such behaviour, I advanced upon him. What did I intend to do? I really can't say, but if necessary I was prepared to slap that silly grin off his face. Fortunately for me, although he may not have been able to read books, he could read faces. And on reading mine, he suddenly panicked. Crying, "All right, all right, I'll clean it off," he proceeded to suit the deed to the word. I had come within a whisker of destroying myself as a teacher.

Although as a part-time support teacher I was not required to do playground duty or to stand in for absent staff, wishing to help my hard-pressed colleagues I volunteered to do both. This fit of generosity did not last. While awaiting the bell on my first stand-in, I surveyed the classroom: cupboards locked, desk locked, no books, no directions for me. Came the bell and a torrent of boys. To my astonishment, they immediately began pushing the desks together; and then, with not so much as a glance in my direction, they fished out decks of cards and began dealing them out. I looked on sourly until they had settled down, and then I spoke. "Right, put the cards away and move the desks back. We're going to have a test." Jaws dropped and the hubbub ceased. A test? Their turn for a surprise. Well, at least they did some work that period – a general knowledge quiz that I made up as I went along. After that, I continued to do playground duty but did not offer to stand in again. I could not condone mere baby-sitting.

"How are things your end?" I asked the policeman, a veteran who was in the school on official business one day. He looked at me, his face serious. "Just about keeping the lid on," he replied. Perhaps I wasn't the only one to feel he was in a lunatic asylum.

Came the day, towards end of term, when I knocked on the door of the headmaster's study and marched in without further ado. The head was seated at his desk, poring over some papers with his deputy standing beside him. "That's it. That's it!" I cried, as they looked up. Throwing up my hands, I declared, "I've had enough." I don't know what I had expected, but the reaction I got startled me. "Oh God," the head exclaimed. "Not another one!" And placing his elbows on the desk, he clasped his head in an attitude of despair. "What do you mean?" I asked, feeling a stirring of sympathy for what I was beginning to suspect might be a fellow sufferer. "You're the tenth one," he groaned. Just at that moment the telephone rang. Excusing himself, he answered the call and then turned to his deputy, "There's a crazed sixth former running around upstairs smashing the toilets. See to it, will you." Then he turned back to me. "Listen," he implored wearily, "Can't we discuss this? Which classes are giving you trouble?"

It transpired that some older teachers had taken a hasty early retirement, while others had quit. An exchange teacher from abroad had walked away from the school without giving any notice at all. As for me, I stayed. Again I had come to the brink of ending my career, for I doubt whether I could have mustered confidence enough to try another school. Only an impulse of sympathy for a fellow had saved me.

I kept my first two classes – they at least were prepared to make an effort – but dropped the last two. Although the second formers were no trouble, I couldn't bear to see them wasting their time. As for the remedial fourth formers, they were beyond any power of mine to help. I could only feel sorry for the poor devil who had to take my place. For the boys' sake I hope he was more competent than I. In their stead I was given two others, including one of top band first formers. The latter became a joy to teach – once I had slippered a few backsides.

All the boys wore uniform, of course, although some were about as grubby as might be expected in a largely working-class district. It was among the staff that the scruffiest persons could be found – a pair of ill-dressed, bewhiskered characters with unkempt hair (fine teachers for all that, I'm sure). The contrast between their appearance and that of the other staff suggested they were making a statement of some kind. Probably middle-class leftists masquerading as working class.

The staff room was divided by a folding plastic curtain. Whether this reflected a division of feeling among the staff or not I don't know. As an inveterate introvert, I am not sensitive to social nuances. I knew there were divisions of a kind. Staff belonged to different unions, for one thing, and some were from the secondary modern and some from the grammar school. Whatever the truth, I gravitated towards the smaller section, where the bridge-players were, and became a regular at the table. My fellow players, who included two department heads, joked about my "antediluvian" bidding style, but their acceptance of me as a fellow professional went far towards restoring my confidence. I was beginning to feel solid ground beneath my feet once more.

ଷ୍ଠ

The Hymn

It is spring. Together with my class I am in the old building, attending an assembley for first formers. With so many boys in the school, full assemblies were not practicable. After a brief address by the housemaster, the boys are called upon to sing a hymn. I do not catch its title. At Garibaldi we had no singing except at Christmas, and then students were reluctant to sing carols themselves, preferring instead to listen to the school choir. But this is England, and the boys sing out loud and clear, their

Morning has broken, like the first morning,
Blackbird has spoken, like the first bird...

treble voices filling the assembley hall. The hymn is new to me. Attracted by it, I attend closely to the words. The voices rise and fall. Such little boys – only eleven! How well they sing! And I think of the boy whose singing at Banstead had touched my heart with the sheer beauty of his voice. And of a

Sweet the rain's new fall, sunlit from heaven,
Like the first dewfall on the first grass...

boy who had collected wildflowers there and who had sung "To Be a Pilgrim" at an assembley in another school. A boy soon afterwards to be terrified out of his wits. He was a little boy, too – younger, only ten. And I'd been cursing him for returning to haunt me. The boys' voices, the hymn and my

Mine is the sunlight! Mine is the morning,
Born of the one Light Eden saw play...

memories meld and become as one... Suddenly, a wave of emotion overpowers me and drives me hurriedly from the hall. The passage outside is dimly lit, fortunately deserted. And there, with my head resting against the wall, I fight to hold back the tears.

☙❧

I saw the school year out and stayed on for another. By that time the school was earning a good reputation. Little thanks to me. I was not a good teacher in London. Given my state of mind when I started there, I am astonished that I survived as a teacher at all. But survive I did. It was time to return to Canada. After applying to the Maple Ridge School Board for re-instatement, I received a telegram offering me the only position open – one in an elementary school. With some trepidation I cabled my acceptance.

In August, 1975, on the day following the farewell party which begins this memoir, I left to spend the night at an airport hotel. There I thought of my sister. I had been right. When Linda left school to become a student nurse and insisted on sharing an apartment with another girl, Pauline had been devastated, so much so that she had become physically ill. Given her hang-up of feeling unwanted, she felt as if she had been rejected by her own child. "I don't know," my mother exclaimed one day, "There seems to be something wrong with my bloody kids!" Since then, Linda had finished her training and become married. Pauline had long accepted the inevitable but at heart still mourned the "loss" of her child. Hoping to cheer her a little, on the one soiled piece of hotel stationery gracing my table I wrote, "If things get bad, hold on to one thought – that there are a number of people who love you dearly and so you do not belong to yourself alone."

Next morning I boarded my flight to Vancouver. The hotel failed to give me the wake-up call I had requested.

CHAPTER TWENTY

Epilogue

1
Back in Harness

Before reporting to the Maple Ridge School Board, I dropped by my old school to see Larry Davies. He was the teacher I had replaced in 1961. After some years as principal of an elementary school, he had returned to Garibaldi as vice-principal and now was the principal. As I had expected, he was in his office, working on the timetable. "Hi, Larry," I greeted him, grinning.

He looked up in surprise. "Phil Condon!" he exclaimed, half-rising from his chair to shake my hand. Then, "Are you back?" he asked.

"Yes."

"Where?"

"I don't know. Some elementary school," I replied. "It was the only position open."

Already reaching for the phone, he said, "Oh, no you're not!" For a minute or so he conducted a quiet conversation with someone and then, replacing the receiver, he turned back to me. "You have come at just the right time. One of our English teachers has got herself pregnant, and I've been looking for a replacement. Welcome back to Garibaldi."[24]

I found my first year a little difficult. It was my first full load in years, after all, and all English. Also, more than half my classes were juniors, which is not the level I prefer in that subject. In succeeding years, however, I had the classes I wanted: Grade 8 social studies (I liked the medieval period and geography) and senior English. I was back where I belonged – a square peg in a square hole.

In the years that followed, I had even less social life than before, but I was not bothered overmuch. I was now resigned to the idea that I would probably have to live alone for the rest of my life. As for my sex life, outside of my brief marriage and the one misadventure it has been zero. And that hasn't bothered me as much as one might expect, either. If you have undergone radical surgery, you don't complain of a hangnail. It's the loss of my wife's love that mattered. Over the years, I have dreamt of her often. Except for one, the dreams had a common theme – she no longer loved me – and I would awaken feeling upset. Clearly, they reflect my sense of loss. In the one exception, we were sitting side by side at a banquet. Leaning over, I whispered in her ear, "I love you".

As for casual affairs, I am not interested. "Love-making" without love is a pale, rather sad reflection of the real thing – the desire for union between two who love each other deeply. The union is not physical alone. I am no prude. Like the no doubt apocryphal English lady, I don't very much care what people do – as long as they don't do it in public and frighten the horses. The truth is that I have good reason to avoid casual affairs. The one I did have was unsought. Though painful, it was also illuminating. I have no wish to be ungallant, for the lady was attractive enough, yet I found the sex boring. I was fond of her – but as a friend. As I did not love her, the sex act seemed insincere, pointless. (Another possible reason occurs to me – perhaps I'm just too lazy!)

The affair also confirmed what I had long known – that my sense of responsibility makes me vulnerable. Just as another

---

[24] Several years after we had both retired I reminded him of this fortuitous event. For a moment he hesitated. Then he said, "Well, it didn't happen quite like that"!

might be trapped by his if his girl friend becomes pregnant so I felt trapped by mine over the sex act alone. As a result, I had remained to face the music:

"Of course, you realize that you've given me the perfect excuse, don't you?" It was late, and the husband and I were alone in the farmhouse basement, cutting up a heifer he had slaughtered. (We were being very civilized.) He was working at one table and I, less expertly, at another, with parts of the carcass strewn over other tables as well. As he posed the question, he waved his bloody knife, and the one naked light bulb cast a huge shadow of him on the wall behind. It was like a scene from the Grand-Guignol. "Yes," I replied glumly. *The excuse to do what,* I asked myself feverishly, *carve me up with the heifer or saddle me with your wife?* Somehow I didn't fancy either prospect.

Fortunately for all concerned, he had done neither. Guardian Angel may have been immensely entertained by my situation – but he had nonetheless rammed his point home forcefully.

And so I live a semi-recluse. Though I cherish family and friends, I avoid large social gatherings whenever I can. They make me nervous. Besides, my hearing is damaged; and if several people speak at once I cannot make out what anyone says. (To be frank, I often find that a convenience, as I have little interest in small talk anyway.)

Kathy and Les had moved to Cadboro Bay in Victoria. Until both had died, I spent Easter and Christmas at their home as before. As for the summers, most have been spent exchanging visits with my family. Mum and Pauline were the first to visit me – the first time we had been alone together since Conway days. I rented a Class A motor home and took them on a tour of the Rockies. The weather was perfect and we saw a wide variety of wildlife. It was, they agreed, the best holiday of their lives. After a brief illness, Mum died at the end of 1982, and Pauline kept her ashes until the following summer, when I could come for the burial. It was my last visit to England. Since then all the traffic has been the other way, with Pauline and Reg alternating with Linda, her husband Nik and their children, Ben and Kim.

Following my return to Maple Ridge in 1975, for a few years

I put up in a cheap motel. Providing I could cook my meals, play my music and work in peace, I cared little how modestly I lived. However, a colleague who cared more than I did persuaded me to move into an apartment. That proved quiet, too, but really little better; and more years saw me shunting between school and a box. Eventually, the fates relented and I was rescued by John Hale, one of the school's counsellors. The house he'd built for his parents had fallen vacant and he asked if I would like to rent it. As I knew the place, I agreed readily. It was on his hobby farm, an oasis of eight acres away from the din of a noisy civilization. And there I live still.

᠗

Ah, but a man's reach should exceed his grasp...
- Robert Browning

As I have said, in the twenty-two years I taught En. Literature 12 there was not one failure – although a few dropped out voluntarily. In spite of the unworthy suspicions of one District Superintendent ("Of course, we all know how it was done"), there was no fiddle. To take the course, a student needed only a pass in the previous year's English. If my students were selected, it was true only insofar as they had selected themselves by choosing to take the course. Moreover, in reviewing the Department of Education statistics, I found that the class marks awarded in other schools were significantly higher than mine. I suspect that, in the hope of encouraging students, other teachers were too generous with their marks. This kindness, perhaps justifiable with juniors, I believed misplaced with seniors, as it might give them a false idea of their progress and so lead to unpleasant surprises at university. Thus most of the credit goes to my students, who took the course out of interest and were willing to do the work necessary to succeed in it.

And so, like some latter-day Mr. Chips, I centred my life on the school. When the children of former students began to appear in my classes, I realized that the time for my graceful departure

425

was drawing near. But it was not to be – not graceful, that is. At an age when many of today's teachers enjoy early retirement, I took responsibility for creating two new programs: one for Advanced Placement English and one for gifted students. The first was successful. The second was not. This failure preyed on my mind and brought about another breakdown. The fact that it occurred suddenly while I was at a meeting with district officials and my peers only compounded my humiliation.

The following year I taught half time and then took my mandatory retirement. When this was announced at our awards assembley in June, 1991, students, parents and staff leapt to their feet and gave me a long ovation. Taken by surprise, I could no more make the expected speech of thanks than fly. Instead, like the Queen, I remained seated, nailed to my chair by acute embarrassment and wishing everyone would shut up and sit down.

I did not enjoy the first years of retirement. My colleagues were more understanding, but I felt I had ruined a reputation built over thirty years. Disoriented, I quit smoking and almost caused another breakdown. Then, after nine months' abstinence, I rebelled. To hell with it, I thought, and lit up again. This act of defiance seems to have stimulated my creativity, for it was then that I began work on this memoir.

Meanwhile, I continue to live on the farm, smoking and drinking rather too much and sharing our green haven with assorted cats, large dogs, chickens and cattle. Red-tailed hawks and bald eagles ride the air above. Squirrels and small birds fill up at our feeders. Bears, coyotes and deer grace us with their presence from time to time. And in the spring and fall, wild geese fly honking by. As for John, his wife Wendy, and their grown children, Andrew and Monica (both of whom I taught) – they insist that I consider them my Canadian family and keep a watchful eye out for me.

Perhaps I do have guardian angels, after all.

෯෯

2
This world means intensely, and means good.
- Robert Browning

My life appears to have followed a frustrating pattern – of repeated attempts to fly that resulted only in my being brought back to earth with a thud. No high flight, then, but circuits and bumps. Following my last breakdown, I was at times tempted to ask why. But always I heard the same reply: You have little cause for complaint and much to be thankful for. It is true. I have loved and been loved and have experienced joy. I come from a loving family, have fine friends and have had remarkably good health. (Voice from the back of the classroom, "Mr. Condon, aren't you ever _ill?_") For most of my career I have been a good teacher. And I have lived untouched, though not unmoved, through more than seven decades of the bloodiest century on record. Blue Jowls has scarred me, it is true. Still, the loss of my wife aside, all the disappointments, however painful, were merely blows to my pride, after all. And let's face it, the best of us need a boot in the backside now and again. I feel I should have done better, of course, but we all can say that.

No, to complain would be childish. I am not nearly as self-absorbed as this memoir might suggest. Over the years I have learnt more about the cruelty and suffering in the world than I care to know. With nature able to inflict pain on a scale and in ways that would sicken a medieval hangman, one would think that the struggle to cope with this alone would suffice us. But as if driven by inner darkness, we have to make things worse, not only with wars – which could be considered as part of the struggle for survival, I suppose – but also with atrocities such as the Holocaust and the butchery in Rwanda. When we recall that, on a lesser scale, similar obscenities and horrors are perpetrated somewhere in the world every day, Mephistopheles' boast, "Why, this is hell. Nor am I out of it," seems only too chillingly credible.

Does life have to be so hard? If we assume that life has a purpose and that we have free will, it probably does. In driving evolution, it is the struggle for survival that helped create the biosphere in the first place – and most present life forms are needed to maintain it, something we have been slow to realize. By evolving technologically, however, we have greatly increased our power, and the consequences of misusing it are becoming more and more severe. It is as if reality is taking us by the scruff of the neck and telling us to grow up.

The fact is that, despite advances in science and technology, we haven't noticeably increased in wisdom. We are still thralls to greed and power, still subject to mass insanity. The 13th Century Albigensian Crusade has been easily matched in the Cambodian killing fields and surpassed by the Holocaust. The Old Man of the Hills lives still, only he has multiplied like dragon's teeth and his assassins are armed with bombs and nerve gas instead of knives. Despite our greatly increased wealth, much of humanity remains poor, ill-educated and malnourished. Even in the West, the gulf between the haves and the have-nots is growing. For the few, millions and mansions; for the many, today's equivalents of bread and circuses. As for the barbarians, they too are alive and well, not hammering at our gates but dwelling in our midst. Yes, human nature being what it is, I believe things must be the way they are. Like the old miner with his donkey, reality has need of a big stick merely to gain our attention.

Meanwhile, it has fallen to the present generation and their children to be faced with the greatest challenge yet. To my mind, the most significant event of the past century is not the "giant leap" into space or the harnessing of nuclear energy but the human population explosion from two to six billion in one lifetime, with a further three or more forecast for the next fifty years. While nature encourages fecundity, when a species stresses its environment a cull usually follows. To avoid it a species limits its numbers, adapts its behaviour or migrates. In our case, because we are stressing the entire biosphere, with perhaps a mass extinction of other species and a catastrophic climate change in the offing, the last option is not open to us. Reality's stick is truly formidable this time.

While no one can predict the future, not even a week ahead, I can not imagine a worldly utopia, unless it be the ersatz variety of a super nanny-cum-Orwellian state. We shall always have challenges. Many will be met through the use of science and technology; but new technologies create further problems and lead us we know not where. Until now, in striving to master our environment, we seem to have succeeded mainly in ruining it. Thus, after studying us, the spider remarked to his mate

"Thinks itself a god, Sweetie. Now that's a laugh
– a clever, bare-arsed monkey, and master
   not even of itself!"

No doubt we are driven to evolve technologically, but perhaps reality is suggesting there are more ways to evolve than in the material sense alone. Instead of seeking to "master" our environment – an ambition, surely, that borders on hubris – we need to co-operate with nature and strive to master ourselves. Given the perversities of human nature, this last is likely to be the most difficult challenge of all.

Assuming that life has a purpose implies of course that the universe has a creative intelligence behind it. Horrified by Auschwitz, a newly-arrived prisoner exclaimed in despair, "There is no God!" Despite this understandable conclusion, I rather believe that there is. Although we have no more chance of comprehending a Being capable of creating this universe than an ant has of understanding Einstein, we are given some pointers to His nature. Hindus believe the divine spirit to be in all living creatures. In her *A Revelation of Love* Julian of Norwich goes further in saying that God "is in the mydde poynt of allthynge."[25] God is not only transcendent, that is, but also immanent. "I it am that is heyest," her "dereworthy lord" tells her; "I it am that is lowist; I it am that is all." The highest, even all – yes. But the lowest? In what sense? An earlier mystic, Angela of Foligno, sheds light on this, for in a vision she was shown not only something of God's power, which is everywhere present, but also his profound humility.[26] The first fills her with awe, but it is the latter that metaphorically impels her to her knees.

Thus Lord Acton's dictum, that power corrupts, does not apply here, for God balances power with humility and is motivated by love. In fact, Dame Julian tells us, He *is* Love:

Fro that time that it [her revelation] was shewid I desired

---

[25] Marion Glasscoe, ed., *Julian of Norwich, A Revelation of Love*, University of Exeter, 1976.
[26] See Evelyn Underhill's magisterial *Mysticism*, Meridian Books, New York, 1957.

oftentimes to witten what was our lords mening. And…I was answerid…thus: "Woldst thou witten thi lords mening in this thing? Wete it wele: love was his mening. Who shewid it the? Love. What shewid he the? Love. Wherfore shewid it he? For love."

My father, the old soldier, had come to the right conclusion after all – and he had never even heard of Dame Julian.

In referring to the Last Judgment, Christ says that whoever has helped or harmed another in effect has done it to God. Does he mean that literally or not? Unless Christ and the great mystics are badly mistaken – and he would be a rash man who would claim that, as they agree to a remarkable degree – then God was present at Auschwitz and shared in the suffering there. The Christian image of a crucified God contains a great truth. Our part in the scheme of things is clear enough. It is, as Christ tells us, to love God and our neighbour as ourselves. More easily said than done! As a mere beginner in love, however, I do not consider myself fit to discuss it further.

There remains the problem of pain. I once believed that no one is afflicted with suffering greater than he can bear. Now I'm not so sure. Whether the belief be true or not, the fact is that many are broken by life. Yet many sturdy souls rise above the most appalling handicaps, and some resist torture unto death. Even in Auschwitz, a survivor noted, although "some prisoners became demons, others became angels." In a letter, Keats calls this world a "vale of soul-making." I doubt whether souls made in a Disney universe would amount to much. It is only in this tough old world that we can, through our actions, prove our courage and our love and in the best of us discover something of the true dimensions of the human spirit. In the words of my mother's favourite proverb – usually quoted, alas, as a gentle reproach to me – Handsome is as handsome does. And pain is the measure.

❦

As a youth I climbed mountains. Now eighty, I get out of breath climbing a few stairs and have difficulty recalling the very words I need. Then I knew little, was sure of much and took much for granted. Now I know a little more, but am sure of less and am filled with wonder. I have even come to believe in miracles. I don't mean weeping statues and such, of course. And I doubt whether Christ walked on water or fed multitudes with a few loaves and fishes. To me, that smacks of magic, and somehow I don't think God operates that way. He is more subtle. Nonetheless, I believe the universe to be a miracle, one that combines simplicity with infinite complexity and is grand beyond our conceiving. As for life, as Whitman says, "a mouse is miracle enough to stagger sextillions of infidels." So is the fact that we share DNA with every living creature, whether it be baboon, banana or bacterium – which means, in effect, that we are all cousins. "But that makes us cannibals!" exclaimed my sister when I mentioned this to her. Yes, even the vegetarians. Perhaps this sheds light on the Eucharist, that mystery over whose meaning kindly Christians once burned one another at the stake. And as for man, that baffling creature whose behaviour ranges from the demonic to the saintly and whose abilities are equally varied and wide, he is perhaps the greatest wonder of all.

Not the least part of the price of long life is to see much of what one loves vanish from the earth. Although I fall short in faith and love, I do entertain the hope that all that is beautiful, all that is loveworthy, continues to exist in God – the ground of our "beseking," as Christ tells Dame Julian. Many years have passed since I last felt close to God. Yet my sense that He is nonetheless present in the silence has sustained me even during those times when I felt my life to be unendurable.

But I cannot claim to *know*. Should my belief that God exists be misplaced, then the great mystics, of whatever religion, will have shared a common illusion. And I would be sorry for it. But it would be a magnificent illusion. Whatever the truth, I am not so enamoured of myself as to wish to live for ever, not as my present personality, anyway. I grow a little tired of it – as perhaps does the reader.

Appendixes

1. Cherry Blossom   435

2. Letters to a Friend   437

3. Sources   473

Cherry Blossom
Vancouver, April, 1957

"*Oh,*" you breathed, "*how proud it must be!*"
And as we paused in silence, arm in arm,
wondering at the glory of its bloom,
the cherry seemed to tremble in my sight
and stretch adoring arms towards the light.

Two lovers standing rapt before a tree,
a scene of common, even hackneyed, charm
- but for the shadow of November's gloom,
when death had served you notice, as of right,
that he'd elected you to boast his might.

And so it was: with sly economy,
using your own sweet self to work you harm,
he fingered through your body's rosy loom
and laboured diligently day and night
until both breath and life were stifled…quite.

Ah well, let death enjoy his victory.
You looked upon his face without alarm:
until his sour presence filled the room,
your spirit, like the cherry, blossomed bright,
and with its blither courage shamed his spite.

Had all been known that morning in the street,
where stood the tree and we two side by side,
the cherry would have gladly rent its pride
and cast its tattered glory at your feet.

❀

1994

"A fine conceit!
You silly, dear, old-fashioned thing
- 'should have', you should've said.
Trees shed their bloom, as we do tears
- but not for us.

"As earth played
rounders with the sun
and spring returned,
the cherry shed its pride again
– but not for me.

"And that morning when I slipped away,
in Maytime, pretty may time,
while birds sang matins to the sun
and earth had never seemed more fair
– no tree, no bird shed pride or tear.
Remember, dear?"

Yes, I remember well, my love.
The earth was bare.

•

In Memoriam JAC [1932 – 1958]

1998

[NOTE: The following have been included as I believe they complement the memoir. They contain my views on it and on poetry generally – and perhaps reveal a little more of my prejudices.]

LETTERS TO A FRIEND
1994 – 2001

Monday, December 5, 1994

Dear Gerry,

In the fall of 1959, during the first term of my fifth and final year at UBC, I used to immure myself in my Ford Prefect between lectures – lectures in the College of Education that were so lifeless and uninspired as to make me feel almost ill – and read St. Augustine's *Confessions*: "Dear Lord, make me chaste, but not yet" – you know the sort of thing. It was a sort of exercise in self-therapy – for me to read it, that is. Somewhere, if not in his *Confessions* then elsewhere, he wrote, "Love, and do what you will." Christ had reduced the Ten Commandments to two, and here St. Augustine had reduced them to one! "Crafty bugger!" I thought, for the two parts of the dictum are contradictions – although not absolutely, for there still would remain ample room for freedom. As a rule to live by, it is not too useful, for of course everything depends upon what he meant by "love". I suppose the real value of the dictum is to get the reader to think about that very thing: Love – what is it, and what is its place in the scheme of things? Now, *what* it is, I believe, cannot be expressed in words but can only be comprehended through experience. I am reminded of a chat I had with Jerry Potts, our old science teacher in the 'Sixties. He was white-haired, pot-bellied and wrote poetry, claiming (too generously) that my enthusiasm for poetry had inspired him. "I did not know what love is," he said, "until I had my daughter – and then I knew

I would have done anything for her, anything!" Reminded me of David mourning over Absalom ("...would God I had died for thee, O Absalom, my son, my son!"), only Jerry found out in good time. Experiencing love of that kind suggests the answer to the second question – but I shall leave that up to you.

Your style of writing, which you describe as "literary" and "artificial", is, I think, too abstract. Be simple, and illustrate to show what you mean. Your amusing chat for the radio is like that. (I enjoyed it, by the way.) As to your topic – the nature of love, religion, and where, I presume, evolution is taking us – well, I suggest it is rather too grand in scope for an essay. If you are going in for reasoned argument, as you seem to be, you'll end up with a tome – and with many a monumental headache before you finish it. You are venturing into deep waters, old friend. Still, soldier on. You'll find that the topic will impose its own discipline and form and direction. And you'll no doubt end up writing, not what you thought you were going to write, but something else altogether. You'll enjoy a voyage of discovery, in other words.

As to those very clever writers in the "posh" newspapers – think not of them. I marvel at their cleverness, too – at their power to "bewitch" the intelligence with language, to paraphrase your quote from Wittgenstein. However, behind the bewitching web they weave, which often suggests certitude, even omniscience, I usually find little of substance. The buggers blind you with science and yet manage to sit on the fence, as it were. In the RAF we had a saying – bullshit baffles brains!

...Dick came over for a visit a week or so ago. We had Chinese food and nattered about this and that. Jack is well, still swimming miles a week. ("The bugger will outlive us all," says Dick.) Dick and I are well, barring the usual failings of aging men. In 1993 I quit smoking for nine months. Had a much more difficult time than when I quit for ten months in the 'Sixties. Psyche started unravelling again because of the stress. Even used the "F" word before my sister when she came visiting in the summer. Got pissed off with all the virtue and will-power and crabbiness around December and started to smoke again. Since then I have written about ten poems. My sister talked me into attempting autobiography and so far I have reached page 80 and the ripe old age of 12. That, and doing the Weekly Telegraph crosswords, keeps me from becoming brain dead. I am 190lbs at last weighing, feel like a pig, am the leader of our pack of three large, hairy dogs – and am beginning to smell and look like them. Cats turn up their noses when I pass. I also drink rather too much – which reminds me, I am out of booze and I'd better finish off this letter so I can catch the mail and visit the liquor store. Oh, and neither Dick nor I have heard any more of Bagley since his incarceration. Now Bagley should write his memoirs! Cheers!

⟡

Sunday, December 3, 1995

Dear Gerry,

...Yes, Christmas again. As you remark, it doesn't bother me, although I appreciate communicating with distant relatives and hearing from old friends. But like you, I suppose, it's not the cheerful jingling of sleigh bells that I hear, but the dong of a different bell. Another year gone. Rats! And in my case little to show for it, although I have been pecking away at my memoirs. Sounds pretentious I know. Blame my sister. It was her idea. Actually, I am enjoying myself – tossing off an effortless paragraph here, sweating for hours over a sentence or two there. Odd the way things go. Like my half dozen poems. Two of the best were done in a matter of three or four hours each; another one I have been struggling with for over eighteen months – and the bloody thing still won't come out!

You might try your hand – at memoirs, that is. You don't have to tackle your whole life – just incidents in it. In the process, you could work in some of your ideas "on human love, divinity" and abandoned morality, and so forth. You might find the anecdotal form a relief from straight exposition. I suppose it's normal to take stock as one approaches three score years and ten, and putting one's thoughts on paper can be a helpful exercise. What has been important in my life? My childhood, my family, Jan, my friends, books, music, mountains, flying, teaching. I can't say that I feel burdened with sins committed – even if I did once commit adultery with the wife of a good friend (no one you know, I hasten to add). Though I emerged from that comedy of errors feeling like Judas decked out in cap and bells, our guardian angels must have laughed themselves sick. I am amused when persons such as Luther, Bunyan and Donne beat their breasts and wail that they are chief among sinners – though I understand why they do so – while murderers, rapists and so on emerge from prison claiming to have "paid their debt to society"!

No, in my case, I find that the sting comes from sins of omission, and they are plentiful enough. But that's all by the way. I have read some autobiographies – Laurie Lee, Dirk Bogarde, for example. I certainly cannot match their skill in writing or the drama of their lives. How do they manage to remember the details of conversation, the weather, the landscape? Did they keep notes as they went along? So, even if I finish, I don't expect publication. I'll leave that to a remote descendent of my sister's – if there is one. Remembering one's childhood is fun, though. I'm including a couple of paragraphs for your amusement.

Dick has been over a few times this year. We chew the fat over a few beers and enjoy a meal together. Last time I fed him some curry. Next time it will be toad-in-the-hole, with bangers from Marks and Spencer's. (Yes, I not only cook but also plan my meals – as much as a day in advance….) I must say that Dick looks well. And Jack, I'm told, still swims miles a week. Other than that I have little news from this end. We had a bit of a heat wave over here, mostly in June, with temperatures in the 80's and 90's. The ground became baked and our spring dried up. I began to dread the summer. However, the weather turned cool and cloudy over July and August – just to annoy the kids. Once school started again, we enjoyed a magnificent fall – plenty of sun, with temperatures going up into the 80's in October! I tell you, the leaves were reluctant to turn. Then a sudden frosty period brought them tumbling with a rush. Since then we have had the pineapple express, with record-breaking rain (over 14 inches in Abbotsford) and floods in November. But I like the rain, as you know, and I squelch around the farm happily with my pack of dogs.

Just about out of steam. I won't comment on the morality of today, for that will only fire up steam of a different kind. I began to feel the times were "out of joint" with the onset of the 'Sixties.

Have a good family Christmas. I hope that the new year deals gently with you all. Cheers!

☙❧

Saturday, June 22, 1996

Dear Gerry,

59° F and already the sun is on its way back south. We had snow on the higher passes and in the Okanagan a couple of days ago and altogether have had only about three days when the thermometer registered in the seventies. A decidedly cool spring, in other words. Not that I mind. The only weather that I loathe is the heat wave, and so I listen to general complaints about the lack of sun with equanimity.

I enjoyed your anecdote about Christmas Day at the "Y". "The best-laid schemes o' mice and man gang aft agley"! But your Christmas scheme did not really gang agley, did it. There are one or two suggestions I could make. The title needs tarting up. I suggest "A Turkey Christmas at the Y.M.C.A." – or some such thing. You could also introduce a little drama and suspense between the invitation to the "12 gentlemen" and the disconcerting arrival of the unexpected 36. Make a little more of it. You know the sort of thing....

As for my own writing, I am sorry to say I haven't written a thing for about three months now. I entered some poetry in a CBC contest – and was rejected. Some talented female who churned out about fifteen poems in a month won it. I also entered a memoir about evacuation days. Likewise, not even among the finalists. They provide no critical comment, of course, and I find it difficult to judge my own work. I also entered four poems for the Arvon competition in England. Two of them I thought better than most of the previous winners and so I felt I stood a chance. Wrong. After reading scads of modern poetry, I find to my dismay that I am about fifty years out of date. Today, rhyme is frowned upon – for prettifying serious thought, as one "post-Modern" poet expressed it. (One of the winning poems of the previous Arvon competition centred on the finding of a pubic hair in the food at a restaurant!) As for the use of metre – that is a definite no-no. As in the art world, there is an "establishment" or at least a fashion in poetry, although here and in England some efforts are being made to encourage metrical and rhymed verse, preferably stuff that is understandable. I am reminded of the early days of the Romantic poets, when for many poets and most critics poetry wasn't poetry unless it was composed in heroic couplets. I am enclosing a snippet from Auberon Waugh's column in *The Telegraph* that sheds some light on the subject. If you could send me a copy of the *Literary Review* I would appreciate it.

As for the slow-up in my memoirs – I'm up to page 200 and about to enter the RAF – it is not out of discouragement so much as dread of what is to come. The fact is that my life up until 30 was interesting enough with its ups and downs, but from then on the only real bright spots were my marriage to Jan (joyous but brief) and the classroom (for 23 of the 26 years, anyway). Outside the classroom I had to struggle with depression and the horrid feeling that my mind was like an eight cylinder engine – with three of the cylinders grinding away in reverse. As with your stammer, the cause was a childhood trauma. Remember when you asked me – so long ago now – if your "Pip" could call me "Pip"? I reacted with a violent "no". The reason was simple enough. When I was ten years old, fresh from seven months in an orphanage and emotionally vulnerable for the first time in my life, like Dickens' Pip I was suddenly pounced on by a man and terrified out of my wits – shocked and traumatized, in short. In my case he had seized me before I even saw him (He had been in hiding.) I forgot all about the matter for years. Blue Jowls, as I call him, first reappeared in a recurrent nightmare when I was in my twenties. Although I did not recognize it as him then, for a few days I was afraid to go to sleep. He re-invaded my waking life – or rather his doppelganger did – three weeks before my wedding – a fine time to cut a man's balls off! And it happened with all the suddenness of the original attack. I was working at Kitimat at the time, if you remember. Within hours, hundreds of men knew that I had behaved like a terrified boy. Worse than the bitter humiliation was the sense of having been betrayed from within. I did not know then that I *had* been a terrified boy. I was in a state of dissociation, of course, helpless to control myself. All I could do was to refuse to run and hide and to finish the last two weeks there walking upright like a man. Difficult. Reading about Pavlov and his bloody dogs for an essay a couple of months later, I understood what had happened to me.[27] But it didn't help much – and I have never been able to trust myself again. I am afraid that the twin shocks of the Kitimat affair and the loss of Jan very nearly shattered me. How in spite of everything I managed to have a successful teaching career I cannot imagine. But the price was a life of solitude and a couple of breakdowns – in 1971-72 and in 1990.

Now why am I telling you this? Up till now I have told only Jan (to give her the chance to call off the wedding), my sister – and some prick of a psychologist I consulted on the National Health in London in 1972. He listened to my explanation of why I was profoundly depressed – oh for all of five minutes, I suppose; then, visibly bored, he shrugged his shoulders and said, "Merely a panic attack. What do you expect me to do about it?" "Give me some of your damned pills, I suppose," I said….

Why tell you, then? Well, in your letter you said "Do you plan to present yourself in all naked human vulnerability or are you going to create a persona?" My answer is that I do not intend to create a persona. But present myself in all naked vulnerability? I don't know whether it is possible. How well does one know oneself? With all the baggage we carry in our brains – the subconscious, unconscious, chemicals, hormones, remnants of our reptilian ancestors – and our infinite capacity to fool ourselves, to use our much-vaunted powers of reason to rationalize, I don't believe it is possible to present ourselves as we really are. Etc. In any case, you can understand now why I dread writing about the last 40 years. If I ever get around to it, I shall probably compress it into a chapter. That would be appropriate, really – about thirteen chapters for the first thirty-two years and the remainder of my life cabin'd, cribb'd and confin'd into one. Somehow, though, I don't think I shall make it. "Ecclesiastes" haunts me – "All is vanity".

I am enclosing a poem I wrote in 1989. I thought at the time it

---

[27]   An episode of dissociation is like temporary possession, not by a demon, but by one's traumatised self – in my case a terrified ten year old child in a state of regression.

would get Blue Jowls out of my system. In the event, about eight months later he struck again, and my ten-year-old self leapt out to humiliate me once again – in a meeting with district education officials and my peers. A reputation built up over twenty-five years destroyed in a minute. If I were paranoid as well as depressive, I might consider fate to be toying with me. The timing, for the third time, was perfect.

There now – I have no doubt embarrassed you. But be of good cheer. I am not depressed all the time, and those occasions when I feel my psyche unravelling into a fuzz ball are fortunately rare. Most of the time I am healthy-minded enough and view the slings and arrows with sardonic humour as a mere peccadillo compared with the horrors many unfortunates have to put up with. Besides, I think the world is crazier than I am. Cheers.

Plumstead
1936

Very well, Blue Jowls,
I forgive you.
You could not know, when
    with a sudden pounce
    you seized the boy,
    how vulnerable he was,
or that your face would leap,
    years later, from the dark
    to shame the man.

Ah well, I gain humility
    and humility, God knows,
    we need. But then
I think of other children
    defiled or terrified:
chance cruelty
    (like yours, old Face)
    we may expect,
for all young innocents

are warned
"Beware the bogeyman,"
and soon enough we learn
the human face
may mask the spider;
but when the predator
is teacher, father, priest
– *there* is betrayal to give us pause!

What ails us? Could it be
a dearth of millstones?
Or is our world
a cosmic psychiatric ward
and we both nurse and inmate?

Predator or victim?
If I *had* to choose, I'd choose
to be the victim still.
So might I earn
what sometimes I have wished
– annihilation.
In the meantime,
I must learn
to love.

1989

⚬❀⚬

Thursday, August 22, 1996

Dear Gerry,

Thanks for the "Literary Review". It has some good stuff in
it, but I don't think that I shall cough up a subscription. I've been
taking the "Good Book Guide" for a year. Drooled at some of the
books reviewed, bought a few, but cannot really afford to support
my reading habit by purchasing books *and* booze and tobacco
– and the books I want are seldom to be found in our library. So I

am dropping the guide. Senseless, tormenting myself by thinking about the mounting pile of books I shall now never read. Really I requested the "Lit.Rev." because Auberon Waugh mentioned that the poetry contest was intended to encourage a return to a more formal verse and I wanted to see what kind of verse he meant. I doubt whether I would enter any of the contests, though. Most of the dozen or so poems I have written stem from personal experience and I have dried up for over a year now.

I see Waugh is the editor. I read his column in the *Weekly Telegraph*, which I get largely because I cannot stomach the local rags, and find him moderately amusing – especially when he aims satirical barbs at the idiocies of the police and the law. (Latest snippet, from another English paper: Judge Pickles frees sex attacker on the grounds that he was "too shy" to approach women normally. Poor sod.) Like his father, Waugh peers dismissively down his nose at the lower classes – and that includes you and me, dear friend. I think that funny. The old fool is also totally besotted with Princess Di and seems to regard himself as a knightly champion, romantically cocking a lance (or something) in her defence. Oh well, we are all fools one way or another.

That I should send the same poem to you twice doesn't surprise me at all. I have the distinct feeling that I have afflicted the ears of some of my friends with the same stories several times over. They haven't exactly starting avoiding me yet, but…. It is not merely a case of aging or worn-out neurons. Ever since a ghastly attack of stage fright at UBC, I have dreaded having to make speeches and over the years I have had a few awkward experiences, such as suddenly drying up completely and having to stand exposed on the podium with a completely blank mind. It often happened in the classroom, too, usually when I was illustrating some point with an anecdote. I would sometimes become so involved with the illustration that I would forget the point. My students enjoyed it immensely. They also enjoyed occasional Spoonerisms such as "those well-known second generation Romantic poets Sheats and Kelly – I mean Kelly and Sheats." Ay me. (The CBC committed a splendid Spoonerism a couple of years ago when the newsreading face solemnly came up with an "announcement from the Department of Wealth and Helfare".) And then there was the day that I walked into my favourite fishmongers and declared in a loud, hearty voice that I fancied a "nice piece of tail" …. We all have these lapses of memory, or gaps between synapses, I suppose.

You ask why I "assert so firmly" that my childhood was a happy one. Did I do that? Well, it wasn't happy all the time, of course. Let's see. Age five (Can't remember anything earlier) to ten, what were happy occasions? Ah, yes. The long sea voyage when I was seven (It was a day trip to Clacton and back on *The Crested Eagle*. I never remember going on a family holiday, other than a day trip, until my parents quit running pubs, you see. Seven days a week job, that. And then they didn't have the money afterwards, not until 1939.) Then there was my eighth birthday, when the authorities permitted me to join the public library. This ended a period of book famine. I had been able to read well by the time I was five, but had to content myself with *Wizard*, *Hotspur* and the occasional book I received as a Christmas or birthday present…. During this time I saw little of my father except during Sunday dinner, and he was usually half pissed then. He and my mother were unhappy together – frequent thundering rows. And so I could go on until I reached the happiest period of my life – the four years in Wales before I joined the RAF.

And yet, on the whole I *was* happy during my first 14 years. Why? I thank my mother. I had her undivided care and attention during my first three or four years, and by the time I was five I was emotionally secure. She was the sun who provided the light and warmth in my family, and she was always there – except when she was ill (hence the orphanage) and when my sister and I were evacuated. Thanks to her, I was a resilient little bugger and kept bouncing back up. Then there were books and the good old BBC, music. I lived a lot in my head. My sister was not so lucky. Still, she grew into a fine woman – and is more compassionate than I. I tend to be more hard-nosed.

As for my father's advice it depends on how you interpret it. He wasn't advocating that I should walk around with a chip on my shoulder, looking for offence, or that I should launch sudden sneak attacks – hitting before the bell, as it were. What he meant was that I should stand up to bullies, that if a fight was inevitable I was not to waste time prancing about but get a good punch in right away as I might not be able to later. I understood that. I thought then that it was "sensible manly advice" – for boys. In practice, I was then, and am now, very inhibited against striking the first blow. Only once did I hit a boy without provocation. I was twelve and trying to impress my cousin. I was immediately ashamed of myself. Otherwise, I avoided fisticuffs whenever possible and refused to be provoked by insults. Physical provocation was another matter. One has a right to self defence.

Now, the second half of my memoirs. The expression I used was "compression", not "skating over". There is a difference. I am not unwilling to discuss unhappy or unpleasant events, only I am unwilling to spend too much time on them. You know the old saying – "Laugh and the world laughs with you, weep and you can piss off." There is only so much you can say about mental torment. Those that have experienced it can understand and sympathize. The others can't. To go on and on about it is to invite the charge of bitching, moaning and whining. Let's face it, most people sympathize with physical suffering, but if you mention that you feel your personality is disintegrating then they begin to edge nervously away, convinced either that you are exaggerating or that you are a nut case….

(Cont.) Thursday, August 29

A week since I took the break! After a couple of cool days following last Monday, when I had to drive thirty odd miles through a steam bath to a luncheon party in Vancouver, it is sunny once more, 88F, and I shall be sitting by my fan getting half pissed until the early hours. No doubt I shall curse the weather man when he proudly forecasts continuing fine weather with only a slight "threat" of possible showers over the weekend. My runner beans are wilting and getting stringy, our spring has dried up, and forest fires rage all over the West – yet these city-bound idiots continue, in effect, to bleat "Hot and sunny good. Wet and cloudy bad." Tell me, do weather forecasters on British TV feel thay have to be comedians? (Damn it. Something's gone wrong with the justification on the computer.) Sounds as if I am in a thoroughly bad temper, doesn't it? Actually I am in high good humour, having just finished Kingley Amis's *Lucky Jim* and laughed myself sick.

...Let's see. Where was I? Ah yes – It is difficult to describe mental states such as dissociation and depression without boring people silly, like that prick of a psychologist, or whatever he called himself. Also, I would have to mention the positive aspects of the experience without seeming to be clutching the tattered shreds of my pride on the one hand or tootling my own horn on the other. The self, says St. Augustine somewhere or other, is an abyss. I have peered into its shadowy depths and experienced dread. Only the fact that the self has unknown heights – at least that is what I sense – saved me. Also of course there is the problem of overdramatization of one's own piffling little problems – and then one enjoys a jolly good belly laugh. The task is daunting, you see. I shall probably press on. I have to as my sister has extorted a promise from me – and I have little else to do. As I am over 200 pages now I might have to divide the thing in two, ending the first with boarding the *Aquitania*, for my RAF days were part of my youth – I was mucking about with the boys.

Thanks for your poem. I see you are more in tune with the modern style than I. That's not an altogether back-handed compliment, for free verse can be excellent, witness Arnold's "Dover Beach". I like a number of things – the first stanza, for example, the sudden turn, like a shifting of the wind, in the second – but what the f--- are "Freudian fields"? Like hapless Canon Dixon appealing to Hopkins, I request a crib.

Poor old Roy, your description of him at Oxford busying himself as a gofer for various Dons reminds me of Lucky Jim and Professor Welch. Now, I know of a man who spent his adult life as a humble helper in a monastery kitchen. He really wished to be a monk but did not think himself able or worthy enough. In fact he proved to be a saint. Fancy that! Don't grieve over your friend as having had a wasted life. Better a fine ironmonger than a lousy historian. His life may have served a purpose ye wot not of. (Well – it's a nice thought, anyway.) Cheers!

PS   I meant to ask you: Are you pissed off with "political correctness" as much as I am?

Thursday, December 12, 1996

Dear Gerry,

Christmas rushes on us once more and I find myself wondering where the year has gone and how I have managed to accomplish so little with it. Poetry come to a screeching stop, memoirs hung up ten pages into the RAF, and but one game of golf. At my age, I should be feeling a sense of urgency, one would think. I really should stop watching the tv news and reading about the parlous state of the world. All that does is either infuriate me or fill me with weltschmerz – and both states are sapping, causing me to reach for the bottle and to light up another fag, while recalling some lines from Shakespeare that I stumbled upon when reading his plays in the Yukon (so long ago now!):

> But man, proud man,
> Drest in a little brief authority,
> Most ignorant of what he's most assured,
> His glassy essence, like an angry ape,
> Play such fantastic tricks before high heaven
> As make the angels weep.

Or make them laugh themselves silly! What does Shakespeare mean by man's "glassy essence", I wonder? Always puzzled me. A "glass" in Shakespeare means not something you drink beer from but a mirror, a looking-glass in "U" vocabulary. A phrase from your letter to Freeman suggested an answer – "the point that all of us are the prisoners of our contemporary culture."

Aha! We all tend to mirror the world we are brought up in. I know I do. I feel like a relic from the 'Thirties and 'Forties looking with dismay upon a world gone awry. Of course, my sense of the "world I was brought up in" was largely illusion. You know, – "Jerusalem", "Land of Hope and Glory", the "Nelson touch", "British is Best". (Yeah, the best of British bullshit.) The world, of course, was awry long before I was born. And then there are those who not only reflect the world they were brought up in but who are determined to reflect the very latest fashions. The "with it" crowd, the "beautiful people", the sickeningly politically correct, those who go around in mobs bleating "Four legs good. Two legs bad".

Ah, dear friend, as you can see, I am in my Ecclesiastes mood.

"'Vanity,' saith the preacher, 'all is vanity'" At least, that's how Browning puts it. Nature will sort us out, bring us to where we must face up to reality. Whatever that is. Only I feel a chill at the prospect. Her sorting-out can be sharp, a "terrible swift sword"....

Well, I didn't intend to sound apocalyptic. It's unseasonable. Blame it onto the Shakespeare quotation. I got carried away.

Thank you for the card and the two letters. Shall answer later. Meanwhile, it is getting dark and I have to drive into town to send off my English mail and buy myself some food and tobacco. Cheers.

PS   As penance for sending you the same poem twice, I am enclosing one that may amuse you. I admire A.E. Housman's work immensely, but "Loveliest of Trees" always vaguely irritated me. When I eventually realized why – he introduces the image of the Resurrection, then ignores it and proceeds to whine about having only "fifty springs" left to look at blossom – then the enclosed poem resulted:

The Cherry
(With apologies to A. E. Housman)

Dear Housman, were those fifty springs
Enough for viewing bloom and things?
Or did you beat at Heaven's door
To stretch your span to seven more?

Alas, my three score years and ten
Will not see sixty-nine again.
Let's see – a dunce could count the score
- That leaves me only one spring more!

Well – let the cherry flaunt its snow
And daffodils their trumpets blow.
I'll take the wine and fill the cup,
I'll drink the whole damned bottle up,
And then *I'll* push the daisies up!

December, 1995

Saturday, December 28, 1996

Dear Gerry,

The old year is wearing away, and as a parting gift has given us a white Christmas, only the seventh in sixty years, apparently – for Vancouver, that is – and record-breaking lows. Actually, we had ten inches of snow dumped on us in mid-November – two and a half feet in the Abbotsford area, lucky people. By the time we got rid of that lot, the Christmas present arrived. Right now my thermometer reads 14° F and we have eight inches of snow, with more forecast for tomorrow. Just as well I was able to get out yesterday and stock up with food and booze. Now, so long as the power stays on, I am content.

Many people are not, needless to say. Lines at the food banks continue to grow, and accommodation for the homeless is limited and crowded. In the name of fiscal responsibility, the powers that be are dismantling the health service and the social safety net, while claiming, of course, that they are doing nothing of the kind. "Jobs, jobs, jobs," promised the Liberals during the election campaign. What we have had since they assumed power (The Progressive Conservatives got only one seat!) has been cuts, cuts, cuts. Included in the many cuts are the Coastguard, lighthouses (replacing people with electronics – as in the U.K., I notice. Too bad a few seafarers will drown!) and the C.B.C. The unemployment rate for the whole country is 10% – up to 19% for poor bloody Newfoundland – and it is not likely to come down, either. There are plenty of jobs for those highly skilled with computers, but otherwise thin pickings…. I fear that many of the kids in school now will never have regular employment. The best they can hope for is part-time or contract work, both highly favoured by employers because of course they don't have to bother then about benefits such as pensions. Companies are downsizing, i.e. laying people off, and realizing juicy profits, while the stock market roars ahead. What they are doing, of course, is laying off one another's customers and preparing the way for considerable social unrest. It all adds up to interesting times ahead.

(Cont.) Sunday, 29th December

More than a foot of snow on my roof now and it's still snowing like buggery. Forecast is for more snow, with the possibility of rain or freezing rain to come. O frabjous joy! Outside, it manages to combine a feeling of raw dampness with a temperature of 19°F. Odd. All highways east of Mission closed. Nothing can move through Hope from any direction. Up the Fraser Valley beyond Abbotsford, outflow winds up to 50 mph are creating blizzard conditions, with drifts of fifteen or more feet. Hundreds of motorists trapped in their cars. One farmhouse up the Valley is sheltering forty-five people from a stranded tourist bus, and a church basement has over a hundred. I hope their septic tanks hold out. Rescue columns, travelling in convoy behind heavy snow-cats borrowed from ski resorts, are chewing their way through the drifts to check for motorists who might still be in their cars. Even a special train has been sent out, and some farmers have rescued people with their tractors. I'm lucky here – just on the fringe of the storm, with relatively little wind.

Victoria has been really dumped on. CBC reported two metres of snow there! But that must have been a mistake. I can't imagine Victoria with seven feet of snow. (Those talking heads have little appreciation of the meaning of numbers. I recall one smiling blonde announcer mentioning the sixty million Jews killed in the Holocaust! Difference of only one zero, right?) ... Final report was four feet, with over two feet falling in a twenty-four hour period.... The dogs look a little puzzled by the excessiveness of it all, but they are not unhappy. The cats, of which we have around seven now (I *told* John, I told him *months* ago, to get them spayed), take a sourer view. If they try to move around, they just disappear. Biggest snowfall around here in living memory, so they say (Not the cats)....

Yes, occasionally I too descend upon the astronomy and physics section to see what's new. I too have wrestled with quantum theory – or rather explanations of it – and have been puzzled. Many dimensions, possibility of parallel universes, electrons that seem to know what their mates are up to, particles that pop up out of nothing and then disappear back into it, Shrödinger's cat and wave functions that promptly collapse when they detect the presence of an observer's eye. Enough to give poor old Sir Isaac the willies. Mind you, I am deeply suspicious if anyone suggests that the observing eye can only be a human one. That sounds pre-Copernican. Regardless of what quantum theorists say, I'm sure the poor bloody cat knows whether it is dead or not before someone opens the box. As for time reversal, postulated in the case of the universe collapsing in on itself, presumably our experience of it will reverse also and so we will be spared the ordeal of walking around backwards, hoovering up shit and spitting out strawberries. But it is a rum old world right enough, odder perhaps, as someone or other said, than we shall ever know. Certainly that would be the opinion of Dame Julian, for Christ told her in a vision that we shall come to know His purpose – essentially the realization of love – but nothing of other thing without end. But, then, she was a mystic, not the sort of person to appeal to your Antony Freeman.

Incidentally, how does the blighter – Freeman, that is – justify going around disguised in shepherd's clothing when he does not believe in God? I found your letter to Freeman interesting. But I perceive that our thinking parts company, old friend. Your final sentence reminds me of the temptation scene in *Paradise Lost*, where Satan urges Eve to eat the fruit of the Tree of Knowledge. "You shall be as gods," he claims. Strangely enough, it was only this morning, on good old CBC radio, that I heard some such claim, by an expert beavering away diligently on the problem of artificial intelligence. The substance was this: that there will come a time when we shall be able to "download" the contents of our minds into a machine, that we shall then become immortal and be able to stride from star to star until we are masters of the universe, and that we shall then be as gods. Sure we shall. He's been playing too many virtual reality games. Somehow I think that if I had the contents of my mind so "downloaded" and then had my body disposed of – perhaps as food for the mink farm – then I should be very dead. I am more than the "software" of my brain. I am also the "hardware" – and something else. I have a level of consciousness above my "thoughts", a critical observer who can survey the passing thoughts, approvingly or disapprovingly (usually the latter, sod it), and can cease to think altogether while remaining very much aware. Anyhow, I find the idea of becoming immortal with my present personality less than appealing.

No, admire my fellow man as I might – and as I do, such people as Mother Theresa and Leonard Cheshire, for example – I cannot see us becoming gods, not even given millenia in which to try. I rather think that there is more to godhood than knowing a lot and having power, even if it is tempered by human love. We are not, and never shall be, fit for absolute power. (You know what Lord Acton said about that.) We shall always have with us our egos – stubborn things, egos – and our subconscious evolutionary baggage. I rather think that we shall go on as we have been – screwing things up and being straightened out (temporarily) by what Graham Greene calls "blessed reality". That's wot I think, anyway – and I don't even know whether God exists or not. (Although I am inclined to suspect that He does.)

(Cont.) Tuesday, December 31

Freezing rain early yesterday morning encrusted the snow with half an inch of ice and clad every twig in crystal. Very pretty. Fortunately, the temperature then climbed over the freezing mark and we had regular rain. I say "fortunately" because the last time we had an "ice storm" branches came tumbling down all over the place, snapping off with reports like rifle shots under the weight of the ice. With every twig having a half inch sheath of ice, each tree must have been supporting tons of it. Mind you, when the sun came out for a moment – the trees blazed. Incredible sight.... Now they have forecast up to seven inches of rain by Thursday – the pineapple express from Hawaii. Vast puddles everywhere. Victoria is still mostly closed down, but Vancouver airport is beginning to move people out. Highways are gradually being opened, except where avalanche danger exists, but remain very slippery. They have begun to call our little adventure "the blizzard of the century".

You are overmodest (or should I say immodest?) in claiming your poem to be something not very good but scribbled in a moment. Come, I'm sure it took longer than that. It sometimes takes me more than a moment to remember why I have got to my feet! I liked it as much as the two Larkin poems you sent me, if that means anything to you. Anyway, it depends what one means by "very good", doesn't it? Some of Wordsworth's poetry is very good, some bloody marvellous ("Tintern Abbey", for example), and some – well, what do you think of this?

> ...though little troubled by sloth,
> Drunken Lark! thou would'st be loath
> To be such a traveler as I.
> Happy, happy Liver,
> With a soul as strong as a mountain river
> Pouring out praise to the Almighty Giver,
> Joy and jollity be with us both.

Well, I ask you…. And he couldn't even claim it as a product of his declining years. It was written about the same time as his "Intimations" ode. Most of my very, very slim output was produced in a matter of a few hours apiece, with some hours of tinkering afterwards (and not finished yet!). But one I laboured on for _weeks_, with about fifteen versions – a half-inch-thick wad of paper, eventually emerged as both flawed and pretentious. I look at it now with distaste and resentment. Damn it. Shall I ever have another go at it? Dunno. As I remarked to a colleague in a letter, determination and perseverance can carry us only so far. We can't all be Sheats and Kelleys. There is the matter of talent….

Apropos rhyme and regular metre. I don't think I have made myself clear. I have no objection to poetry that avoids both. Pope's heroic couplets, marvelously varied and flexible though they are, eventually begin to irritate me. On the other hand, Donne's "Meditation 17" ("No man is an island…") is I think pure poetry. True, it is classified as prose – but it has such complex and subtle rhythms, not to mention imagery, that it is really poetry. No, what I object to is something being dismissed because it does not conform to the current fashion – and that objection applies to those critics who panned "Cockney" Keats for not writing "proper" poetry (i.e. heroic couplets) and those who today spurn some poetry merely because it uses traditional forms.

Weather forecast: Victoria – heavy rain, with winds to 90 kph; Vancouver – heavy rain, winds to 70 kph; Fraser Valley – wind, heavy rain, freezing rain, snow, depending on location. Roof collapsed on a hangar at Victoria airport, roof collapsed on a shopping centre, signs of flooding here and there, avalanche danger one notch below "extreme". How's Lloyd's doing for cash? 1996 is going out with a flourish here!

(Cont.) Saturday, January 4, 1997

There, this has now become my first letter of the new year. Nothing left of the snow but a few dirty patches – around here, anyway. Hundreds of avalanches in the Fraser Canyon and other places in the interior. Boston Bar, with dozens of motorists and trucks, was isolated by avalanches for a week. Had to supply the town by helicopter. They escorted out the first convoy yesterday – well spaced out on a single track in case of further avalanches. Floods in the US Northwest are horrendous. But you are fed up with reading all of this, especially with Siberian air clamped down over Europe.

Could Evelyn Waugh write like an angel without being a shit? Could Bobby Fisher play chess like a fiend without being a nutter? Could Spike Milligan and Tony Hancock be so funny without being absolutely miserable in their private lives? I wonder. What if we could, via computers, machines and genetic engineering, construct a new breed of human, programmed to be handsome, healthy and happy? What then? Somehow, I don't believe in utopias. Let's face it, we all need a good kick in the backside from time to time to keep us human.

And that's about all…. Cheers!

◦◦

May, 2000

Dear Gerry,

Received your e-mail OK. Clicked onto attachment. Instead of opening, a notice came on asking if I wanted to save it. Clicked "Yes".

Next problem – where was it? Found it in "Documents" section. Clicked on. Notice: "attachment cannot be opened as the application program that created it couldn't be found".

Curses. Trashed it.

I'd rather not receive attachments. My niece a couple of times has sent me commercial greeting cards. First one I couldn't open at all. Second opened with picture but no sound. Then she sent me another attachment about six weeks ago. Took me three days to figure out.... So, for long attachments, use snail mail. Less frustrating....

Hope you are sorting your computer out. They really are not user-friendly. I use MacOS, of course, which is usually quite good but still has some idiot features. EG: Computer crashes. Notice comes up "Sorry – Error type #@%$%#! has occurred." Very helpful. I know something's wrong and their info is useless to me. What I want to know is what to DO about it. Bloody Twits. Trouble is programs are compiled by smart young idiots whose liberal education has been neglected. Regards, etc.

◦◦

Friday, December 8, 2000

Dear Gerry,

This is the third time I have started this letter. At the end of the first para of the first draft, I said to myself, "What am I using the word-processor for? I should be using e-mail." So I trash it and start on Eudora. Then, "Wait a minute. I'm not sending this by e-mail. That's all cocked up. I'm enclosing this with a card." So, back to square one. You see, I am becoming vague and confused, even though I can still do the Times crossword (though with a little cheating sometimes)....

Are we communicating, or is there a cock-up somewhere? Or are you sinking into rain-sodden melancholia because of the awful weather you have been having (with January and February fill-dyke still to come)? Or, worse, are you ill? I sincerely hope that the last is not the case. For in one of your recent communications you said you were planning to return to the Algarve next March.

A little over two weeks to Christmas as I write this, and just over three weeks to the beginning of a new century and a new millennium. (In contrast to my neighbour, who strongly believes 2000 to be the beginning, and to the millions who celebrated it last year, I maintain that the year 2000 is the last year of the 20th Century and January 1, 2001 the beginning of the 21st Century. But, then, in these days of instant gratification appearance is all and substance unimportant. And words and numbers mean what you want them to mean. The significance of the occasion is overblown anyway. The billions of people who are non-Christian have their own calendars.) But I blather on.... Where was I? Ah yes – "time's winged chariot". Curious thing, time. Elastic. Flits by when you are happy or merely contented and stretches out into an eternity when you are in pain or bored out of your wits. Some physicists now wonder if time is discontinuous – broken into little packages, quanta, the way the physical universe is. A mystery...

I am, I am grateful to say, in reasonable health, despite the rattling marbles. In fact am due to play golf next Tuesday, weather permitting. Still a lousy player, despite a fluky eagle last month. I sincerely hope that you and yours are in good health, too.

Have a pleasant family Christmas – and good luck to you all in the new year. Cheers!

☙❧

Wednesday, December 20, 2000

Dear Gerry,

Sorry to be so long answering your e-mail. (That's more or less how you started yours, wasn't it.) By now I guess you have my Card explaining troubles with computer. Turns out it wasn't a glitch in the computer but the fault of my server. Silly buggers had changed their domain name without informing me first. So I was off line for a week. No e-mail, no internet, not that I spend much time on the 'net.

Shortly following my reading your letter came four inches of snow and a wind. Very Christmassy. However, a loud thump around two in the morning proved to have been a large tree falling across my driveway, missing my garage by about three feet. So the next day I helped my landlord and neighbour, John, clean it up. Took most of the day. Sawing most of the tree up was a cinch for him – chain saw – but the time was consumed in stripping off the ivy and carting it away. Seemed to be tons of the stuff. Now I know exactly what "clinging like ivy" means! Nothing like experience for illuminating the meaning of words, is there?

The following morning, as I was watching an English Premier League soccer match, the power went off. Turned out to be our power pole. Like the tree it had decided to take a dive. So no lights, no water, no heat and no cooking for the next thirty-odd hours. Again, experience makes one feel sympathetic towards the birds and squirrels – and to poor sods who get flooded out at this time of year. Nothing quite like experience – or contact with reality. "Blessed reality", Graham Greene calls it. Not quite the adjective that would occur to victims of the holocaust, but one grasps his point. But for reality, we would no doubt become totally insane.

Yes, the war was fun for us. But we were both young and lucky. I recall what my father said of his first experience of war as an 18 yr old artilleryman at Mons in 1914. "I thought it a lark at first," he said, adding in his direct soldierly way, "but I soon realized it wasn't shit they were throwing. The buggers were actually trying to kill us!"

Ah, Dickens! Like Chaucer, Shakespeare, Tolstoy, etc., the creator of a world, only I have felt almost a participant in his. Smoky old London of the early 'Thirties, when my parents ran a little pub on Goswell Road, where Mr. Pickwick once stayed, and not far from the foggy old Thames of "Bleak House". Then, like Oliver, without warning or explanation whisked off to an orphanage. Fortunately, although unsettling, it was no Dotheboys Hall. Then within three months of returning to my family, now in Plumstead and not all that far from the marshes of "Great Expectations", like Pip I was suddenly seized by a man (Good old Blue Jowels) and terrified out of my wits. He proved no benefactor to me, though…..

Have a good family Christmas, the last of the 20th Century. I hope you enjoy better health in the new year – and celebrate many more Yuletides in the new century. Regards to all. Cheers!

August, 2001

Dear Old Friend:

As I may have told you, my sister and her husband are staying with me for an extended visit (two months) – at my invitation, I hasten to add. Even with family, though, one has a certain responsibility to entertain one's guests. Not always easy. Nowadays, I do not like driving long distances. Something to do with my eyes, I think, for I tire easily and have difficulty concentrating, especially if I'm driving in unfamiliar territory. I'd hate to have an accident and wipe out most of my remaining family. However, my sister has lower back pain and various other complaints that septuagenarians are prone to and doesn't like sitting in a car for long. So long trips are out, fortunately, and short local trips, such as they are, are in.

Went off to Dick's for dinner several days ago, and then to a luncheon party in North Vancouver the following day. Sounds like a social whirl, doesn't it? But it hasn't been quite like that. Mostly, the darlings have been fixing up my garden and weeding my landlord's garden. That after whizzing around cleaning up my house for the umpteenth time. Sister claims the work helps to loosen the stiffness. In addition, they have re-covered my footstall, re-upholstered an old chair on my porch, and in spite of my protests have upholstered a little stool I use to save bending in the garden. "Blimey," I said, observing this, "I'm buggering off. You'll be upholstering me next."

Living here is normally quiet, with few comings and goings from one week to the next. Just as I like it, for the more the world stays away from my doorstep the happier I am. Unfortunately, Landlord's son is getting married in a couple of days, with the ceremony to take place on the property. And so hordes of people will be swarming all over the place – over 150 guests, I'm told. Thus for the past five weeks, landlord and family have been as busy as bees. Hanging flower baskets by the dozen everywhere, repairing fences, gates, repairing part of my house, repainting the outside of the workshop and my house. Building and painting a wooden arbor to frame the happy couple. (Bride wanted to arrive on a horse-drawn cart. Fortunately, commonsense prevailed – the hill to our property being so steep the horse would have had to be towed up! Like living in a fishbowl or on a construction site. Sister, husband and I helped with the housepainting, though. Kept us all occupied for the better part of a week. "You're all invited to the wedding," says John. "Thanks," says I. "But I don't have to come to the reception, do I?" I adds hopefully. "Of course you must. Don't be a miserable old sod. Besides, you'll know most of the guests." Scads of former students and their families. I won't recognize half of them and certainly won't remember their names….

Evenings tend to be tedious. One can't talk all the time (although my brother in law, a lovely man, tries – and then whistles when he runs out of steam), and summer TV is all re-runs, including numerous American sitcoms from the '60's. Bloody boring. I suppose I am becoming a bit of a misanthrope. (Becoming? perhaps I have always been one! Although, to be fair, I get along with people in small numbers – five or fewer at a time. Any more and I get the feeling of being trapped. Intelligent conversation becomes impossible and social interactions become so much gas.)

As for the world of man – endless idiocies. IRA – still piling up arms and training, with the dirty work delegated to so-called splinter groups, no doubt really surrogates – has the lying British gov't by the balls. Israelis and Palestinians still at it, as they have been since at least the 30's. Troubles in the Balkans – as there have been for centuries. Greed and general decadence in the West. General dumbing down and pandering to the ill-educated and people who think they're as good as anyone else, even though they may be useless slobs. "The World Turned Upside Down" it seems, except that the world has always been that way. Phooey! And yet man has landed on the moon; the Vietnamese, after thirty years of war, outsmarted and defeated the US; and the Russians, despite 20 million dead (and ignoring the millions of dead from the Revolution, Civil War and Stalin's purges), defeated the Germans and within five years of the end of the war were scaring the pants off the Americans. Just as one despairs of humanity one is staggered with wonder and admiration for its strength and achievements. Too bad it doesn't have more sense. As for the world of nature, it is complex and grand beyond our imagining, and filled with beauty, from the quiet beauty of the English countryside to the awful beauty of a hurricane, of Antarctica, of the stupendous reaches of outer space.

And yet the machinery of life – work or starve, kill or be killed, the survival of fittest – sometimes gives us pause. No doubt it has to be like that, and the image of a snake consuming its own tail is an apt symbol for it. Nature doesn't give a damn for the individual, not even for the species – and perhaps the odd asteroid or comet knocks out an inhabited planet. Tennyson, as you know, went into all of that in his "In Memoriam" – a poem I found profoundly moving – but then Browning comes along and dismisses the whole grand scheme of things as "machinery just meant to give the soul its bent." The universe is what it is (whatever that is) – and it challenges the soul, enables the soul to measure itself against reality and discover its true dimensions. The trouble, old friend, is that we are not all heroes, and even those who are get tired and worn out. Some few strong souls go on from strength to strength, and like Nelson can die murmuring "Thank God I have done my duty", but most of us become only too aware of our shortcomings and weaknesses.

It's not weltschmerz that possesses you, although there is that. Perhaps your pills; or perhaps a powerful attack of depression, something with which I am only too familiar and which Churchill called "black dog"; or perhaps it is the curse of the introverts – the doubt of one's own worth, the dissatisfaction with self. If the last – and I guess that is what it is – then it is a healthy state, as long as one does not become too morbid about it. Most counsellors and psychiatrists would not agree with me, of course, and spend their time trying to convince the most worthless that they should feel good about themselves. I'm reminded of the woman whose child died through her neglect. While awaiting her trial, the social welfare agency (in England, of course) treated her to a yacht trip to France on the grounds that she must be feeling bad about herself and needed cheering up. My view is that she bloodywell ought to have been feeling bad about herself!

Well, I am not going to tell you to snap out of it. In my downs I feel like murdering anyone who suggests that to me. But it is a temporary state. I am reminded of Hopkins, who in verse has expressed states I have from time to time enjoyed…. I have at times thanked God for the mercy of sleep, and have perceived that perhaps death could be the greatest mercy of all…. Well, you'll be familiar enough with his "terrible sonnets". At least they show we are not alone…. Personally, whatever they may think of themselves, I prefer the Hopkinses and Gerald Richardsons of the world to those self-satisfied souls who would love to be themselves for ever. (Now there's a definition of hell!)

One final thought (one I gave to my sister when she was at a low ebb. I wrote it while spending the night at an airport hotel just prior to my return to Canada in 1975, after enjoying a four-year breakdown and convalescence in England): "Just remember that you do not belong to yourself alone. Others love you – and that in itself justifies your existence and gives you a responsibility." Cheers!

❧

September, 2001

Dear Gerry:

After a stay of two months my sister and her husband have returned to England and my house is empty once more. I shall miss them. There was not much I could do for them in the way of entertainment, I fear. There are only so many scenic drives and places of interest within reach, and the quality of TV programs over here, particularly in the summer, is appalling. So it has been very much a working holiday for them – much gardening and assisting with the painting of the outside of my house…. I think they enjoyed their stay, though. Reg loves nothing better than gardening, and my sister is a non-stop cleaner and tidier.

Their return flight was delayed two days because of the emergency. Then they had to leave at the ungodly hour of 0505hrs, arriving at Gatwick the same day at 2345hrs. It was 0300 before they arrived home, dead tired. I'm told they slept for fourteen hours straight. At least they avoided the tremendous line-ups of the previous few days.

I hope you found something in my previous e-mail that was cheering. Not much, perhaps, in the light of the recent obscene atrocity. As you know, I have been expecting something of the sort for some time. The wake-up for me was the nerve gas attack on the Tokyo subway, which showed the willingness of religious fanatics to kill as many people as possible. This rising tide of hatred, religious fanaticism and outright stupidity is profoundly depressing. One sometimes despairs of the human race. (And it's not just religious nuts. Did you know that, after signing a treaty with the US, agreeing to ban biological weaponry, the Russians secretly redoubled their efforts at research in that field, even under Gorbachev and with his knowledge? They have also experimented in genetic modification of deadly organisms, for example crossing smallpox with the ebola virus, in an effort to develop strains that come as close as possible to a 100% fatality rate! I find it difficult to comprehend such unutterably evil folly in people who after all are political leaders of a great nation or intelligent, well-educated scientists! Their stockpile of biological weapons presumably still exists and, since some people are willing to sell anything or anyone for money, may be made available to the highest bidder and find their way into the hands of terrorists.) Well, at least the world in general is now aware of the danger. I hope. But God help the next generation....

Well, that's enough cheering up for one letter. I do hope you and yours are well – and would appreciate a line or two. Cheers!

PS I see Bush spoke of a "crusade" against evil-doers. I cannot think of a word more likely to enrage Moslems generally. Doesn't he know what the word means?

ᘐᕐᕬ

September, 2001

Dear Old Friend:

Like you, I have a distrust of all religions. Though no doubt all the major religions at one time or another have had truly spiritual members, even holy ones perhaps, too often priests, rabbis, mullahs and such are neither. John Calvin, for example, originator of Presbyterianism, that most dour form of Protestantism, started out as a French lawyer. And the simple message of the original inspiration gets fogged up and loaded with intellectual baggage. So Christ's original message of love – Love God and thy neighbour as thyself" – is forgotten, and Christians eventually get around to burning one another at the stake for not toeing the party line, as it were. What a strange, stubborn creature man is!

I haven't read St. Thomas Aquinas, that pillar of Catholic theology, because I probably wouldn't have understood him and because towards the end of his life he himself dismissed his monumental effort to reconcile Catholic theology with Aristotle's philosophy as mere "straw". I prefer St. Augustine, whom I have read…. No, I am a simple man and I prefer Julian of Norwich (1342 – c. 1429). When she was thirty years old, she had a religious experience in which she enjoyed a conversation with Christ, who told her "I am ground of thi beseking". At the end of her book, "A Revelation of Love", she writes

> "Fro that time that it was shewid I desired oftentimes to witten what was our lords mening. And xv yer after and more I was answerid in gostly vnderstanding, sayand thus; 'Woldst thou wetten thi lords mening in this thing? Wete it wele: love was his mening. Who shewid it the? Love. What shewid he the? Love. Wherfor shewid it he? For love. Hold the therin and thou shalt witten and knowen more in the same; but thou shalt never knowen ne witten therein other thing without end.'"

Well, that's clear enough, despite the early 15th c. spelling. I'm not sure, though, about the last clause (translation: You'll never understand the universe, though.) Was that intended for Julian alone or mankind as a whole? If the latter, then good luck Stephen Hawking!

"The letter killeth; the Spirit giveth life." The Bible is right on.

All of which you may or may not find interesting. In any case, if God exists, I don't think he gives a toot[28] whether you believe he does or not. What counts is how much you love.

Now I am going to prepare my dinner – sausages and mash with the last of the runner beans. Keep your pecker up. Cheers, Phil

⟶✥⟶

---

[28] I wrote this to comfort an atheist. Christ enjoins us to love God, of course, and we are told that God very much desires our love. The idea, held by some, that God consigns the unbeliever permanently to hell or at best to limbo is, I think, silly.

November, 2001

Dear Old Friend:

Just before 2.00 am yesterday morning, as I was sipping my third drink and peering through the murky depths of the North Atlantic at the shattered remnants of HMS Hood, I was startled by a loud stamping and the entry of my 6' 2" neighbour. In the unlit hallway, clad in large wellies, heavy mackinaw and a toque, he looked more like a rampant 7-foot grizzly. "Would you turn your kitchen light off, Phil. Andrew and I are going to look for falling stars and we want to get our eyes accustomed to the dark. You should come out too." "Good idea," I said. "I was intending to go out myself in a few minutes." Switching off the light, I finished my drink, donned boots and coat and went out. "Where are you? I asked, addressing the night. "Over here in your driveway," a voice called. "Can't even see the damned driveway," I complained. "Besides, I'm half pissed." My feet, however, could feel the wheel ruts and I felt my way some fifty yards and came across them. They were lying on a pad they had thrown down. "Here," said John, patting the pad between him and his even taller son, "make yourself comfortable". And there, like three large sardines, we lay for nearly an hour, staring up at the heavens....

Well, though the Leonids put on quite a show, I would hardly call it the experience of a lifetime. But the night was magical, for all that. And I thought of other times I had stared up at the stars – in Kent, where I had first escaped the lights of London; on a midnight mountain in Wales; on a beach in the Gulf Islands; and on a sandbank on the Peace River, with lightning flickering about the horizon. Now, as I lay there, staring up, my eyes gradually adjusted themselves and the night filled with light. There, shining steadily, were the constellations of my youth – the Great Bear, standing on his tail with his faithful beacons pointing the way to Polaris; and Orion the Hunter, striding the night with a companion, I noted, for next to Castor and Pollux, the Heavenly Twins, a brighter body shone. Jupiter, probably. That is how the "fixed stars" appeared to our grandparents, and that is how they will appear to our grandchildren long after we have gone. Of course, we know now that the stars are not "fixed". It is only an

467

illusion created by immense distances and the brevity of our lives, which, like the Leonids, blaze only for a moment and leave fading trails which vary according to fate and the brightness of our endeavours. So thought I. At last, beginning to feel cold (it was a brisk 38°F), we decided to retire and bade one another goodnight. Then I went inside and poured myself another drink.

Did you know (I'm beginning to sound like Michael Caine, aren't I?) that astronomers have recently made a remarkable discovery? After painstaking study of dozens of supernovae in remote galaxies, they have come to the conclusion that the expansion of the universe, far from being slowed by gravity, is actually speeding up!

"Curiouser and curiouser," exclaimed Alice. "If I throw an apple into the air, it should fall back down again!"

"Pooh!" said the Red (or White) Queen, "not in my realm. The apple would keep going...!"

In other words, something out there is overcoming gravity and giving us a gentle shove. But what? Empty space, say the astronomers. For "empty" space is not empty at all but filled with a seething quantum stew of particles which, like surfacing dolphins, continually leap into existence only to disappear back out of it. This is the source of the required energy. 'Struth! It's hard enough to imagine a universe suddenly popping up out of a singularity. Now we have particles doing it all the time. Continuous creation! 'Tis a mystery. Mind-boggling!

Dear Gerry, my old friend, best man at my wedding – Remember? – it is painful to think of you lying there, fighting for breath. I suppose the last thing you want is to be boggled. But still, I am only trying to cheer you a little. You may insist, with Prospero, that our little life is rounded with a sleep. As I pointed out in my last e-mail – did you like the quote from the Lady Julian, by the way? – it matters little what we believe. But in a universe in which, to borrow from Walt Whitman, "a mouse is miracle enough to stagger sextillions of infidels", there is always room for hope. One way or another, I hope you will soon be more comfortable.

With love, from one who is glad to call you "friend" – Philip

Tuesday, December 11/01

Dear Gerry,

Sorry for the long silence. Had to repair my hard drive, which necessitated re-installing all softwear – and that knocked me off the internet, rendering me blind and dumb for about five days. Not that I use the internet much. Useful for specific research but otherwise largely a waste of time….Well, Christmas is just around the corner, a time whose magic vanished for me a long time ago. Still enjoy the snow, mind you, but hope that it knows its place and keeps to the mountains…. I don't suppose the thought of Christmas makes you wet your knickers with excitement either. I hope, though, that the day finds you comfortably esconced at home in your own armchair with your family around you.

Played my last golf of the season two weeks ago. 102! Not bad for me, especially since I was putting badly and had to paddle around the course. After about twenty years of teaching myself, I at last know how to swing a golf club. Knowing how and doing it, though, are seldom the same thing, and I still have a distressing tendency to hit the ground instead of the ball. Not much other news for you. I believe I have already told you that we have lost two of our three dogs. Can't remember. Oh, I see the Turner awards for modern art have been handed out. The winning entry, to the tune of £30,000, was an empty room with lights going on and off. When asked what it meant, the proud artist – a tall streak who looked in need of a wash and shave – mumbled that he couldn't actually say what it meant. One of the judges had a go, though, with some drivel about possible profundities. Two other entries were a blob of something resembling sticky plasticene and a ball of crumpled paper. Talk about the emperor's clothes!

Well, I'm about written out. I hope you are recovered enough to begin flirting with the nurses. Cheers!

Thursday, December 20/01

Dear Gerry,

The sun is out today and has chased the frost from the upper meadow. Quite a pleasant change after weeks of gloomy skies, rain and wind. Not that I mind gloom and rain. After all, what do you expect of November and December? But wind can be annoying, often bringing down power lines. And that is tiresome – no heat, no light, no water and no cooking. The signs point to a green Christmas on the coast, which suits me fine. Snow belongs on the mountains not on my driveway.

Well, all my cards and presents are done and the frenzied part of the season is over. Good thing, too. And just in case the weather plays a trick on me and snows me in, I have enough food, booze and tobacco to last me a week. Now I can relax. I hope.

A while back I was visited by some old friends from West Vancouver. We see one another about once every three years, as they don't like driving out here and I avoid Vancouver like the plague. We have enough mad drivers here. He's an uppercrust Englishman and his wife is a Swedish Finn from Australia who talks with a U-English accent. (Can you work that one out?) I met her when she was substituting at the schools here in Maple Ridge in the 60's. "What part of England are you from?" I asked her husband. "Oh, some place in Kent that you've never heard of," he answered. "Where?" "A little village called Boughton Monchelsea," he said. That's what he thought. In 1939 my sister was evacuated to that very village and I went to one about three miles away. Small world, isn't it?

One often hears evacuee horror stories, of snotty-nosed slum kids billeted on middle class country homes piddling and defecating in the corridors. Evelyn Waugh is very amusing on the subject in his war trilogy,[29] which I've no doubt you've read. ("How could such a shit write so sublimely?" you said of him – or was it of Philip Larkin?) Anyway, one of his seedier characters becomes a billeting officer who farms out a trio of his ghastliest children on the poshest homes. Within a week the distraught owners are willing to pay him anything – anything – to move

---

[29]   My memory was at fault. The seedy billeting officer, Basil Seal, is to be found in *Put Out More Flags*.

them somewhere else, and he makes a tidy sum out of the process. But the reality was not always so. The reverse, in my sister's case.

I gave my friend a cut-down version, complete with poem, of [our experiences as evacuees], and he found it fascinating. Like all of us, he had little idea of what was going on in his own backyard.

Well, I've got to get my dinner now and I'll sign off. I've not heard any news of you since Chris's e-mail, and so I'm hoping no news is good news – and that you are comfortably convalescing. Cheers! Phil

[My last letter. Gerry died a few days later.]

In Memoriam

Gerald D. Richardson – d. December, 2001

Sources

NOTE: Following are sources of some quotations in the text. The alert reader will notice others, some acknowledged and others not.

Page

35 "turn from praise...not purely"
   – See E.B.Browning, "How Do I Love Thee?"
42 "as that busy old servant, the sun...across the way"
   – adapted from Dickens, *Pickwick Papers*
51 "To travel hopefully...."
   – Robert Louis Stevenson, "El Dorado"
53 "The Mezzotint"
   – M.R.James, *Ghost Stories of an Antiquary*
57 "The world of books lay all before me...."
   – Adapted from end of John Milton, *Paradise Lost*
79 "Stone walls do not a prison make...."
   – Richard Lovelace, "To Althea, from Prison"
80 "What's in a name...."
   – Shakespeare, *Romeo and Juliet*
   "You spotted snakes..." and "I know a bank...."
   – Shakespeare, *A Midsummer Night's Dream*
82 "One law for the lion ...."
   – William Blake, *The Marriage of Heaven and Hell*
83 "My mind to me a kingdom is"
   – Sir Edward Dyer, "My Mind to Me a Kingdom Is"
89 "And because I am happy...."
   – Blake, *Songs of Experience*
91 "his eyes looked most powerfully...into his"
   – Dickens, *Great Expectations*
135 The King is quoting from the following poet
   – Minnie Louise Haskins (1875 -1957)

146 "with the joy of elevated thoughts", "life and food...."
  – William Wordsworth, "Tintern Abbey"
157 "nameless, unremembered acts...of love"
  – Wordsworth, "Tintern Abbey"
166 "less of body...soul"
  – Adapted from Robert Browning, "Fra Lippo Lippi"
168 "Ah, but a boy's reach...his grasp"
  – Adapted from Browning, "Andrea del Sarto"
183 "Evil into the mind of God....", "wayfaring Christian"
  – Milton, *Paradise Lost*, "Areopagitica"
184 "But what good came...at last"
  – Robert Southey, "The Battle of Blenheim"
193 The world "means intensely and means good"
  – Browning, "Fra Lippo Lippi"
194 "A leaf of grass...of the stars"
  – Walt Whitman, "Song of Myself"
194 Thomas Traherne, *Centuries of Meditation*
194 "the true success is to labour"
  – R.L.S., "El Dorado"
195 "... glory and the dream"
  – Wordsworth, "Intimations" ode
196 "renovating virtue", "I have felt..."
  – Wordsworth, " Prelude", "Tintern Abbey"
224 "Whoever degrades another degrades me."
  – Whitman, "Song of Myself"
267 "To adapt Walt Whitman...poet"
  – See "When Lilacs Last in the Dooryard Bloom'd"
298 "'Tis not what a man Does...but what man Would do"
  – Browning, "Saul"
328 "Some lines of Henry Vaughan" – from "The World"
334 "To adapt lines from RLS" – See "Christmas at Sea"
369 "The best-laid schemes..." – Burns, "To a Mouse"
411 "If the sun and moon should doubt...out"
  – Blake, "Auguries of Innocence"